GILLES VILLENEUVE

GILLES VILLENEUVE

The life of the legendary racing driver

Gerald Donaldson

Canadian Cataloguing in Publication Data

Donaldson, Gerald
  Gilles Villeneuve : the life of the
legendary racing driver

Includes index.
ISBN 0-7710-2846-6

1. Villeneuve, Gilles, 1950-1982.   2. Automobile
racing drivers – Canada – Biography.   I. Title.

GV1032.V54D66 1989   796.7'2'0924   C89-093456-8

Printed and bound in Canada

McClelland & Stewart Inc.
The Canadian Publishers
481 University Avenue
Toronto, Ontario
M5G 2E9

CONTENTS

ACKNOWLEDGEMENTS

I am indebted to all those who helped during my research. Although I covered Gilles Villeneuve's first and last Formula 1 races and many of those in between, the material in this book includes contributions from many others. Often they are mentioned in the text, but I would like to pay specific tribute to several people.

First of all, I wish to thank Joann Villeneuve and Gaston Parent for their help and co-operation. Without their assistance the book would not have been possible.

Of the many others interviewed, special thanks are due to John Lane, Jody Scheckter, and Ray Wardell, who went out of their way to help. Others who generously gave of their time were René Arnoux, Mauro Forghieri, Kris Harrison, John Hogan, Marco Piccinini, Keke Rosberg, Antonio Tomaini, Brenda Vernor, and Jacques Villeneuve.

Among the motorsport journalists I would like to thank Len Coates in particular for making available material for the book he was planning to write with Gilles. Special thanks also is due to Nigel Roebuck, who generously shared insights and anecdotes about his good friend Gilles, and checked over this text.

Other journalists who provided useful information include: Pino Allievi, Derick Allsop, Didier Braillon, John Blunsden, Alan Brinton, Jabby Crombac, Mike Doodson, Maurice Hamilton, Alan Henry, Jeff Hutchinson, Innes Ireland, Denis Jenkinson, Gordon Kirby, Franco Lini, Bob MacGregor, Jean-Louis Moncet, David Phipps, Giorgio Piola, Johnny Rives, Patrick Stephenson, Rob Walker, Peter Windsor, and Eoin Young. Thanks also to the photographers, who are credited on their photos.

I am also grateful to the following people for various forms of assistance: Maria Bergamin at Alitalia, Philippe Belay, Harry Calton at Ford UK, Peter Dick, Dott. Guiseppe Giraudi at Fiat, Dott. Gozzi at Ferrari, Yvonne Horwitz, Laurence Kimber at *CBC Sportsweekend*, Elizabeth Lane, Judy Lester-Stephenson, Sheila Piper, Dan Proudfoot, and F. David Stone. Thanks also to the manuscript editor, Richard Tallman. Finally, I am especially grateful to McClelland and Stewart for commissioning the book.

Primary sources of information for race reports and results include issues of *Autosport*, edited by Quentin Spurring, and the annual editions of *Autocourse*, edited by Maurice Hamilton. Other publications consulted, used for reference, and/or quoted from are: *The Champions of Formula 1* by Keith Botsford; *Ferrari's Drivers* by Michele Fenu; *Formula Villeneuve* video produced by Yves Hébert; *The Globe and Mail*; *Grand Prix* by David Hodges, Doug Nye, and Nigel Roebuck; *The Grand Prix Drivers* by Maurice Hamilton, Alan Henry, Denis Jenkinson, and Nigel Roebuck, edited by Steve Small; *Grand Prix Greats* by Nigel Roebuck; *Grand Prix International*; *The Grand Prix of Canada* by Gerald Donaldson; *Gilles Villeneuve* by Alan Henry; *Gilles Villeneuve* by Nestore Morosini; *Gilles Vivo* by Cesare De Agostini; *Keke* by Keke Rosberg and Keith Botsford; *La Cometa Gilles* by Enzo Russo; *La Dernière Virage* by Christian Tortora; *Marlboro Grand Prix Guide* by Jacques Deschenaux and Werner Haefliger; *Motor Sport*; *Road and Track*; *SCCA Media Guide*; *To Hell And Back* by Niki Lauda and Herbert Volker; *Toronto Star*; *Villeneuve* by Allan de la Plante, Pierre Lecours, and Linda Press Fisher.

Gerald Donaldson
Toronto, Canada

PROLOGUE

Saturday, May 8, 1982
Zolder, Belgium

It was 1:52 p.m. in the pine forests of eastern Belgium. There were just eight minutes to go in the final qualifying session for the Belgian Grand Prix. The sky was dull and grey after morning showers, but the track surface was dry. The drivers were trying to improve their grid positions for tomorrow's race.

None was trying harder than the French Canadian in the red number 27 Ferrari. He came powering through the chicane on full throttle and disappeared over the hill toward Terlamenbocht, one of the most difficult curves on the Zolder circuit. It was to be his last lap.

The engine noises stopped. An eerie hush spread around the 4.26-kilometer track. Spectators whispered nervously at the unexpected silence. Suddenly the track announcer began screaming hysterically about a huge accident involving one of the Ferraris.

Moments later, the scene at the right-hand Terlamenbocht corner bore awful testimony to the enormity of the crash. Bits and pieces of wreckage of the Ferrari were strewn along the circuit for some 200 meters. There, in the middle of the track, was the utterly destroyed chassis, shorn of all bodywork, with only the right rear wheel remaining and the entire front of the car sheered off at the point where the driver once sat.

Beyond the car, amid the tangled wire of the catch-fencing on the outside of the curve, distraught track marshals stood wringing their hands in anguish. Quickly, they held up a curtain of blankets to shield onlookers from the view. Their agitation increased as running crowds converged on the area and the marshals, joined by police wielding truncheons, began physically to beat back the spectators.

At 2:03 p.m. the track announcer said Gilles Villeneuve was being taken by helicopter to a nearby hospital. Shortly after came another announcement from the organizers. Couched in careful terms, it was given first in Flemish and then in French, the official languages of Belgium, then in English: "The front left wheel of the number 27 car hit the right rear wheel of the number 17 car. Car number 27 was then thrown in the air, and having come down several meters further, the driver was ejected from his seat into the catch fences. The driver is very seriously injured."

In the pits the Ferrari team closed the steel doors of their garage. Personnel on other teams exchanged worried glances. People stood around in small groups, talking quietly. Some, who watched the accident replayed on television monitors, wept unashamedly, as had certain drivers who had stopped at the crash site.

The remaining eight minutes of practice resumed but only six cars went around for a few half-hearted laps. The teams packed away their equipment for the day. The Ferrari team loaded everything, including the twisted pieces of metal that once were the number 27 car, into their transporters and left for Italy.

In the Zolder press room journalists sent the news to a waiting world, updating it with the periodic announcements issued by the doctors attending the accident victim. At 5:40 p.m. it was officially announced that Gilles Villeneuve was unconscious and suffering from severe injuries to his neck and brainstem. His vital functions were being maintained by intensive care.

Then a last bulletin was issued from the University of St. Raphael Hospital in Louvain, Belgium. "Gilles Villenueve died at 9:12 p.m."

The members of the international press went back to file their final stories. Several of them were crying. One veteran writer from Brazil spoke slowly: "You know, my greatest regret today is that I hardly knew Gilles at all. I couldn't do anything about it. I was so impressed by him that I hardly dared talk to him . . ."

/

/

"It was a clear, hot summer's day with no one around but us, so my father let me drive. What a thrill!"
— Gilles Villeneuve

Joseph Gilles Henri Villeneuve was not born on January 18, 1952, as most record books show. He was two years older than that but hid it from public view in the belief that his real age might be a barrier to progress in his career. He was a relative latecomer in his chosen profession because, given his unexceptional beginnings, Gilles Villeneuve needed extra time to achieve his extraordinary success.

His father was an itinerant piano tuner. Seville Villeneuve lost his father when still a young boy and left school early to work as a handyman and jack-of-all-trades, picking up the necessary skills along the way. As a teenager Seville was taken in by a married couple, the Montagnes, who had no children of their own, and Seville came to regard them as his foster parents. Monsieur Montagne, a piano tuner, discovered that Seville had an ear for music and for many years the two of them travelled to the far corners of the province of Quebec to ply their trade.

Seville was twenty-three when he married Georgette Coupal, whose family owned a small construction business. Their wedding took place on June 21, 1947, in Chambly, Georgette's home town on the Richelieu River about 30 kilometers east of Montreal.

For several years they lived just across the river in the town of Richelieu. At six in the morning on a frosty January 18th in 1950, Georgette gave birth to Gilles in the Saint-Jean-Sur-Richelieu hospital. Another son, Jacques, was born on November 4, 1953, and the Villeneuve family was complete.

The Villeneuves were close but Georgette and the boys were often left alone for lengthy periods of time as Seville's piano-tuning took him hundreds of miles away to such places as the Gaspé Peninsula. Her husband's income was modest but Georgette was a good mother and homemaker and their household was a happy one. Little Gilles was fascinated by anything mechanical, particularly the construction equipment operated by his uncles. His favourite toys were bulldozers and trucks but they had to be realistic, with exactly the right number of wheels and axles, or he wouldn't play with them. He would take them apart and put them together again, no matter how complicated they were. Seville built him a sandbox in the backyard where Gilles amused himself for hours on end, painstakingly building miniature roads and bridges with his toy machines. When his roads were built he pushed the machinery around the curves as fast as he could, accompanying them with high-pitched noises in imitation of engines being stretched to their limits.

A quiet but adventurous small boy, he showed high degrees of courage and determination from the beginning. Too soon, he asked his father to remove the training wheels from his first small bicycle and Gilles promptly fell over. He persevered and, after a few spills, mastered the technique of two-wheel travel. Learning came easily to him in elementary school, where he entered the first grade in 1955. He took his studies very seriously then and, while there was no real pressure from his parents, he felt he had to be the best. If he didn't come first in his class he would rush home in tears.

He wasn't a precocious child, but he was very bright for his age and competitive beyond his years. Though he was something of a loner, his playmates tended to be older children and he enjoyed the stimulation of having to work harder to keep up with them. These associations developed an aspect of perseverance in his budding character as Gilles continually pushed himself to improve. When he challenged a naturally faster friend in a foot race, he delighted in coming closer each time they ran.

He set unusually high standards and continued to test himself as if searching for something in which to excel. There was always a piano at home and with his father's help he soon became quite proficient at the keyboard. Flushed with that success he decided he wanted to become a professional musician and became obsessed with learning to play the trumpet. Schoolwork and playtime played second fiddle to this new passion. Determined to master the technique, he practised five and six hours a day until he became quite accomplished. When he gave it up, several years later, he said it was because the shape of his upper lip changed as he grew older and it hurt his mouth to play. Given his penchant for perfection, he may have set the trumpet aside when he realized his skill level would never meet his own high standards.

When Gilles was eight the family moved to Berthierville, where the Montagnes were living. Here, about 70 kilometers northeast of Montreal on a quiet tributary of the St. Lawrence River, Gilles spent the formative years that were to determine his future. The first settlers had come to this part of New France to farm the surrounding flat and fertile land and today Berthier, as the French Canadians call it, is a sleepy town of about 4,000 people, the kind of place where the inhabitants stare curiously at strangers. The townscape is dominated by the large Roman Catholic church, Sainte-Genevieve-de-Berthier, and the sturdy, square frame houses are brightly painted in the Québécois tradition.

The Villeneuves moved into an old farmhouse on the outskirts of the town, where Seville set about rebuilding the interior and Gilles delighted in helping him, pounding away with a hammer and nails. As he grew older, he much preferred physical activity to scholastic tedium. When his parents enrolled him at the Seminaire de Joliette, where he was to be educated by the religious brothers, he was only home on the weekends and holidays. Joliette is only about 25 kilometers away but Gilles was a boarder and had to eat at the school. He detested the regimented institutional discipline – and the food.

"I hated it. I hated the fact that when the meal bell rang, everybody ran to get into the line. I hated the idea of waiting in line, especially the idea of waiting in line to eat this awful, disgusting, inedible food." Ever resourceful and independent-minded, Gilles solved this culinary catastrophe by smuggling in food from Georgette's kitchen, mainly cakes and jars of peanut butter. He said he survived on one meal a day, breakfast, when he would hide his precious peanut butter beneath the table and surreptitiously slather it thickly over slices of toast when the brothers weren't watching. When he went home, he gorged himself on his mother's cooking. "But even then I was a picky eater. Meat, especially hamburger, and chicken with potatoes were okay. But no fruits, vegetables, or fish. I must've driven my mother crazy. Stranger still, I was never sick."

He got plenty of fresh air and exercise. In the summers he and his friends rode around the streets of Berthier on their bikes or played tag and hide-and-go-seek when the hay was high in the farmers' fields. In the winters they cleared rinks on the frozen river where they skated and batted around hockey pucks or they skidded down snow-covered hillsides on sheets of cardboard. He made the best of the harsh climate in this part of the world where the year is said to be ten months of winter and two of poor sledding. His idea of a good time was to bundle himself up against the cold and run out into a raging blizzard. "I loved winter storms. There was always someone to dig out, or snowbanks to crash through to get to my grandparents' house. The sheer excitement, the sheer challenge of getting through, or going where they said you couldn't go, was a real thrill."

For a while music helped distract Gilles from the boredom and ritual of school. He studied classical music and played trumpet in the marching band at the seminary in Joliette. In his spare time he played improvisational jazz on his trumpet and occasionally performed disc jockey duties, choosing and playing records at school dances. But a new passion had taken over his life – cars, especially cars driven quickly. He came by it naturally. As a passenger in his father's car he was seldom driven slowly.

Seville Villeneuve was in many ways a methodical and meticulous man. He took pride in his work and would labour diligently over the most neglected and out-of-tune piano until he was satisfied that it was absolutely perfect. When he took up golf he was dismayed at his lack of ability and would endlessly practise his swing and spend many minutes positioning himself perfectly over the ball. Though he was prepared to exercise infinite patience in his pursuit of perfection, the elder Villeneuve was always in a hurry behind the wheel of a car and was noted for it in the community.

Jacques Villeneuve, who also inherited the family taste for speed, recalls those early days on the roads around home. "Our dad was a very fast driver. He was a high speeder, always overtaking people and always in a rush. And he had some big crashes, like at over 100 miles an hour. It's hard to say if we got our driving skills from our father but for sure we got the feeling of speed and driving fast from him." Their age difference meant Jacques and Gilles were not particularly close in their formative years, though Jacques followed a very similar development pattern to that established by his older brother. Later, when racing took over their lives, they became good friends.

Before his boys could see over the dashboard of the family Ford, Seville let them sit on his lap behind the wheel. Gilles was to say, "I loved it when the tires squealed. I can remember yelling, 'Faster, Daddy, faster!' or 'Pass him, pass him!' Maybe that is why he was always being caught for speeding!"

Shortly after moving to Berthierville, Seville and Georgette set up a small women's clothing business they called Industrie Seville. It evolved from Georgette's working at home sewing women's clothing as part of a local cottage industry that supplied larger Montreal manufacturers. The Villeneuves organized their own work force of neighbouring women and as it prospered Seville was able to join his wife in the enterprise. One of his duties involved driving into Montreal to get fabrics, and when their financial circumstances improved Seville bought a new Volkswagen van to ferry the materials. This was to be the first vehicle Gilles drove by himself and it remained his most vivid childhood memory.

"It was in 1959 or '60. We were driving down one of those long, straight country roads near Berthierville. It was a clear, hot summer's day with no one around but us, so my father let me drive. What a thrill!"

2

"Gilles doesn't feel fear at all. He always drove very fast, at the very limit. He always made everything he drove go as fast as it would go."

— Seville Villeneuve

When he was ten years old Gilles was given one of the first ten-speed racing bicycles to be seen in Berthierville and he always used it for its intended purpose, working the gear lever continually and pedalling just as hard as he could. But it couldn't compare with the pleasures to be had on four wheels. He pestered his father until he was allowed to putter around in the driveway with family vehicles and when he was eleven Seville let him loose in the nearby fields with a battered pickup truck. There Gilles bounced around in a cloud of dust and euphoria: ''I was crazy about that old truck!''

Not content with conducting himself just at speed, Gilles was interested in the mechanical aspect of his motorized fun and tried his hand at manufacturing his own vehicle. He commandeered the lawnmower, removed the engine and wheels, and slapped them onto a primitive chassis he'd cobbled from scraps of plywood and two-by-fours. He adapted the drive belt from the mower to the rear axle of his machine, fashioned a tensioner from a piece of wood, and putt-putted proudly around the property. Though the Villeneuves' lawn grew to resemble the nearby hayfields, Seville took a tolerant view of his son's enterprise, in fact, encouraged it.

When Gilles was fifteen his father presented him with a decrepit red 1958 MGA two-seater he'd bought from a neighbour for $100. A tattered manual from the manufacturer was included in the price and Gilles, who understood very little English at the time, relied on the diagrams and his own ingenuity to figure out what made the car tick. With the help of a couple of interested friends he took the engine apart and managed to fit most of it together again so that the vehicle was occasionally roadworthy. Until he could effect more permanent repairs he overcame the problem of the broken steering wheel by fastening vice grip pliers to the steering column. Thus equipped, he motored slowly down the driveway and toured up and down a strip of abandoned highway behind the house.

He was still legally confined to such minor off-road adventures since he had another year to wait to get his Quebec driving licence. Gilles became impatient and began to lust after the new family car, a 1966 Pontiac Grand Parisienne. It was a green two-door model with bucket seats and, while it had an automatic transmission, the shift lever was on the floor and the speedometer was calibrated up to 120 miles an hour. In exchange for his washing it, Seville let him try it out on the road around the house. The temptation to take it further became too great for Gilles and he had a separate pair of keys made.

One Friday night Seville drove Gilles and a neighbourhood friend to a teenage party a few miles away and dropped them off. After midnight, when the Villeneuves were asleep, the two desperadoes returned to the house and pushed the Pontiac silently out of the driveway. When it was safely out of earshot Gilles brought his secret set of keys into play and they drove off toward Joliette. Despite the fact that heavy rain was falling he quickly discovered the top speed of the car was 108 mph. He was doing close to this along a straight section of highway when he was suddenly confronted with a sharp curve. He lost control, skidded off the slick pavement, clipped off one telephone pole, then planted the Parisienne firmly against a second one. In fact, he wrapped it completely around the second pole, pushing the door on the driver's side almost into the transmission tunnel, and Seville's pride and joy was in a sorry state of disrepair. Fortunately, his son had suffered only a banged knee while the friend was unscathed, if very scared.

The accident happened about five miles from Berthier and the two shaken survivors decided the best course of action would be to hie on home as quickly as possible and hope for the best. They set out on foot in the pouring rain, ducking into the ditch whenever the headlights of an approaching car appeared. They separated near their homes and it was with considerable trepidation that Gilles entered his. He had just gotten into bed to think things over when the police, who had traced the licence plates, called to inform Seville his car had been stolen and wrecked.

While his parents allowed him considerable latitude, there were certain codes of behaviour to be observed at all times, among them absolute honesty. This came to the fore now as a chastened Gilles sheepishly recounted the night's misadventures. The police came around and he filled in an accident report. Because an unlicensed driver was involved, Seville was unable to collect insurance. The car was a write-off, as was the $4,000 he'd borrowed to buy it. Gilles was not severely reprimanded for what he had done, his parents believing that the crash and the cost had driven home the point.

■ ■ ■

Gilles's motoring adventures were more subdued for a while, then accelerated shortly after his sixteenth birthday as he celebrated the increased mobility afforded by his driving licence. There followed a succession of vehicles, including another MGA, this one black and somewhat more roadworthy than the first one. Besides his developing automotive passion, the teenager was experiencing a burgeoning interest in the opposite sex. A girl in Joliette had captured his fancy and one evening he hopped into the black MGA to visit her.

En route down the country road he came up behind a Dodge Roadrunner, a lumbering device with high-performance pretensions that Gilles saw as a challenge to his nimble British sports car – and his blossoming manhood. He attempted to pass, his adversary floored the Dodge, and the chase was on. It ended abruptly when the Dodge slewed to a halt, mere inches from a herd of cows a farmer was bringing across the road into his barn for milking.

In effecting his makeover of this MGA, Gilles had neglected to adequately refettle the brakes and his car was reluctant to stop in time. Seeking immediate evasive action, he jerked the steering wheel to one side. The car flew off the road and into the ditch, sending up a shower of mud and grass, flipped over onto its side, then careened back onto the pavement, landing upside down and in a considerable state of disrepair. The wisdom of wearing seatbelts in an open car lacking a roll bar was debatable, though immaterial in this case. The MGA didn't have them but its driver had managed to hang on during his wild ride. Gilles crawled out from beneath his totally destroyed car with severe head cuts caused by flying glass from the broken windscreen.

Early the next morning the Villeneuve home received a call that the remains of their eldest son's sports car were lying outside a nearby garage. Shortly after came the news that Gilles was lying in the hospital in Joliette with eighty stitches in his scalp.

■ ■ ■

Having destroyed examples of American and British engineering, Gilles remained undeterred about the perils of speed gone wrong and also gave his attention to an ancient little car of Czechoslovakian origin, a Skoda. He drove this ungainly rear-engined contraption much more quickly than its makers had intended, or the rules of the road in Quebec allowed. The car had a defective starter and usually needed a push to get going, but the accelerator pedal was in fine working order. Gilles's persistent rapid velocity began to attract the attention of the local constable, Claude Page, who later recalled: "I used to catch him quite often doing 80 in a 30-mile zone. He never argued. On the contrary, he was always very polite and paid the fine – it was $10 at the time – immediately. He would say, 'Good, you caught me. But the urge to drive fast is stronger than I am.' "

Fortunately for Gilles, these misdemeanours came before the Quebec policy of losing points and then one's licence for driving violations was instituted; the price he paid for speeding in the Skoda was only financial. There was no question in his mind that it was worth it, for himself and the carload of friends he used to ferry about to local dances and parties, and he recalled the Skoda escapades fondly: "I don't think I ever enjoyed myself, felt as completely free, as I did that summer."

Part of the challenge of this car was to try to corner it on two wheels and, at slower speeds, try to roll it over. He was unsuccessful in this latter manoeuvre, attempted during a couple of low-key slalom events he entered in the Skoda. These were held in the parking lot of a shopping centre on a tight course laid out with traffic cones. This type of competition proved to cramp the Villeneuve style and he tended to leave a trail of scattered cones in his wake.

His vigorous cornering technique brought him a certain amount of notoriety in neighbouring St. Thomas, which he passed through more frequently now on his way to see the girl in Joliette. The Skoda's squealing tires heralded his progress around the tight corner in the centre of the village and several times Gilles noticed he had an audience of interested St. Thomas citizens. It happened frequently enough for him to realize they were anticipating his arrival and he looked forward to entertaining the people on their porches – his first fans.

■ ■ ■

The girl in Joliette was Joann Barthe. She, too, was French Canadian but had lived for some time across the U.S. border in Connecticut before returning to Quebec. When she was eight her father abandoned the family, leaving Joann, her older brother, and two younger sisters with their mother. Mrs. Barthe was born with a heart defect and was often too ill to be able to work to support her children. They were frequently impoverished and needed financial assistance from the government welfare bureau. Joann attended a convent school run by strict nuns who stressed piety and moral virtue. In her early teens she began to work after classes and on weekends as a cashier in a variety store. At home she helped her mother around the house and sewed her own clothes to save money. Her life was not easy, but Joann was an attractive, optimistic, and self-reliant young woman when she met her future husband on a blind date.

Her sister Louise had a boyfriend who had a friend Louise thought Joann should meet. Teenage custom in the 1960s dictated that socially active boys and girls should "go steady" and the desirability of those who hadn't achieved this status was suspect. Several times Joann refused her sister's matchmaking attempts, thinking that if this guy couldn't get a girlfriend of his own then she didn't want to be stuck with him even for one evening. Louise persevered until finally Joann relented, agreeing to make up a foursome to attend a Saturday night dance in a hall outside Joliette.

Gilles, too, was a reluctant party to their first evening together. "My friend told me she was pretty but I didn't believe him. Most blind dates are a joke, but not this time," he said of Joann. She wasn't immediately swept off her feet by her date, who was a year older, and found him to be just "so-so." He was handsome enough, she thought, with a baby face and brown hair worn long in the fashion of that time. He was slight in stature and she wondered if he was perhaps too short for her, though in reality they were about the same height, five-feet six-inches. He was very polite, and while a bit shy, he seemed quietly self-assured, though she thought she detected an air of vulnerability and innocence about him and was struck by his complete honesty and sincerity. He told her he had been accepted by the Quebec Conservatory of Music as a trumpet player, but he was unsure about devoting his life to music and found the prospect of several more years in school somewhat less than thrilling.

Their first evening together passed comfortably enough and they continued to see each other occasionally on weekends. It transpired that Joann's reservations about Gilles's desirability to the opposite sex were unfounded. When she discovered he already had a steady girlfriend named Ginette she was furious. They had a spat and a week later Joann had a new boyfriend. This in turn made Gilles very jealous, especially since Ginette had terminated their relationship when she discovered she had a rival named Joann. After a period of estrangement Gilles called up Joann, and they patched up their differences and became a steady twosome in August of 1967.

3

"I love the smell of burning rubber."

— Gilles Villeneuve

Joann soon learned that life with Gilles would revolve around motor vehicles. Following his stint in the seminary he spent a year in the Sainte Rose school, where he studied publicity. Then, aged seventeen, his formal education ended, but he continued to pursue his own course of study—all about cars. He subscribed to many motoring publications and his room at home was filled with them and the walls covered with posters of racing cars. He pored over his magazines and they contributed to improving his understanding of English. He had studied it briefly at school and learned a bit from his father, who had acquired a fair command of Canada's other official tongue from his travels and work. Gilles found that the magazines were speaking his language and was delighted to discover that his twin loves of motors and speed could be combined in competition, that people actually made careers of doing what he did every day on the roads around Berthier. Accounts of races inspired his imagination and he sought practical experience.

On one occasion Joann found herself bundled into the trunk of Gilles's latest acquisition, a 1967 Mustang with a 289-cubic-inch motor. Joann's confinement was to avoid paying the admission price at the entrance to a local drag strip. For a while this stomp-and-go type of racing was an outlet for his competitive urges, and he entered the Mustang in drag races in the small towns of Napierville, Sanair, and Lavaltrie. He modified the Mustang, jacked up the rear springs for more traction, and replaced the 289 engine with a massive 427 unit to better tear up the pavement.

In everyday motoring Gilles saw each stoplight changing from red to green as a signal to blast off as fast as was mechanically and humanly possible. He loved the sensation of flooring it, the spinning wheels, the squealing tires, the blue smoke from burnt rubber, and the thunder of eight cylinders being tortured. He revelled in the sudden acceleration from zero to full tilt and practised the quick gear changes necessary to reach this state of euphoria at every opportunity. Drag racing enabled him to do this legally.

Joann found the drags a complete bore. As a passenger in a car with Gilles there was never a dull moment, but now she had to sit in the spectator stands all day with only periodic moments of interest when he was performing. Her boyfriend began to think likewise. The problem with this form of competition was that the thrill was over far too quickly: a short burst of excitement down a quarter-mile strip of flat and straight asphalt and that was that. Gilles viewed this as a mere preliminary to more prolonged racing adventures.

Most of all, the drags lacked corners on which to test one's mettle the way he did on the roads. And the idea of jockeying for position, wheel to wheel with other cars, on a proper racing circuit with curves had more appeal for him. The most basic form of this kind of racing took place on oval tracks, essentially two parallel drag strips linked by curves at each end. In his racing magazines Gilles read about the exploits of brave USAC drivers like A.J. Foyt and Roger Ward, who screamed around the oval at Indianapolis at over 150 miles an hour in single-seaters. On banked ovals, at places like Daytona and Talledega, larger-than-life heroes like Richard Petty and Junior Johnson manhandled lumbering American sedans at amazing speeds.

Gilles could relate most easily to these NASCAR drivers south of the border – their cars looked more like his Mustang. In fact, a primitive form of NASCAR-style racing took place almost within earshot of the Villeneuve home on a dirt-track oval once used for harness racing. The necessary equipment was a very-used family sedan, gutted of all passenger comforts and with the licence plates removed. Gilles bought one of these clunkers for a few dollars, gave it a basic race preparation once-over – mainly scrawling numbers on the bodywork – and entered his first motor race. The noise, chaos, fender-bending, and sliding sideways in the dust were enjoyable enough, but he soon tired of going round and round in circles. Just sitting there with the steering wheel cranked on left lock and his foot to the floor was curiously unsatisfying.

To express himself fully, to provide the real test for his skills and his cars, Gilles needed a variety of topography to negotiate. He wanted to be more involved, to shift gears, apply the brakes, and explore the limits of adhesion – and his courage – around corners of different types. This was what he did on the open roads around home, and reading about the great road-racing events in Europe set the wheels in motion in the youthful Villeneuve's mind.

In *Road and Track* he was enthralled by the wonderfully evocative race reports by Henry N. Manney III from such places as the mighty Nürburgring in Germany. Here, famous drivers such as Jimmy Clark and Chris Amon hung onto their exotic, frequently airborne Lotus and Ferrari Formula 1 cars to maintain incredible average speeds of over 100 miles an hour around the over 170 curves of the 14.150-mile circuit in the Eifel Mountains. Then there was the amazing Targa Florio, where the bearded

Swede Jo Bonnier and the handsome Italian Lodovico Scarfiotti corkscrewed their Porsche and Ferrari sportscars as fast as they could possibly go, up hill and down dale over the tortuous 44-miles-to-the-lap mountain road circuit in Sicily.

Thus inspired, Gilles would take to the back road from Berthier to Joliette. In the Villeneuve imagination, the winding highway became a circuit like the Nürburgring or the Targa Florio, with the village of St. Thomas serving as somewhere like Campofelice in Sicily. Or it became a town on the road from Rome to Brescia in the famed Mille Miglia race in Italy. The seventeen-year-old boy in a Mustang in Quebec was transformed into the dashing Spaniard, the Marquis de Portago, racing his Ferrari to the finish line, there to meet his beautiful actress friend Linda Christian at the chequered flag.

Alfonso de Portago had been killed in that race in 1957 and now, ten years later, Gilles's magazines too often contained solemn obituaries for racing heroes killed in action. But Gilles didn't dwell on that; he was too full of life and cars and speed and Joann to linger over motor racing's tragically negative side. His own accidents hadn't blunted his taste for automotive adventure and having a girlfriend in Joliette gave a new purpose to his fast driving. Joann was a goal at the end of the road and reaching her more quickly promised the spoils of victory sooner. The two were becoming quite close and their rendezvous in Joliette were more frequent.

Nowadays the curves between Berthier and Joliette have been straightened and much of the driving challenge is gone, but Jacques Villeneuve, who later cut a dashing figure on the same route, remembers what the 15-mile trip was like and how his brother used to drive it – faster than a mile a minute. "It was winding like hell, some short straights, but just winding, winding, winding, so it was a really gutsy road if you wanted to test yourself. And Gilles was always doing that. He used to make it in eleven, ten, sometimes nine minutes."

■ ■ ■

While Gilles and Joann were a steady item, he still had a few wild oats to sew with the boys on nocturnal outings. He was the quiet one in his group, yet with a natural aura of authority, augmented by his astonishing bravado behind the wheel, that commanded respect from his peers. Most of their escapades were of an automotive nature and, in the great Canadian tradition, these often took the form of loading up the trunk of the car with a case of beer and hitting the local weekend dances. Following one of these Gilles and his carload of friends decided to pay an impromptu visit to the newly built road-racing course near St. Jovite in the Laurentian Mountains. The fact that it was now past midnight in Berthier and Le Circuit Mont Tremblant was over a hundred miles away to the northwest was no deterrent. Laden with tents, sleeping bags, and beer coolers, they set off in search of sport.

Arriving at their destination in the mists of early dawn, and in high spirits, they sneaked through the fence and set up camp. Twice their revelries were interrupted by the police, who promptly threw the ticketless offenders out of the circuit. Each time they returned, and by the time activity began on the track Gilles and company had settled down enough to become interested spectators. The circuit was spectacularly beautiful, 2.65 miles of twisting, undulating asphalt hacked out of the rugged Precambrian shield and surrounded by forests, lakes, and rivers.

The day's racing consisted of regional events for production sports cars and sedans, single-seater races for Formula V and Formula Ford machinery, and the main event was for modified sedans in the Trans Am category. Gilles had mixed feelings about what he saw in his first road races. "It all looked completely inaccessible to me. The cars cost so much money. But I was looking at the drivers, too, and I figured about 90 per cent of them were 'wankers.' They hit the brakes too soon, they took the curves all wrong. I thought it was easy. When you're on the other side of the track that's the simplest thing to say. But I thought I could do better."

4

"Every winter there would be three or four huge flights and I know what being thrown on the ice at 90 miles an hour means."

— Gilles Villeneuve

Gilles's plans and prospects for the future were vague. He had completed a basic secondary education to Grade 12 but going on to university did not appeal to him and, besides, it would be expensive for his parents. Having given up on music, the only other conventional line of study that held any interest for him might be engineering. He began a correspondence course in that subject but his enthusiasm waned and it was never completed.

Although formal schooling was at odds with his independent nature, he had developed an exceptional ability to learn anything he set his mind to. No wiring diagram was too complicated for him to sort out and few of his friends were as knowledgeable about the internal workings of the combustion engine. He always described himself as "basically lazy" but, left to his own devices, Gilles was prepared to spend as much time as was necessary to get things right. This often meant many laborious hours because, in matters he considered important, he became a very demanding perfectionist. On the road he might flog his cars to the brink of their mechanical limits, and frequently beyond those limits, but he would labour over them at length to set them right again.

For a while he financed his carousing and courtship of Joann by working for his parents in their clothing business. Then he found employment with his uncles, who had a contract with Hydro-Québec to construct the foundations for the pylons that carried electricity from the generating sites. He drove trucks ferrying equipment, then he operated a transit and level on a surveying crew that checked the foundation construction for accuracy. The precision required in working with the instruments, following plans and engineering drawings, and drafting and plotting the results of field surveys held Gilles's interest for a while. And the driving, even heavily laden trucks over rough terrain, was great fun. Less pleasurable was having to get up at five in the morning to go to work, and Gilles's forays into the routine of the normal workaday world ended before he left his teens.

His native land receives an average of over five feet of snow (161 centimeters) each winter so, like many Canadians at this time, Gilles welcomed the new popularity of the snowmobile. A fellow Québécois, Armand Bombardier, had invented it in 1937 in Valcourt and now L'auto-neige Bombardier (Bombardier Snowmobile) had many competitors to their famous Ski-doo models. The devices, consisting of two short skis and motorcyle-style handlebars at the front for steering, have a moving rubber belt with cleats powered by a small-capacity engine for propulsion. Their proliferation in the late 1960s opened up the winter and most people used them as recreational vehicles to explore previously inaccessible back country. Bombardier's original name for his contraption was "ski-dog," and for fur trappers and the Inuit in the Far North snowmobiles became utilitarian vehicles to replace sleds drawn by dog teams. For Gilles Villeneuve they became another form of horsepower to be raced.

Snowmobile manufacturers began to field racing teams to promote their products and amateurs were welcome to compete against them. Seville Villeneuve bought a snowmobile and Gilles entered several events near Berthier, most of them held on oval circuits used for horse racing on the grounds where small communities held their annual fall fairs. He took to the sport like a duck to water and was immediately quick and a race winner.

Inherent raw bravery and the development of certain skills brought him to the fore and kept him ahead of competitors who drove equipment with similar performance potential. In those days, before the courses were iced as they were later, a snowmobile race was conducted in a cloud of flying snow thrown up by the whirling treads of the machines. It was like driving in a howling blizzard and Gilles pressed on regardless, into the fearful void of the whiteout, leaving more timid rivals in his wake. With a steadfast belief in his own ability, he kept the throttle lever on one handlebar pressed wide open while the brake lever on the other was seldom brought into play.

He developed a finely tuned sense of balance and an almost delicate sensitivity to know just how far he could tempt the centrifugal force that contrived to throw his mount off into the haybales surrounding the slippery circuit. His point of no return became much farther than most as he honed his reflexes to a lightning degree and trusted them to rescue him from the brink at the very last instant. The skis provided little grip at the front and the spinning rubber track helped maintain adhesion. Gilles's machine was in a continual powerslide and he kept it on course with minute throttle and steering applications. It wasn't road racing at the Nürburgring, but roaring round and round in a freezing blizzard was exposing him to the kind of things he had often read about in car racing.

"You can't see a thing," said Gilles of his rapid progress in the snow and cold. "You have to build quick reactions to whatever the machine does. That kind of thing teaches you to react to everything. You can also get very cold on a snowmobile. Sometimes your hands feel as if they want to fall off. But, of course, you must hang on, whatever happens. It helps, you know, to build a big heart."

His headlong approach also provided him with firsthand experience in crashing. "Every winter there would be three or four huge flights and I know what being thrown on the ice at 90 miles per hour means. But I never hurt myself on a snowmobile." His mechanical skills were exercised, too. "Few people realize just how sophisticated those machines are. They have many of the same characteristics as cars . . . they understeer and oversteer and you must set up the suspension just as you would in a car."

After just a few races on his father's machine the name of Gilles Villeneuve was becoming one to be reckoned with in snowmobile circles. When he was eighteen he was given a modified production machine to race by a family friend, Gilles Ferland, who sold Skiroule snowmobiles. Gilles won several races and the Ferland dealership prospered. The next winter, 1969-70, he was hired by the Skiroule factory as a driver/mechanic on their Quebec team. Now he was actually getting paid to race and was enjoying himself hugely.

Joann, who accompanied him to many of these weekend races, was not always having fun. "It might be fun if you're spectating for a couple of hours and when you're cold you can go inside and warm up with a coffee. But not if you arrive at six in the morning and you're outside standing alone and bored stiff in the cold until late in the afternoon. Still, it was a lot easier to go and watch him race than to stay at home and worry, not knowing what was happening to him. So I accepted it."

Joann accepted her lot in life because she was about to become Gilles's wife. She had not gone back to school and their relationship had reached a crucial stage – for she was pregnant. They decided to make the commitment and, for better or for worse, were married on October 17, 1970, in a small wedding attended by their families and a few friends. Led by the newlyweds in a borrowed, noisy, souped-up, bright orange Boss 429 Mustang, the wedding party left the church and toured through the streets of Joliette with exhausts blatting and horns blaring. Following a reception at a nearby hall, the new Mr. and Mrs. Gilles Villeneuve spent their one-night honeymoon at a nearby motel.

5

"I left the road several times. But I really enjoyed myself and won 70 per cent of the time."
— Gilles Villeneuve

Three days before his betrothal, Gilles had learned his services were no longer required by Skiroule. There was a suspicion that the head of the racing department, himself a racer, was jealous of Gilles because he was faster. There were Canadian and American divisions of the factory team and Gilles was asked to stay north of the border while he felt he was good enough to cash in on some of the big paydays in the U.S. races. Gilles refused to agree with the Skiroule request and was now an unemployed new husband and expectant father.

Refusing to be defeated, especially by politics and not on a race track, Gilles went shopping for another snowmobile ride. He found one with another manufacturer, Motoski, which gave him three machines and some technical assistance, and expense money to compete on a private team basis. Now he was literally racing for his daily bread, for any prize money he won was his only extra income. But he kept the larder reasonably full, becoming champion of Quebec in his class and topping off that season by winning the 440cc World Series title in New York state. Shortly after that, on Good Friday, April 9, 1971, the Villeneuves became the proud parents of a son, Jacques.

With his life now having such a pronounced vehicular aspect, it seemed logical to Gilles that his house should also be movable. He made a down payment on a 72-foot-long mobile home, towed it away from the dealer, and parked it on a two-acre parcel of land across the road from his parents' house. These portable, prefabricated structures come ready to use, with most of the comforts of home built in, so Gilles plugged in water, electricity, and telephone lines and left Joann to get on with the homemaking.

Around his machinery her husband was fastidiously neat and tidy and meticulously well organized. Joann soon discovered he was almost the complete reverse in most other manifestations of his private life. The nineteen-year-old bride and new mother had to contend with an overturned oil drum instead of steps into her new home, not the ideal way to make a grand entrance with a baby boy and his carriage. She eventually overcame this obstacle by arranging to have rudimentary steps installed.

Their abode was perched precariously on concrete blocks and lacking a proper foundation, so its underside was exposed to the elements. When that first winter howled south to Berthier from Labrador the water pipes promptly froze solid. Gilles's solution to this problem was to buy a blowtorch for Joann. On the worst sub-zero mornings she would find herself crawling around beneath the floor applying a flaming blowtorch to frozen water pipes. On particularly cold days the pipes would burst and the hard-pressed heating system malfunctioned, leaving Joann's blowtorch and all the clothes she could find for herself and Jacques as sources of warmth.

Meanwhile, Gilles was mechanically occupied, busying himself with such distractions as an old yellow school bus. He called it Big Bertha and divided it into two sections: the front to serve as sleeping quarters at the races and the rear to function as a combined transporter and workshop for his snowmobiles. In the winter of 1971-72 these were Alouettes and he repeated as Quebec champion, winning ten of fourteen races. Mechanical failure prevented him from completing the four races he didn't win. It was quite a respectable record, but Gilles was dissatisfied with any imperfection and worked at length developing modifications for the fragile rubber-belt transmission systems that caused his retirements.

By now he had a prominent position in snowmobile racing. His flamboyant style and flair for the spectacular made him a major drawing card at the races and his services were in demand by the event organizers. The next season he expanded his horizons, logging many miles in Big Bertha and travelling to events outside Quebec, and finished up as overall Canadian snowmobile champion. He was away from home for longer periods, but at least he was bringing back more money – about $5,000 that winter. He would need it and more, because on July 26, 1973, Joann presented him with a baby daughter, Melanie.

■ ■ ■

The responsibilities of fatherhood did nothing to diminish Gilles's enthusiasm for racing and there was no desire to settle down and get a "proper" job. Increasingly, he saw his winter racing as a means of livelihood. To earn more money, he would just have to enter more races and win more of them. The problem of what to do when the snow melted remained, and when it was suggested his talents on snowmobiles might be transferable to cars Gilles was all ears. One of the snowmobile engineers he knew was an émigré from France, where he had been involved in car racing. He knew some of the people in Quebec road racing, explained to Gilles how the licensing system worked, and recommended the Jim Russell driving school at Le Circuit Mont Tremblant as a starting point.

Gilles made an appointment with the school director, Jacques Couture, and showed up at the circuit one rainy morning. Couture, a former Canadian driving champion, arrived to find his obviously keen pupil waiting at the front gate. Other students arrived and in the preliminary classroom session the would-be racers listened intently to pointers on seating position, the proper grip on the steering wheel, gear-shifting tips, and so on. Gilles absorbed Couture's instruction on braking, traction limits, cornering techniques, skid control, and the like and realized he already knew most of it from reading his racing magazines and from his practical experience in the Gilles Villeneuve School of Advanced Motoring on the road from Berthier to Joliette. But he was his usual quiet and polite self and showed no impatience while the others tried to grasp the basics of operating a car at speed.

When the school Formula Ford cars were fired up and the students buckled in for a first tentative whirl on the damp track one car immediately shot into the lead and left the others behind in a cloud of spray. Couture was taken aback that his most diffident pupil should be so quick so soon. ''It rained during most of the classes and I was just a little bit nervous about how fast this kid Villeneuve was able to go in comparison to everyone else.'' But Gilles was in his element, and Couture relaxed when it became obvious he knew exactly what he was doing. The next weekend Gilles returned to Le Circuit in his current road car, an English-built Ford Capri, and was again the fastest at the school. He passed with flying colours and was immediately granted a racing licence.

Gilles came away from Mont Tremblant with more than a piece of paper. His first road-racing experience left him exhilarated and thirsting for more. The sensitivity and handling of the spindly little Formula Ford on its skinny tires were a revelation to him and he itched to get his hands on one again. He conferred with his snowmobile engineer friend, who introduced him to Jean-Pierre St. Jacques, a driver/mechanic who built his own Formula Fords. Gilles put a down payment on a rusty two-year-old car that St. Jacques was prepared to part with. Big Bertha was pressed into summer service and Gilles went racing in the Quebec provincial Formula Ford Championship Series.

It took him just a few laps to find his way, then he was gone. He finished a fighting third in his first race and won his second. The FF cars, using basic 1500cc British Ford engines, were very reliable, so Gilles didn't need to spend much time preparing his car and could concentrate on driving it – fast. On asphalt his style was similar to that on snow: flamboyant and spectacular rather than smooth and controlled and his decidedly sideways cornering technique owed much to snowmobiling. Occasionally his inexperience and exuberance tested the all-terrain capabilities of the unsophisticated but durable St. Jacques chassis.

''Most of my friends and rivals thought I was stupid to drive such an old car,'' he said later. ''It wasn't the most competitive car around at the time, but it was very sturdy and that was just what I needed most at this stage of my career. I left the road several times. But I really enjoyed myself and won 70 per cent of the time.'' Competing at Mont Tremblant, Sanair, and Trois-Rivières, he won seven out of ten races and was named Rookie of the Year as well as becoming FF champion of Quebec – all of this in an older car against more experienced road racers.

6

*"He came home and said, 'I've sold the house to buy a
car.'"*

— *Joann Villeneuve*

Now firmly in the grip of racing fever, Gilles eagerly anticipated
the coming snowmobile season. Before winter arrived he set up
a drafting board at home and worked on his own design based
on racing-car principles. While Joann attended to the needs of
little Jacques and baby Melanie, Gilles had his head down at the
board for many hours, detailing an innovative wishbone suspension system similar to those he'd seen on road-racing cars. It
would enable his machine to better apply the power to the snow
by making the chassis more flexible and adaptable to terrain
changes for improved traction.

Brilliant though it was, the Villeneuve suspension was not an
immaculate conception and took some time to prove reliable.
And Gilles's inventiveness and need to tinker with his equipment
required special tools he couldn't afford. But his racing passion
was so great that it overruled his sense of propriety and during
this period he resorted to "borrowing" tools from a nearby Canadian Tire hardware store. When his needs went beyond the
scope of his rudimentary tool kit, he would walk out of the store
with the required item concealed beneath his jacket. This dis-
honesty was quite out of character in an otherwise completely
forthright young man. He wrestled with it in his conscience for
many years and later went to great lengths to make amends.

He was less contrite regarding his behaviour to his family and
sometimes oblivious to the needs of those nearest and dearest to
him. They suffered another winter of hardship as Gilles took Big
Bertha further and further away from home. Racing weekends
became weeks – three, four, and five of them at a stretch. During
Gilles's prolonged absences Joann would often find herself snowed
in and fighting with frozen water pipes yet again. On most days
the refrigerator in her kitchen was completely superfluous. Her
in-laws helped whenever they could but were often away on
business.

Gilles would think nothing of spending their last $20 on a fuel pump, leaving her struggling to find enough money to feed and clothe the children. Bills were run up at local stores, debts mounted, and Joann despaired at her husband's apparent lack of concern. She complained often but he didn't seem to realize how difficult it was for her. And her own resourcefulness worked against her: after all, she had learned to handle the blowtorch well enough. "I think he just thought that, well, she can cope with anything, so it's not a real problem." And so he left her to get on with it.

Joann was without any means of transport and had to trudge through the snow to the shops in Berthier. Sometimes a kindly neighbour took pity on her and shovelled a path to the road, but on one occasion Joann's plight reached a crisis point. She had arranged a doctor's appointment for Jacques and awoke that morning to find snow drifted high around the front door and lying deep between there and the ploughed road. A taxi had been called and was waiting so there was no option but to wade out through 100 meters of winter's worst.

"Jacques was about two then and Melanie was just a few months old so I couldn't leave her behind. I had to carry both kids and their diaper bags and my bag and the snow was up to my waist. I thought, I'll never get there, and I was calling to the taxi driver to please come and help me. He yelled back that he didn't have any boots on and I thought, Oh God, why does this have to happen to me?"

■ ■ ■

At least Gilles was meeting with continued success during this 1973-74 snowmobile season. He rented a former pigsty in Berthier and hired a mechanic to help him prepare his self-designed machine. Fortunately, the freezing temperatures helped mask the odour of the building's former tenants and the Alouette chassis was substantially modified. Incorporating the Villeneuve suspension system, it also had enclosed bodywork so that it resembled a racing car and was sure to be noteworthy among snowmobile racing fans.

Big Bertha's decks were cleared to become a workshop while Gilles and his mechanic had a fifth-wheel rig, a camping trailer towed by a pickup truck, as living quarters. He was asking for, and receiving, appearance money from race promoters and the winter ended with a full-fledged world championship. Joann, taking her first weekend off in over a year, farmed out the children to her mother-in-law for the weekend and travelled with Gilles to Eagle River in Wisconsin. There she watched him tear up the track to win the 650cc title against the best international competition.

Nonethleless, his snowmobile earnings of nearly $13,000 disappeared quickly to pay accumulated bills and the family remained well short of a state of affluence. But Gilles was not to let that interfere with his now firm commitment to progress further in the various formulae that ultimately led to Formula 1, the international series for the world championship. After his sweeping success in FF, Gilles was looking much further down the racing road and the possibility of reaching the pinnacle existed in his mind. Many years later, at the beginning of his final F1 season, Gilles confessed how he felt after his first attempt at road racing. He was never one to boast and it wasn't articulated at the time, but he thought to himself: ''Boy, if I never make it beyond Canada the world will miss seeing a very great driver.''

Formula Atlantic was the top category of single-seater racing in Canada and that is where he decided to go. The Atlantic formula consisted of sophisticated chassis using slick racing tires and powered by modified 1600cc Ford Cosworth engines from England. Through the racing grapevine Gilles heard about a team called Ecurie Canada being put together by a Montreal driver/entrepreneur, Kris Harrison.

Harrison, who also ran a garage and racing shop, remembers his first meeting with Gilles. ''This kid walked in, introduced himself, and ordered a driving suit and some gear. Then he said he wanted a drive in Atlantic and asked me what it would cost. I told him I wasn't interested in anyone who wasn't experienced. Before he left he told me to call Jacques Couture.''

Harrison was impressed by the Villeneuve confidence but wondered how a snowmobiler with only ten FF races to his credit could possibly help his fledgling Ecurie Canada Formula Atlantic team. But he talked to Couture, against whom he had raced and with whom he had had business dealings in the past. ''Jacques told me to do a deal with this guy. He said he was sensational. When Gilles phoned a week later I told him to come in. He did, we shook hands on a business deal, and that was it.''

That was it as far as Kris Harrison was concerned because, as he was told by Couture and came to learn firsthand, ''Gilles's word was his bond.'' But for Gilles there remained the very expensive task of living up to his part of their bargain. The deal required him to provide the basic funding, which Harrison would use to help import two March 74B chassis and a supply of Ford BDA engines. Depending on the number of races entered, the 1974 season would cost Gilles between $50,000 and $70,000.

''I didn't have a penny. When I think about it I wonder how I made it. It was kind of a hard year. I put down $20,000 which I didn't have and even now I don't really know how I came to pay it back. I had a house which I sold. . . .'' That was Gilles's hazy recollection of what then transpired.

Joann remembers it clearly. ''He came home and said, 'I sold the house to buy a car.' '' A rather one-sided domestic quarrel immediately ensued, but the deed was done. ''It didn't make any difference to him because he had decided that was the way it was going to be. If you like it, fine. If you don't like it, scream if you want. That was the way he was.''

The mobile home wasn't really his to sell since the bank still held a substantial mortgage on it, but Gilles turned over a cheque to Kris Harrison right on schedule. And of course he had a solution to his family's immediate housing crisis: Joann, Jacques, and Melanie would travel with him to the races across Canada in Seville's pickup truck with the little camper on the back. As it developed they were not to join him until the third, and most disastrous, race of the season because Joann suffered a severe migraine attack that kept her in or near a bed for six weeks.

7

"Maybe, I thought, he's a little bit crazy."
—Joann Villeneuve

Besides his own cash contribution, Gilles brought a few dollars from the Cyma watch company, whose name he would display on circuits across Canada, while Kris Harrison had arranged some sponsorship from Schweppes beverages and the Goodyear tire company. Still, the Ecurie Canada team was underfinanced and the budget was further dented when Gilles destroyed both March chassis in pre-season testing at St. Jovite. Though he hoped his driver had now found his limits, Harrison was not particularly upset and made no attempt to curb the obvious Villeneuve speed. Repairs were made and, with only enough racing tires to last four events, the team travelled west to begin the 1974 Player's Challenge Series for Formula Atlantic cars.

Over three thousand miles later the little Ecurie Canada band arrived at the scenic Westwood circuit outside Vancouver, where they scored an encouraging third place in a field of over twenty cars. The winner was the experienced American, Alan Laider, and Gilles had driven from the middle of the pack to finish ahead of more affluent opposition. So the team was optimistic as it trekked back through the Rocky Mountains to the next race at Edmonton. Gilles qualified sixth on the grid but was delayed by a malfunctioning engine to finish a distant 22nd behind the winner, veteran Canadian driver Bill Brack.

Two weeks later, after a long return journey across the Canadian Prairies, Gilles was again sixth in qualifying but that was the highlight of his weekend at Gimli in Manitoba. Engine problems intervened once more and he did not finish. Things could only improve at the next race, at Mosport in Ontario, where Gilles looked forward to seeing Joann and the kids again.

By now the team's supply of rubber was threadbare, the Villeneuve sideways cornering technique having worn away much of their usefulness, and tires were rotated to get more mileage. This was a distinct disadvantage around the swoops and swerves of the hilly Mosport circuit and Gilles could only qualify 15th. The race, held on July 1, Dominion Day in Canada, attracted a large holiday crowd and there were many witnesses to the accident on lap nine on one of the fastest of Mosport's curves.

The yellow number 13 car was the most exciting of all to watch, broadsliding wildly through every turn on the ragged edge of control as if driven by a man possessed. Often it was completely sideways on the track and sometimes the rear wheels were in the dirt. Suddenly it flew off the circuit and disappeared in a big cloud of dust. There was a grinding crash of metal as the car banged heavily into the steel guard rail. The dust settled and the stricken car could be seen buried in the barrier with both front wheels off and the nose pushed in.

Yellow flags were waved as marshals struggled to extricate the injured driver from his crumpled March. The race continued while Gilles was gingerly placed aboard an ambulance and driven to the Mosport emergency centre. The track doctor assessed the damage done to his left leg: it was badly broken in two places, but Gilles refused to believe him.

Gilles's several off-course excursions in his previous races had not hurt him. How could this be? he asked Joann, who was translating the doctor's diagnosis into French. "He was really annoyed that he might not be able to race again. He kept telling the doctor, 'My leg cannot be broken,' and the doctor kept looking at me and saying it's very broken. Both bones were cut through as if they'd been sawn. It was quite obvious to everyone else but Gilles's main reaction was, Well, now I know what it's like to run into a guard rail and it's really not so bad."

But it was bad. Joann began to wonder about her husband as she tried to convince him that he was seriously injured. "Maybe, I thought, he's a little bit crazy. I started thinking, does this mean I'm going to have to go through this kind of thing all the time? Wasn't it dangerous enough on snowmobiles?" But she kept her misgivings to herself and eventually, when his shock wore off and pain set in, Gilles reluctantly agreed to be taken to hospital, though he did it only to humour the others, for he was sure the x-rays would prove that he was right and everyone else was wrong.

■ ■ ■

Outfitted in a cast from hip to toe, Gilles returned home to Berthierville in despair. He was even more upset when he heard his seat for Ecurie Canada had been taken by an up-and-coming driver from the U.S., David Loring. Gilles, immobilized in a wheelchair, was an infuriated spectator at Sanair, the next race in the series, and vowed to get himself back on track as quickly as possible.

He was a very bad patient and continually fiddled with his cast, pulling bits of it away and asking Joann to help him cut it off. She refused but agreed to take him to various doctors to get their opinions. Finally they found one younger doctor who was willing to exchange the hip cast for a smaller one that would enable him at least to bend his knee and ankle. As soon as he was able to move the leg, which had begun to atrophy from lack of exercise, Gilles pronounced it ready to operate a clutch and himself ready to race again. His doctor, Joann, and everyone else disagreed and after a fierce argument it was decided he could race only if he was able to extricate himself from the March cockpit in sixty seconds, this being the minimum safety margin should his car catch fire.

The Villeneuve family Mustang set off on a journey to Canada's far east and the next Atlantic race in St. John's, Newfoundland. Gilles did much of the driving during the trip, exercising his wounded limb in what he termed the Villeneuve System of Physiotherapy. He gritted his teeth through thousands of clutch applications but sitting in the spacious front seat of his Mustang was quite different from making a hasty exit from the cramped confines of a racing car. He failed the sixty-second test and was not allowed to compete. His disappointment was alleviated somewhat by the indisputable realization that his still quite severe pain would be difficult, if not impossible, to race with.

In August, six weeks after the Mosport accident, Gilles was able to resume racing at Atlantic Motorsport Park, near Halifax in Nova Scotia. He had to be lifted in and out of the car but his determination and pain tolerance brought him to a seventh-place finish, despite a spin.

The season ended at the beginning of September in a race through the streets of Trois-Rivières in Quebec. Gilles qualified in mid-field, 13th on the grid, but his race ended on the first lap when the circus high diver cum racing driver, Gary Magwood, spun in front of him and the two collided.

The year-end results were not very impressive: one third place and 16th overall in the series, several wrecked cars, one badly broken leg, and a crippling bank debt amounting to $14,000.

This might be enough to deter most people and to suggest that another line of work might be more suitable. But Gilles was confident that all his bad luck had been used up and more Formula Atlantic would surely bring improved fortune. It was certainly needed.

He had been supplementing his income with unemployment insurance but someone had notified the authorities that Gilles was earning money from snowmobile racing. The government demanded that part of the insurance funds be paid back. To do that Gilles borrowed money from his two uncles and ploughed much of it into further snowmobile escapades. Then the Alouette company went bankrupt and Gilles was left without any factory support for his racing program.

Gilles's entrepreneurial flair came to the fore as he capitalized on the potential crowd-pulling capabilities of his entry. He contacted the race organizers and demanded more appearance money. His previous reputation as a winner earned him the desired sums up front and L'Equipe Villeneuve, hauled by the faithful Big Bertha, showed up at races throughout Quebec and Ontario. The celebrity driver quickly showed a previously broken leg was no handicap, thrilling the crowds with his customary dash and flair and covering his pursuers in spewn snow. The perfected suspension system worked wonderfully well and the sleek device won a major share of the race purses.

For a very short time Joann thought some of the winter winnings might be used to find more suitable accommodation for her increasingly nomadic family. Following the disposal of the mobile home, Joann, Jacques, and Melanie lived in Berthier and Joliette, alternating between rooms in the Villeneuve homestead and Joann's mother's house. The arrangement was completely unsatisfactory for all concerned and that fall she finally told Gilles they couldn't live that way any longer. He then rented them a tiny apartment near his parents' place and, since his own main abode was in the back of a camper truck or in Big Bertha at the races, Gilles was surprised to learn that his nearest and dearest were still not comfortable. He decided he would rescue them by resurrecting his plan of the previous year: his family would accompany him to the Formula Atlantic races across Canada, for that was where he was headed once again.

2

QUICK TIMES: 1975–1976

I

"Gilles always knew exactly what he wanted and always did what he felt he had to do in order to get it – no matter what the obstacles."

– Kris Harrison

Despite the hefty Villeneuve-inspired repair bills for the Ecurie Canada racing machinery, team owner Kris Harrison invited Gilles to return for the 1975 Atlantic series. He'd had a year's seasoning and Harrison thought that Gilles's was a diamond-in-the-rough driving talent that only needed polishing to shape into winning form. And Harrison was willing to overlook their frequent differences of opinion.

"We disagreed on many things. He was extremely strong-willed and for me to survive in the racing business I had to be that way too. He wanted to test every day but we had no budget for that. He didn't want another driver in a second team car. He wanted number-one status. For him, our organization was a means to an end. My objective was to build a successful racing team. So we were often two people of similar character going in opposite directions at that time. Still, I was happy to have him back, though he was sure that he could run a team better than anybody else."

In the end Gilles missed the deadline to secure the Ecurie Canada drive when the potential sponsors he had been counting on backed out. Harrison signed up the quick Swedish driver, Bertil Roos, and Canadian veteran Craig Hill.

Three weeks before the season began Gilles still didn't have anything lined up and he became very depressed and was ready to give up. It was the first time Joann had seen him feel this way. "Even though I was completely against racing, I couldn't stand to see him so unhappy, so destroyed. So I encouraged him, not necessarily to race, but to at least try everything possible to succeed. I said to him, 'Order the car, buy the engine, have them sent over and we'll worry about paying for them later.' " A new March 75B and a Ford BDA were ordered from England and the Villeneuve team was mechanically set, though still financially destitute.

Once again snowmobiles provided the impetus to get Gilles's road-racing aspirations into gear, and his increasing shrewdness as a negotiator came into play. Those winter performances on his modified snow machine had attracted the attention of his former employer, Skiroule, who invited him to return to the fold the next season as its star driver.

This was just one week before the first Atlantic race and, though he was desperately keen to leap at the opportunity, Gilles held his enthusiasm in check long enough to see some light at the end of that long, cold snowmobile tunnel. Yes, he would be happy to race for Skiroule, providing they agreed to one condition: they would sponsor his Formula Atlantic car during the summer. He pointed out that the Skiroule name on his car, a frontrunner of course, would keep the name before the public year round.

It was a big gamble on Gilles's part because a negative answer might have left him without a ride on snow as well as the roads. But Skiroule agreed to come up with enough funds at least to get the Villeneuve Atlantic show on the road. He made arrangements with an engine expert in Montreal to help when his Ford BDA motor needed rebuilding and hired his snowmobile mechanic to travel with him to the road races. Joann would be the team's timekeeper, chief cook, bottlewasher, and babysitter for Jacques and Melanie, and Gilles would look after the rest. In mid-May the tiny team set out from Berthier in Seville's camper truck with the shiny new March on a trailer behind.

The first race of the 1975 Player's Challenge Series, in Edmonton, showed Gilles just how difficult it would be for his shoestring operation to challenge the more affluent opposition. On paper, the Atlantic formula decreed that the cars were equal in performance so, in theory, driving ability would win at the end of the day. But in Edmonton Gilles came to realize that another factor – money – was likely to influence the results.

The wealthier section of the paddock was full of large transporters from which crisply liveried personnel unloaded the best equipment money could buy. Most of the name drivers had spare cars: people such as the 1974 championship winner, Bill Brack, who owned a prosperous car dealership; the Mexican playboy, Hector Rebaque; and Americans Price Cobb, Howdy Holmes, Bobby Rahal, Elliott Forbes-Robinson, and Tom Klausler, who either came from affluent backgrounds or had the reputations and/ or connections to attract healthy budgets. Some teams had crates of new engines and stacks of tires, and elaborate tool chests that looked as if they cost as much as L'Equipe Villeneuve had for the entire season. Gilles looked on enviously as he and Joann polished the number 69 green-and-white March with the Skiroule name hand-lettered on it while swarms of mechanics poured over the rival machinery.

Besides the very obvious financial disadvantages, Gilles knew he was also still short on racecraft compared to most of the others and could only hope that his underdog enthusiasm would overcome his lack of experience. It didn't in Edmonton and he was buried in the results of the Alberta race, finishing 15th behind the winning Ecurie Canada car of Bertil Roos. The Swede was undoubtedly speedy, but Gilles was convinced he had been out-engineered rather than out-driven and put down his defeat to better preparation by the opposition.

He concentrated on fine-tuning his March for the next race, at Westwood in British Columbia. There, he was more on the pace and qualified an encouraging eighth on the starting grid. Unlike the flat and featureless Edmonton circuit, Westwood's twists and turns were more a test of man than of machine. Gilles threw his March around with great verve to finish a fighting fifth in the race, just half a minute behind the winner, again Bertil Roos.

■ ■ ■

A spirit of optimism helped the miles fly by as the nomadic Villeneuves drove back across country to Gimli for the June 22 race date. Gilles took to the track with a vengeance in qualifying but various mechanical problems relegated him to 19th fastest and his chances for a good showing in the race seemed slim.

Then fate intervened in the form of a deluge from the Manitoba skies and the airport circuit was awash in a torrential downpour for the race. Gilles was to describe Gimli in 1975 as "worse than a nightmare," and the driving conditions were, but he turned it into a dream come true. "I'll never forget that race. I felt I was given a chance that would never happen again."

He seized the opportunity with both hands in sink-or-swim weather that put everyone in the same boat. The rain was the great equalizer that placed him on the same, if desperately uncertain, footing with his soaked rivals. Skill and daring overcame equipment and experience differentials as he sailed inexorably up through the pack. Fearlessly, he dove into the balls of spray thrown up by the cars ahead and left everyone in his wake. Visibility was virtually non-existent and he relied instead on instincts sharpened in the whiteouts of snowmobile racing and uncanny car control. His mastery wasn't enough to prevent him from spinning many times, but so did everyone else, and Gilles pressed on regardless and took the sodden chequered flag first, 15 seconds ahead of the next man, Bobby Rahal.

"I couldn't see anything on the straightaway and only the orange marker cones ahead on the curves told me when I had to start braking," said the drenched but happy victor after the race. "I drove right off the track twice, but still managed to finish." His driving suit was soaked with as much perspiration as rain from the supreme effort. As the Villeneuves loaded up their gear in Gimli it was their turn to be the subject of some envious looks from the rest of the paddock.

That Gilles's performance at Gimli was no flash in the pan became obvious at the following race, at St. Jovite, where he qualified fourth and finished second, a mere six seconds behind Elliott Forbes-Robinson. In Halifax he was seventh in qualifying but fell back to 14th in the race (won by Bill Brack), the victim of mechanical problems again, and his lack of point-scoring finishes affected his position in the overall results of the series. Brack won the championship once more, with 112 points, and Roos was second with 94, while Villeneuve's 69 points earned him fifth place in the final standings. Still, such a highly respectable showing from a relative rookie and impoverished privateer earned Gilles a much more prominent position in the estimation of the racing establishment.

His growing reputation was further enhanced at an end-of-season, non-championship event, the Molson Grand Prix at Trois-Rivières. The organizers of the street race in the Quebec town invited several name drivers from Europe to augment the Formula Atlantic regulars and Gilles found himself competing for grid times alongside Italian Vittorio Brambilla, who had just won the Austrian Grand Prix in a March Formula 1 car. There were other Grand Prix drivers from France, including Jean-Pierre Jarier from the Shadow team and the Tyrrell driver Patrick Depailler, as well as Formula 2 frontrunners José Dolhem and Jean-Pierre Jaussaud.

Gilles was unimpressed by the celebrity drivers and flung his March around the exacting Trois-Rivières track in his customarily aggressive, stylish manner, registering faster and faster times on Joann's stopwatches. He qualified an astonishing third, right on the heels of Jarier and Depailler, immediately overtook the latter at the start of the race, and set out in hot pursuit of Jarier. Alas, the brakes of his March were unable to withstand the punishment being given them and he began to fall back, much to the relief of the imported stars. They were not at all unhappy when the absence of stopping power forced the upstart French Canadian into retirement on the 60th lap.

■ ■ ■

Back on the snowmobile ovals that winter Gilles had his best-ever season. He entered thirty-six races, dropped out three times because of mechanical failure, came second once and won thirty-two times for Skiroule. Undoubtedly, the Villeneuve family's much improved domestic circumstances contributed to his success. In lieu of Skiroule paying for his flights, hotel rooms, and restaurant meals, he convinced the company to give him a lump sum of expense money. He bought a 26-foot motorhome, fully outfitted with beds, kitchenette, toilet, and shower. It was a home he could call his own and, better still, it could travel. Joann, the kids, and the newest member of the family, Princess, an Alsatian, accompanied him to most of the winter races and Gilles was very content.

His mind was also unencumbered by worry about his immediate road-racing future because the deal for his 1976 Formula Atlantic season was already secured. After his sudden rise to prominence at Gimli, reinforced by his showing against the international hotshots at Trois-Rivières, Gilles's services were in demand. He received attractive offers from several Formula Atlantic entrants, including Doug Shierson, Pierre Phillips, and Ecurie Canada again.

Skiroule had already agreed to help fund his Atlantic efforts for another year, which was useful since Gilles was, as he put it, "extremely flat broke" as usual. At least there was some momentum in their life, and Joann, gradually becoming resigned to her husband's ambitions, began to take a greater interest in his progress. Now, with her advice, he was able to choose what he felt was their best opportunity.

The season on their own had taught them the value of skilled personnel to provide the essential backup services and teamwork for a racing driver. Foremost in Gilles's mind was the need to be able to concentrate on driving and not have his attention unduly diverted by the mechanical side of the sport, setting up the car and maintaining it. "No way can you drive well and be your own mechanic. You're too tired. When I first started I did all my own work. But I couldn't afford anything else. Now I don't want to touch the car. Sure, maybe to help align it, but things like changing an engine – I hate it."

Another prerequisite was to be with a team with enough resources to fully service its driver's needs, and a two-car team might not be able to do that. Doug Shierson Racing was also negotiating with Bobby Rahal, who had emerged as another promising driver, and Gilles was to be the American's teammate. Harrison, too, was talking to Rahal and Joann suggested to Gilles that Rahal's family money might become a factor in a two-car entry when the choice of the best equipment might be given to the driver who contributed most to the team coffers. Perhaps, she suggested, Ecurie Canada might be persuaded to have Gilles as its only driver, and he would have the full weight of a familiar team behind him. On the weekend of October 5, 1975, all interested parties were at Watkins Glen in New York to watch the U.S. Grand Prix and there Gilles signed a contract with Ecurie Canada for the 1976 Atlantic series.

■ ■ ■

While he remained wary of personality clashes with Harrison, the deciding factor for Gilles was the presence of Ray Wardell. "Kris Harrison and I were not really getting along," Gilles said. "We never understood each other too well. But Ray Wardell was coming with him and I knew him just a little bit because he had come to Trois-Rivières to help Depailler and the other Europeans. I thought he was the best guy in the business and when we talked I said, 'Okay, I'm driving for you.' "

Ray Wardell, a widely experienced race engineer from England, had worked for the March organization for some years in several European formulae. He was also responsible for customer liaison and attended the annual Trois-Rivières event, where Kris Harrison customarily entered the top European March drivers under the Ecurie Canada banner. Previously, Wardell had worked with the likes of Niki Lauda and Ronnie Peterson early in their careers. At first, both were wild and prone to crashes, then they matured to become two of the biggest names in the sport, Lauda a triple World Champion and Peterson one of the fastest and most colourful drivers. Wardell thought he saw similarities in Gilles Villeneuve at Trois-Rivières in 1975.

"The talent was there. He reminded me of Ronnie and Niki in their early days. While you couldn't say he was going to be as good as either of them, you could tell that here was a young driver with an awful lot of drive."

Wardell used the state of the equipment as a yardstick to measure the driver. "Working with the team you don't get to see much out on the track itself. I would look at the condition of the cars after the drivers had used them and look at the times they were able to do. What Gilles was doing with a car that had no right to do those times was amazing. He really had no brakes on it at Three Rivers. I tried to give him some advice but he was on his own and didn't have any money or backing to improve the situation. But you couldn't help but be impressed. He was going to put out an awful lot of effort if you could give him a car that worked. Gilles was one of the main reasons I came to Ecurie Canada.''

2

"He knew what his own limits were. Those limits
happened to be different from the average driver and
Gilles was prepared to use those limits more often."
— Ray Wardell

Gilles now abandoned snowmobile racing and his first road event of 1976 was in late January at an endurance race in Florida where he was invited to share the driving with Maurice Carter in his Chevrolet Camaro. Mo Carter, a car dealer from Hamilton, Ontario, was a perennial winner in his lumbering, modified sedan in shorter races but would require help for the 24 Hours of Daytona. His choice of co-driver proved to be inspired, in terms of speed.

In his first time behind the wheel of a car he had never driven on a track he had never seen Gilles was two seconds quicker than Mo, but their equipment was not up to the task of running around the clock. Gilles's driving stint ended after seven laps when the 450-cubic-inch engine blew to smithereens as he was motoring briskly down the straight. He managed to wrestle the massive machine to a safe halt and an engine change was made in the pits, but the equally fragile replacement gave up the ghost ninety minutes later with Carter driving.

Early that spring, while the snow was still receding from the northern part of the continent, the Ecurie Canada team went south to Atlanta, Georgia, to get a head start on the Formula Atlantic season. By now this was the most important single-seater series in North America, with the American International Motorsports Association (IMSA) running four U.S. races for the category to complement the Player's Challenge events north of the border.

Ray Wardell was pleased with the performance of the new Skiroule-liveried March 76B in Georgia but somewhat taken aback at the antics of his new driver in another car. ''I didn't yet know the bloke very well and on the second day of testing he drove me to the track in a rental car. There was a gate we had to open and I got out to open it while he drove through. I closed it and all of a sudden the right rear wheel of the car just lit up in smoke and he stood there and burned that tire until it virtually burst. The whole place was full of smoke. I thought, Geez, this guy's a real cowboy.''

Wardell was given further revelations when the two were sitting in the rental car in front of the pits discussing racing. Bobby Rahal, who was testing with the Shierson team, and Ecurie Canada's engine man, Dave Morris, drove by in their rental cars, cruising around slowly examining the circuit. The Wardell/Villeneuve conversation abruptly ceased as Gilles saw the opportunity for some sport. ''He fired the thing up and off we go after them. I'm not particularly brave when it comes to being a passenger. Well, I had the most frightening drive I've ever experienced.

''I was hanging onto the door handle and my feet were in his lap. His rental car was the slowest of the three but he caught the other two, who tried to race with him, and just blew them off. By the time he'd finished the tires were complete junk. When we returned the car to the rental agents at the airport Gilles remarked that it was just terrible the way they equipped their cars and told them the tires had given him so much trouble.''

When Wardell had recovered his equilibrium he began to see the method in the apparent Villeneuve madness. ''It made me realize the ability Gilles had, standing that thing on two wheels around every corner. I think he had such a good feel for any automobile that he had to find the limit of everything about it. He didn't do it to entertain people. He felt this was the way to go. And he knew what his own limits were. Those limits happened to be different from the average driver and Gilles was prepared to use those limits more often.

''You might say that as he matured he should learn that you don't have to do that all the time. Gilles looked at it in a different way. He thought his job was to deliver every time he got into a car. That's the way he worked. That's how he lived his life. His life was motor racing and he delivered every time. He always gave an honest effort and he expected the same from everyone else. But if you didn't, you weren't going to get along with Gilles Villeneuve.''

Under Wardell's tutelage Gilles was able to grasp the mechanical intricacies of setting up a car, but his failure to come to grips with the financial side of racing continued to cause friction with his team owner. Kris Harrison remembers that it was ''fun to work with someone who was so single-minded and one-directional,'' but the two seldom saw eye-to-eye outside racing cars and Wardell often found himself acting as mediator between his race-oriented driver and his business-minded partner in Ecurie Canada. As had been the case during their previous season, whenever Harrison had to close the pursestrings on more testing or buying better equipment, Villeneuve saw it as a threat to his racing and arguments ensued. Wardell tried to mediate. ''It was fortunate that I could stand back from that. Gilles could never see Kris's side and would think of him as a bad guy. He couldn't appreciate what the business side was all about and anything that might sacrifice the effort of the team he couldn't accept at all.''

■ ■ ■

As Wardell became more involved with Villeneuve, they developed the closest engineer/driver relationship of Gilles's career. After each practice session they would pore over a map of the circuit and spend hours discussing the driver/car situation according to the configuration of the track. Wardell would go into the details of each turn, asking Gilles exactly where he was shifting gears, what kind of revs the engine was pulling, whether the car was neutral or in an oversteering or understeering attitude, and so on. Wardell would translate his driver's comments and feedback into mechanical adjustments on the March and they came to have a deep understanding, mutual trust, and respect.

Villeneuve's insights into the technical side of racing invited further comparisons with Wardell's former charges. ''Of all my drivers, Peterson and Lauda included, Gilles was the best to work with by far. Ronnie had pure ability and no technical understanding. Lauda was all understanding and thought every single thing out in great detail. The best combination of those two was Gilles.

He had an excellent understanding of the car, not to Lauda's degree perhaps, but he certainly had Ronnie's ability and would give you 100 per cent aggression every time.''

Their superlative qualities were not enough to prevent Lauda and Peterson from having very bad accidents: the Austrian was to come close to death from terrible burns in 1976 and the Swede eventually paid motor racing's ultimate price in 1978. And Wardell, a sensitive and emotional man, had learned from painful experience to keep a certain distance between himself and his drivers.

At the Dutch Grand Prix in 1970 Wardell was the chief mechanic on the March Formula 1 car of the Swiss driver Jo Siffert. By coincidence Siffert's March went missing during the race at the same time as the De Thomaso of Piers Courage. The Englishman, a member of the prominent brewing family, was the victim of an appalling accident and from the pits Wardell saw the thick clouds of black smoke billowing up from out on the circuit and knew something was desperately wrong. He thought it was Siffert's March, though it wasn't, and assumed the worst. There was little consolation when he learned that Courage burned to death that day in Zandvoort and Wardell suffered ''a kind of breakdown.'' He couldn't be a mechanic on a car after that and switched to race engineering and management.

A year later Jo Siffert, then driving a BRM, was killed in a fiery crash at Brands Hatch in England and Ray Wardell was only too aware of the potentially disastrous side of his sport. ''You accept that this is a dangerous business and if something goes wrong, it can go wrong horribly. But you put that to the back of your mind and do the best job possible for your driver. Because that's what he wants to do. I wouldn't get into the car but he's made the decision to do it and so I accept it.''

Thus, while he had the closest possible working relationship with Gilles, they were not as involved socially. But then few people were because nearly all of Gilles's non-racing time was devoted to his family. Wardell marvelled at their closeness. ''They were a very tight unit, right down to the dog, Princess, who was very protective and loyal. Nobody could get near her other than the family and Gilles loved that because this was his family . . . he created it.''

3

"Joann and the children were absolutely part of him. They were his life. They were Gilles. It was critical to him that they were there all the time."

— Ray Wardell

During that season the Villeneuves had the closest and happiest time of their lives as a family. Remembering her own fatherless childhood, Joann had been worried about the effect of Gilles's prolonged absences on their children. Now they were to be with their father twenty-four hours a day and the family, with the faithful Princess in tow, had a surfeit of togetherness, living like gypsies as they navigated the continent in their motorhome. If travel is the best education, Jacques and Melanie, now aged five and three, had a wide-ranging kindergarten experience that took them from coast to coast in the U.S. and Canada.

One thing they weren't exposed to was the variety of cuisine in the different regions they visited, and Joann's grocery shopping en route was made easy by her husband's insular culinary preferences. Gilles was strictly a meat-and-potatoes man and variations on that theme, topped off with sugar pie, a French-Canadian favourite, for desert, were standard fare from Joann's kitchenette. Gilles loved to stop at the plethora of fast-food joints in America to feast on hamburgers, chips, and Coke and often presided over barbecues at the campgrounds where they stayed overnight. With Princess (now in an advanced state of motherhood) as a most effective canine security system, the family could sleep securely anywhere and the lights in their camper went out early most evenings.

To help pass the long miles on the road Joann tried to keep the children amused with puzzles and games. Up front, behind the wheel of a vehicle that wouldn't go nearly fast enough for his tastes, Gilles occupied himself with endless racing reveries. He engaged in mental exercises to keep his mind in technical trim. A favourite pastime was counting off the mileage markers along the highway and comparing them to the motorhome speedometer tallies. In this way he discovered the instrument was fractionally inaccurate and thereafter relied on his own calculations to mark his progress. Other parts of the not terribly well-constructed motorhome were unable to keep pace with the driver's often indelicate treatment. Pit stops for repairs frequently interrupted the family's progress but Gilles took these in stride, indeed delighted in mending the damage he'd done. Now that others were looking after his racing machinery, the motorhome was the main opportunity for him to wield wrenches himself.

At the race circuits Gilles parked the motorhome near the fence in the paddock and instructed the kids to stay away from the pits when racing cars were around. But his son was already showing signs of being a chip off the old block. Jacques had a plastic three-wheel tricycle he pedalled furiously at all times. Inspired by a certain Ecurie Canada March that tended to spin its wheels frequently, Jacques learned how to apply a burst of power so as to spin the large front wheel of his mount and did so at every opportunity. When the real racing cars were out on the track Jacques and Melanie wore adult-sized insulated headsets to prevent hearing damage. During the races they cheered loudly for their daddy and it seemed to work . . . because he nearly always won.

■ ■ ■

In mid-April the Villeneuve motorhome pulled into the Road Atlanta circuit in Georgia for the first race of 1976. Gilles manoeuvred the vehicle into a strategic corner of the paddock near the Ecurie Canada pit, plugged in the electrical cord, and went off to meet with his team. He loved to watch the two Ecurie Canada mechanics work on his car and would sit, often in the cockpit, talking shop with them and Ray late into the night. Joann would have to keep his meat and potatoes on the back burner for lengthy periods while Gilles was ''bench racing.''

Gilles particularly liked to hear about Ronnie Peterson, his favourite F1 driver. He had seen Peterson's spectacular sideways displays in races on television and in person at the Canadian Grand Prix at Mosport in 1971. He and Joann stood on the outside of Turn One in the rain watching the cars of the stars tiptoe around in admittedly terrible conditions. The exception was Peterson, who powered his rain-tired March up from sixth on the grid to engage polesitter Jackie Stewart in a tremendous tussle.

He muscled past him into the lead and stayed there for thirteen laps until he clouted a backmarker (the Canadian driver George Eaton in a BRM). Peterson continued to drive in total disregard of the weather and the bent nose of his March. Stewart won, with Peterson second, but it was Ronnie who impressed Gilles.

Peterson's famous cornering technique, with the tail out and the front wheels on full opposite lock, struck a responsive chord in Gilles. This was the way he had always negotiated the bends around Berthier in his road cars. And for him, the supreme pleasure of throwing a much more sensitive and responsive racing car sideways and controlling it was a major reason for choosing this profession. Yes, people like Jackie Stewart won more races with a smooth, unruffled style, but Peterson always looked faster and Gilles was sure the daring, uninhibited Swede was enjoying himself more than the canny, controlled Scot. Any comparisons Wardell made between Gilles and Ronnie were particularly welcome.

At the Road Atlanta race Villeneuve showed the best of both schools of thought regarding driving technique: he threw his car around wildly – and he won. Most of the Formula Atlantic front-runners had returned for another season and the field was full of equally eager young rookies, but none were able to catch the French Canadian in the Wardell-engineered March. Gilles lit up the tires from pole position and was never headed, finishing 13 seconds ahead of American Tom Pumpelly.

There was a repeat performance at the next IMSA race, at Laguna Seca in California, where the best the opposition could do was Elliott Forbes-Robinson's second place, a minute behind the flying Villeneuve. Even more success followed at the next California stop on the tour, at the Ontario circuit, when Gilles added fastest race lap to his pole position and win over Forbes-Robinson.

The Villeneuves celebrated the U.S. sweep with a side trip to Disneyland before heading north for the first round of the Player's Challenge Series at Edmonton. Again Gilles was quickest qualifier, led from start to finish, and set the fastest race lap, but it was no runaway this time. Gilles had to work hard to win, as he explained after accepting the victor's laurels and prize money. "It wasn't easy, because Bill Brack was hot on my heels all the way and I couldn't afford to make the slightest mistake.'' Princess commemorated the win by giving birth to half a dozen offspring in Edmonton and the motorhome was even more crowded until homes were found for the puppies.

The euphoria in the Ecurie Canada camp was dimmed at the end of May at Westwood, where the infamous Vancouver weather rained on their parade. Gilles started from his now customary pole position and his enthusiasm was certainly not dampened by the diabolically wet conditions. Alas, his engine was. He was leading by eighteen seconds when the Ford BDA momentarily cut out – the rear wheels lost adhesion, he slid off the track, and his race was over. Ray Wardell had never run an Atlantic car in the rain and had prepared it as he would an F2 car. He took full responsibility for the carburetor malfunction that caused the problem and was impressed that Gilles never faulted him for this, the team's only DNF (did not finish) of the year.

■ ■ ■

The score now was Villeneuve four, the opposition one, and word of this North American phenomenon had spread to Europe. An invitation came from Ron Dennis (who later masterminded the McLaren F1 team into prominence) to drive one of his March F2 cars in the annual race through the streets in Pau, France. Early in June, Gilles, accompanied by Ray Wardell, flew to the attractive city in the Pyrenees to test himself against the foreign talent. During the flight they talked about how the usual route to the big time was up through the European formulae: Formula Ford, Formula 3, Formula 2, then Formula 1, and Gilles wondered whether he should do more racing abroad to get noticed. Formula Atlantic was probably closest to F3 but took place some distance away from the talent spotters. However, now that Ron Dennis had noticed him, Gilles began to consider his chances of circumventing the established farm system.

In the past, several Canadians, including Bill Brack, who was now a mainstay in Formula Atlantic, had competed in the annual Grand Prix of Canada, hiring a car for the weekend. George Eaton, a member of the wealthy department store family, had rented a more permanent ride for part of a season with the BRM team, but F1 was essentially a European show. The last American to make it was Mark Donohue, who had come in the back door, so to speak, driving a Penske for the American entrant Roger Penske. Donohue's career had ended in disaster when he was killed in the warm-up for his fifteenth F1 race, at the Austrian Grand Prix the previous August. And Wardell, worried about his charge wanting too much too soon, cautioned Gilles that motor racing's big time was still likely a long way down the road.

There was to be no great leap ahead at Pau. Gilles qualified his unfamiliar March 762-Hart well enough, 10th overall on a difficult circuit he had never seen before. His opposition included such F2 regulars as Tambay, Cheever, Laffite, and Arnoux, names he would would later come to know well. Gilles powered his way through the twisting streets with great gusto and was soon challenging for a position among the top six. Jacques Laffite set the fastest lap and René Arnoux won his first important race. But Gilles was waylaid by an overheating engine and was forced to park the March, which bore advertising for the upcoming Grand Prix Molson Trois-Rivières. He would have to wait for that race to confront the Europeans again.

■ ■ ■

Meanwhile, there were more Atlantic races to be won, and his domination continued at Gimli with another visit to the top step of the victory podium, this time ahead of Tom Klausler. The Ecurie Canada team headed east to Mosport cautiously optimistic about their chances of winning both North American championships. But it was still by no means a sure thing because Klausler, Price Cobb, Bertil Roos, and others had scored consistent finishes in the points and there were three Canadian races and one U.S. event remaining. Also, the team was still running close to the bottom line financially, and Kris Harrison was relying on Gilles's prize earnings and winner's status to attract other smaller sponsors to supplement the Skiroule budget.

A few days before the Mosport race Harrison was shocked to learn that the last cheque from Skiroule had been declared NSF by the bank and the cheques he had written to pay suppliers were bounced. Harrison had been supplementing their income with appearance money for his driver, now regarded as the top drawing card in Atlantic racing. A sum had been agreed to by Mosport and now Harrison asked for more or his team wouldn't be able to compete. The Mosport management, headed by chartered accountants who had rescued the circuit from receivership, refused to up the ante. They had had to cancel the F1 Grand Prix the previous year over another monetary disagreement and still had no extra money to spend on star attractions.

Negotiations continued right up until the last minute, with Harrison adamant that he couldn't afford to race without more money up front. Gilles sat fuming in the motorhome, where even the appearance of his kids, who were black from head to toe after playing in the spent embers of an abandoned barbecue firepit, failed to distract him from his profound gloom. He was furious that all his supreme efforts behind the wheel could count for nought because of financial embarrassment. His anger became despair when he had to sit out the Mosport race.

Harrison was very worried about the Skiroule situation and the team huddled together to find a way to make the starting grid of the next race, at St. Jovite on July 11. Everybody pitched in, including John Lane, an American who was now a member of the Ecurie Canada entourage. He offered to buy the two March chassis from Harrison at the end of the season for $25,000. As a businessman, Lane's reasoning was that the Marches would be a desirable commodity if Gilles were to win the championships with them. But he was also a friend of Gilles and was willing to stretch his own resources to get him racing again.

John Lane had become involved with the team at the California races earlier in the season. He had made money in the government securities business in California, but the excitement and challenge of motor racing had always attracted him. Previously he had sponsored a Formula 5000 team on the West Coast, with John Cannon (an expatriate Englishman who had emigrated to Canada) as his driver and Ray Wardell as the team manager. When Wardell joined Ecurie Canada he and Kris Harrison made overtures to Lane about sponsoring their effort but Lane felt he had ploughed enough money into the sport and declined.

But when Wardell invited Lane to the Atlantic races at Laguna Seca and Ontario in California to help with the lap scoring, he leapt at the chance. Lane's own team hadn't had much success in F5000 but his first Formula Atlantic experiences were entirely positive when Gilles won both events. And, despite their different cultural backgrounds, the two struck up a friendship. "Gilles and I were about the same age, though he looked to me like he was about eighteen. He was very small, very quiet, and spoke only a little English at that point, but he was very aggressive and impressive on the track and we got along well."

Lane, then in the process of moving his business to New York to be closer to Wall Street, responded to the lure of racing again. Taking a cue from the travelling Villeneuves, he sold his house in California, bought an expensive motorhome, and, with his wife Elizabeth and their two small daughters and their two dogs, hit the road with Ecurie Canada. On race weekends the French-Canadian and American families were usually alone overnight at the circuits. Jacques and Melanie were older than Courtney and Lindsay Lane, but the children played together around the motorhomes, overcoming the language barrier by developing their own pidgin tongue, which was incomprehensible to their parents. Jacques taught Courtney the finer points of wheel-spinning her tricycle while the adults sat around the barbecue with Joann translating any complexities of English for Gilles. It had been a happy carefree time – until Mosport.

■ ■ ■

John Lane's contribution to the team coffers was enough for Harrison to see his way clear to attend the next race and they all headed up into the Laurentians of Quebec to Gilles's home circuit of St. Jovite. When Lane took Jacques Couture's driving course at St. Jovite, Gilles kidded him about trying to take away his Ecurie Canada driving job. But following the Mosport crisis, Lane was one of those Gilles had to thank for helping preserve it. He resumed his winning ways but the result came only after a disturbing accident during testing.

Ecurie Canada had arrived early for private practice and was the only team there. Gilles was lapping very quickly when Ray Wardell and the pit crew suddenly became aware that their driver, who was due around again, hadn't appeared. Wardell: "It all went very quiet and we started getting very nervous. There were no marshals on duty and we shouldn't really have been testing under those conditions. There was this old beaten-up ambulance which you were expected to use yourself, so we hopped in this thing and went looking for him, wondering, 'Geez, where has he gone off.' "

They found Gilles trudging up the hill just after the pit straight, apparently none the worse for wear, though his car lay in ruins in the bottom of a ditch. He was unable to explain the cause of the crash but Wardell, more concerned about the state of his driver than the wrecked car, was astonished by Gilles's attitude. "Thankfully he wasn't hurt in the slightest but he must have been badly shaken. All he wanted to do was get in the spare car and get going again, which is exactly what he did. It didn't slow him down one bit."

"Classic Villeneuve" is how John Lane describes the ensuing performance at the Mont Tremblant circuit. "After a really big shunt Gilles went on as if nothing happened. In qualifying he would set the quickest time, then Klausler or Rahal would go out and break that time. Villeneuve would get mad, get back in the car and go break their time. This went on over the two days of qualifying. Finally somebody had beaten his time by a fairly decent amount and Gilles just got back in the car and completely obliterated that time."

Gilles kept his pole position advantage throughout the race, set the fastest lap, and finished comfortably ahead of Klausler. The winner was in a buoyant mood in post-race interviews, where he explained the Villeneuve philosophy of racing: "Before the season started I didn't want to win the championship by placing second and third. I've always believed that the best way to win the championship is to win all the races."

Scarcely had the victory celebrations peaked when along came another plunge in the roller-coaster ride of circumstances that marked that year. Skiroule declared bankruptcy and Harrison was forced to pull the plug on any further racing. Instead of moving east to the next event, in Halifax, Ecurie Canada loaded the equipment and drove away in the opposite direction, back to its headquarters, which was now in Toronto. For Gilles Villeneuve's career to continue an immediate influx of cash had to be found, and with the Halifax event less than a month away it became a race against time.

4

"I look at this kid and notice he's very animated and when he talks about racing I can see him actually vibrate."
— Gaston Parent

Ten days before the August 8 date at Atlantic Motorsport Park in Halifax there was still no glimmer of hope for Gilles. Kris Harrison had done his calculations and arrived at a sum of $5,000 that would be required before Ecurie Canada would race again. Gilles didn't have even one-tenth of that amount to call his own, in fact, could hardly afford to put gas in his car to travel around treasure hunting for potential financial saviours. But he persevered and presented his plight to one of his contacts, Robert St. Onge, who was involved in promotional work for Molson, the brewing company that sponsored the race through the streets in Trois-Rivières.

St. Onge was employed by Gaston Parent, a successful Montreal entrepreneur who had built up what began as a graphic design organization into a group of nine companies involved in various aspects of advertising, communications, and promotion. Parent, then fifty-three, was thinking of retiring to enjoy such favourite pursuits as big-game hunting in Africa. Parent owned a percentage of the Alouette football team and had a privileged seat for the Canadiens hockey games in the Montreal Forum. But while his client, Molson, invested in motorsport, and Parent's staff under St. Onge looked after it, Parent himself knew very little about any kind of racing other than the sport of kings for horses. Becoming involved with a young driver was the furthest thing from his mind. But he listened dutifully to St. Onge's explanation of the Villeneuve saga, about how he was something special and looked like he might go places in the racing world. Finally Parent agreed to meet him, as long as it wouldn't cost him any money.

"I come into my office one Monday morning and see this young guy sitting in reception. He looked like he was about seventeen and I just walked right by him into my office. About ten minutes later St. Onge came in, followed by this youngster, and I was introduced to Gilles Villeneuve."

The two visitors sat down in front of his desk. Parent fondled his goatee and listened as they ran through the details of the season to date and the financial predicament. He watched Gilles, who seemed shy and nervous, constantly rubbing his hands together and his eyes were watery, perhaps with emotion. A colourful character with an entertaining manner of speaking, Parent remembers the occasion well.

"I look at this kid and notice he's very animated and when he talks about racing I can see him actually vibrate. He has conviction in his voice and says he can win the Canadian championship easily. Not only that, he tells me he can win the American title and the Molson race in Trois-Rivières. Nothing can stop him . . . except $5,000.''

Parent, a shrewd judge of character, was impressed by Gilles's complete honesty. "He told me the whole story, about his wife and kids living in that motorhome and that he was mortgaged to the hilt. He didn't have a pot to piss in but he had charisma. I saw a young man full of hope and confidence he could make it.''

Parent was becoming intrigued and, being a man of action himself, the sense of urgency appealed to him. The Halifax race was on the coming Sunday, just six days away. He picked up the phone on his desk and placed a call to Kris Harrison in Toronto. Their conversation was cordial. Harrison knew of Gaston Parent and knew his cheque for $5,000 would be good. But Harrison, at the end of his financial tether, insisted on having the money in hand before he would release the car. "I figure, you son of a bitch Harrison, I'll show you. I was annoyed and my wanting to help Villeneuve race became stronger. It became more of a challenge for me to get the money there and get the car released than having Villeneuve in my debt.''

Parent called in his comptroller from an outer office and instructed him to transfer the money to Toronto. Forty-five minutes later the deed was done and "Villeneuve was practically jumping out of his chair, saying Wow! And he says to me, 'Look, you're the sponsor now, how do you want the car painted?' '' One of Parent's companies had designed the fleur-de-lis logo for the province of Quebec for Canada's centennial celebrations in 1967. "I had nothing to sell to the public, so I said just paint the car white and get the goddamn fleur de lis on it.''

■ ■ ■

A week later Robert St. Onge came into Gaston Parent's office with the morning papers. He showed him a photo of a white racing car, decorated with the lily of Quebec insignia, taking a chequered flag. In another photo Parent recognized the grinning young driver with the laurel wreath around his neck. In the sports section Parent read that Gilles Villeneuve had dominated the race at some place named Atlantic Motorsport Park near Shubenacadie, outside Halifax. He won pole position, was the fastest driver in the race, and beat the second-place man, Bill Brack, by 16 seconds.

Furthermore, said the article, his Halifax victory meant that Villeneuve was the winner of the Player's Challenge Series for Formula Atlantic cars, finishing up with 120 points, 48 more than the runnerup, some Swedish driver named Bertil Roos. This made him the Canadian Driving Champion and, it was noted, Villeneuve seemed set to win the American version of the series at the last race in Atlanta. And there was speculation about how he might fare against the European stars who were coming to Trois-Rivières early in September.

Parent found himself "a little bit proud" of this course of events and was happy to receive another visit from Gilles Villeneuve. "So the kid comes bouncing back into my office and says, 'I got my money I won! I won 10,000 bucks in Halifax!' Then he tells me that 30 per cent of that was going to Harrison, so he had $7,000 in his pocket and he was ready to pay me back.

"I had looked around a bit more and found that Villeneuve was really up to his goddamned neck in debt. But I'd talked to St. Onge again and he advised me that the kid is really very, very good. So I said to Villeneuve, 'Take that $7,000 and do something else with it, pay something off.' Then he tells me he needs $12,000 for Harrison to take the team to the next two races. I told him, 'Look, I'll put up the $12,000 but I want you to give me the right to recoup my money.' And he said, 'Fine, no problem,' and he was all set to go racing again." Thus began a business relationship that developed into a personal one, almost like father and son, between Gaston Parent and Gilles Villeneuve.

In mid-September Parent's Monday morning newspapers again informed him that Villeneuve had won everything at the Road Atlanta circuit in Georgia, starting from pole, setting the fastest race lap, beating Tom Gloy to the finish line. His four wins in as many U.S. races gave him 80 points to Price Cobb's 45 and Gilles Villeneuve was the 1976 IMSA Formula Atlantic Champion. But that story was almost anticlimatic because it was preceded by the non-championship race in Trois-Rivières, where the news generated by Villeneuve made headlines everywhere in the racing world.

■ ■ ■

Following their first meeting Gaston Parent had been busy organizing the Gilles Villeneuve Fund. He lunched at Montreal's exclusive Beaver Club with several influential friends, including representatives of the top management level in Canada Steamship Lines, Loto-Québec, and the Bluebonnet harness-racing track. Parent explained his idea of using a young Québécois racing driver to enhance the image of the province by sponsoring his racing car at Trois-Rivières and Atlanta. The Fund would invite corporate and public contributions, the former would reap promotional benefits, and the people of Quebec would have the excitement and satisfaction of being involved with a unique form of charity. His luncheon companions knew as little about motorsport as Parent, but armed with Villeneuve's results he convinced them of his scheme's merits.

Important personages were appointed to the board of directors of the Gilles Villeneuve Fund, which was launched at a Parent-arranged press conference in Montreal. Parent looked after the publicity and was amazed at the reaction. The biggest corporate donor was CSL, which chipped in $600, but the public response, five and ten dollars at a time, was overwhelming. In a few weeks the goal of $12,000 was reached and a multitude of investors in the Fund were in attendance to watch "their" driver race on the Labour Day holiday Monday, September 5, 1976, at Trois-Rivières.

The last Grand Prix du Canada for F1 cars held at St. Jovite was in 1970, after which Mosport in Ontario secured the annual world championship event. The Grand Prix Molson at Trois-Rivières was now the most important race in Quebec and the presence of the invited F1 stars gave it international stature. This year the celebrity drivers were led by the swashbuckling Englishman, James Hunt, who was just four races away from becoming the 1976 World Champion. Appearance money of $10,000 helped persuade Hunt to interrupt his pursuit of the F1 title in his McLaren. And since he was to drive in an Ecurie Canada March 76B identical to the one that had won nearly all the North American Formula Atlantic races, there was little chance of Hunt's image suffering through inferior equipment. The fact that his teammate at Trois-Rivières was to be Gilles Villeneuve was of little consequence.

Also competing was the rugged Australian Alan Jones, who was beginning to make his mark with the Surtees team in F1 (and would be World Champion in 1980, with Williams). The flamboyant Italian March F1 driver, Vittorio "The Monza Gorilla" Brambilla, a favourite with the Trois-Rivières fans, was back again, as was the Tyrrell F1 rising star Patrick Depailler, who would also line up in an Ecurie Canada car for Kris Harrison. Another Frenchman, the handsome young Patrick Tambay, who was making his mark in F2, was also in attendance. These were the invited guests against whom the leading Atlantic runners would test themselves. Gilles Villeneuve summed up the significance of the race: "I'd gladly trade all my wins for a victory at Trois-Rivières. In my opinion it's the most important event of the season. European teams and foreign reporters are interested in the race. It's very important for me to win."

5

"Here Gilles was, with exactly equal equipment, and he was streets ahead of the Formula One guys."
– Kris Harrison

In the Ecurie Canada pits Ray Wardell readied three Marches for Hunt, Depailler, and Villeneuve. Kris Harrison had done a deal with Ramada Inns to sponsor the Hunt car, while the Villeneuve version featured the corporate identity of Direct Film, a film-processing company that came through with a last-minute donation to the Villeneuve cause sizable enough to gain visual prominence on the car. Joann and John Lane got their stopwatches ready for qualifying, which would be all-important on this tight circuit made up of ordinary streets where passing opportunities in the race were few and far between.

Gilles took to the track in a rush and immediately entertained the crowd, though his antics had Kris Harrison worried and embarrassed for him. "He would come through a right-hand corner just past the pits where he spun I don't know how many times, right in front of everybody. I thought, gee, we're about to lose the car, right in front of the F1 guys. This is going to be a disaster and Gilles is going to make a fool of himself. I said to Ray, 'Let's pull him in and cool him off.' But Ray said, 'No, no, he's going to be fine. Don't worry about him.' And Ray was right. Here Gilles was, with exactly equal equipment, and he was streets ahead of the Formula One guys. He was super-motivated and if he could outqualify them and win the race it would say all he wanted to say."

Timing one of those first laps, John Lane glanced up from his watch to see Gilles shooting through the corner between the houses – backwards: "In typical Villeneuve fashion, he never lost sight of where he was, kept the car running, whipped it around in a cloud of blue smoke, and kept right on going. It only cost him a second. I couldn't believe my watch and asked Ray about it. He just shook his head and laughed."

Wardell noted that Gilles could wind himself up right from the word go, with very little warm-up, and "He also has the ability to spin the car and know exactly where it is and what it's doing. In fact, he's the only driver I have ever seen who seems able to do that."

Harrison, with the Goodyear tire concession for Formula Atlantic, had plenty of rubber for his cars, which used up a set of sticky qualifiers every three or four laps, less in the case of his Direct Film entry. "He'd burn up a set, come in for another set, then go out and clock another fastest time. The two F1 guys on our team tried to do the same thing but they simply weren't in the same league. It was an extraordinary performance."

Ray Wardell was busy overseeing the pit operations and trying to keep all his drivers happy, particularly the featured Formula

1 guest. "I asked James what he wanted from his car, which was one of Gilles's regular cars. He said, 'Villeneuve's car seems to be going well, you tell me what I need.' We did everything we could for his car. But, with Gilles's attitude, his experience in the car, and this being a familiar circuit for him, there was no way that anyone was going to compete with him."

As Gilles later pointed out, part of his spectacular pursuit of pole position was due to handling problems left over from his St. Jovite practice accident. "The car was just on opposite lock everywhere. It wouldn't turn in at all and the moment it hit the apex of a corner it would just go into a long, long slide. I was only quick because I was using every inch of the circuit, sometimes scraping the rear wing against the walls, and being very, very brave. We tried everything in practice and qualifying, but couldn't get rid of the oversteer. And what was annoying me a little bit was that James wasn't complaining about anything. He said there was a bit of oversteer in his car, but that it was just nice, and when James Hunt says that people listen. But when I also drove James's chassis at the next race (Road Atlanta), I realized it was much better than mine. Anyway, I was right in Trois-Rivières because on race morning we tried wider rims on the back and my car was much better."

Gaston Parent, with several of the Gilles Villeneuve Fund dignitaries in tow, paid a visit to the pits and, at first, wasn't exactly bowled over by what he saw. "I didn't know what the hell was going on. Villeneuve had Wardell and the mechanics around him and we couldn't get close. I didn't like the smell and all the noise. Then all of a sudden the race took off and there's our car ahead of everybody and beating them all. The whole place went nuts and Villeneuve wins by something like ten seconds ahead of a Formula One guy named Jones."

The view from inside the number 69 car was equally spectacular, and while he was fully occupied performing in the manner so entertaining to his audience, Gilles was able to extract some pleasure from their reaction. He particularly took note of the corner just past the pits where photographers were leaning out over the concrete wall to better focus on his furious progress. "I was always tail out and all sideways coming through there, looking like I was going to hit the wall – and sometimes believing I would hit it! Every lap the photographers would scatter, running like mad. That made me laugh. On corner two I could see John Lane with his stopwatch, see him quite clearly. You don't have time to look at these things, but the eyes, the peripheral vision registers them.''

On his victory lap with the chequered flag through the streets of Trois-Rivières, Gilles witnessed the effect his epic drive had produced: many of the wildly cheering spectators were weeping with joy, ecstatic that one of their own had won. The race organizers, too, were mightily pleased that a native son was victorious and there was little resentment from the Formula Atlantic brigade. Granted he had beaten them all in nine of the ten races he entered (it would be ten of eleven after Road Atlanta), but a Formula Atlantic driver had now shown the world just how strong their series was. And the Formula 1 drivers were duly impressed, particularly James Hunt, as Gilles noted. ''James was a real gentleman about it and said some great things about me when he went back to England.''

■ ■ ■

The European motoring press gave great prominence to the Trois-Rivières story, expressing some wonderment at how an ''unknown'' could so soundly trounce drivers like James Hunt. No doubt it was in his own best interests, to preserve his reputation as a prime contender to win the title as the best driver in the world, for Hunt to stress that Villeneuve was indeed extremely talented and would surely be able to acquit himself well against any F1 opposition. In fact, Hunt spoke very highly of Villeneuve to his boss, Teddy Mayer, suggesting that Villeneuve would not be out of place in a McLaren F1 car. Hunt also spoke to John Hogan of Marlboro, the cigarette company that sponsored McLaren and paid a large portion of Hunt's considerable retainer. Hunt said, ''Look, I've just been beaten by this guy Villeneuve and he's really magic. You really ought to get hold of him.''

Meanwhile, others were showing an interest in the French-Canadian phenomenon as the Formula 1 teams were now involved in the traditional end-of-season scramble to find drivers for the next year. The motoring press and the grapevine were full of rumours and Gilles learned that Bernie Ecclestone, owner of the

Brabham team, might be considering him as a replacement for Carlos Reutemann, who was reportedly going to Ferrari in 1977. Gilles also knew that Walter Wolf, a wealthy Canadian businessman, was planning an F1 team and the Villeneuve name was being mentioned as the driver of an all-Canadian Wolf entry.

Gilles had misgivings about beginning his F1 career with a new team in an untried car, but the Wolf possibility ended when Walter Wolf announced he had signed South African Jody Scheckter. The Brabham opportunity evaporated at the Canadian Grand Prix at Mosport, where a spectating Gilles met Ecclestone and discovered there was unlikely to be any future for him with the abrasive Englishman. The two developed a mutual dislike, one of the very few such relationships in Gilles's life, which blossomed into full-fledged loathing later on. But at the upcoming F1 race in the U.S. Gilles's chances of closer involvement with the McLaren team were to improve.

At Trois-Rivières John Lane had invited James Hunt to use the Lane motorhome during his weekend with Ecurie Canada. Hunt, always one to take full advantage of all available creature comforts, enjoyed Elizabeth Lane's cooking and was delighted to find that her husband was a competent backgammon player, a game for which Hunt had a passion. Hunt asked the Lanes to come to the Canadian Grand Prix at Mosport and there the Lane motorhome became the McLaren team headquarters. James won the race to gain valuable world championship points over his rival, Niki Lauda. (Lauda, in only his second race after suffering nearly fatal burns earlier in the season at the Nürburgring, finished eighth in his Ferrari.) Jochen Mass was fifth for McLaren and Teddy Mayer asked the Lanes to accompany his team to the race at Watkins Glen the next weekend.

At Mosport, Gilles, still unsure of himself in such exalted company, stayed away from the McLaren entourage in the Lane motorhome. At Watkins Glen he found the courage to come closer. It was typically cool and blustery October weather in upstate New York and the Lane vehicle was crowded between practice and qualifying. Inside were Teddy Mayer, his McLaren partner Tyler Alexander, Hunt, Mass, John Hogan of Marlboro, and Hogan's assistant, Patrick McNally. (Later McNally achieved some notoriety when his ex-girlfriend "Fergie," who was formerly his children's nanny, married into the British royal family.)

For some time John Lane had noticed someone dressed in a sports jacket standing outside, huddled up against the cold. Lane had been talking to Mayer about how his friend Villeneuve's terrific talent deserved him a chance in F1, but Mayer thought Lane was prejudiced. Lane took a closer look at the person hovering outside. "Since I had never seen Gilles in anything remotely resembling a sports coat I had no idea it might be him. Normally he would just knock on our door and walk in. We could be standing there stark naked at the sink and Gilles wouldn't bat an eye. After about fifteen minutes I realized it was him standing out there waiting to be invited to come in. I brought him in and introduced him to everybody but Gilles seemed very uncomfortable, no doubt partly because of the sports coat! He didn't say much, just listened in on the conversations. But I knew he was feeling like a kid in a candy store. When he left Teddy Mayer, who is basically a taciturn person and can be sarcastic, gave Gilles what from him was like the *Good Housekeeping* seal of approval. Mayer said: 'He seems like a fairly nice kid.' "

■ ■ ■

The facts were that Gilles Villeneuve was no longer a kid. Despite his perennially youthful appearance and the myth of his 1952 birth date now being perpetuated, he would be twenty-seven years old in January. James Hunt, only a couple of years older, was nearly on top of the world as a driver. Niki Lauda, born in 1949, just a year before Villeneuve, had already won a world championship in 1975 (and he would win it twice more in his thirteen-year career) and had already been "To Hell And Back" (as he was to call one volume of his autobiography) since his F1 career began in 1971. So Gilles was becoming impatient.

At the end of October he read that Hunt was declared the 1976 World Champion in Japan, where his third-place finish gave him just one more point than Lauda for the season. Lauda had dropped out of the Japanese race after only two laps because he considered the torrential rainstorm at the Mount Fuji circuit made conditions too dangerous to race.

Gilles had mixed feelings about Lauda's decision. No one could question the man's courage. Following his brush with oblivion in Germany, in August, Lauda had finished fourth just six weeks later, in Italy, with blood from still unhealed burns seeping through his facemask. But Gilles loved to race in the rain; that wet Formula Atlantic race at Gimli had helped propel him into prominence, and he wondered if he would ever get the chance to do it in a F1 car.

Shortly after the McLaren team arrived back at its headquarters in Colnbrook, near London, Teddy Mayer summoned Gilles to come to England, at McLaren's expense, to talk about his racing future. Gilles could scarely contain himself. He immediately called Gaston Parent and asked him to accompany him. Parent, pleading ignorance about the intricacies of racing matters, declared himself too busy and deputized Robert St. Onge to go with Gilles. When they met with Mayer and John Hogan, Gilles was offered an option contract with Marlboro McLaren for 1977.

The deal was for him to drive "selected" races later in the season, up to five in all, in a third car alongside Mass and Hunt. The British Grand Prix was mentioned as his probable debut race, with the Canadian and U.S. events also likely for Gilles. There was also the possibility of Marlboro sponsoring him in some F2 races that didn't conflict with his F1 dates. There would be a signing bonus of $25,000 and Marlboro McLaren would have an option on his services for 1978. Gilles Villeneuve's signature was applied to the contract as quickly as he could make the pen fly.

3

MARKING TIME: 1977

I

"No doubt about it, Gilles was abnormally brave. To race against, he was the hardest bastard I ever knew, but absolutely fair. He was a giant of a driver."
— Keke Rosberg

His arrangement with McLaren was formally announced in December of 1976 when Gilles explained his rationale for signing as a part-time driver with the world championship winning team. "I feel it's better to do part of a season with a good team than a full season with a bad one. Formula One is what I want, but I want to do it right. If you get with a poor team, you can't do well and nobody thinks about you after that. I don't want to blow it. I want to stay in it, not just be able to say to my children that I once sat in a Formula One car."

While the $25,000 seemed like "a mountain of money" to Gilles, in Gaston Parent's opinion "It wasn't much but that wasn't important. The important thing was to sit his fanny in Formula One." They had now begun a commercial partnership and Parent pledged his intention to "wrap and sell" Gilles. "When he asked me to be his manager I said, 'I'll take you on as long as I can sell you like a can of beans.'"

And Parent, while demanding ironclad, lawyer-vetted contracts with sponsors, required no such document with his racing driver client. A simple three-paragraph letter, signed by both parties in May of 1977, sufficed. It was intended as an interim measure prior to working out an elaborate contract, but Parent soon decided further documents were unnecessary. "With Villeneuve I didn't need a contract. Unlike most people, he never had two angles. His true feelings were always on the table. He was one of the most honest people I've ever met."

Gilles's first racing venture of 1977 made him wish he had opted for another winter on snowmobiles instead of the Phillips International Formula Atlantic Championship in South Africa. The four-race series took him on a warm sightseeing tour in January and February but left him with little more than a tan to show for his travels.

In the events, held at the Roy Hesketh, Kyalami, Goldfields, and Killarney circuits, Gilles drove a Chevron B39-Ford BDA in a field where March cars were obviously superior. He managed only two finishes, a third and a fifth. South African driver Ian Scheckter, whose younger brother Jody was making a name for himself in F1, won the first three races in his March. In the last race Gilles was unable to avoid an accident between Scheckter and Nols Niemand and was happy to leave for home with only his pride damaged. The mediocre results, sixth overall in the series behind the winner, Scheckter, detracted from his North American successes and Gilles could only write off his South African misadventures to experience.

Also brought home to him was the value of having the right equipment, though he was sure Ray Wardell could have extracted more performance from the Chevron. These truths, and the failure of any concrete F2 plans to materialize quickly, were enough for Gilles to decide on another season of Formula Atlantic in Canada to supplement his F1 appearances. Direct Film would sponsor him for the season, the firm's owner having become an immediate Villeneuve fan on witnessing his Trois-Rivières victory. This season there were to be no American races and only seven events in the Labatt Challenge Series, renamed in deference to the brewery that also sponsored the annual Canadian Grand Prix. There were also some changes at the Ecurie Canada team that would interfere with the hugely successful Wardell/Villeneuve partnership.

Kris Harrison and Ray Wardell had come up with a scheme that in effect made them supporters of the 1977 Atlantic series in Canada through an engine program. Ecurie Canada imported a supply of 1600cc Ford BDN motors modified by Cosworth Engineering and made them available to all the Formula Atlantic competitors. Everyone was to have equal power and it would be politically wrong, they felt, for Ecurie Canada to be too closely involved with the 1976 series winner.

They formed a new team, the Motor Racing Company of Canada, and appointed Dave Morris as manager. Morris, a medical doctor and mechanical wizard from Edmonton (he built one of the first mechanical hearts and installed it in a cow), had been responsible for Gilles's engines in 1976. Now he would perform Ray Wardell's function in the MRC team, which would field two March 77B cars: one for Gilles and another for Richard Spenard, an up-and-coming Québécois driver from Montreal.

Gilles was not pleased about Ray Wardell disappearing into the distance of management and worried about the absence of his invaluable input in sorting out his car. Also, while he was the team's number-one driver and would take over Spenard's car should anything happen to his own, not having the undivided attention of the MRC crew was a source of concern for Gilles. The entry list for the Labatt series didn't make him rest any easier. Most of the leading lights had returned: Bill Brack, Price Cobb, Bobby Rahal, Tom Gloy, and all; and Keke Rosberg, a widely experienced and very quick journeyman driver from Finland, was another name to contend with.

It would be very difficult, almost impossible, for Gilles to duplicate his 1976 runaway, and he warned his growing public of this before the season began. "Last year was like a dream and it will be very hard to do as well in 1977. I have no trouble sleeping and thinking about the McLaren deal, as I know I'll be ready for that. But I'm not so sure about the Labatt series. Everyone will expect the same performance as last year, but if I lose a few, it might start to look bad, which won't help my career. But I'll be driving as hard as I can right from the start and hope everything goes well."

■ ■ ■

Gilles's misgivings proved prophetic at the season opener, at Mosport, where he found he would need every ounce of his abundant determination and derring-do to re-establish his authority in Atlantic. The Motor Racing Company's brace of March 77Bs arrived from England just five days before the May 22 race date and were brought to Mosport unsorted. Forced to use the first day's practice and qualifying periods as test sessions, Gilles found himself behind Keke Rosberg and Bill Brack on the grid. In final qualifying Gilles picked up his still recalcitrant March by the scruff of the neck and threw it around Mosport's ten turns like a man possessed, which of course he was.

No way was The Flying Finn (as Keke Rosberg was customarily called by alliteratively inclined journalists) going to outdrive Gilles Villeneuve on Canada's best road-racing circuit. It was a matter of pride and in a scintillating last lap, clocked just as qualifying ended, Gilles stopped the watches two seconds quicker than he had previously, and over a second faster than Rosberg's best time, to capture pole position in no uncertain terms.

Keijo "Keke" Rosberg and Gilles were two of a kind. Both from northern climes, they also shared a mutual racing philosophy: go flat out at all times. But Rosberg, who had rally enthusiasts for parents, was much the more experienced driver, having begun racing go-karts with his father in 1965 at the age of sixteen. When Gilles was still puttering around the Villeneuve driveway in Berthierville, Rosberg was Finnish, then Scandinavian kart champion. His competitive instincts won out over a career as a budding computer systems analyst and in 1972 he borrowed money for a Formula Vee car, toured around northern Europe with it, and won all the championships in 1973. There were similar results when he moved up to Super Vee and he had showed well in F2 in 1976. At the end of that year he won the Formula Pacific Series in New Zealand driving a Chevron for Fred Opert, the U.S. importer of Chevron cars. Now he was with Opert's team in a Chevron at Mosport and being outqualified by someone named Gilles Villeneuve did not leave him overawed.

At the start of the race Rosberg lit up his Chevron's rear tires and outdragged Villeneuve's March into Mosport's Corner One. They hied off into the rolling landscape of southern Ontario as if tied together. Several times the March belligerently nosed up alongside the Chevron and sparks flew when the rival makes banged wheels. On the fourth lap they shot over the brow of one of Mosport's hills side by side. They became airborne in unison, wheels came into contact again, both cars teetered on the brink of lost equilibrium, then the March spun off in a cloud of dust. The Chevron straightened out and continued at unabated pace while the March regained the circuit and resumed the chase. Rosberg's engine eventually blew up but Villeneuve motored on madly, setting the fastest race lap and picking off backmarkers relentlessly until he crossed the finish line in second place, less than a quarter of a minute behind the winner, Price Cobb.

"Gilles and I had some mighty battles that year," recalls Rosberg, grinning at the memory. Now safely retired and a wealthy man, he was declared World Champion in the ill-fated year of 1982. "Gilles was extremely talented, very, very quick and very, very brave. He was just an awfully hard driver and very ambitious. Our battles were always fair and most of the time I was the one who was chasing him. We always had a good professional relationship because we both played by the same rules. I don't remember deliberately pushing him off at Mosport but I do remember that Joann didn't talk to me for a long time after that!"

The Villeneuve motorhome was again a fixture at the Atlantic races and Joann, Jacques, Melanie, and Princess continued to have the Lane family and their dogs for company. They decamped from Mosport and headed west through Ontario's endless panorama of forest, rocks, lakes, and trees to Manitoba. At Gimli, the largest Icelandic community outside of the mid-Atlantic island and the scene of two previous Formula Atlantic triumphs for Gilles, no hat trick proved possible. His motor expired on the 27th lap, leaving him well behind his pace of the previous season and anxious to make up for lost time. On the long haul across the flat and lonely Prairies, John Lane in his motorhome soon lost sight of the Villeneuve version as Gilles sped away to Edmonton on the other side of the horizon. There he started from pole and in the race became involved in a sensational struggle with Keke Rosberg.

"It was just a war," is how John Lane remembers the Villeneuve/Rosberg battle at Edmonton. "They were touching everywhere. The track was way out in the boondocks from Edmonton and there were only about 12,000 people there but they were going insane. It was probably one of the better races between two drivers that's ever been. The two of them had a ball and they were both laughing about it afterwards. Gilles wasn't really angry with Keke about their Mosport incident. His attitude was that beating him was the best revenge. That night in Edmonton I bought dinner for the team and Melanie sat on my lap. Her dad was the happiest I'd ever seen him at that point. That kind of battle represented what Gilles loved about motor racing.''

Rosberg found their duel "hilarious" and gave a detailed account of one lap in particular in *Keke*, his volume of memoirs. "Gilles was leading and I was hauling him in. I knew that with a 'bastard' like Gilles I wasn't going to get too many chances. Then suddenly he made a mistake and I was able to get right up to him and we did the whole of a long corner side by side banging into each other. The pair of us ended up off the track on opposite sides and the pair of us still in full swing came back in off the grass and down the bank at full speed at exactly the same spot and banged into each other again. Gilles won, I came second. At the end of the race my car looked like a piece of cake with a big slice taken out of it. His rear rim had cut through my bodywork all the way into the tub.''

"Gilles was a hell of a racing driver and I have very fond memories of him,'' admits Rosberg, but he tempers his admiration with a critical assessment of Gilles's attitude. Given that Rosberg himself had a reputation for absolute aggression and a press-on-regardless, damn-the-consequences approach to racing, his thoughts are somewhat surprising.

"Gilles took all his races personally. It was as though he had his own personal barrier he wanted to break through. He would shunt one car and five minutes later he'd be out in his spare shunting that. I'm amazed when people think I drove like that. I think I was as self-protective as you can get. Maybe my limit was a bit higher than some people's. Gilles's was probably too high.

"I liked him a lot as a driver, I liked the way he raced. The man had guts, skill, and intelligence. His courage was far beyond normal standards. I'm not fearless at all. Gilles was. Racing with him in Atlantic I was just taking what I got. Back then I might have taken the same risks. But in my book, not in Formula One. I don't think driving like that has any place there. The machines are too quick, too dangerous for that kind of driving.'' And

Rosberg agrees with those of his peers who censured Villeneuve and Arnoux for their controversial no-holds-barred Edmonton-style battle in the 1979 French Grand Prix.

From Edmonton, Rosberg went on to win his first Canadian Formula Atlantic race, in July at Westwood, while his main rival was busy making his F1 debut with McLaren at the British Grand Prix. Before that Gilles took advantage of an unexpected opportunity to try another formula: Can-Am.

2

"I've only known one driver in the world who had the car control Villeneuve has, a guy who always knew where he was in the car no matter what. That was Jimmy Clark."
— *Chris Amon*

The Canadian-American Challenge Cup Series was first organized in 1966 and until 1974 was the top form of road racing in North America. The sleek, two-seater sports cars with their bellowing big-capacity American engines presented an impressive spectacle. The series attracted large crowds to watch the cars thundering around in the hands of famous international drivers who enjoyed the challenge of handling brute horsepower. Mario Andretti, Mark Donohue, Dan Gurney, Denny Hulme, Bruce McLaren, Jackie Stewart, John Surtees, and several others found their Can-Am machines could sometimes be as quick as their F1 cars.

The most successful equipment was designed and built by the New Zealander, Bruce McLaren, who with his compatriot Denny Hulme dominated the series for several years in their "Bruce and Denny Show." McLaren also founded his own F1 team in 1966, the one Gilles Villeneuve was about to join, but McLaren was unfortunately killed testing one of his Can-Am devices at Goodwood in England in 1970. It was another New Zealander, Chris Amon, who provided the link for Gilles to drive a Can-Am car.

After a two-year hiatus the series was resurrected for 1977, based on the mechanical components of the now defunct F5000 single-seaters. The new era Can-Am cars, with production-based engines of 5000cc or racing engines of 3000cc, and using enclosed sportscar bodywork, were very quick. In fact, they were so quick on the ground that, having attained the speed of a plane taxiing on a runway, they were capable of emulating one.

At the opening race of the series, at St. Jovite, the Lola Can-Am car of the English driver Brian Redman crested a rise and, with its flat underside acting like an aircraft wing, took off. The car did a complete backflip and Redman, who had been the star of F5000, was hospitalized with severe injuries and would take nearly a year to recover. Redman's accident was a prime factor in making another Can-Am competitor reconsider his motor racing future.

Chris Amon was thirty-four years old and in the twilight of a career that included ninety-six Grands Prix with several teams, notably twenty-six races with Ferrari. While he was tremendously skilled and often a frontrunner, he never won a world championship race. A gentle, somewhat timid, and often indecisive man, Amon was praised by Enzo Ferrari as "a good test driver, a clean and refined driver." (Though he was usually accused of caring more for his cars than his drivers, Ferrari developed a special fondness for Amon, as he was to do with Gilles Villeneuve. They stayed in contact and fifteen years after he'd last driven for him, Enzo Ferrari sent a fortieth birthday card to Amon at his home in New Zealand.) But as a driver Ferrari thought Amon's main weakness was a lack of confidence, saying, "He should have encouraged himself more during the races . . . a strength which he often lacked."

Amon later agreed with this judgement: "I always put the champions on a pedestal, at a superior level. I considered them to be supermen." But during his Ferrari years he had been optimistic about reaching the top, saying, "I would like to be the best driver in the world, but I don't want this kind of job for the next ten years." However, he stayed on the job in F1 for fourteen seasons, finally retiring in 1976 after a disastrous year, including two bad accidents in an Ensign. He had signed to drive Walter Wolf's Can-Am car for 1977, but after St. Jovite he had had enough and was ready to hang up his helmet.

Walter Wolf, who in 1960 came to Montreal from Austria with seven dollars in his pocket, was happy to spend large quantities of the millions he made in construction and oil on his real passion, motor racing. His self-sponsored Formula 1 team ran in the blue-and-gold Wolf corporate colours decorated with the Canadian flag and was headquartered in Reading, England. Walter bought himself the best team his money could muster, hiring accomplished Englishmen Dr. Harvey Postlethwaite as designer (he later worked at Ferrari with Gilles Villeneuve) and Peter Warr (from Team Lotus) as team manager. Wolf's driver was Jody Scheckter, who had previously won four Grands Prix with the Tyrrell team.

It cost him several million, but the brand new Wolf WR1-Ford DFV won its first-ever race, the 1977 season opener in Argentina. That unprecedented achievement in F1 was followed by three more top-three placings, then another Walter Wolf Racing triumph at the Monaco Grand Prix in May. There Scheckter received the victor's laurels from Prince Rainier and Princess Grace and a jubilant Wolf served champagne to everyone in sight, saying, "No problems at all. Winners don't have problems!" But now he had problems on the other side of the Atlantic, within his Can-Am team, which was administered from office space donated by Wolf's good friend in Montreal, Gaston Parent.

Early one morning Parent had an unexpected visit from a very bothered Chris Amon. "He was a very nice guy, honest and sincere, but not young any more and a very safety-conscious driver. Chris wanted to quit, then and there. Walter had this Dallara, an odd-looking car, and Chris couldn't do anything with it. He thought it was simply too dangerous to drive. And he said, 'Look, I don't want to do this to Walter. He's put a lot of money into this thing and I don't know how to tell him.' Then Walter's girl Friday, Dana, a very nice British girl who was his co-ordinator and worked in the outer office I was letting them use, comes in and is very upset. She's wringing her hands and doesn't know what to do about telling Walter. This was on a Monday morning at nine o'clock and here I am confronted with a racing problem which I need like a hole in the head. Anyway, I told them to take it easy. I would call Walter in and sort it all out."

Wolf (who also had residences in England, Switzerland, Austria, and the south of France) had a flat in Montreal that had previously been owned by members of the Molson family. He was there when Parent called him and the two met in Parent's office behind closed doors. Parent explained the problem to Wolf. "Then I said to him, 'I have the answer.' He said, 'What's your answer?' I said, 'Villeneuve.' "

Wolf immediately agreed that this would be the perfect solution. "Walter said, 'Fine. It's settled.' I told him, 'Not yet. I have to talk to Villeneuve. I don't know know if he wants to go Can-Am racing.' So I called Villeneuve in Berthier. He was home. Without exaggeration, thirty-five or forty minutes later he was sitting in my office. I was so goddamned surprised to see him! I figured an hour and a half at least."

Parent called in Wolf, Amon, and the secretary. "Walter was saying to Amon, 'No problem, no problem,' and Dana was very relieved. Walter said to Gilles, 'You've got the car and here's the guy who's gonna manage the team.' Amon. Walter said, 'You're the racer now, go and rent a track and practise. Do anything you want, I'll fork out the money.' Gilles lit up, literally lit up. He was on cloud nine. Here he was getting a car without having to pay. They all shake hands and are ready to walk out of my office. I say, 'Hey! Hold on, wait a minute. How much are you going to pay?' Walter asks me how much. I said, 'Two thousand dollars per race plus expenses.' Walter agrees and Gilles is this high off the ground. He didn't want the money. He just wanted to race. But all of a sudden, for the first time in his life he's getting paid to race."

Chris Amon's lack of confidence in the Walter Wolf Racing Dallara WD1-Chevrolet proved to be fully justified. Amon had called it a "pig" and Gilles went beyond the "cochon" label to pronounce it "absolutely undriveable." It was subject to constant problems, such as the suspension pulling away from the chassis, the handling was atrocious, and after a few laps fading brakes made it nearly unstoppable. Yet Gilles had a great time in it.

Everyone knew the car was a dud and anything he could wring out of it would be a bonus. There was no pressure on him and he thoroughly enjoyed the challenge of flogging it around at Watkins Glen, his first Can-Am race. After many spins he managed to qualify it fourth on the grid but only travelled four laps before the brakes disappeared and he retired. The race was won by the Lola of the French driver Patrick Tambay, who was replacing the injured Brian Redman.

John Lane was with the team at Watkins Glen and after dinner one evening he and Amon stayed up late talking shop. When Lane asked him for his opinion of Gilles's ability, Amon said: "I've only known one driver in the world who had the car control Villeneuve has, a guy who always knew where he was in the car no matter what. That was Jimmy Clark."

The great Scottish driver, who was killed in an F2 accident at Hockenheim in Germany in 1968, was considered the greatest F1 driver of his era and one of the best ever. (He was also very much admired by Gilles, who had read about him in several books.) This was the highest praise Amon could bestow on Gilles and he elaborated on it to Lane. "When I was driving and got into a spin, I was just a passenger. Gilles isn't. When he's spinning he's always thinking ahead, how to get out of it, which way to go, when to drop the clutch, and he always brings the thing out going the right way."

Amon and Lane agreed that Gilles, who entertained them with tales of his wild escapades on the roads around Berthierville, had probably come by his spinning prowess through experience, particularly doing "bootleg" turns on highways. This manoeuvre (accomplished by jerking on the hand brake at speed and cranking the steering wheel, which spins a car around through 180 degrees to face the other way) was reputedly used by bootleggers in the southern United States to escape pursuing federal agents bent on relieving them of their cargoes of illicit moonshine.

That Watkins Glen weekend, John Lane was treated to more examples of the Villeneuve mastery over machinery. Lane's personal transport was a Honda Accord he had had modified considerably, including turbocharging the motor. On race day, as he often did, Gilles had slept in and asked Lane to let him drive the Honda from their motel to the circuit. "Like a fool I said yes. About a mile from the circuit the traffic was backed up bumper to bumper and hardly moving. Gilles pulls over into the left lane and floors it. He reels off snap shifts up to 80 miles an hour and we did that the whole way. I've only had the car three weeks and I'm thinking, Oh, my God! We blast through the gate at the track and he's looking for a parking space. He finds an opening about six inches longer than my car. I told him to get going and get ready for the race, I'd park it. He said, 'Oh no, it'll just take a second.' And it did. He backs the rear of the car in, cranks the wheel as hard as he can, revs it up to about six thousand, pops the clutch, and hops the front end in with three inches to spare. Amazing!''

Gilles had three more Can-Am adventures that summer. His only finish came at Elkhart Lake in Wisconsin in July, where he started from pole but dropped back to finish third behind the winner, Peter Gethin. He failed to finish at both Mosport in August and Trois-Rivières in September and was classified a lowly 12th overall in the 1977 SCCA Citicorp Can-Am Challenge Series. The series sponsor, an American bank, made much publicity hay from their product (Yankee dollars), which was awarded to competitors. The $14,920 Gilles earned for his team was a fortune to him but wouldn't keep Walter Wolf in cigars. At the end of the season Wolf gave the car to the automotive department of a Toronto technical school, where students dissected it like a cadaver. Patrick Tambay, who won six of the nine races, was the runaway champion and won $95,380 for his Haas/Hall Lola team. Tambay won the series again in 1980 (and Gilles's brother Jacques, managed by Gaston Parent, was the winner in 1983), but Gilles did no more Can-Am racing.

3

"I said to myself, that's Scheckter and that's Andretti and I can keep up with them. I was well pleased."
– Gilles Villeneuve

Right after that Can-Am race at Watkins Glen, Gilles flew back to England to practise and try to qualify for his F1 baptism with the McLaren team in the British Grand Prix. The main event was scheduled for Sunday, July 16, 1977, at the Silverstone circuit in Northamptonshire. Formerly a World War Two airfield, the flat, 2.932-mile (4.719-kilometer) track makes up for the absence of significant elevation changes with half a dozen high-speed corners to test the mettle of racing drivers. The lap record of 1 minute, 18.81 seconds had been set by James Hunt in 1976 and worked out to an average of 133.932 miles per hour (215.543 kph). This was really very fast considering the drivers had to slow down to a walking pace at the Woodcote chicane, an obstacle installed in 1975 to slow down the cars from speeds judged to be too dangerous. A major factor in deciding on this modification had been a huge first-lap accident at Woodcote in 1973 occasioned by a driver named Jody Scheckter, in only his fourth F1 race, spinning in the middle of the pack. Scheckter was driving a third McLaren entry then, having been given a contract similar to that of Gilles Villeneuve.

Gilles had first seen Silverstone the week before the Grand Prix, prior to his Watkins Glen Can-Am outing, during a special two-day test session organized by the Formula One Constructors' Association (FOCA) for the regular F1 teams. Gilles was given a red-and-white Marlboro McLaren M23-Ford DFV, James Hunt's old car, while Hunt and his teammate, Jochen Mass, were using the latest M26 models. Hunt's car bore the number 1 in honour of his being the reigning World Champion, and Mass's was number 2, while Gilles's was number 40 and was being looked after by a separate pit crew from the main McLaren team.

At first, Gilles took it easy, feeling his way around Silverstone to see which way it went and familiarizing himself with a chassis and engine completely new to him. He kept a close watch in his mirrors to make way for those famous Formula 1 names who might be trying to overtake. Soon, surprisingly soon for those who didn't know him (and few did), other drivers had to watch for the oncoming number 40 McLaren in their mirrors as Gilles began lapping very quickly.

His accelerated progress was accompanied by spins, many of them. He spun at Copse, Becketts, Stowe, Club, and Woodcote, at nearly every one of Silverstone's historic corners, sending up showers of grass and turf as he slewed off the tarmac. Miraculously, it seemed, he missed hitting any of the solid earth banks or "sleepers," the unforgiving wooden walls made from stacked railway ties. On one occasion he applied the power too quickly on the exit from Copse and spun through three complete revolutions at very high speed, coming to rest just inches from a wall of sleepers. This contretemps was witnessed by many in the pits and there were some mutterings from the F1 establishment about dangerous wildness and an impetuous newcomer who might be out of his depth.

While there did seem to be an element of desperation about this Villeneuve character, whoever he was, a few keen observers noticed his times dropping ever lower and began to see just what he was driving at. They watched him more closely, particularly his spin recovery technique. While still rotating, he simply selected first gear and, when the car was facing approximately where he wanted it to go, tore away again to resume his private chase. They saw that he seldom spun in the same place twice. Gradually it dawned on them that here was a driver who was finding the limits of his car at each corner by starting over the top and working down.

It was a crude but effective method: take the car beyond the limit of adhesion, take note of that limit, and don't exceed it again. In this way Gilles spun his way around Silverstone an estimated twenty times in all (though he thought that was an exaggeration) during a total of 169 laps of testing, practice, and qualifying.

Later, he explained what was going on in his mind at the time. "All I could think about was getting out of Atlantic, making it in Europe, getting into Formula One. This looked to me like my only chance . . . I had to learn about the car and the track very quickly. I needed to impress everyone in that race. For me, the quickest way to learn the limits of the M23 was to go quicker and quicker through a corner until it spun. Then I knew how quick was too quick."

During that pre-race test session his best time was was a highly respectable 1 minute, 20.90 seconds, 12th fastest overall, about halfway down the pack of F1 regulars. Fastest was Mario Andretti in his Lotus; James Hunt was third, followed by the Ferraris of Niki Lauda and Carlos Reutemann. Jody Scheckter's 10th fastest time was fortunate to be established at all after he got a terrific fright. His Wolf was speeding through Maggotts bend at about 150 mph when its rear wing flew off and the car became airborne, then spun like a top on one wheel as it touched down. The car was competely undamaged but a thoroughly shaken Scheckter admitted, "I really thought it was all over for me."

■ ■ ■

Scheckter was one of those who had criticized the influx of untried rookies into Formula 1, saying, "Some of these guys think their mirrors are just for shaving in." Of the forty-one entries at Silverstone, fourteen were newcomers, who either had the talent to earn a tryout or the money to rent a ride. It was decided all of them, regardless of how they got there, would have to undergo a special pre-qualifying session and times would tell. The fastest five would earn the right to join the F1 regulars in the usual qualifying sessions, which would establish the final grid of twenty-six cars for the race. Pre-qualifying was held in two sessions on the Wednesday before the race.

Gilles was quickest of the lot, winding up with a time of 1 minute, 19.48 seconds, just .07 seconds faster than another debutant, Patrick Tambay, who was driving a Theodore Ensign for the colourful privateer Theodore "Teddy" Yip. Tambay was Yip's replacement for his 1976 driver, Chris Amon, and the Ensign was so new Tambay was using Amon's seat from last year.

Regarded as one of the ten richest men in the world, Teddy Yip had varied sources of income around Hong Kong and Macao, including gambling interests and the Far East Hydrofoil Company. Noted for his lavish hospitality and retinue of beautiful women, Yip regarded motor racing as his elixir of life. Tambay's performance at Silverstone gave him a shot in the arm. In his late sixties, Yip was fond of saying, "Without racing I would be dead within three years."

It is also possible to drown in the fountain of youth, and while racing made Teddy Yip come alive it very nearly did the reverse to English driver David Purley at Silverstone. A former paratrooper and given to such thrill-seeking pursuits as hang-gliding, Purley was attempting to pre-qualify his Lec car. His time in the first hour-and-a-half session wasn't quick enough and in the second he pulled out all the stops. He had turned the fastest lap to that point when the throttle of his Lec car jammed wide open just as it was entering the right-hand turn at Becketts at very high speed. The car cut across the inside of the corner and slammed head-on into the bank on the outside of the curve, coming to rest from 120 mph in about two feet – the approximate length of the crumpled ball of twisted metal that was all that remained of the chassis.

It took nearly an hour for rescuers to extricate the gravely injured driver. His wounds were later diagnosed as a dislocated collarbone and heels, seven broken ribs, five fractures to the pelvis, eight breaks in the left leg, two breaks in the left foot, and seven in the right. Today, the wrecked Lec can be seen on display at the Donington Motor Museum in England, resembling an eccentric piece of abstract sculpture more than an ex-racing car. It seems impossible the driver survived, yet David Purley recovered and even raced again, though not in F1. (Sadly, he was killed in 1985 when the plane he was piloting crashed.)

The Silverstone proceedings continued in a sombre mood as the Purley incident rekindled memories of the horrible accident at the South African Grand Prix in March. Tom Pryce, the very promising young Welsh driver, died when a track marshal ran out in front of him. The marshal, armed with a fire extinguisher, was rushing to the aid of another car and failed to notice Pryce's speeding Shadow. Pryce was hit by the extinguisher, the marshal was also killed, and the driverless Shadow sped down the circuit for some distance before crashing. A few days later the Brabham driver Carlos Pace was killed in a plane crash in his native Brazil. There was a sense of uneasiness among the superstitious, who felt Formula 1 racing was in for another of the accident-filled years the sport was prone to.

■ ■ ■

Though Villeneuve frequently looked on the verge of disaster, people began to realize it was fabulous car control, not lack of it, that was responsible for the remarkable angles being assumed by the number 40 McLaren. While the spins lessened in frequency, there was still a great deal of sideways motoring to observe and more and more people were sitting up and taking notice of this new phenomenon.

When final qualifying positions were posted on Saturday afternoon the F1 establishment was astonished to see Villeneuve firmly ensconced in ninth place on the grid. His best lap of 1m 19.32s was a mere .43 seconds behind the polesitter, James Hunt, the World Champion and master of Silverstone, driving a new and improved version of Gilles's car.

Next to Gilles on the fifth row of the grid, and a tenth of a second slower, was his hero, Ronnie Peterson, who was taking part in his 102nd Grand Prix. Peterson's experience and entertaining powerslides were not enough to overcome the handling deficiencies of the eccentric Tyrrell-Ford six-wheeler. And behind Peterson was Jochen Mass in the other McLaren M26. Lauda had qualified third quickest but Villeneuve was ahead of the other Ferrari driver, the veteran Carlos Reutemann, and another favoured debutant, Tambay in the Ensign.

Much of the press interest at Silverstone was focused on the Renault car that Jean-Pierre Jabouille had qualified in 21st place. It was the first appearance of a 1500cc turbocharged engine in the current formula, the others all conforming to the 3000cc normally aspirated variety of motive power. After final qualifying the yellow-and-black factory-entered device from France was surrounded by scribes and photographers anxious to see the curiosity close up. The Renault was to retire with a broken turbocharger after 16 laps in the race, but it was an historic occasion, heralding the approaching turbo era.

Before the race only a few journalists saw enough historic potential in the French-Canadian driver of the third McLaren to seek him out for an interview. They found him sitting with his wife on a pile of tires behind his pit; Joann was busy sewing a Marlboro patch beside the Canadian flag on Gilles's driving suit. He seemed a bit shy, but was quite friendly and approachable and responded easily to their questions in quaintly accented (compared to the drivers from France) but proficient English. They asked him about his racing background and he patiently gave them a précis of his snowmobile successes and what he had accomplished in Atlantic, paying special tribute to the man he felt had helped him most. "I owe a lot to Ray Wardell. Without him I wouldn't be here today. I'm really thankful to him. He's one of my best friends."

Someone asked him about his interests outside racing. Did he have any hobbies? ''I don't really have any other interests. But at home I like to work on my street Mustang. I modified the engine myself. I also have an old school bus and a four-wheel-drive Ford pickup that I used to haul my snowmobile trailer on. I have the biggest tires on it and a winch and in the summer we take the kids and go into the mountains on rough trails for picnics. The dirtier and tougher the trail the better. I like to get stuck and get out again. I guess I should be playing golf or tennis. They're probably more normal Formula One hobbies.'' He laughed at that, and it was noted that here was a driver with a sense of humour and a refreshing lack of pretension.

He laughed again when he was asked to describe his Silverstone experience to date. ''Yes, I spun a lot but I didn't hit anything, touch wood. I hope it's always going to be like that. I can throw the M23 around a bit now and at places like Stowe and Club it gets really sideways. It's kind of hard on the heart! By the end of the day I felt as if I was driving a Formula Atlantic with an extra-powerful engine. I was hoping to be somewhere between 20th and 12th, so I'm actually very pleased to have come ninth.'' When asked to compare asphalt to snow and ice, he said there was an affinity between them, at least the way he drove. ''You slide on one just as on the other. And driving a Formula One car is like sliding – sliding very, very fast!''

The questioning continued. Why did he race? Because it was fun. He did it not for money or popularity but because he loved it. No, he didn't like the travelling so much and preferred to be at home with Joann and their two kids. Joann would rather he did something else for a living but came to all his races. In North America, he explained, the family travelled together in their motorhome. They were just normal people, he said, from a small town in Quebec and no matter what happened in his racing future, even if he got rich, they intended to live as they did now.

The journalists scribbled away, using words like polite, sincere, unassuming, and likeable to describe his character. His talent was labelled as promising, and they talked to Teddy Mayer, who pronounced the team ''very pleased with his progress.'' One of the McLaren mechanics assigned to him had more praise. ''He's exceptionally bright. He's got a computer up there and he can relate directly to the car and tell us what he needs. He's got his eyes wide open.'' More eyes were to be opened wide in the race.

■ ■ ■

Traffic carrying 85,000 spectators choked the narrow country lanes leading into Silverstone on a warm summer Sunday. Many people, anxious to get to their favourite viewpoints in the covered stands and on the grassy banks that line the circuit, abandoned their vehicles out in the hinterland and walked five or six miles to take up their positions. With Hunt on pole and John Watson from Northern Ireland beside him, the chances of a British victory looked good.

At the start the roar of twenty-six F1 engines drowned out the cheering crowd. Against a backdrop of waving Union Jacks, Hunt faltered with a troublesome clutch and Watson seized the advantage in his Brabham-Alfa Romeo. Lauda's wailing Ferrari was next, followed by the Canadian flag-bedecked Wolf of Scheckter. Hunt held his McLaren in fourth, just ahead of the Lotus teammates, the Swede Gunnar Nilsson and the American Mario Andretti. At the end of the first lap the pack snarled through Woodcote and rocketed down the pit straight in that order with – and most spectators had to make a quick check of their programs to identify it – the McLaren of Villeneuve in seventh place, ahead of more familiar names: Mass, Brambilla, Peterson, and sixteen others.

The thundering herd reeled off more laps, with the newcomer in the number 40 car keeping pace with the best drivers in the world. Behind him Rupert Keegan left the circuit on three wheels after losing one in a coming-together with Reutemann's Ferrari. Peterson's Tyrrell retired with all six wheels intact but the engine in pieces; Tambay's first F1 race ended prematurely when electrical troubles halted his Ensign; and Ian Scheckter spun his March out of contention. His brother, urged on by an excited Walter Wolf leaning out over the pit wall, continued in third place, hard on the heels of Watson and Lauda. Hunt held fourth, Andretti and Nilsson were next, but there was trouble brewing in the cockpit of the Villeneuve McLaren.

Gilles noticed the needle of his water temperature gauge creeping up, and on the 10th lap, when it finally reached the boiling point, he peeled out of the pack and pulled into the pits. It was a long journey from the Woodcote entry down the crowded pit lane to the far end where his unexpected arrival met with a flurry of activity. He pointed to the gauge and his mechanics swarmed over the back of the car looking for the problem. Two laps had gone by before one of them leaned over to scream the diagnosis into the helmet of the driver sitting impatiently at the controls: "The gauge is just fucked up!"

The McLaren crew scattered as Gilles dropped the clutch and blasted back out onto the circuit, leaving two strips of black rubber on the pavement behind him. He rejoined the race just as the leaders went by on the 13th of their 68 laps and he slotted in behind Watson, Lauda, and Hunt and just ahead of the pursuing Scheckter, Andretti, and Nilsson. Gilles, aware that Scheckter and company in his mirrors were fighting for race positions while he was now effectively out of contention, politely moved over and let the trio by. Then he pulled in behind them and stayed right with the frontrunners until the end, establishing the fifth fastest lap of the race (after Hunt, Watson, Nilsson, and Scheckter) and was classified 11th overall in the results. Watson, Scheckter, and Andretti dropped out with mechanical problems, leaving Hunt, Lauda, and Nilsson as the top three finishers.

Gilles was very happy with his showing but demonstrated no extravagant displays of emotion: "I'm a calm person, I guess, and it takes an awful lot to make me jump in the air. I don't get excited easily."

Calmly, and with both feet on the ground, he described his British Grand Prix. "If I ignored the gauge and the engine blew it would have been the action of a dumb beginner who wasn't paying attention to the gauges. I didn't want that tag so I pulled into the pits. After I went back out and let the others pass I was driving at my own pace. And I realized I was keeping up with them. I said to myself, that's Scheckter and Andretti and I can keep up with them. I was well pleased."

Were it not for what turned out to be an unnecessary pit stop, Gilles was surely destined for fourth place – where Jochen Mass finished. His performance earned him the Allied Polymer Group "Driver of the Day" award and accolades from such influential journalists as Franco Lini, who reported back to Italy: "Quite amazing for one who races for the first time in F1 and he scores nine on his report card in qualifying and earns laurels as the most impressive man in the race.''

The British motor-racing press agreed. Denis Jenkinson, the famed ''DSJ'' of *Motor Sport* who had been covering racing since the 1947 season, paid tribute to ''the smooth, confident way he had driven.'' Villeneuve ''was undoubtedly the man of the meeting.'' Writing in *Autosport*, Nigel Roebuck (who was to become a close personal friend of Gilles) said, ''Villeneuve demonstrated enormous natural talent'' and was ''tremendously impressive.'' In the same magazine James Hunt, who could now take some credit as a talent spotter, talked about ''being very impressed with his obvious talent and his professional approach'' in Trois-Rivières. In *The Times* the highly respected F1 journalist John Blunsden called him ''racing's brightest new star,'' who was sure to become ''a regular member of the Grand Prix circuit. Anyone seeking a future World Champion need look no further than this quietly assured young man.''

4

''I could not understand why Mayer changed his mind. I could not work out why I should suffer this backward step. My morale took a serious blow.''

– Gilles Villeneuve

Gilles returned to Canada without learning which of the remaining seven Grands Prix McLaren wanted him to drive in. Anyway, he was faced with a busy month of August, beginning with Formula Atlantic races on consecutive weekends in Halifax and at St. Félicien, Quebec. Gilles came back to the series in fourth place behind Rosberg, Rahal, and Brack and needed to make up for lost time. After starting from pole in Halifax, Gilles spun out on the 19th lap and Brack won, with Price Cobb in second place to push Gilles down to fifth in the standings.

At St. Félicien, a circuit near Lac Saint-Jean in Quebec, Gilles parlayed another pole into a race win, but the pole was hard-earned. With only a few minutes of qualifying remaining he was only third fastest and trying hard – too hard. The Direct Film March careened wide at a corner, thumped into a protective wall of used tires, and came to rest, rather bent, against a cement wall. Gilles extricated himself from the mess, ran back to the pits, commandeered his teammate Richard Spenard's car, shot back out onto the circuit, and secured his pole-winning time with just seconds to go in the session. He won the race nearly a minute ahead of Tom Gloy, while both Brack and Rosberg crashed.

One of his rivals at St. Félicien was a young driver over from France, Didier Pironi, who was an invited guest in a Fred Opert-entered Chevron. Pironi introduced himself and told Gilles there was gossip in Europe that Gilles's name was being associated with Ferrari in F1 and that Gilles and Eddie Cheever were to test with the Italian team, the best one to get the drive.

Gilles was astonished and thought Pironi (who would later be his teammate at Ferrari) must be joking. "I said, 'C'mon, don't kid me. I've never heard anything from Ferrari.' I didn't believe him. It never dawned on me that Ferrari would ever even think of me." Besides, he explained to Pironi, he already had a contract with McLaren. A few days later Gilles discovered that piece of paper had lost a great deal of its significance.

He was entered in a doubleheader at Mosport, a Can-Am race preceded by the Molson Diamond Six Hours, an event in the World Championship of Makes. In the endurance race Gilles would share the driving of a privately entered BMW with Eddie Cheever, the twenty-year-old American-born resident of Italy who was expected to have a bright future in racing, and now, according to Didier Pironi, perhaps a rival of Gilles for a seat at Ferrari. Another BMW, for Ronnie Peterson and David Hobbs to drive, was entered by Team McLaren. Teddy Mayer was at Mosport to supervise its running and, it transpired, to give some bad news to Gilles.

■ ■ ■

The Villeneuve/Cheever combination was victorious in their Group 5 class in the race and finished third overall. Gilles's Dallara, as usual, was classified as DNF (did not finish) in the Can-Am race the next day. On the podium during the awards presentation Gilles threw up twice, having over-indulged in liquid refreshment – pop and milk – during his rest stints.

And Gilles returned to Berthier with a lump in his throat, but not because he was still physically ill. He was upset at what happened at his Mosport meeting with Teddy Mayer. "He told me that if any other Formula One teams made me an offer, I should not let my contract to do the McLaren races hold me back. And he did not intend to keep his option on me for 1978."

The McLaren rejection was like a bolt out of the blue to Gilles, who wondered if his F1 career had already come and gone. It was also a blow to his ego since Mayer had a reputation as a shrewd judge of talent and organizer of world championships. Besides giving Scheckter his start, he had rescued Hunt from relative obscurity in March and Hesketh cars, where he had only won a single race. Hunt then became World Champion in his first season with McLaren. Prior to that Mayer hired Emerson Fittipaldi away from Lotus, where he had been the 1972 champion, and the Brazilian repeated as the title winner driving for McLaren in 1974. Now Mayer had taken a look at Villeneuve and decided not to keep him. Gilles was bewildered.

"I said to myself, 'Holy shit! Not looking good.' Since Silverstone I had been sure Jochen Mass would be out and I would be a McLaren driver for the coming year. I wanted to go to McLaren because they were a winning team. I liked the people there and I was very sad that it wasn't going to work out. It really bothered me. I could not understand why Mayer had changed his mind. I couldn't work out why I should suffer this backward step. My morale took a serious blow."

Mayer had decided to replace Jochen Mass with Patrick Tambay for the next season. In later years Gilles took great relish in telling the tale of being spurned by Mayer, who in turn was often asked why he let Villeneuve go. There were rumours of an impending sponsorship deal with Elf, the French oil company, which required a driver from France in the team. Marlboro paid the greater portion of the McLaren drivers' retainers and it was said that Marlboro's parent company, Philip Morris, wanted a European driver because their Marlboro brand was not marketed through motor racing in North America. Another version on the marketability theme had it that Tambay was the more promotable of the two. Handsome, sophisticated, debonair, and from a wealthy French family, he was fluent in English, had attended university in America and married Dana, a girl from Hawaii. John Hogan denies that Marlboro had anything to do with the McLaren decision and the world is left with Teddy Mayer's explanation: "Gilles looked as though he might be a bit expensive and, anyway, Tambay was showing almost the same promise in the Ensign, which perhaps wasn't as good a car as our M23."

The news spread quickly and Gilles put on a brave front in response to press queries about his future, saying, "I've had a lot of offers from other people if I don't go to McLaren, so I really don't mind that much if it doesn't work out. The other offers are just as good. There is nothing definite yet. Right now it's a game of musical chairs." Gilles ran down the list of rumours about possible driver movements that might lead to an opening for him. They included the departure of Peterson from Tyrrell, Lauda and maybe Reutemann from Ferrari, Nilsson from Lotus, maybe even Jody Scheckter from Wolf.

In fact, Gilles had no firm offers at all, though Walter Wolf was again thinking about having Gilles on his F1 team and discussed it with Gaston Parent. "Walter was throwing money around like wild rice," says Parent. "At the time he had money coming out of his ears. He wanted to form a truly Canadian team. At the end of the summer he came to me and talked about maybe signing Gilles and running two cars. Jody and Gilles. And he tells me if he gets Villeneuve he's gonna practise him so goddamned much he might win the title."

Wolf was talking about next year. Parent's more immediate concern was the McLaren deal that entitled Gilles to several races in 1977, and there were now only four F1 events remaining. Parent was aware that Teddy Mayer had been a lawyer in his native U.S. before turning to race management and it was unlikely McLaren would leave itself open to breach of contract.

■ ■ ■

Meanwhile, Gilles had another doubleheader to deal with at Trois-Rivières in early September. The Can-Am race was another DNF for the Wolf Dallara and a win for Tambay's Haas/Hall Lola. But Gilles had the pole for the Molson Grand Prix, ahead of

Rosberg and two Fl drivers, Depailler and Laffite, who were imported by Rosberg's entrant, Fred Opert. As usual, the race did not count in the Formula Atlantic series, but Gilles's uncertainty over his future left him feeling he had more to prove than ever. And because of this he gave a ragged performance.

He began by inadvertently squeezing Rosberg into a wall and retirement in the opening laps, then fell foul of pace-car intervention while he was in the lead. With just four laps remaining a collision between two backmarkers, David Oxton and Gregg Young, partly blocked the track and the pace car was sent out to hold the field in check while the debris was cleared. Gilles, busy watching the queue of cars lining up behind him, was slow to notice the green flag for the restart. Three cars shot past him before he recovered and in his desperation to catch them he overcooked it and spun. Price Cobb was declared the winner, ahead of Howdy Holmes and Patrick Depailler, with Gilles taking the chequered flag in fourth place. But this result was not what Gilles thought it should have been and he returned to the pits in a rush, slammed on the brakes, jumped out of his car, and stalked off, angry with himself and not terribly pleased at the rest of the world.

Behind the scenes, the next few days in that September of 1977 were among the most eventful in his career. And, although the new developments were of a much more positive nature, Gilles's preoccupation with them again seemed to interfere with more immediate matters: namely, the Formula Atlantic season finale on the September 25 in Quebec City.

Though no less than seven drivers had a mathematical chance of winning, the Labatt Challenge Series had ostensibly narrowed down to a three-man title fight among Brack (who led in points), Villeneuve, and Rosberg. This last race, on a new 1.2-mile circuit located in the exhibition grounds of the ancient city, would decide the championship. All the Atlantic regulars were there to do battle, as were two Formula 1 drivers, Patrick Depailler and Jacques Laffite.

Gilles's troubles began on the first day, just five laps after the circuit was opened for practice. His March came twisting through the chicane at full tilt only to be confronted with Tom Gloy's recently spun March sitting in the middle of the road. There had been no yellow flags of warning and the two Marches met abruptly, the Villeneuve version coming out much the worse for wear with a damaged tub. While Kris Harrison's MRC team effected repairs to the chassis, Gilles took over Richard Spenard's mount and was sitting in it in the final qualifying session watching in exasperation as the times of Brack and Rosberg come tumbling down and the time remaining for him to beat them was running out.

Ray Wardell, still politically prevented from helping him, was watching nearby. "I never once saw Gilles actually lose his temper. But you could see pressure build up if anyone else started to go quickly. If he was being held up in any way by the crew, you could see the hands start going in the car and he would be wondering what's going on back there. I was standing there at Quebec and could see the guys weren't doing the job right for him during the last ten minutes of qualifying. He wanted to be out there and they were taking too long with the adjustments. I remember saying to John Lane, who was beside me, 'They're doing it wrong and they shouldn't let him out.' But they let him out and he stuck it straight into the wall. It was so obvious it was going to happen."

Gilles screeched out onto the circuit moments after Brack had set the quickest time and three laps later he disappeared from view. John Lane went looking for him. "He went off somewhere out on the back side of the course behind an arena which was being used for a garage. I walked in there and Gilles came through one of the doors at the other end. He walked toward me with this sheepish grin on his face and I asked him if he was okay. He said, 'Yeah, I'm fine, but the car she is fuck-ed.' "

■ ■ ■

With his team's second car thus ravished, Kris Harrison was left wringing his hands, Richard Spenard was left out of the race, and Gilles was left in third place on the grid, sitting behind polesitter Brack in his STP Oil Products-sponsored March and the Excita Condoms Chevron of The Flying Finn. Rosberg flew away in first place at the start, then half spun to give Brack a momentary lead that was soon usurped by Villeneuve. Rosberg clouted Rahal on his way back onto the circuit, had to pit for repairs, and was effectively out of the championship chase. Brack fell back clutchless and eventually stopped after losing an argument with a wall. Villeneuve's immediate pursuer, Rahal, took advantage of a moment that forced the Direct Film March into an excursion up an escape road. Villeneuve was making inroads on Rahal's seven-second lead when Rahal was forced to call into his pit for quick repairs to bodywork and engine damaged in the earlier altercation with Rosberg.

Gilles still needed to finish first and he did, 20 seconds ahead of Rahal and third-place runner Depailler. Hence, Gilles Villeneuve was declared Formula Atlantic champion for the second year in a row, this time with 114 points, followed by Rahal with 92, and Brack with 67. The winner described his mid-race detour, made necessary when his brakes, which were biased at the back, failed to retard his speed. "Maybe I could have made the corner, but if I did not I would have ended up on the guard rail and I would have been out of the race."

Then came an interesting comment from one who was later thought to be interested only in winning races, not championships. "I took the easy way and went straight off down the escape road, turned around and came back. I knew it might cost me the race but I also knew I had to finish high to take the championship." In response to the inevitable "How do you feel?" question, Gilles replied, "It was better winning this year because we had some troubles. Last year it was too easy."

Gilles's Formula Atlantic career was now over. In all, he won thirteen of the twenty-six Atlantic races he entered, a record that still stands in that formula. (His brother Jacques continued the family tradition by winning the title in 1980 and the next year and scored eight career victories.) Now Gilles was about to begin his career in the most important formula of all, with the most famous team in motor racing.

4

THE CHANCE OF A LIFETIME: 1977

I

"Enzo Ferrari himself called me and said, 'Are you ready to drive for us?' And I said, 'Of course I'm ready!'"
— Gilles Villeneuve

Following his rejection by McLaren at Mosport, Gilles drove the motorhome, more slowly than usual, back to Berthierville and parked it in the field across from his parents' house. He hooked up the electricity and telephone lines and moped around while Joann cleaned up the accumulated clutter from their race weekend in Ontario. Jacques and Melanie played outside with Princess and Gilles stared at his red-and-black helmet. Joann had helped him with the design, a stylized variation of the letter V, and he wondered if it would have to be packed away or put on display along with his trophies, to become just another memento of his former racing career.

Other than the upcoming Quebec City race there was nothing on the horizon for him. Another season in Atlantic, while possible, would be tantamount to failure, a dead end to his so-far rapid progress up the motor-racing ladder. Indycar racing in the U.S. was a possibility but had nothing like the allure of competing against the best international drivers at road-racing circuits around the world. No, Formula 1 was the place to be, and his experience at Silverstone had convinced Gilles that was where he belonged. And, though it was certainly not a priority for him, the money being earned by the top Grand Prix drivers was the quickest way Gilles could repay Joann's years of sacrifice and deprivation. Here he was, twenty-seven years old and with only one trade: racing driver. He had to think about providing for his family, getting out of debt, giving the kids a more stable future. They were growing fast, the motorhome was becoming too cramped . . .

Gilles's reveries were interrupted by the sound of the telephone ringing. Joann answered it and assumed a puzzled expression, straining to listen to what seemed a faraway voice. She turned to Gilles. "It's for you. It's long distance. Somebody speaking English with a foreign accent, I think." Gilles grabbed the phone to hear a voice saying, "One moment please, Ferrari is calling."

Another person came on the line and identified himself as Ennio Mortara at the Scuderia Ferrari headquarters in Maranello, Italy. He said he was speaking on behalf of Mr. Ferrari, who had asked him to contact a certain Gilles Villeneuve in Canada. "That's me," said Gilles. The message was in the form of a question: "Would you be interested in driving for Ferrari?"

Gilles was incredulous and whispered the question to Joann, who remembers their reaction. "At first we thought for sure it was someone playing a joke. How could Enzo Ferrari know where to find Gilles or even have heard about him? Then the caller said Mr. Ferrari had seen the race at Silverstone on TV. But we wondered how he could judge him on one race alone." At that point the Villeneuves recalled Didier Pironi's mention of Gilles's name in connection with Ferrari.

Mortara, fluent in English and French, was Enzo Ferrari's mediator in matters where those languages were concerned. He asked Gilles if he would prefer him to speak in French. Gilles said no, he understood perfectly, and, yes, he was very interested in driving for Ferrari. Mortara then told Gilles that Mr. Ferrari would like to meet him and he should book a flight to Milano immediately. Ferrari would pay his fare. Gilles booked his flight and any remaining doubts about the authenticity of the first call were dispelled by another in which Mortara asked for his arrival time in Milan.

On Monday, August 29, Ennio Mortara met Gilles at Milan's Malpensa airport and drove him east on the autostrada toward Modena for his first audience with the man considered to be the

Pope of motor racing. Indeed, it was said that the Pontiff in the Vatican in Rome and the Commendatore at Maranello near Modena were venerated on fairly equal terms in Italy. Gilles was dressed for the occasion in his usual style, well-worn blue jeans and nondescript shirt, and carried only a small shoulder bag. He slept most of the way to the exalted destination on the Via Trente e Trieste in Maranello.

■ ■ ■

"Well, well, young man, how much do you need to be content?" These were reportedly Enzo Ferrari's first words to Gilles in their meeting, which lasted about an hour. They sized each other up, the shrewd, eighty-year-old, silver-haired patriarch in the dark glasses, and the slight, baby-faced French Canadian whom he was considering as a candidate to drive one of his famous scarlet racing cars.

Gilles was not intimidated by the venerable presence sitting behind the big desk and surrounded by trophies and photos of legendary Ferrari cars and drivers. He explained that he was still under contract to McLaren. He was guaranteed more races with them this year and, though Teddy Mayer had told him he should accept any other offers and that Tambay would likely drive for him next year, Gilles's contract still contained the option clause for 1978. The document still existed, Gilles was legally bound to it, and he would have to get a written release from McLaren before he was free. Ferrari, vastly experienced in the permutations of F1 politics, assured Gilles that would be no problem.

The meeting ended cordially, with Ferrari saying he would be in touch. Gilles got the impression he could have signed then and there, and he left Maranello a worried man that he had not done so. He knew that Ferrari's interest was more than casual because Niki Lauda was fully expected to leave the team at the end of the season. Others knew it, too, and Gilles had heard several names being mentioned to partner Carlos Reutemann in the 1978 Ferrari team, most prominently Andretti and Scheckter. People like Watson, Jones, and Cheever were also said to be in the running, all very experienced drivers (even the twenty-year-old Cheever, who had been Italian kart champion at the age of fifteen), and Gilles wondered if his insistence on bringing up the

McLaren contract might have sabotaged whatever chances he had.

The importance of his meeting with Enzo Ferrari was further underlined when Gilles saw that the occasion had already been discovered by the ever-vigilant Italian press. On the way out of the Scuderia Ferrari front gate the paparazzi snapped photos of him in the white Fiat 131 being driven by Ennio Mortara.

In fact, the newsmen were after bigger game, Niki Lauda, who was also visiting Ferrari that day. Lauda, World Champion in a Ferrari in 1975 and so nearly killed in one in 1976, was now odds-on favourite to win the 1977 title. At his summit meeting with Ferrari that day Lauda announced his intention to drive for the Brabham team in 1978. Lauda (who previously had assured ''the Old Man'' that he would never leave as long as he was there) gave loss of motivation as the factor behind his decision. But Ferrari thought his $800,000 per season deal with Brabham, courtesy of team sponsor Parmalat (an Italian dairy products firm), was surely a factor. The Lauda/Ferrari meeting, which ended in a shouting match when Ferrari accused Lauda of betrayal, meant the race for the coveted ride in the Italian cars was well and truly on.

Gilles heard the news as soon as he returned to Canada and was very agitated: ''The situation was impossible. I couldn't move legally until my contract with McLaren expired on October 31st. In the meantime Ferrari wouldn't want to wait for McLaren to let me off the hook. I had the feeling that everything was going to be up in the air for me. The idea of going to Ferrari seemed too much. It's like looking at a beautiful, beautiful woman and knowing you'll never have her.''

But he continued to be wooed by Ferrari. They invited him to the Italian Grand Prix at Monza, a few miles north of Milan, where Gilles watched the Lauda Ferrari finish second to the Andretti Lotus. In the pits, rumours were rife that the Italian-born American would replace the departing Austrian in 1978. Andretti and Ferrari would be a match made in heaven for the fiercely partisan Italian fans, the *tifosi*, and a relative unknown named Villeneuve seemed an unlikely third party in the triangle. But Gilles was filled with resolve and during the Monza weekend he spent considerable time talking with Teddy Mayer and John Hogan, whose cigarette dollars were instrumental in consummating the original McLaren/Villeneuve relationship. The company also had previous associations with Ferrari drivers and now Hogan could see no harm in having the Marlboro logo, featured front and centre on Gilles's helmet since Silverstone, displayed in a Ferrari.

Eventually Mayer agreed, but the McLaren release would be conditional on Gilles signing only with Ferrari and not with any other team, particularly Walter Wolf (whom Mayer had heard was interested in Gilles), otherwise McLaren would keep the option on him. This curious proviso was felt by some to be related to an anti-Wolf movement then afoot in F1. There was a certain amount of resentment that the brand new Walter Wolf Racing organization was so successful against the establishment F1 teams, several of which had been around since the world championship was formally organized in 1950. Wolf's Scheckter was even now a contender for the world championship, fighting with Lauda and Andretti.

While Scheckter might himself go to Ferrari next year and Walter Wolf had only spoken in very general terms about hiring Gilles, Mayer was using his leverage to prevent Villeneuve from driving with any team but Ferrari. Perhaps that prospect seemed so unlikely as to make Villeneuve's McLaren contract an insurance policy for the team, to be brought into play should Tambay (whom, it was later revealed, had been formally signed in late August, 1977) not pan out. Whatever, Gilles left Monza with Mayer's blessing to negotiate with Ferrari and he returned for another visit to Maranello.

■ ■ ■

This time he met more of the people in the Ferrari team and was taken to Fiorano, their private test track just around the corner from the factory. There Gilles was strapped into Niki Lauda's 312T/2 and sent out to explore Fiorano's fourteen curves. The three-kilometer circuit was designed expressly to test the behaviour of Ferrari's racing and road cars – and racing drivers – under different conditions. Top speed at Fiorano is only about 280 kph but terminal velocity is not the point of Ferraris, or of road racing. More important is the average lap speed, then about 150 kph (it's now about 170 kph), and every twist and turn of Fiorano is fitted with speed traps, sensors, and photoelectric cells (forty-four in all) that supply continuous data to a central computer system located in a control room at the circuit's start/finish line. The control centre also features a wall of television monitors, which receive pictures from several mobile cameras strategically positioned around the track.

Gilles Villeneuve's first appearance in a Ferrari registered no major blip on the Fiorano Richter scale of performance. He was watched by a small, select group of the Ferrari inner circle: Enzo Ferrari, his son born out of wedlock, Piero Lardi Ferrari, the team's chief mechanic, Antonio Tomaini, and Ferrari's technical director, Mauro Forghieri, who remembers the occasion vividly. ''Gilles was putting too much heat on everywhere and made many mistakes. First, he spun because he was way over the limits of the car. Then he was braking so hard he almost stopped the car when entering corners. At this stage he was using the car like it was a Formula Three, normal for a guy coming from Formula Atlantic. I knew that when a young driver first goes into Formula One he feels immediately that it's a very safe car and very easy to control – until a certain limit. After that first time, Gilles was maybe afraid that he was not ready to go racing because of the difficulties at the Fiorano track.''

Privileged members of the Italian press were invited to watch the test and documented every move of ''il piccolo Canadiense,'' the little Canadian. Previously they had noted that Mario Andretti arrived for his test in a Rolls-Royce and sported a large diamond ring on his finger. Here was Villeneuve arriving in a Fiat 131 and wearing jeans and simple sport shirt. The press detailed Villeneuve's movements: at 2:30 p.m. on Wednesday, the 21st of September, he gets into the car; adjustments are made to the pedals for Villeneuve, who is 1.68 meters tall, while Eddie Cheever, who had tested in the car the day before, is 1.86 meters tall; Villeneuve does a few slow laps, then speeds up and spins on his fifth lap; at 4:20 p.m. he does his fastest time, 1 minute, 14.38 seconds; at 5:40 he spins again and at 6:00 the test ends.

The Italian journalists interviewed Villeneuve and asked him how he came to be invited to the Ferrari test. Gilles replied: ''I don't know who recommended me to Ferrari. It might have been

106

Marlboro. In any case I have to be grateful to whoever it was
that gave me this opportunity." Villeneuve was asked for his
first impressions of Fiorano. "I've never seen anything like it!"
And what was it like out there in the 312T/2? "I need to work
very hard. The steering is light and precise, the motor very powerful, and the gears are what interested me most."

Privately, Gilles was unhappy with the car's handling, but at
this point he wisely refrained from saying anything negative about
a Ferrari. "I found the T2 very hard to drive. I had to be extremely
careful. It was set up for Niki Lauda and he has a particular way
of driving and I have another. Maybe he can drive a car adjusted
for me, but I can't drive his. I find it very soft, both the springs
and the roll bars, and I can't get used to it."

The next day Villeneuve's best time of 1 minute, 13 seconds
was duly recorded and, when compared with the circuit record
of 1.09.341 established by Carlos Reutemann, found to be less
than earth-shattering. Enzo Ferrari, watching from his post in the
control booth in front of the closed-circuit TV monitors, then
called a stop to the test and pronounced himself satisfied. "He
can learn here. He needs to work a lot. You can see by the way
he enters a curve that he knows what he's doing. But we really
can't be too hasty. We saw all this at Silverstone and it was
pointed out to me by Wolf and Amon."

Now Gilles knew two of those he had to thank for his summons
to appear before Ferrari. (Ferrari had also heard a recommendation from the son of one of his executives who worked in
Canada and followed Gilles's Formula Atlantic achievements.)
Walter Wolf, a great admirer of the Old Man and the owner of
various examples of his super-fast road cars, had struck up a
friendship with him. Ferrari had even allowed Walter Wolf Racing the use of the Fiorano facilities to test the Wolf F1 car, the
only time he ever did this for a rival team. So, besides talking
about hiring Gilles for his own team, Walter had spoken very
favourably about Villeneuve to Ferrari: "Walter Wolf had talked
to me about this young man's courage when he was racing his
Can-Am car."

And when Wolf's Can-Am team driver-cum-manager, Chris
Amon, echoed the praise, Ferrari, who had great respect for his
former driver's opinion, listened intently. In Amon's estimation,

"Villenueve has tremendous natural talent and unlimited enthusiasm. At the moment he spins a lot but this is only a matter of
finding his limits. His control of the car is amazing and I think
he is a tremendously brave driver."

Shortly after Gilles's outing at Fiorano, Andretti announced
his decision to stay with Lotus in 1978 and there was one less
rival to worry about. But, said Gilles, "When I came back home
I was doubting very much that I would go to Ferrari. Still, they
told me that they would call me in a couple of weeks. But two
weeks later I was ready to leave for the last Atlantic race at
Quebec City and I still hadn't received a call from Ferrari. Things
were looking rather grim."

Back in the motorhome in Berthier, Gilles was stewing over
the lack of response and the fact that he was shortly going to
have to disconnect the telephone, his umbilical cord to Maranello.
Joann was busy packing and stowing gear for what, she hoped,
was their final race weekend of the year. "Gilles said, 'Now I
have to leave and they're not calling.' I told him to just call
Ferrari up, think of any old excuse. But he said, 'I'm not going
to call and say, Hey listen, have you made up your mind yet?'
Finally I told him to call and ask them about the expenses for
his trip to Monza, which they were going to pay. So he did that."

"I spoke to a secretary," said Gilles. "They said the money
had been sent but they didn't say anything else to me and I
thought, 'Well, that's it.' But then five minutes later, Enzo Ferrari
himself called me and said, 'Are you ready to sign for us?' And
I said, 'Of course I'm ready!' But I still didn't have the release
from McLaren, so on the Monday after Quebec City I went to
England and got the release, and then I went to Italy and did it."

2

"Meeting Ferrari was like an audience with the Pope."
– Gaston Parent

On the 26th of September, Gaston Parent and Gilles set off on
the momentous journey to visit first McLaren, then Ferrari. Gaston Parent did all the talking . . .

"We stopped to see Teddy Mayer in his office near the London airport. He had his nose stuck in his files and all he wanted was to get out of paying us the $25,000. He said if we sign for Ferrari we're all square. I said, 'If we don't sign for Ferrari you've got a breach of contract.' Gilles was saying, 'Forget it, forget it, let's sign with Ferrari.' Anyway, Mayer paid us $6,000 and said, 'If you make a deal with Ferrari I'm out of this contract.'

"Mortara meets us at the Milan airport and we drive to Maranello with Gilles asleep in the back. Instead of going in the front entrance we get driven down this side street to a big door in a wall. The door opens and we drive in. We're shown into a dusty old office, with dirty glass cases full of trophies and so on and only a table and a couple of chairs. You could tell this place wasn't used much. My impression was, Jesus Christ! this is some kind of inner sanctum. Meeting Ferrari was like an audience with the Pope.

"We sat down and the Old Man came in with Della Casa, his administrator and signing officer and, for us, the interpreter. The Old Man would only talk in Italian, although he could speak beautiful French. He hands us copies of a piece of paper that said 'Verbal Agreement' and it had a list of conditions and said Ferrari was paying so many dollars for Gilles Villeneuve to race for them in 1978. I had never negotiated a contract in my life and didn't know what the hell to ask for. Before I left I talked to Walter Wolf, who said that Gilles has got to sit in a car in every race. Walter said that McLaren sat him on the bench, so Ferrari must supply Gilles a running car at every race. So I asked for that clause to be put in.

"On the flight over I had six hours to get to know Gilles better. One thing he said was 'There's no goddamned way anybody is going to stop me from doing what I like to do because of car racing.' He used the example of a surgeon, saying that even if a guy uses his hands to operate with, he goes skiing or whatever. Gilles said he didn't want anybody trying to run his life because he raced for them. He wanted to keep doing his own thing and to be his own person. So I said to Ferrari that Gilles wanted to own his own person. This was my way of expressing that he wanted freedom for himself as a person.

''Ferrari looked at me and asked me if I was a lawyer. I said no. Then he asked Gilles if he was a lawyer, and Gilles said no. Then Ferrari said okay, Gilles could own his own person. But they interpreted it to mean Gilles wanted to own everything on his person, so he owns his driving suit. I didn't know it at the time but we found out that it meant Gilles could sell his suit and we got control over that except for Marlboro and a couple of other sponsors.

''So Della Casa scribbles all this down. Then I said to Ferrari, 'Gilles cannot race if his family's not there. I want expense money for the family to follow him to every race.' The Old Man said, 'No, we don't want to deal with kids. If an accident happens we've got enough to deal with the wife, without the kids.' I asked him why an accident should happen and he told me a strange thing: 'Every time a driver takes off, we write him off in our book. When he comes back it's a bonus.' He may have been joking. Anyway, I said Gilles doesn't go racing unless his family's there. On the plane Gilles had told me about wanting the family with him. So I asked Ferrari for expenses for the family to travel, $15,000 a year.

''Now Gilles wasn't just excited about signing with Ferrari. He was out of his goddamn head! I'm sure if the Old Man had asked Gilles for $50,000 to race in one of his cars, he would have paid it. Earning money was not his motivation. So there he was sitting beside me and telling me to shut up. From the minute I started to negotiate with Ferrari, Gilles was telling me to take it easy. He was very nervous and kept whispering about let's take the deal. He was getting harassed because I wasn't signing fast enough for him. When the Old Man got up to go and pee or something, Gilles said, 'Jesus Christ, let's get this thing over and get out of here.' I told him to take it easy.

''When Ferrari came back I said I wanted 50 per cent of all the sponsorship on the car. I didn't know my ass from a hole in the ground and Ferrari says, 'Uh, uh, it's never been done.' I said it was time to start. In the end we walked out of there with $75,000 for the year for Gilles to drive for Ferrari, plus 25 per cent of the car, plus the extra $15,000 for the family. But we didn't have a contract. They put everything on a new verbal agreement and it was signed, sealed, and delivered by 9:30 that night.

"They put us up in a hotel in Modena and Gilles and I went with Mortara to the restaurant. Right away everybody knew what was going on and the owner asked for Gilles's autograph. Gilles looks at me. He's been a Ferrari driver for about an hour. Here he is signing his name for fans already. The restaurant owner gave us souvenir plates and about eleven o'clock we go up to the hotel room Ferrari had reserved for us. Gilles spent the whole goddamned night on the phone. He phoned his old man and his mother, he phoned his friends. Then he got calls from the press in Montreal. Geez, we didn't sleep all night.

"We went to Fiorano in the morning and there were a bunch of dapper dans watching with Ferrari. Gilles gets in the car, takes off, and spins right into a field of high grass. The front wing of the car mowed all the grass down like a grasscutter. He gets back onto the track and tears round and round, the car is full of grass, and he keeps going like nothing happened. I look at Ferrari and see him smiling.

"They had a big press conference with Reutemann there and we found out the plan was for Gilles to race with him and Lauda at Mosport, in a few days, at the Grand Prix du Canada. Then he's going to race in Japan. We went to the plastic department in the factory to get a seat for Gilles. There was not time to mould him a new seat so they cut down a seat of Lauda's. Gilles was smaller, so they put some foam in and we ended up with a seat formed to fit him that we were supposed to take with us back to Canada.

"There had been an air strike on and they drove us to Rome. We get to the Rome airport and it's full of stranded people backed up from the strike. I said to Gilles, 'The first thing we do is get rid of that seat, put it in the baggage.' He says, 'No goddamn way. I can't afford to lose this seat. It stays with me.' Okay. So the next problem is all the planes are full. We go to the Alitalia manager's office and I explain we've gotta take off. No way. Then the guy finds out this is Villeneuve, the new Ferrari driver, and all the doors opened like a charm. The seat went with us. It's like transporting a mummy, this goddamn thing. They put us in first class with a separate seat for Gilles's racing seat.

"We take off and the captain announces that on board he's got the new driver for Ferrari. Gilles sinks down into his seat trying to hide. He was embarrassed. Then the captain comes up to Gilles and wants to show him how the plane works. And every three minutes a hostess comes around wanting to know if he wants champagne or orange juice. Gilles says he doesn't like the taste of champagne. It makes him sick. He takes the orange juice."

3

"I like to think that Ferrari can build drivers as well as cars. Some people called Villeneuve crazy. I said, 'Let's try him.' "

— *Enzo Ferrari*

Gilles Villeneuve was the seventy-first driver to be hired by Ferrari and probably the least experienced of any of them. It seemed a strange decision at the time but it was completely in character for the living legend who created the most illustrious of all racing teams. Gilles once said that "Ferrari is devoted to racing cars like no man who ever lived." They were kindred spirits.

Enzo Ferrari was born on February 18, 1898, just after the history of motor sport began. No other individual contributed more to that history. Even the word Ferrari, symbolic of fast red racing cars driven by brave men, is ironically appropriate. The family name Ferrari comes from the Italian word for iron: *ferro*, as does the word *ferrare*, which means to shoe a horse. Enzo Ferrari's father was the proprietor of a small iron working shop in Modena. When Enzo's life became devoted to harnessing mechanical horsepower crafted in metal ("I build engines and put wheels on them."), he chose as his personal emblem a prancing horse.

At first, the young Ferrari wanted to be an opera singer—a tenor—or a sports journalist. Though he couldn't carry a tune (unlike another Modenese, Pavarotti), he did have a way with words and for a while reported on soccer games for local newspapers. (Later he wrote eloquently in several books, notably *My Terrible Joys*, a volume of memoirs published in 1963.) But these youthful ambitions soon took a back seat to motor racing. The grand passion of his life began one day in 1908 when his father brought him to see the great Felice Nazarro win in a Fiat at nearby Bologna. "That day I felt a profound emotion."

Like many of those who later drove his racing cars, the road to success was paved with hardship and heartbreak for Ferrari. He had only seven years of formal schooling. During World War One his humble position in the Italian army was that of caretaker for a pack of mules in a transport section. He was devastated by the deaths of his older brother Alfredo and his father during the war years and was himself discharged in 1918 with a lung ailment. He applied for a job with Fiat in Torino but was rejected because there were not enough jobs for all the returning war veterans. He went to a park and sat on a bench, where "I wept with loneliness and despair."

He eventually found work as a test driver with a small car-manufacturing concern in Milano, CMN, and even did some racing for them. In 1920 he saw a girl in the Torino rail station: "She was a fine looking girl, blonde, elegant, vivacious, minute." Her name was Laura and they were soon married. Ferrari then was hired by Alfa Romeo, for whom he acted as a car distributor, competition manager, and, as a weekend bonus, racing driver. In the latter pursuit he competed forty-seven times (from 1919 to 1931) and won thirteen events. It was a quite respectable record but Ferrari felt his mechanical sympathy was a limitation. "I had one big fault. I drove always with consideration for the car, whereas to be successful, one must on occasion be prepared to ill-treat it."

Speaking of those many occasions when Gilles Villeneuve mistreated his cars, Ferrari was philosophical, referring to his "destructive powers" as a factor in improving the Ferrari product. "Villeneuve contributed a lot to us with his intense competitiveness and his talent for taking anything mechanical and utterly destroying it. He continually brought us face to face with our limitations, with the most extreme tests for our cars that our engineers had ever encountered and had to solve, and he indulged in some of the most hair-raising acrobatics I have ever seen in

the process. Transmissions, gearboxes, driveshafts – all were subjected to the utmost punishment. He was a high priest of destruction but his way of driving showed us how much we had to
improve those parts so they could stand the assaults of any driver.''

At one of Enzo Ferrari's race wins, near Ravenna in 1923, he
was introduced to the parents of Italy's leading fighter pilot in
the war, Francesco Baracca. His plane had been decorated with
a special insignia, *Il Cavallino Rampante*, The Prancing Horse,
on a shield and Baracca's daring exploits in the air had made it
a symbol of courage and audacity. It turned out that the late
Alfredo Ferrari had served on the ground crew of the same wartime squadron and after the Ravenna race the Baraccas befriended
Alfredo's younger brother. They presented Enzo with their son's
insignia for his personal use. When he established his own racing
team in 1930, the Scuderia Ferrari, Enzo added a yellow background (the official colour of Modena) to the black horse on the
shield and his cars have carried it ever since.

Following the birth of his son Dino in 1932 Enzo stepped out
of the driver's seat to mastermind his team, and the Scuderia
Ferrari Alfa Romeos became the powerhouse of racing in Europe
in the early thirties. Financed by wealthy partners, Ferrari was
able to engage the services of brilliant designers and remarkable
drivers like Tazio Nuvolari. In 1935 the tiny, fiery Nuvolari drove
Ferrari's Alfa P3 to an amazing victory over the nine cars entered
by the mighty Auto Union and Mercedes-Benz teams. This effort,
around the over 170 curves per lap of the daunting 14.17-mile
Nürburgring course in Germany, remains one of the most extraordinary drives of all time.

For Ferrari, Nuvolari's performance in that event epitomized
all that a racing driver should be. ''He was a driver who, in any
type of car, in any circumstance and on any track, always gave
everything and ended up being, on the whole, the best. Nuvolari,
in contrast with many drivers of yesterday and today, never started
out beaten because he had an inferior car.'' When Ferrari hired
Villeneuve he noted a physical similarity to Nuvolari – both were
small men – and it helped influence his decision to hire him.
''When they presented me with this 'piccolo Canadiense,' this
minuscule bundle of nerves, I immediately recognized in him the
physique of Nuvolari and said to myself, let's give him a try.''

■ ■ ■

Ferrari's arrangement with Alfa Romeo ended in 1938 and during the ensuing war years he built machinery to make ball bearings. His workshop in Modena survived two bombings and in 1946 he moved his premises down the road to Maranello to take up racing on his own. That it soon became a thriving enterprise was only a secondary benefit for Ferrari, who said: "I race because I am an enthusiast. Others do it as a business."

The first all-Ferrari car, the 125 V12, was designed by Gioacchino Colombo and became successful in the hands of drivers like Alberto Ascari and Luigi Villoresi in the late 1940s. Ferrari sports cars first won the epic Mille Miglia and Targa Florio races held on public roads in Italy in 1948 and the historic Le Mans 24-hour endurance race in France the next year. Ferrari began producing road cars based on his racing machines and they soon became the most desirable vehicles for wealthy automotive enthusiasts and exotic status symbols for the rich and famous.

For Enzo Ferrari his "civilian" cars were simply a by-product of his competition department and racing, especially single-seater cars, remained his first love. When the Formula 1 world championship was formally organized in 1950 it became his main interest. Although Ferraris won races in nearly every category of road racing (over 5,000 wins to date), it was putting his cars to the Grand Prix test that mattered most to the founder of the team. Here, too, Ferraris were the most successful (94 wins versus 79 for Lotus, as of 1988), but in later years the man behind the name hardly ever saw them race in person. He restricted himself to watching the events on television because, he wrote, "It offends me to see the machines I have created being driven to death."

However, many people thought his absence from the circuits was prompted by Ferrari's profound sorrow over the cruel death of his son Dino from muscular dystrophy in 1956. The grieving father even contemplated suicide: "Work was my only salvation, the anchor I had to grasp in order not to find myself adrift." Ferrari once told a friend that "Every morning I wake up with Death in my pocket." Following Dino's funeral Ferrari began every day with a visit alone to his grave, then said prayers for him in a chapel dedicated to his son's memory. When his wife

Laura died Ferrari became closer to his illegitimate son, Piero Lardi Ferrari, who is now head of the company.

A complicated man of apparently conflicting emotions, Ferrari was to say of Gilles Villeneuve, "I loved him like a son." But he was also accused of being a hard man who cared more for his cars than his drivers. There had been a great public outcry when the Marquis Alphonso de Portago's Ferrari went off the road in the 1957 Mille Miglia, killing himself and many spectators. Ferrari was charged with using unsuitable tires, then exonerated. But all too often, it seemed, race drivers were killed in Ferraris, and after Luigi Musso died in the wreckage of his Ferrari in 1958, no native Italian appeared in his famous red racing cars for several years. "The reason why I don't have any Italian drivers in my team," said Ferrari, "goes back to 1958 when the Italian newspapers said I was the devil eating my own sons."

In 1963 Ford tried to buy Ferrari, but he refused to sell to the Americans. Then, in 1969, Fiat, the Italian state-owned conglomerate, bought a controlling interest in Ferrari, leaving Enzo in charge of motor racing, and he was able to devote himself exclusively to the Scuderia. He was in his office each morning by 7:30 and (even at the age of ninety) knew each of his employees in the racing division (200 of them before his death) by name. A win in an F1 race was "like a blood transfusion" for Enzo Ferrari, said one of his recent drivers, Michele Alboreto (who had the number 27 made famous by Gilles Villeneuve), and his passion for the sport undoubtedly prolonged his life. (He died on August 14, 1988.)

"I have known men who have undoubtedly loved cars as much as I have," Ferrari wrote. "But I don't think I've known any who have been as obstinate as I have, motivated by the same wholehearted passion that has left me without either the time or the inclination to do anything else. I have no other interests apart from racing cars. Whoever follows in my footsteps inherits a very simple doctrine: to keep alive the desire for progress which was pursued in the past, pursued at the expense of noble human lives."

In his later years Ferrari spent much of his time in a converted farmhouse located within the Fiorano test circuit, where he surrounded himself with racing memorabilia. It is a veritable Ferrari museum crammed with photographs and trophies, even a life-size bronze sculpture of a prancing horse. Pride of place in one corner is given to a wall hanging created by Georgette Villeneuve to commemorate her son's first win in a Ferrari, the 1978 Grand Prix of Canada. And outside the entrance to Fiorano, on the corner of the Via Gilles Villeneuve, is a bronze bust of the French-Canadian driver from Berthierville.

According to Ferrari, his hiring of Gilles was based on a hunch, a gamble that he would develop into a winner. "I admired Villeneuve," he said. "He's the product of a bet I made with myself. When I engaged him I thought no one would ever have put any money on him. It is a well-known fact that many times in life one acts under emotional impulses rather than cold reason. There was a chorus of criticism when I engaged him because he was an unknown entity. Taking into account that I had taken Lauda on as a virtual unknown, well, if Lauda was out there there must be others out there, too, others who can climb to the top. I like to think that Ferrari can build drivers as well as cars. Some people called Villeneuve crazy. I said, 'Let's try him.' "

4

"He'll get better. It's too soon to judge."
—Antonio Tomaini

On his return from signing at Maranello, Gilles went to the Grand Prix at Watkins Glen as a spectator and watched the race from the Ferrari pits. There he was confronted with the kinds of demands made on Ferrari drivers by journalists who wanted to know his innermost feelings. "Well, of course I'm absolutely delighted. Every driver dreams about joining Ferrari. I've been very lucky because of a series of opportunities which favoured me in the race for Lauda's place. It will be very difficult for me to fill the gap he leaves, to repeat some of his achievements. I'll try my best." Yes, these last few weeks had been very nervous ones for him. And it was true that Ferrari's choice of him was probably quite a bit further down the line behind Andretti and Scheckter (who had re-signed with Wolf for 1978). "But," said Gilles, "there's no disgrace in being behind those two, right?"

In the U.S. Grand Prix, Andretti and Scheckter were second and third behind the winner, James Hunt. But Lauda's fourth place meant he was assured the 1977 world championship and his teammate Reutemann scored a point for sixth place to assure Ferrari of another Constructors' title as the year's most successful team. The Formula 1 circus then folded up its tents and headed north across the border for the next weekend's race at Mosport. It was to be the last F1 race at that circuit and the date, October 9, 1977, would be an auspicious one for several reasons, including Gilles's first race for Ferrari.

The action began in the Ferrari pits at Mosport before the cars even took to the circuit, when Niki Lauda had a flaming row with the team. The brusque Austrian had a reputation for speaking his mind and did so now. First of all, he was fed up with the internal politics at Ferrari. Second, he was furious over the dismissal of his faithful mechanic, Ermanno Cuoghi, who had been sent packing at Watkins Glen after Ferrari discovered he was negotiating terms with Brabham to accompany Lauda to that team next season. Lauda's third bone of contention was the appearance of Gilles Villeneuve in a third Ferrari, which Lauda felt was one car too many for the team to handle.

The Ferrari team manager, Roberto Nosetto, responded to Lauda's grievances by contending that the World Champion-elect had lost his motivation after clinching his second title. The matter was resolved when Andreas Nikolaus Lauda stalked out of the pits, collected his $5,000 promotional fee from the race sponsor, Labatt, and promptly flew home to his sumptuous estate at Hof near Salzburg.

So Ferrari, which had actually brought two engines and two new mechanics for its third entry, was again a two-car team and there was increased pressure on the new Canadian driver to fill the breach left by the departed Austrian. Gilles's diplomatic skills were also called upon. "Ferrari is very demanding because they have good cars. Drivers must be willing to give a lot. But if they've had problems in the past it's none of my business. I'm usually very calm and easy to work with. Of course problems will arise, you expect that. But I'm sure we'll be able to talk them over and work things out.''

Gilles had the benefit of anonymity at Silverstone but here he was not unaware of the multitude of his countrymen on hand to view his Ferrari baptism. ''I'm going to have a lot of pressure on me now. It makes a big difference when you know that every move you make will be watched closely by thousands of people. But this whole thing is a dream come true for me. Now I have to prove that I can do it.''

■ ■ ■

Lauda's absence left twenty-seven drivers from twelve different nations vying for the twenty-five grid positions. As it developed the only car not to qualify was Jean-Pierre Jabouille's Renault RS01. Dubbed by an unkind press as ''the yellow tea kettle'' for its propensity to trickle into the pits in a cloud of steam and smoke from another blown V6 turbo motor, the car again lived up to its infamous reputation. Another vehicle was eliminated from competition in a horrifying accident in the first practice session on Friday.

The Englishman Ian Ashley, driving for Lord Alexander Hesketh (James Hunt's former patron), crested the brow of Mosport's Mario Andretti Straight at 290 kilometers an hour in his Hesketh 308E. The car became airborne and flew out of control, somersaulting three times, then vaulting over the armco barrier and impaling itself near the top of a six-meter-high television camera tower. The car and the tower lay in a tangled heap of wreckage well inside a spectator viewing area, which was fortunately deserted at the time. It took forty minutes for rescuers, among them the McLaren driver Jochen Mass, to free Ashley, who was whisked away by helicopter to a hospital in Toronto. Under the circumstances, with his Hesketh totally destroyed and his helmet having come off during his wild ride, the injury report on the unfortunate Ashley seemed relatively good news: both ankles and wrists broken and a slight concussion.

Later on, the McLaren of Jochen Mass spun backwards at Corner 1 and thumped into the steel barriers, which gave way under the impact when the wooden support poles snapped. Mass was unhurt, but the drivers' complaints about inadequate safety measures at Mosport (they were also unhappy at the confusion and delay in attending to Ashley) were a major factor in this being the last Formula 1 race at the sixteen-year-old circuit. But the proceedings continued, including the crashes, one of them involving Ferrari's new recruit.

Gilles's teammate Reutemann blamed lack of grip for his relatively slow times, and lack of adhesion was at the root of Gilles's Friday afternoon miscue. Granted, his continual tailout style was a contributing factor, but Gilles also confessed that he found the car extremely twitchy and difficult to drive on the limit. He went beyond that limit on Friday afternoon and into a wild spin down the chute on the approach to the Moss Corner hairpin. His Ferrari gyrated viciously, knocking its extremities against the rails and coming to rest with crumpled front and rear wings and bent right-side suspension.

Rain on Saturday washed out the possibility of any quicker times so the grid was set from those established the previous day. Andretti's Lotus 78 was on pole with a time of 1 minute, 11.385 seconds, with Hunt's McLaren next up. Jody Scheckter was back in ninth place with his Canadian flag-bedecked Wolf, while the Ferraris, further hampered by the failure of their Goodyear tires to warm up properly in the cold weather, were well back. Reutemann was 12th on the grid at 1m 13.890s and Gilles's 1m 14.465s made him 17th fastest. This put him two places behind Patrick Tambay, his former rival for McLaren affections, driving an Ensign. By now, their paths had crossed many times and Patrick and Gilles were becoming good friends, but talent comparisons were still being made between the two.

At Silverstone, Gilles had logged laps equivalent to several Grands Prix in distance and was able to dial in the McLaren M23 to suit his preference for oversteer. This condition during cornering, when the rear of the car has a tendency to want to precede the front through a corner, was the crux of Gilles's technique. And his method of powering through turns, with the tail out and the front wheels cranked on opposite lock to counteract the sliding rear end, was what made him so spectacular to watch. The reverse condition of understeer, when the chassis is set up so that the front of the car predominates over the rear in cornering, was Niki Lauda's preference.

At Mosport, Gilles's Ferrari T2 was still set up to understeer for Lauda and Gilles was having to fight it all the way, hauling it around corners with the steering wheel rather than the accelerator and his reflexes. In addition, Gilles had been able to confer directly with his English-speaking crew at Silverstone; at Mosport there was still a communications gap in his dealings with the Italian team, and technical chief Mauro Forghieri was concentrating on Reutemann's car. Chief mechanic Tomaini oversaw the repair operations to the Villeneuve-bent Ferrari, and he seemed impressed by the depth of Gilles's interest in the technical side and how he hardly ever left the team pits except to drive. But Tomaini was hesitant to comment on his performance: "He'll get better. It's too soon to judge."

Journalists, though, wanted to know more details about the driver of the number 21 Ferrari, and they chased down his wife in the Villeneuve motorhome parked in a corner of the Mosport paddock. They kept a cautious distance from a rather fierce-looking Alsatian standing guard near the door and questioned this sweetly smiling young lady with two cute kids by her side. Why were they camping out here in the boondocks instead of staying in the posh hotel room reserved for them by Ferrari? "We don't like hotels," Joann replied. "We like the motorhome. It's a nice warm place to stay. I can cook here and it's much better for Jacques and Melanie. I'd rather eat my own cooking and Gilles is happy as long as he gets a steak. Sure, we live like gypsies. But we like it and I don't think we'll change. We may have a bit more money from now on, but we aren't going to change our lives."

And what about the dangers of her husband's profession, doesn't she worry about him? "When Gilles races I am always afraid. But I know he's a good driver and that's why I don't freeze up when I look at him on the circuit. He will continue to improve and polish his performance. Then the public will judge him and time will take care of the rest."

When Gilles arrived on the scene he was asked about his wife's role in his life. "Joann is very important to my career because, even though she doesn't like it, she supports it. When I need to talk to somebody in confidence, she's there. We are very close that way. And being married lessens the temptations that come to a racing driver. Let's face it, there are lot of pretty women in racing and a lot of parties. Being married," he smiled, "I skip all that. I'm better rested on race day."

Race day dawned cold and blustery under sullen grey skies. This did not deter 60,000 fans, dressed in full winter regalia, from crowding up to the fences around Mosport's 3.957-kilometer length. All were in high spirits for the 1977 Labatt Grand Prix of Canada, some of them influenced by copious quantities of the sponsor's product. Their local hero was to have mixed fortunes while a battle royal raged around him. And for Gilles, his eyewitness perspective gave him a close-up view of just how serious this Formula 1 business was. It made his previous racing experiences seem like child's play.

■ ■ ■

Andretti outdragged Hunt at the start, and as the pack tore off into the countryside to sort itself out on a hectic first lap, two cars promptly fell out. Gianclaudio "Clay" Regazzoni's Ensign managed only two of Mosport's ten corners before it was sidetracked into the scenery to the detriment of its nose. Six corners later John Watson lost an outbraking competition with Ronnie Peterson – his Brabham flew over a curb and landed quite heavily, then hobbled into the pits rather the worse for wear. Peterson, with Brabham-inflicted damage on the rear wing of his Tyrrell, motored on briskly, as did the rest, to complete the first of 80 laps.

Super Swede Peterson then used his aggressively driven Tyrrell to hold back Scheckter's Wolf, his chopping and hacking being described by a closely shadowing Alan Jones as "a bit rude – there was dust and muck flying up everywhere." Jones's vision in his Shadow was cleared somewhat when Peterson spun out of contention on lap 11. Sweden's misfortunes continued when Gunnar Nilsson found the throttle in his Lotus sticking wide open as he sailed down the high-speed straight named after his teammate and the race leader, Andretti. With Corner 8 approaching at a terrific rate, Nilsson was able to arrest his progress only slightly before he sailed off into the catch-fencing in a shower of shredded Lotus fibreglass. He was unhurt but through for the day.

Reutemann retired with fuel pressure problems, leaving Gilles to fight the Ferrari battle alone, his ill-handling and gripless T2 oscillating around in 10th place, albeit in a spirited struggle with Tambay's Ensign and a rent-a-drive McLaren hired by the rich American Brett Lunger. At least Gilles was avoiding intimate contact with his rivals, unlike Rupert Keegan and Hans Binder, who tangled wheels at Corner 9 in a painful misunderstanding that saw the Englishman's Hesketh and the Austrian's Surtees fly up into the air alarmingly. The cars returned to earth spinning and both ended up welded to the guard rails, leaving Binder unhurt but Keegan with a broken ankle and minor cuts.

Meanwhile, the Andretti-versus-Hunt clash continued at the front. Such was their pace that they had lapped the field except for Hunt's teammate Mass, and on lap 60 they appeared in his mirrors. Pulses quickened, in the cars and among the spectators, as the opportunity arose for the McLaren duo to conspire against the leading Lotus. En route into Stirling Moss's Corner, Andretti moved up alongside Mass to find the McLaren somewhat wider than it had previously been. The Lotus was forced to place two of its wheels in the dirt, nearly spun, and Hunt went through to claim the lead, though Mass was still in front of him. Mario was not pleased at the manoeuvre: "Bloody Mass nearly had me off!" the normally calm resident of Nazareth, Pennsylvania, later expostulated.

Nose to tail, in the order of Mass-Hunt-Andretti, the threesome pelted past the pits to begin their 61st lap. Sweeping into Corner 3 Mass dutifully moved to the outside and, according to Andretti, "waved Hunt through, then lost it." The Mass version had it that his teammate hit him in the back when Mass was forced to lift off early because he was taking the more slippery outside line. In any case, Teddy Mayer's two cars touched and departed from the track at considerable speed, leaving the road clear for Andretti. Mass eventually emerged from the dust cloud and resumed running, to eventually finish third, but Hunt was left behind in a towering rage.

Momentarily trapped in his distinctly secondhand McLaren, he extricated his undamaged but considerably agitated self from the car. Hunt's nickname for Mass was "Herman the German," but when the native of Frankfurt came around on his next lap

Hunt was hollering much less complimentary names at him. He was also shaking his fist, then proceeded to apply it to the face of a track marshal who tried to prevent the irate Englishman from crossing the circuit. The marshal went down for the count and Hunt went storming back to the pits on foot to be met with a $2,750 fine for his outburst.

Andretti continued on his merry way, ahead of Scheckter's Wolf and Patrick Depailler's Tyrrell, only to hand them first and second places when the Cosworth V8 in his Lotus exploded with just a handful of laps to go. Andretti coasted into the pits in his stricken machine, followed by a dense cloud of smoke and a trail of oil, the latter greasing the wheels of the chaos that then ensued in Corner 9.

Riccardo Patrese's Shadow hit the oil first, skated off the circuit, and caromed into Keegan's abandoned Hesketh. Patrese immediately leaped out and bounded over the rail, a prudent move as Vittoria Brambilla's Surtees executed a piroutte identical to the Shadow and piled into the scrapyard of waylaid machinery. Brambilla, ''The Monza Gorilla,'' had been so engrossed in his battle for third place with Depailler that he failed to notice the oil flags being waved by the marshals. Poor Vittorio (whose only Grand Prix win, in Austria in 1975, ended in ignominy when he took both hands off the wheel to celebrate the unfamiliar chequered flag and promptly crashed) walked into the pits at Mosport in tears. Next on the scene was the Penske of the Hawaiian Indycar veteran Danny Ongais. He managed to sort out his spin and continued, but not so Gilles Villeneuve.

■ ■ ■

Earlier on Gilles had climbed up to eighth place, but he was having a rough ride in a chassis he compared to a lurching, yawing Cadillac. ''I don't know why I didn't crash a dozen times on the first two or three turns where it was the worst,'' he remarked later. He finally did spin at Moss Corner on lap 72 and lost two hard-earned places. Now he came charging into the Corner 9 debacle intent on making up for lost time. He spun, managed to steer clear of the accumulated carnage, and came to rest unscathed, though broadside in the middle of the track. He kept the V12 running throughout the gyration and then popped the clutch, a trifle over-exuberantly it turned out, for a driveshaft was unable to take the sudden application of power and snapped in two. His race was run, and a dejected Gilles walked the short distance into the pits.

Though it was not to be Gilles's day, it was a day of days for Walter Wolf and his adopted country when his car won the race. "These days don't come up every year. They're once in a lifetime. Coming home to win a race is very satisfying," said a jubilant Walter with his arm around Jody Scheckter on the victory podium. But his driver, in keeping with the tone of much of the day's events, was in a foul mood. His car "had run like a train," said Jody, but that !*%#?*& Peterson had run like an idiot (or words to that effect). "Five < +/%&# times he almost had me off going down the &%$#@?! straight!" he fumed, and Jody had to be restrained from going head-hunting for Ronnie.

While he was also frustrated, Gilles was more restrained in post-race interviews. And, when talking about his demise, he impressed with an honesty that was refreshing to the jaded journalists who were accustomed to hearing every excuse in the book from drivers who seldom laid the blame for any miscue at their own feet. "I saw the oil too late and spun around without hitting anything. Then, when I tried to get back into the race, I dropped the clutch, overdid the revs, and a driveshaft broke. It was my fault."

The spectacular rate of attrition left only five cars running at the end of the race and Gilles, had he made it to the end, would probably have been fifth. As it was Patrick Tambay finished in that position, while Gilles, who had remained in the fray longer than many, was classified 12th overall in the final results. He would have one more chance in 1977, at the Japanese Grand Prix in two weeks.

5

"Attends-moi, ce ne sera pas long." – "Wait for me, I won't be long."

– Gilles Villeneuve

The second-ever Japanese Grand Prix was held on the Fuji International Speedway against the dramatic backdrop of the snow-capped volcanic peak after which it was named. The previous year Fuji-san had been obscured by torrential rain and beneath it the season ended in damp disappointment for Ferrari fans when Hunt secured the world championship after Lauda's controversial decision to stop racing in the admittedly diabolical conditions. Now Lauda was World Champion again but absent from the proceedings, leaving Reutemann and Villeneuve to carry the Ferrari cudgels. Lauda, now in deep disgrace at Maranello, had had his Ferrari slate wiped clean and Gilles's car was carrying his number 11.

With the championship no longer an issue and just seventy-three laps of racing remaining in the 1977 season, the atmosphere along pit lane was more relaxed than usual. When opening-day practice was delayed because no doctor was present at the track, spectators were entertained by several drivers and members of the Ferrari crew who raced each other on foot between the Ferrari timing beams on the pit straight. After the medical man arrived and the F1 teams got down to business, the Ferrari frivolity ceased. Their cars were again on less than equal footing with the frontrunners.

Taking full advantage of Colin Chapman's ground-effects design, which effectively glued his car to the road in cornering, Andretti was quickest and the Fuji front row was the same as at Mosport, when Hunt qualified his McLaren M26 next to the Lotus 78. Reutemann ended up on the fourth row of the grid and was a very bothered Argentinian. His time of 1 minute, 13.32 seconds was only a second and a bit slower than the polesitter but it had been very hard to come by. "I try everything, everything, but nothing makes any difference. It has a fantastic engine but I just cannot get any traction. Something is very wrong with the geometry." He then described some of the lurid details about the behaviour of the car on Fuji's several lengthy swoops and pronounced it all "really dangerous."

Reutemann's new teammate was even more concerned. Despite frequently desperate-looking attempts, he was only able to manage a 1m 14.51s lap that put him 20th fastest. "I'm really worried about this and I don't really know the answer," said

Gilles, who was getting lots of oversteer now, though he had little say in the matter. The T2 seemed to have a mind of its own, snapping out of line regardless of any input from the driver. He couldn't remember ever having driven a worse-handling car. "I have to drive like an old man around the corners and press the throttle on the straight, or else I spin. About the only thing that's worthwhile on this car is the brakes, I just don't know what to do . . . ."

Sunday, October 23, was warm and sunny and 70,000 enthusiastic Japanese spectators were jam-packed into the Fuji circuit. In the pits Joann helped Gilles with his last-minute preparations before taking up her position in the Ferrari timing stand along the pit wall. It wasn't necessary to talk; their routine was established many races ago and Joann knew Gilles was concentrating deeply, thinking about the start, planning his moves and, here, wondering how he was going to compensate for his car's deficiencies. She handed him his flameproof balaclava and driving gloves. Just before he pulled his helmet on Gilles leaned over to her and whispered the words that were the final moment in their private pre-race ritual: "Attends-moi, ce ne sera pas long." – "Wait for me, I won't be long."

As the lights turned green Andretti let his revs drop too low and flubbed the start, giving Hunt the advantage over Scheckter. Andretti, who had dropped to eighth, became overzealous to catch up and hit Jacques Laffite's Ligier in the middle of a fast corner. The Lotus broke a steering arm in the clash and slewed off the road out of control, smashing hard into the barriers. Andretti was lucky to walk away from the wreck, one wheel of which landed in the middle of the track. In trying to avoid it, two following cars collided, the Surtees of Hans Binder and the Kojima of Noritake Takahara. Both the Austrian and the Japanese were out of the race on the spot. All this brought out the ambulances on the first lap. Fortunately they weren't needed then, but soon all the Fuji emergency services were called to the scene of a disaster on another part of the circuit.

Gilles was charging hard and had already passed four cars but had several times experienced locking brakes that sent up clouds of blue tire smoke. In practice and qualifying he had praised his car's stopping power; now the brakes were overdoing their job and locking up unpredictably. At the beginning of his sixth lap the number 11 red Ferrari roared down the pit straight at about 260 kph, tucked right in behind the blue-and-white six-wheeled Tyrrell of Ronnie Peterson. Ahead of them was Devil's Curve, the sharp right-hand bend at the end of the straight that required heavy braking on a bumpy track surface. Under braking, the Ferrari ran into the Tyrrell's right rear wheel and was launched high into the air. As the Ferrari soared overhead, the Tyrrell spun away violently, losing its rear wing but otherwise intact.

The Ferrari, having lost very little momentum, dropped down nose first, then cartwheeled off to the outside of the circuit. It somersaulted several times, shedding pieces of bodywork, then scythed sickeningly into a group of people who were standing in a prohibited area. Two of them were killed instantly, a twenty-five-year-old amateur photographer and a twenty-one-year-old track guard who was trying to move the spectators out of harm's way. Ten people were injured, seven seriously, many being cut from flying pieces of metal.

All that remained of his car, now lying in a ditch 130 meters off the track, was the monocoque, in which he still sat, and the engine behind him, but Gilles was completely uninjured. He quickly unfastened his seat belts and ran back to the pits. Ronnie Peterson was also unhurt and Gilles went up to him, the driver he most admired, and apologized, saying his brake pedal had gone to the floor. Peterson then gave his version of what happened. "On the straight I saw him in the mirrors and I was concentrating on the curve. I think inexperience lies at the bottom of what happened. He probably forgot that he had 200 liters of fuel on board. He was certainly bloody lucky the Ferrari did not catch fire."

Joann, unaware of what had happened, was surprised to see Gilles appear on foot in the pits. She thought he seemed grim and upset and assumed something must have gone wrong with his car. "I didn't say anything because when he's in that kind of mood it's better to just be quiet. Then Patrick Tambay came running up and asked me if Gilles was okay. I thought that was a silly question and said sure, he was all right, just mad. Then Patrick told me Gilles had had a very big accident and I just about flipped. We went to find him, he was in a small camper at the back, and when Patrick asked him about it all Gilles knew was that he had touched some people and probably hurt them. He didn't realize anyone was dead. He was just very angry with himself.''

James Hunt won the race, then upset the organizers when he refused to attend the awards ceremony, instead dashing for the airport. He was accompanied by Carlos Reutemann, who had managed to climb up to an unexpected second-place finish and now correctly anticipated the legal wrangle about to befall his teammate. Patrick Depailler, who salvaged third for the Tyrrell team, was thus the only driver to appear on the victory podium. Then everyone packed up and went home, everyone, that is, but those involved in the accident. The Ferrari and the Tyrrell cars were impounded and remained exactly where they had landed in the accident, which was now the subject of a police investigation.

■ ■ ■

On Monday morning the parties involved met at the Fuji circuit. Ken Tyrrell argued on behalf of his driver and Roberto Nosetto represented Ferrari's interests. Peterson and the Tyrrell were finally released and allowed to go back to England after Ronnie demonstrated that his car was in good running order by doing a complete lap and performing a brake test. The investigators then poked about the wreckage of the Ferrari but were unable to reach any conclusions. Then they grilled Gilles, asking him how fast he had been going, what gear he was in, how far behind Peterson and so on. Gilles had called Gaston Parent in Montreal (waking him at three in the morning) and was advised to say or sign nothing. Nosetto suggested he plead shock and didn't remember anything.

A team of lawyers arrived with papers, written in Japanese, Gilles was asked to sign. He refused until they were translated. English versions were proffered the next day and he signed a document that simply recounted what had happened. Gilles and Joann flew back to Canada while Nosetto took the remains of the car back to Maranello. A few days later the investigators established that both drivers had driven ''in accordance with the rules of the International Federation of Automobiles,'' the world

The spirited Villeneuve cornering technique set him apart from the beginning. Formula Atlantic at Edmonton, 1974.

(Christopher Waddell)

He said he only ever really felt alive in a racing car.

(The Toronto Star)

She didn't like her husband racing, but Joann was always there. The
Villeneuves with Antonio Tomaini of Ferrari.

(*The Globe and Mail*)

In the early days the family lived like gypsies and Jacques and Melanie
Villeneuve grew up watching their father race.

(*The Toronto Star*)

Sideways all the way at Trois-Rivières in 1976, his performance set the stage for a dramatic Formula 1 debut. *(Pierre Bolduc)*

The Prime Minister, Carlos Reutemann, Jody Scheckter, and a multitude of his countrymen were happy for him when Gilles's first win came at home. *(Lionel Birnbom)*

The adulation became worldwide, but he remained essentially a shy man. Montreal, 1978. *(Parent Collection)*

Gaston Parent began as Gilles
Villeneuve's manager, then be-
came one of those closest to him.
(*Daniel Auclair*)

They had their battles, but Ferrari's Mauro Forghieri thought Villeneuve had a rage to win like no
other driver.　　　(*International Press Agency*)

He was called both a hero and an idiot for trying to continue in damaged cars. Zandvoort, 1979. *(Canapress Photo Service)*

The Villeneuve-Arnoux duel at Dijon in 1979 was one of the most torrid ever seen in the history of motor racing.

(Phipps Photographic)

Villeneuve's number 27 Ferrari in classic form in Argentina in
1981. (*International Press Agency*)

Villeneuve in the rain was in a class by himself. At Watkins Glen in 1979 he was 11 seconds faster than anyone else.

(*Phipps Photographic*)

Against all odds Villeneuve leads Laffite, Watson, Reutemann, and de Angelis across the finish line in Spain, 1981.

(International Press Agency)

Jacques and Gilles, the Villeneuve brothers from Berthierville, at the Grand Prix of Canada, 1981. *(Jan Bigelow)*

He went from rags to riches and spent a lot of money on expensive
"toys." *(The Toronto Star)*

"Wait for me, I won't be long," were Gilles's last words to Joann before the start of each race.
(*W.H. Murenbeeld*)

His last race: Imola, 1982. While Didier Pironi celebrates, Gilles feels betrayed.
(*International Press Agency*)

May 8, 1982: Zolder, Belgium. The last lap.   (*Gerald Donaldson*)

Enzo Ferrari called him a Prince of Destruction, but loved Gilles Villeneuve like a son.
(Phipps Photographic)

Scheckter and Lauda agreed Villeneuve was the fastest of them all. Jody called him the most genuine man he ever knew and Niki said he was the craziest devil in Formula 1, but he liked everything about him.　　　　　*(Dominique Leroy)*

(Noel Neelands)

governing body of motorsport. It was several weeks before the full investigation was completed and no blame was appropriated.

Gilles maintained his silence for some time and never changed his mind about what had gone on in the cockpit that day. Some wondered if he simply left his braking too late in an effort to outbrake Peterson. From his long observance and admiration of Peterson, Gilles should have known he was the last of the late brakers. Another point of view had it that Peterson failed to notice the Ferrari's fast approach on his right-hand side and simply chopped in front of it. Still another concept involved the unique technique necessary to turn a six-wheel Tyrrell that perhaps Gilles was unfamiliar with. Peterson had to take a corner in a series of segments and Gilles mistook one of them for an opening that quickly closed. Eventually the affair subsided and was filed away under the "just another racing accident" category.

Regarding the tragedy, Gilles's position was that the people shouldn't have been where they were and that motor racing was dangerous enough for the drivers without them having to worry about spectators. But he was badly shaken by what happened – not for fear of what might have happened to himself, but at what did happen to others. "I wasn't scared after that accident – just terribly sad about the people who were killed. I know they were standing in a forbidden area and I didn't feel responsible for their deaths, but . . ."

As to his performance to date with Ferrari, Gilles made a terse statement: "At Silverstone I had done 1,500 kilometers and I had gotten used to the car and to the circuit. In Canada and Japan I hadn't. That's all there is to it."

Niki Lauda watched the Japanese Grand Prix on the television in his living room back in Austria. When he saw what befell his successor at Ferrari, Lauda said: "Villeneuve will have a hard time after this. I can imagine how they are shaken up down there at Maranello."

5

MAKING UP FOR LOST TIME: 1978

I

"I hope to win my first Grand Prix halfway through the season."

— *Gilles Villeneuve*

"That boy's in too much of a hurry," was Carlos Reutemann's comment about Gilles's difficult debut with Ferrari. From Austria came the considered opinion of Niki Lauda that his successor was bound to have problems because racing a T2 without sufficient experience was a very risky proposition. There were also negative stories in the racing press, particularly in Italy, about Villeneuve being in over his head, and some speculated that Enzo Ferrari might have lost his gamble in signing an unknown. But in his traditional end-of-season press conference Ferrari defended his choice. "I took Villeneuve on for the talents he has and such as they were pointed out to me. It is still too early to pass judgement on him. He has been unlucky, but I think he has the ability to grow."

On their way back from Tokyo he and Joann stopped off in New York to visit John Lane, who was now working on Wall Street. Lane took them to lunch high above the city in the World Trade Center, where Gilles speculated about his future at Ferrari. While he was pleased to hear about the Old Man's vote of confidence, Gilles also confessed he was worried about how he might be viewed by the Italian press. He knew about the importance of Ferrari drivers in the hearts and minds of the Italian people and the vital role the press played in creating public images. Lauda, formerly the hero who came back from his deathbed to fight again for Ferrari and the glory of Italy, was being rubbished in print for being a traitor to the cause. And his successor would be subjected to the closest scrutiny. If he did not measure up and public opinion turned against him, Gilles's stay at Ferrari might be short.

When they landed in Montreal, Gilles found to his dismay that he was also being treated as negatively newsworthy in his native land. The Canadian media, often accused of subscribing to the theory that bad news is good news, were also labouring under the handicap of knowing very little about Gilles's profession. Except for a handful of knowledgeable motor-racing journalists, who were aware of the fact that the sport is the second most popular in the world after soccer, the scribes concentrated on the traditional North American stick-and-ball games. Now they hurled verbal sticks and stones and Gilles did not like what he read. "The Canadian press was really bad in the way they were reporting what the European press was saying. Lots of papers in Europe said it was an accident that could have happened to anyone at any race. But here, from the accident on, I was being fired about twenty times a day in the press and being replaced by different drivers."

In Berthierville, Gilles and Joann made the relatively few preparations necessary for their new life abroad. In their seven years of marriage they hadn't accumulated much excess baggage in the way of personal possessions. The physical move to Europe entailed no complicated logistical problems, other than what to do with Princess. She was very much a member of the family. The children had grown up with her and there were tears at the parting. But she was given a good home and would remain a Villeneuve dog because Gilles's brother Jacques agreed to take her. And Princess's new master would treat her very much in the manner to which she was accustomed, for he, too, was embarking on a racing career, beginning on snowmobiles, where he would become World Champion three times.

The Villeneuves had narrowed down their house-hunting to the storied south of France, not because of its wealthy playground reputation but for more practical reasons. Patrick Tambay, a resident of Cannes, recommended his part of the world and Gilles had decided on that area. "I have nothing against living in Italy," he said. "But it will be better for the kids if they can continue to speak French. And it's an easy trip from Cannes to Maranello."

They had only a couple of weeks after the Japanese Grand Prix before Gilles was due at Fiorano for testing, not enough time to find a place of their own. Tambay, about to embark on his McLaren sojourn, very generously handed Gilles the keys to his villa in Cannes.

They stayed in the Tambay residence for several weeks, with Gilles commuting to Fiorano in a small Fiat loaned to him by Ferrari. He was away two and three days at a time and when he returned they explored the splendours of the Cote d'Azur and environs in search of a place of their own. Eventually they rented a villa just outside Plascassier, a charming village up in the hills between Cannes and Grasse. They bought furniture for the villa, which was much more spacious than any of their previous premises. The three-year lease was expensive, enough to buy a luxurious house in Berthier, and while it was not a mobile home that could be transported to a variety of scenery, it was splendidly situated with inspirational views in every direction. The higher peaks of the Alpes Maritimes behind it were already covered with snow and the valley below stretched away to the palm-treed beaches of the Mediterranean eight kilometers in the distance. There was a nearby school for Jacques and Melanie, and also neighbours they knew: the Wolf family. It was a favourite among their several international addresses and Walter, his wife, and two daughters were frequently in residence. Joann became quite friendly with Barbara Wolf, a Canadian from Prince Edward Island.

There was no language barrier in their community, though the Villeneuves found their Québécois accents were a novelty to the French. The countryside and climate were indeed glorious but they missed the changing seasons, even looked longingly at the winter snows further inland. The kids used to enjoy playing in the snowstorms after coming home from school in Berthier and Gilles regarded negotiating snowdrifted roads as one of his great driving pleasures. He missed his vehicles, the Mustang and his four-wheel adventures aboard a Ford Bronco in the back country of Quebec. And it took the Villeneuves a while to adjust to the European way of life, as Joann recalls.

"It was difficult for the kids because we were kind of isolated up there and they had to find their way around a new school. They adapted quickly and soon made friends but there was quite a culture shock at first for all of us. We had to get used to little things, like the phones not working so well, the fact that the milkman didn't come to the door and the stores were closed from twelve to three. It took a few months to find out where to buy certain foods and some, like peanut butter and chocolate chips for baking cookies, we had to have sent over from Canada. But there was no real problem shopping for Gilles, no matter where we went in the world. He was a steak-and-potatoes person and that was that. For him eating was a waste of time, something he had to do."

"I'll never be a European," said Gilles, who was not impressed with the fact that two of the world's great cuisines flourished on his doorstep. "I'm a typical North American. I like to drive down the highway and pull in for a hamburger, French fries, and a Coke." According to the *Michelin Guide*, three of the best restaurants in France were within a few kilometers of their villa, but that was of no consequence to Gilles. He was dismayed at the absence of hamburger joints but delighted to discover a restaurant in Nice, Le Petit Québec, which served French-Canadian cuisine, including Gilles's favourite dessert, sugar pie.

"In France," said Gilles, "they don't have quick snacks, just big meals. The bread is as hard as the table. And the only thing they have to drink is water or wine." As long as he had his bacon and eggs and peanut butter on his toast in the morning he was gastronomically satisfied. At lunch breaks at Fiorano, while the rest of the Ferrari personnel might linger over a fine Italian meal at the nearby Prancing Horse restaurant, he would munch on a Kit Kat chocolate bar and wait impatiently for testing to resume. When the day's driving was over Gilles stayed in the nearby Montana hotel, but the sessions at Fiorano always ended too soon for him and he remarked that if the car had headlights he would be happy to continue all night.

■ ■ ■

His every move was detailed by journalists, who monitored his progress as closely as Fiorano's electronic gadgetry. Beyond the mechanical and technical, they probed his character and wanted to know all about his private life. They found that, after racing, Gilles's favourite topic of conversation was his family, and particularly his son. "Jacques is six years old," he told them, "and already he knows how to hold a steering wheel. He sits on my knees, I press the accelerator and he drives. We are already up to 60 miles an hour." Gilles talked of his own boyhood initiation behind the wheel of his father's car and the scribes noted that speed seemed to be in the Villeneuve genes. Gilles spoke of Melanie (who, in the more fanciful press, became the little blonde girl with the big blue eyes who was going to break men's hearts when she grew up) and he described how he had met Joann on a blind date (the sweet young girl with the sun shining in her liquid eyes who appeared to have no other purpose than to enchant the future racing driver) and described their simple lifestyle in Canada, their gypsy travels, and the financial hardship.

These slices of the life of the new Ferrari driver were chronicled and embellished in the press, and they appealed to the Italian love of family and children. And after the unsentimental Lauda (who came from a wealthy Viennese family, who shielded his family from public view, who called his trophies "useless" and gave them away to a local garage owner in Austria in exchange for car washes), the Villeneuve saga seemed more in keeping with the romantic notion of the heroic racing driver with a heart of gold. The big question remaining was: how good was he? He apparently did not lack confidence about his own ability and even seemed a bit audacious. When he was asked what he expected of himself during 1978, Gilles replied, "I will do my best to speed up my times and to learn it all. I hope to win my first Grand Prix halfway through the season."

At Fiorano, his early testing times were two seconds slower than Reutemann, suggesting that Gilles was still a long way from achieving his lofty ambition. But he pounded round and round for hours on end until mid-November, when the Ferrari team went south to the Vallelunga circuit near Rome. Here they could test on another configuration of track where the longer straight sections permitted the cars to stretch their legs. Also on hand was Niki Lauda, whose Brabham had an Alfa Romeo engine, and the English-based team was taking advantage of the Italian connection to test in more favourable climes. Also there, to Gilles's surprise, were several thousand *tifosi*, anxious to get a preview of 1978 and, of course, to cheer for their beloved Ferraris and hurl insults at Lauda.

In the two days at Vallelunga the World Champion's best time was 1 minute, 6.68 seconds. Reutemann toured around quickly and methodically to wind up with a best of 1m 5.83s and the *tifosi* responded with triumphant cheers. Lauda's car might be half-Italian but Ferrari was faster. Gilles's most noteworthy accomplishment in his early laps was a monumental spin from which he emerged in his customary manner, selecting first gear while still in orbit and zooming off without pause. The onlookers yelled their approval and watched him circulate ever faster. His best lap registered 1m 6.25s on the clocks and another burst of cheering in the grandstands. "Villanova," too, was faster than the World Champion!

In the pits Antonio Tomaini triumphantly raised his arms in the air and had words of praise. "He is a diligent pupil. The more time passes the better I like him." And Mauro Forghieri agreed. "Villeneuve is growing. He has taken gigantic strides in a very short time. We are all very pleased with him. He is a driver who will give us a great deal of satisfaction."

■ ■ ■

"A genius, but also a madman" is how Niki Lauda described Mauro Forghieri, and their shouting matches in the pits were legendary. Beyond that, wrote Lauda in *To Hell and Back*, "he has the psychological finesse of a sand viper . . . when the Ferrari went well and all was perfect, he considered me a very good driver, perhaps the best. When things went wrong, I was an idiot."

Forghieri, a Modenese, earned a mechanical engineering degree at the University of Bologna and began with Ferrari in 1959. He became technical chief of the racing department in 1962,

responsible for translating all his boss's aspirations into success
on the racing circuits of the world.

An exuberant and passionate man, Forghieri's volatile personality occasionally boiled over into loud verbalization of his feelings, particularly with drivers who might be in disagreement with
him. Yet his technical genius brought much glory to Ferrari,
including four Constructors' Championships to 1977. And despite
Lauda's acerbic assessment and Forghieri's reputation for feuding
with his drivers, he was also able to help nurture immature talents.
He had worked well with Chris Amon, who was just twenty-four
when he came to Ferrari, as was Lauda. Teamed with Forghieri,
Amon went from backmarker to frontrunner with unparalleled
testing abilities and Lauda developed from a crash-prone non-
entity into a double World Champion during his Ferrari tenure.
Now Forghieri had a much more obscure newcomer to contend
with.

"I watched him at Silverstone," Forghieri remembers, "and
I saw that he was a very highly skilled driver . . . because he
was driving on a very difficult track without any reference points.
I came back and told Mr. Ferrari about this young guy who is
not so bad and looks very promising. He is very inexperienced
but looks promising and maybe it's a nice chance to contact him
for the future. Mr. Ferrari had told me to look around because
he was having problems with Niki. Then Chris Amon also spoke
about Gilles being a good one and Mr. Ferrari soon chose him.
He was a natural driver. The only thing he needed was to learn
to work on a car like Niki. Gilles could be quick in any car but
to be a winner in Formula One you must also develop the best
car. During the winter I pushed him to do a lot of work so he
got a tremendous improvement in his feeling for the car. We had
some fights, Gilles and I, but that's normal. In a family you must
have battles or you don't have a good family."

Joann was often a witness to their family squabbles. "Oh yes,
they screamed at each other a lot, but they got things done and
they progressed. Gilles's attitude was that we say what we have
to say and then it's finished and we get on with it. Gilles thought
Mauro was an extremely bright man and admired him very much
and believed that his excitable way was just part of being Italian.
He thought it was funny."

Gilles was prepared to humour Forghieri because he respected his talents and the two established an early rapport seldom seen at Ferrari. "Forghieri is an exceptional man from whom I've learned much," said Gilles. "I like him because he's strong-headed, someone who doesn't give up when he wants to reach an objective."

Carlos "Lole" Reutemann was another member of the 1978 Ferrari family, and the senior driver after Lauda left. Aged thirty-five, tall, and ruggedly handsome, Reutemann looked every inch the racing driver; though his performances were uneven in that he seemed unable to charge unless he was in the right frame of mind, he was to win twelve Grands Prix in an eleven-year career. He came from Sante Fé, Argentina, where his Swiss-German father and Italian mother operated a pig farm, and his boy-hood nickname "Lole" came from the Spanish for pigs, *los lechones* (though Reutemann took pains to conceal its origins). An introverted and taciturn man, he was never very popular at Ferrari and during his two years with the team only ever met Enzo Ferrari twice. Ferrari evaluated him as "an excellent driver whom nature has not helped by giving him a troubled personality."

Part of Reutemann's reputation stemmed from the fact that he was never very forthcoming with the opinion-makers, the journalists, most of whom labelled him the moody Argentinian. He once confessed that "I give the impression of being a placid man, without problems. Instead, I'm very nervous, although I hide it well. I'm constantly worried by a thousand things going through my head."

During the winter testing at Ferrari, Reutemann was entrusted with the bulk of the work developing the entirely new T3 model, which Forghieri had designed around the tires of the team's new rubber supplier, Michelin. Ferrari had decided to use the French company for 1978 after several years with Goodyear, the American company that supplied most of the Formula 1 teams. Meanwhile, Gilles soldiered on with the 312T-2/78, an interim model intended for use in the early races until the T3 was ready. Gilles continued to find the T2 very nervous and twitchy: "It was still rather vicious and you had to be careful with it." And at first the Michelin/Ferrari marriage was not a happy one so that, as

Reutemann put it, "Ultimately the brunt was borne by Villeneuve and myself."

Reutemann was supposed to be difficult to get along with. Indeed, Niki Lauda wrote that "To have Reutemann for a team-mate was never agreeable, not for one single second." Says Joann, "We had been told about Carlos and we waited for him to be hard to get along with. But it didn't really happen. I remember how he would come up to Gilles, Carlos was really a tall guy, and tap Gilles on the head and say, 'Hi, little chum, how's it going?' "

Early in the 1978 season it was not going all that well for Reutemann's little chum.

2

"The man is a public menace."

– Ronnie Peterson

The first race came just two weeks into the new year, at the Autodromo Municipal de la Ciudad de Buenos Aires. Carlos Reutemann's homecoming began triumphantly when he qualified his T2 on the front row beside Andretti's polesitting Lotus. After he had only spun once on the first day Gilles joked that "It must be a personal record. And the one I had really wasn't my fault. The brake locked up on one wheel of the car." Then Gilles wanted to clear up a misconception about his propensity for spinning, which was rooted in his Silverstone appearance in the McLaren. There, he maintained, he had deliberately spun because it was the fastest way to find his limits. But he wasn't necessarily doing that now, though occasional rotations might come. "It's just that I don't mind spinning a car. It doesn't bother me as long as there is nothing around to hit."

He didn't hit anything, but his progress in the rest of practice and qualifying was punctuated by several spins and emergency excursions up an escape road when he entered a corner too optimistically. All of this earned him seventh fastest time and in the race he had a lengthy battle with Patrick Tambay. It was finally resolved in the McLaren driver's favour when Tambay motored past him in a risky manoeuvre on the inside of a curve. Gilles was nearly forced off the circuit when Tambay slid wide but held no grudge against his former landlord, putting the pass down to a better-handling McLaren that overcame the horsepower advantage of the Ferrari V12.

"I finally managed to finish a race for Ferrari," said Gilles after eventually finishing eighth, just behind Reutemann, who in turn trailed Tambay. Andretti won, followed by Lauda, in what was a rather processional and uneventful race in Argentina.

There was a two-week interval until the next event, in Brazil, and the Formula 1 circus took full advantage of the South American weather and hospitality along the beaches outside Rio de Janeiro. Gilles was also celebrating his birthday, his twenty-sixth according to the press biographies, but in reality his twenty-eighth.

On that day, January 18, he and Joann had lunch with a party that included Jochen Mass, late of McLaren and now of ATS, a team fielded by a fellow West German, Hans Gunther Schmid, who used his Formula 1 enterprise to publicize his ATS wheels. Mass and the others ordered a feast of exotic Brazilian fare while Gilles's birthday meal consisted of a well-done steak, French fries, and a couple of Cokes. Everyone else had wine, at which Gilles turned up his nose. "I don't like wine. It makes me sick."

Gilles lamented that it was impossible to get a decent hamburger in Brazil and everyone made sport of his plebeian tastes. Jochen Mass said, "He'll learn." Mass, who once was a merchant seaman, also lived on the Cote d'Azur, in a villa on Cap Ferrat, where he was a neighbour of Carlos Reutemann and kept his large sailing schooner. Gilles thought Mass was good company and it is very sad that this man, so widely regarded as one of the most pleasant men in racing, was to be involved in the final tragedy of the driver whose birthday he helped celebrate in Rio in 1978.

The birthday festivities were soon forgotten and the irony in Gilles's life continued at the Jacarepaguá circuit near Rio when he had another controversial incident with the driver he most admired. Peterson, now Andretti's teammate at Lotus, was on pole, ahead of Hunt, Andretti, Reutemann, Tambay, then Villeneuve. The race began in heat of 100 degrees Fahrenheit with the humidity hovering near 80 per cent, conditions that contributed to Peterson and Hunt falling back with tire troubles. Reutemann then dominated the race, leading all the way to win the first Grand Prix for Michelin. But his little chum was in trouble.

Gilles was running well in fifth place after having passed Tambay early on, then local hero Emerson Fittipaldi (driving a car of his own manufacture), much to the dismay of the 65,000 Brazilians in attendance. On the 15th lap Gilles encountered Peterson's ailing Lotus dropping back into his clutches. When Ronnie refused to give way in a late-braking duel, Gilles aggressively tried to muscle past by way of an opening the Lotus refused to make for him and both cars spun off. In the ensuing confusion Scheckter tried to sneak by Tambay, the Wolf and McLaren collided, and their races were soon over. So was Peterson's, whose Lotus 78 suffered immobilizing suspension damage in the altercation with the belligerent Ferrari.

Gilles pitted for a new wheel, then continued on until lap 35 when he spun again, in the same place, though this time unassisted, and his car finished up wrapped in the catch-fencing. In truth, like several others, Gilles was suffering somewhat from the heat, but Peterson regarded their second run-in in three races as a replay of the first. "He came into me again from behind, just as he did in Japan. I really think that he has a pretty minimal judge of the distance between things. The man is a public menace . . . he was going so fast that if he hadn't hit my Lotus he would have driven straight off the circuit."

Gilles gave little defence, saying only, "I was alongside Peterson and getting ahead of him when he just came into me." And the anti-Villeneuve movement gained more followers when there was further ignominy in the South African Grand Prix, where Gilles inadvertently spoiled the debut of the Ferrari T3. The only positive thing about the weekend for Gilles was that for the first time he outqualified his teammate, eighth versus ninth on the grid, thus winning a bet with Tambay, who had to pay for Gilles's steak and potatoes that night. The wager was to see which one of them would be first to beat his team leader in qualifying and Tambay was unable to outpace Hunt.

At the front, the race was quite exciting with Peterson victorious after the other leaders – Andretti, Riccardo Patrese (Arrows), and Patrick Depailler (Tyrrell) – were victims of a variety of misfortunes. Patrese's performance was a particularly notable one by a young driver in a new car, though his Arrows failed him in the end, as did the Teddy Yip-entered Theodore of Formula 1 debutant Keke Rosberg. Before his car malfunctioned Gilles's old Formula Atlantic foe caused some excitement with his aggressive motoring.

There was excitement, too, in the Ferrari camp, though Forghieri's new creations were languishing back in mid-field suffering from the wrong choice of Michelin rubber compound. On the 55th lap the V12 behind Gilles's back suddenly erupted in a cloud of smoke as oil from its innards was pumped onto the hot exhaust system – and onto the circuit. The gusher began just beyond the pits and the number 12 T3 deposited a trail of oil over much of the circuit before it was brought in to retire. There Gilles was very shortly joined by his disgruntled teammate, minus the number 11 T3, and together they broke the bad news to Forghieri.

Reutemann had come sailing into Crowthorne, the fast right-hand corner at the end of Kyalami's lengthy straight, at full tilt and failed to notice Gilles's oil (which had itself supplemented an earlier spill by Rupert Keegan's Surtees). Brakes were applied but the T3 continued on at scarcely abated speed to rip through several layers of catch-fencing before coming to a halt. Just as Reutemann was climbing out the brand new T3 burst into flames from a ruptured fuel tank and it now lay a smouldering ruin in the background.

The South African debacle fanned the flames of discontent among Ferrari followers and when Gilles came down with a case of mumps there was a strong recommendation that a replacement for him be tried at the next race. That happened to be at Long Beach in California and it was a month away. Gilles had time to recover from his ailment so the suggestions that, for instance, Elio de Angelis fill in for him at the U.S. Grand Prix West were superfluous. Nevertheless, de Angelis, the son of a Roman millionaire and a hot property in Formula 2 and Formula 3, continued to be rumoured as waiting in the wings should Gilles falter . . . which he did – again – at Long Beach.

3

"The hiring of Villeneuve surprised the public and unleashed a public outcry which might have been justified at the time."

– Enzo Ferrari

The Formula 1 circus, having grown tired of the infamous denizens of "The Bog," a spectator area at Watkins Glen where insensibly drunk "race fans" burned cars and buses for amusement (the record stood at twelve vehicles, three buses included, in 1973), was more receptive to the laidback antics of the southern Californians. But for many Americans the Long Beach Grand Prix was just another curiosity in a city of faded grandeur not far from Disneyland. Long Beach also had on display the Queen Mary, anchored and serving as a hotel, and the Spruce Goose, an enormous wooden aircraft built by the eccentric Howard Hughes to ferry troops during World War Two. Among the other sideshows noted by the visiting race fraternity were a young couple coupling prominently on a balcony, the details of their embrace captured lovingly on a television screen in the press room in front of a cheering audience of international journalists. A person dressed as a lion, or perhaps it was a real lion, was spotted in the paddock, and the patriotic tenants of an apartment building, beneath which "them noisy little furrin racin' cars" roared by, erected an enormous banner reading "God Bless America."

Letting Formula 1 cars loose in the streets of downtown Long Beach was intended by the organizers (led by a transplanted Englishman, Chris Pook) to impart some of the glamour and prestige associated with the Monaco Grand Prix. Other than a shared proximity to water, the Pacific Ocean and the Mediterranean, the two locations were distinctly dissimilar, but the Long Beach event had a not-unpleasant ambience. And like Monaco, the circuit itself presented a multitude of challenges. The 3.251-km route wound through the streets with manhole covers, bumps, curbs, right-angle turns, and other motoring hazards lying in wait to pitch unwary drivers into the unforgiving concrete walls installed for the weekend to keep the race traffic out of the places of business.

Rapid progress in the confines of a street circuit calls for fierce aggression tempered with precision and neatness, the lot working in tandem with intense concentration. In qualifying, Reutemann combined these qualities (with the able assistance of Michelin qualifying tires that worked better than Goodyears here) to claim pole position. While a lot less precise and neat, Lole's little chum sat beside him on the starting grid, just a tenth of a second slower. Gilles was well pleased, especially after being a second and a half behind Reutemann on the first day of qualifying.

Behind the Ferraris, Lauda in his Brabham and Andretti in his Lotus lined up in front of their teammates Watson and Peterson, who shared the third row. The rest of the field was strung out two by two behind them, and with so few passing opportunities available in the Long Beach configuration, they all dialled themselves in for the all-important dash down Shoreline Drive at the start.

With a mighty roar that could probably be heard in Hollywood, the cars accelerated off the line as one. The crescendo shook the ground and rattled windows for miles around and scared the wits out of the many first-time race-goers included in the assembly of 75,000. The Ferraris shot down the kilometer-long Shoreline Drive neck and neck with the two Brabhams in close attendance. All snicked down through their gearboxes and slowed in unison for the sharp Queen Mary hairpin, but Watson, intent on sneaking through on the inside, was first to take his foot off the brake pedal. In fact, his reach exceeded his grasp, for the Brabham teetered on the brink of disaster in mid-corner, forcing Reutemann, Lauda, and Andretti to swing wide in avoidance. There was a certain amount of wheel-banging but all recovered to give chase to Villeneuve, who emerged from the gefuffle in the lead.

Thus, on the first lap of only his sixth Formula 1 race Gilles led from Watson, Lauda, Reutemann, Andretti, Alan Jones, and all. And for nearly half of the 80-lap race he kept all comers in his mirrors and Gilles thoroughly enjoyed the view. "It sure was a nice feeling, being out there in front. I was working hard, ten tenths for the first twenty laps or so. But when John retired, and Niki retired, I began to think about Carlos. I could see he was catching me and I knew he had Alan Jones on his tail. The last thing I wanted was to slow down Carlos and be in a position where Alan got past one or both of us, so when I came up to lap Clay Regazzoni I didn't hesitate.''

On lap 39 Gilles came upon Regazzoni's Shadow, which was busily engaged in a private duel with Jean-Pierre Jabouille's Renault. Gilles sat on the Shadow's tail for half a lap, then, in the middle of a slow chicane, he thought he saw an opportunity and went for it. ''Clay braked sooner than I thought he would because of his battle with the Renault in front of him. I had no chance to brake as well without hitting him up the back, so I tried to go between him and the curb.''

The right rear wheel of the Ferrari rode up the left rear of the Shadow and was launched into space. The flying T3 spun in the air, hurtled backwards into a row of tires fronting a concrete wall, then collapsed in a heap. Gilles quickly undid his belts and jumped behind the wall.

''If I hadn't tried to pass where I did we would have done another half lap before the next chance and anything could have happened by then. That isn't to say it wasn't my fault. You can't blame Clay for holding his line, because you normally don't try to pass at that point. But I also don't think I had an alternative. Besides, Clay was taking a different line than I was at that point, and braking earlier, so it looked to me as though he was making room.''

Regazzoni continued on, albeit with Michelin tread marks along the Shadow's length – and, he was disturbed to discover later, on his helmet. ''He would have been able to overtake me in other places, like on the straight,'' said the disgruntled Swiss, himself an ex-Ferrari driver. ''But on that curve there's only room for one car and I had the right of way. I found Villeneuve on my head!''

Reutemann went on to win splendidly for Ferrari, but though Gilles's intentions might have had his interests in mind, Lole, too, was critical of his impetuous teammate. ''Villeneuve has to calm his temperament. Experience will be a great help when he gets it.'' In Watson's opinion, ''It was a very foolhardy move on Villeneuve's part, wanting to overtake in that spot where you could only succeed with the total collaboration of the driver in front of you.''

Not for the last time would Gilles be criticized by his peers. He was in complete disagreement with future censuring by other drivers, but he was privately furious with himself at Long Beach and became remote and withdrawn, not very good company at dinner that night with Joann and a visiting John Lane. By the next morning he had mellowed enough to look at the positive side. "I was packing my things and got quite a surprise when I picked up my helmet. There wasn't any oil on it or dirt or rubber or anything. That's what happens when you lead, I guess." And he left for the next race, in Monaco, in an optimistic frame of mind. "I know what it's like to lead the first half of a race. Now I want the other."

4

"Villeneuve's personality was such that he captured the crowd right away and became known as Gilles."
– Enzo Ferrari

On his return to Europe, when Gilles touched down at Nice airport on the Cote d'Azur, there were more journalistic vultures circling over his head. "Crazy Overtaker" was a milder term among several that alluded to his propensity for leaving the ground. Other descriptive flights of fancy included "Air Canada" and "The Pilot," and there were jokes that he would soon become a friend of Lauda's (an avid aviator and the proprietor of his own airline, Lauda Air, now a successful commercial enterprise) because they were both keen on flying. Even some of the Ferrari mechanics nicknamed Gilles "Flyer" because "he spends more time flying than he spends on the track."

But while Antonio Tomaini and his work force grumbled about having to labour longer repairing his cars, they appreciated the interest Gilles took in what they did. This was no prima donna who treated his mechanics as servants and showed up at the last minute to drive. Gilles spent hours with his crew, as if he were just one of the boys, and actually enjoyed getting his hands dirty. Then, when the last nut was tightened, he would hop in the car and proceed to use it for its intended purpose to a degree the Ferrari men had rarely seen. Such was the case during qualifying at Monaco where the Ferrari pit watched, with awe and apprehension in equal measures, as Gilles went to work.

Their T3 came hurtling around the corner like some unguided missile, defying gravity and several other laws of physics. At nearly a right angle to the road and a few centimeters from the steel barriers, with the fat rear Michelins sending up puffs of blue smoke and Forghieri's 312B motor screaming just a few revs this side of disintegration, Gilles seemed completely out of control. Barely protruding above the tiny plexiglass windscreen of the number 12 red-and-white winged projectile, Gilles's helmet was cocked in a defiant attitude, his white-gloved hands whirling in a flurry of activity, making vigorous corrections on the saucer-sized steering wheel as he struggled to avoid the surely inevitable accident.

Somehow, at the last possible instant, milliseconds before the T3 caromed into the rails or spun around madly to bite its tail, Gilles gathered it all together and caught the spectacular powerslide. Winding off the opposite lock to straighten out the front wheels in the approximate direction of the Ste. Dévote hairpin, he smashed the gearlever into third, fourth, fifth, as quickly as the words can be said, and catapulted spectacularly sideways down the pit straight in a roar of noise that shook the very foundations of the principality of Monaco.

And the Ferrari pit became animated again, its collective breath was released in a sigh of relief, heads were shaken in disbelief, and words of wonderment issued forth. Gilles had managed yet another lap without crashing, but how long could he possibly keep it up?

Had they been watching his amazing progress up at the exit of Casino Square, Forghieri, Tomaini, and company would have despaired of ever again seeing their precious car in one piece. Gilles's arrival was heralded by the high-pitched howl of twelve cylinders being stretched to their limits and punctuated by squeals of protest from four tortured radial tires, the crescendo of noise reverberating off the walls of the Casino and the Hotel de Paris. His right foot flat to the floor, his helmet inclined to the right in the direction of the turn, his hands sawing away at the wheel,

Gilles would careen over the brow of the hill, as usual, on full opposite lock. The front of his car pointed into the doorway of the headquarters of the Monégasque constabulary on the right while the rear threatened to make a forcible entry into the café on the left.

At the exit of the corner a few brave photographers and journalists cowered behind the rails in front of the news kiosk on the left curb to witness the phenomenon, but their pictures tended to be blurred and their notes indecipherable because they invariably ducked down at the last minute, unable to believe Gilles was not about to plunge into their midst. And, every few laps, even the hardnosed marshals abandoned their positions and ran for cover when the Ferrari's left rear wheel kissed the barriers and sent up a shower of sparks before roaring off down the hill at unabated speed to attack the next corner at Mirabeau.

■ ■ ■

Monaco seems an impossible place to hold a race. Indeed, it is regarded by many as the most dangerous circuit, winding up, down, and around the narrow confines of streets that are difficult enough to negotiate in everyday motoring, let alone high-powered Formula 1 cars. But Gilles thoroughly enjoyed it, describing it as "like a good mountain circuit with a town around it. It's very different from the street circuits I'm used to, which are just straights separated by 90-degree corners. Here every corner is different and delicate. I like streets and, all in all, I like it here better than the circuits in Canada and Long Beach. And this place is unlike any other . . . a Formula One car is very big for this sort of track.''

Throughout the two days of practice and qualifying (Thursday and Saturday, Friday being set aside for the citizens of the principality to go about their normal business) the spectacular Villeneuve show continued in preparation for the Monaco Grand Prix. And Gilles was performing in front of an increasingly appreciative audience now able to get a closeup view of his style around a track where it was often possible to look right down into the cockpit to see the stuff racing heroes are made of. In his previous races, on television, many had viewed his troubles with their hearts in their mouths and, no doubt, his accident-about-to-happen reputation attracted the ghoulish among them. In Monaco he did execute a few wild spins and there were innumerable scary moments, but his phenomenal car control was winning over scores of new fans. They began to recognize his flair, his courage, his passion, and they responded dramatically.

Whenever there was a lull in the cacophony of noise from the cars out on the circuit a new sound was heard, a human sound. It took the form of a rising chant from thousands of voices echoing around the yacht-filled harbour. It came from onlookers hanging over the wrought-iron balconies of the hotels and apartments above the pit straight and from the packed grandstands around the crowded harbour, from the weekend sailors clinging to the masts of the boats, from the throngs sitting among the rocks and trees on the hillside beneath Princess Grace's residence, even from the walls of the palace itself: "Gilles! – Gilles! – Gilles!"

Souls were being stirred, passions inflamed, adulation developing, and the chanting and cheering grew louder, much of it coming from the thousands of Ferrari fanatics who had made the pilgrimage across the nearby border at Ventimiglia.

Following the end of final qualifying on Saturday afternoon, Gilles left the Ferrari pits to attend the team debriefing session in the paddock along the harbour behind the pits. He walked down the circuit past the Rascasse corner and the fans crowded in for a closer look. It was their first opportunity to see him in the flesh and many wanted to press it. They reached out to touch him and tugged at his driver's suit and he began to walk more briskly.

"Ciao, Gilles! Bonjour, Gilles! Guten Tag, Gilles!" the greetings rang out for him in the languages of Europe. People peered intently into his baby face and were surprised to see how small and slight this man who drove like a superman was. He looked young and vulnerable and seemed somewhat shy, not aloof at all, like other racing heroes. Here was someone they could identify with, someone whose innocent appearance made his driving feats all the more extraordinary. Programs were pressed to him, pens proffered, and he began to sign autographs, carefully at first, then in a scrawl as he was engulfed in a sea of humanity. He scratched his name until his hand got sore and finally Gilles made a break for it, walking fast, then sprinting to escape the clutches of the pursuing throng.

He made it into the palisade formed by the huge red transporters from Maranello and there ducked down behind a stack of Michelins to ponder his first real glimpse of superstardom. "Most of them didn't even let me finish writing my name," he marvelled as he caught his breath. "They just wanted to touch me. But it doesn't bother me because there's nothing better than to know people like you and like the sport. Here people really love the sport, I guess, especially Ferrari."

Included among the Villeneuve fans that weekend were the people closest to him. Besides Joann and the kids, Seville and Georgette were over from Berthier and Ray Wardell and John Lane had also arrived. It was the first of many regular trips Gilles's parents made to Europe and he always welcomed them at his home. And Gilles played the perfect host to his guests back at the villa in Plascassier, but in truth he preferred not to have a lot of people around him on race day. Especially for his parents, who were unfamiliar with the chaotic atmosphere at F1 races, Gilles felt responsible and worried that it might interfere with his concentration.

In the final minutes before the thirty-sixth running of the fabled Grand Prix de Monaco, Gilles was concentrating deeply. Strapped tightly in the cockpit of his T3, he was lined up beside Ronnie Peterson, having qualified eighth fastest, a fraction slower than the Swede. Ahead of him, beyond Depailler, Hunt, Lauda, Andretti, and Watson, Gilles could see the rear wing of Carlos's car parked on the pole. But a little while ago, in the morning warm-up with the cars fuelled up and in full race trim, Gilles was fastest of all.

Now in the middle of a mass of vibrating machinery on the starting grid beneath the umbrella pines along the harbour and just across from the royal box where Prince Rainier and his movie star princess looked on, Gilles saw the 30-second board held up at the front. He blipped the throttle nervously and made a quick final mental run over the 3.312-km route that lay in front of him. Sharp right at Virage Ste. Dévote (watch out for the inevitable first-lap accidents), up the long hill with the kink in the middle opposite Rosie's Bar, quick left into Casino Square, quick right past the news kiosk (where there always seemed to be people running away), down to the sharp right at Virage Mirabeau, corkscrew down and around Loews Hotel, hard right out onto Avenue Princesse Grace and then into the darkness of the long, long right-hander of the tunnel under Loews, flat out into daylight and swerve through the chicane, quick right and left swerves around the Olympic swimming pool, slow hard right around Virage de la Rascasse (named after that ugly scorpion fish they use to make bouillabaisse, that awful soupe de poisson), hard right again around the last corner and onto the pit straight where Forghieri and Tomaini waited . . .

Sixty-two laps later, with 13 laps still remaining in the race (which Depailler would win ahead of Lauda and Scheckter), Gilles walked toward the Ferrari pit. He gave scarcely a backward glance at his car, piled in a heap at the exit of the tunnel, minus one wheel and with the other three askew and the bodywork comprehensively modified.

It had been a big accident, starting in the middle of the tunnel where his car smote the rail and lost a wheel while he was travelling at something like 300 kph. The uncontrollable tripod rebounded from rail to rail like a berserk ballbearing in a pinball machine, sending up sheets of flame from metal-to-metal contact. The remains of the car finally smoked and scraped to a halt all too near the most infamous spot on the Monaco circuit, where Lorenzo Bandini had been horribly burned to death, trapped in his blazing Ferrari in 1967.

"As I went into the tunnel I could tell something was wrong. I turned the wheel to the right and the car went towards the apex all right, but after the apex it just went straight on into the barrier." That's what Gilles reported to Forghieri and subsequent investigation showed that the left front tire might have deflated to pitch him out of control. But a close look at the bodywork also revealed that – symbolically – the name "Villeneuve," inscribed in white on a black background, had been partly scraped off in the accident. And Tomaini took Gilles aside for a heart-to-heart chat.

Forghieri was in a distinctly unhappy post-race frame of mind with no good to report back to Maranello. Reutemann had only finished eighth after a poor start and then a pit stop to replace a wheel damaged against another car. Gilles had been running fifth at the time of his crash and was surely destined to score points for Ferrari. Deflating tire aside (and it wasn't yet clear that it hadn't happened during the crash, not before), the facts were that in six of his first seven races for Ferrari Gilles's car had arrived back in the pits on the end of a wrecker. Antonio Tomaini told Gilles that he should take it easy because things were not going at all well for him. He should at least try to finish a race, like the next one in two weeks in Belgium.

When Elio de Angelis won the prestigious Formula 3 race at Monaco the down-with-Villeneuve movement in Italy made a great hue and cry that the time for a change at Ferrari was now. And despite the enormous fan support he'd received at Monaco, Gilles's position looked even more precarious.

In Canada, Gaston Parent became so worried about the negative press reports that he flew to Italy to confer with Enzo Ferrari. "I went in to see the Old Man and asked him about the rumours he might drop Gilles. I asked him if it was true. He said, 'Look, Villeneuve is a champion and a guy cannot be a champion if he doesn't risk and Villeneuve is risking because he has what it takes. So we're not going to drop him from the team.' "

5

"At first, I was a little lost. I guess because I'm a little reserved had a lot to do with it. But now I feel more at home."

– Gilles Villeneuve

Back at Plascassier, Gilles talked things over with Ray Wardell and John Lane, who stayed on for a visit after Monaco. Gilles's position was that the accidents had happened because they happened, he hadn't gone looking for them. Immediately following the Monaco crash, his friends, as they expected, had noticed no apparent sign of emotion, and the view from the cockpit was equally sanguine.

"I wasn't worried about myself. I just told myself, 'Good grief, I'm going to have a big accident!' In that split second all I could think of was that I wasn't going to finish and would lose two points in the championship. Nothing else. I never really think that I'm going to get hurt, it just seems impossible. If you believe it can happen to you, how can you possibly do this job properly? If you're thinking about a shunt, you're not going as quick as you can. And if you're not doing that, you're not a racing driver."

From their Formula Atlantic experiences, Wardell and Lane knew full well the Villeneuve approach to racing, but they strongly advised that he try following Tomaini's recommendation, particularly since Forghieri's patience was obviously wearing thin. Following one of Gilles's spins in qualifying he had shouted, "You've got to stop this! It is not possible that you still don't know the circuit and you still don't know your car!"

Sitting on the verandah of the villa at Plascassier, surrounded by clusters of purple lavender framing the magnificent view to the sea, the three friends discussed the pros and cons of Gilles's philosophy. While his approach to qualifying made Forghieri see red, Gilles saw it in plain black and white. "To attack means two things: on one hand you don't go over the limits that you know well; on the other hand you try to go as fast as possible and that's when you have to go over that limit and at the worst you might spin or crash – but you might also have the best time."

Gilles talked about the adjustments he'd had to make in Formula 1. "It's exactly what I thought it would be, very tough and very serious. But I was affected by all the differences, the longer races, more testing sessions, it was all very intense at first. Everything is much more serious and racing is not a game any more. I still love it, but it's a lot different now."

On the track Gilles was finding he had to fight for every inch of ground and some of his peers were less than accommodating: "They don't gracefully let you pass them." But he was learning from them. "In qualifying I watch drivers who've known the circuits for a long time." And there were other lessons. In South Africa he held up Scheckter during a qualifying lap. "After he passed me he tapped his rearview mirror to show me my mistake." Then, Gilles noted, when he was on a quick lap Scheckter moved over and let him by. And, gradually it seemed, he was being accepted by the Formula 1 fraternity.

Within the Ferrari team Gilles felt he was doing less chassis tuning than he did with Wardell in Atlantic. This was because the team was concentrating on tire work with Michelin, and to Gilles it seemed he was conferring more with Michelin's Pierre Dupasquier than with Forghieri. He spoke with them and Tomaini in French, but there was still a communications gap with his mechanics, whom he had to confer with mainly in sign language. While he was beginning to feel more a part of the team, it had been hard: "At first, I was a little lost," he admitted. "I guess because I'm a little reserved had a lot to do with it. But now I feel more at home."

Gilles had great respect for Ray Wardell and they had even discussed his going to Ferrari to work with Gilles. Now Wardell told him to stop worrying about being fastest on every single lap. He was trying to do too much too soon, in a car he didn't know nearly as well as his Atlantic March, on circuits he'd never seen before. After all, he was competing against the best drivers in the world and it was unrealistic to expect to be able to beat them until he had much more experience. And in the long run, as the old racing cliché goes, to finish first, you must first finish.

■ ■ ■

Gilles went to Belgium suffering from what he thought was the 'flu but which later proved to be an allergy to the lavender growing around the villa at Plascassier. He felt weak and feverish and his first view of Zolder, the circuit that was to claim his life four years later, was no antidote to his condition.

Until 1970 the Belgian Grand Prix had been held on the spectacular and daunting Spa-Francorchamps track where much Formula 1 history had been made (and Spa is again in use, though in modified form). Gilles would have loved Spa, but it had been declared too fast (with lap speeds of nearly 150 mph) and too dangerous (several drivers had been killed), and the dramatic venue in the Ardennes Forest was replaced first by Nivelles, near Brussels, then by Zolder, near Liège.

Zolder is situated near a gloomy industrial area and its twisting 4.262-km length resembles a mangled paper clip in configuration. Built on sandy soil and surrounded by a pine forest, the circuit suffers from a negative ambience, caused in large part by overzealous policemen who exercise their authority vigorously, either mounted on horses and wielding truncheons or strutting around on one end of a leash with fierce guard dogs on the other. In the prison camp atmosphere of the paddock circled by high fences, the Grand Prix circus made preparations to race.

Mario Andretti put Colin Chapman's new ground-effects Lotus 79 on pole with a lap nearly a second quicker than Reutemann's Ferrari T3. Lauda's Brabham-Alfa was next and would line up on the grid beside Gilles. In the Ferrari pit Joann, who was now helping with the timing, and the others thought they had clocked Gilles on a quicker lap than Lauda but were happy to settle for fourth fastest, as was Gilles. "Third, fourth . . . it's still the second row, right? The car is fabulous, I must say," and it was like a shot in the arm for his 'flu, which he felt would be gone by race day.

At the start, Andretti shot off into the distance alone, his lack of immediate pursuers due to mass mayhem instigated when Reutemann missed his shift from first to second. There were several collisions, the main casualties being Lauda, Hunt, and Fittipaldi, whose cars were rendered hors de combat. But Gilles jinked past the faltering Lole and sped away in pursuit of Mario.

Gilles hauled himself up to within shouting distance of Andretti and held his own there wonderfully well, showing his heels to people like Peterson, Patrese, and the recovered Reutemann. Behind him others were stopping to change worn tires and, on lap 39, his left front tire exploded as he braked for the left-hand Sterrewachbrocht curve. The misfortune, accompanied by a puff of smoke and a loud bang, occurred within sight of the pits, thus serving to silence any disbelievers among the Ferrari crew who had doubts about his Monaco tire failure. This time Gilles was able to hold the car, but his brilliant second place quickly disappeared during his crippled lap back to the pits.

Tomaini and the crew slapped on a new wheel and tire and Gilles tore back into the fray, leaving a substantial portion of his rear Michelins behind in the form of two black streaks down pit lane. His lost time had dropped him to sixth place and he forged ahead, hampered somewhat by a front wing bent by the earlier flailing tire. He finished fourth, just behind Reutemann, who survived a coming together with Laffite. Peterson was second behind his teammate, Andretti, who dedicated his victory to Gunnar Nilsson. The popular Swedish driver had won this race the previous year when he was Andretti's teammate but now was suffering from the cancer to which he would succumb later that year.

"Finally!" Gilles exalted over his first finish in the points. "I knew it was going to happen one day. Finally it did, and more than that, I was running second, which was good." Indeed it was, and he also set the fourth fastest lap in the race. If he continued to keep his car in one piece his first victory would surely not be long in coming.

■ ■ ■

The Belgian success helped silence his critics in Italy, where attention was also diverted by wide fascination over the arrival in Europe of the Villeneuve motorhome. Gilles had the 36-foot-long structure, a Fifth Wheel Globestar, custom-made in Quebec to his specifications. It was a fully equipped three-bedroom model, with kitchenette, bathroom, and wall-to-wall carpeting, and was shipped over by container along with the old Ford pickup he'd used for haulage in Atlantic racing. The somewhat secondhand truck, festooned with decals of the Montreal Canadiens hockey team (Gilles was a great fan of the team and became a friend of its scoring leader, Guy Lafleur), towed the motorhome in fifth-wheel fashion. The home-away-from-home was driven to the races by one of Gilles's boyhood friends and his wife from Berthier (who were also babysitters for Jacques and Melanie during the races) and the lengthy device with Quebec licence plates turned heads on the roads in Europe.

It also set tongues wagging in Formula 1 circles, where such a sight had never been seen. Some of the powers-that-were at the time thought the boxy, cumbersome-looking contraption lowered the tone of the paddock. Most of the teams had sleek motorhome-style vehicles, which served as headquarters and a place of refuge for the drivers during the day, but everybody stayed at the best hotels and the paddock was deserted at night. Here was a driver who actually lived, with his family, in a motorhome (moreover, the Villeneuves often sat down and ate with the Ferrari mechanics) and this phenomenon was given extensive coverage in the press.

"Shoes off!" was the greeting to visiting journalists who trooped into the motorhome. Besides a strict no-smoking code, the rule was that visitors must leave their footwear at the door. "We live in here," said Gilles. "I don't want people dragging mud everywhere over the carpet. And anyway," he joked, "people feel uncomfortable standing there with no shoes on—so they don't stay long!"

"No, being enclosed in the pit area for three days does not bother me," said Gilles in explaining his rationale for bringing his creature comforts with him in a caravan. "There is no noise here after ten. I can sleep well in my own bed, not like in hotels where you don't always get a good bed. I can sleep later in the morning and I go to bed when I want, without having to attend the hotel dinners and staying out late. Here I can eat when I want to, we can have barbecues outside, and I don't have to depend on restaurant food. I can't stand certain foods and what a driver eats affects his physical and mental attitude. Not only that, this way I can see my kids grow up. In fact, this is the only way to have a normal life in a moving career."

■ ■ ■

His career moved hardly at all in the next race in Spain, while his teammate's very nearly ended in disaster. Andretti and Peterson led for Lotus and Gilles's tire and handling troubles and a broken exhaust caused him to be classified tenth. But Reutemann was very fortunate to survive a huge accident caused by a broken driveshaft that threw his Ferrari through several rows of catch-fencing and over a guard rail, its somersaulting stopped only by a high debris fence surrounding the paddock of the Jarama circuit. Lole was miraculously unhurt, save for chest pains where his seatbelts had squeezed him during the violent deceleration.

Both Ferraris were two seconds off the qualifying pace at Anderstorp in Sweden. Their handling problems continued in the race, where Gilles finished ninth, just ahead of Lole. Lauda won in a new Brabham, which was henceforth banned from competition. It featured a huge fan at the rear that sucked the car down onto the road but also acted like a vacuum cleaner and blew the dust and debris in the face of following cars.

The Ferraris were in even more trouble at the French Grand Prix on the Circuit Paul Ricard, where they fishtailed around madly with dire tire troubles. Gilles was 12th after two stops for tires and a spin, while Reutemann's four pit stops dragged him down to 18th at the finish.

Michelin brought a new tire compound to the British Grand Prix and Reutemann used it to sensational advantage, winning the Brands Hatch event in what he called ''the best drive of my life.'' Gilles stuck with the usual tires on the front and they only lasted 10 laps before he had to pit. His race lasted just nine laps more before he was sidelined by a broken driveshaft.

Gilles very nearly missed the start of the Grosser Preis von Deutschland at Hockenheim, arriving in the Ferrari pit with just twelve minutes to go. He thought the appointed hour was 2:30 instead of half an hour earlier. He might just as well have stayed in the motorhome because the Michelins were again contrary and both Ferraris were also plagued with fuel vaporization, caused by hot weather. Reutemann did not finish and Gilles sputtered around to eighth place. He climbed out of his car at the end of the race and went quickly to the motorhome to do some deep thinking. Andretti had won the race, his fifth of the year, but Gilles was more concerned with the second-place finisher, Jody Scheckter.

Scheckter had called an impromptu press conference at Hockenheim to announce that he would be leaving Walter Wolf Racing at the end of the season to drive for the Scuderia Ferrari in 1979. ''I have accepted Ferrari's offer because I've always thought that this was the team which would give me the best chance of winning the world championship. Enzo Ferrari is a fantastic character, his collaborators are of the highest calibre, the entire car is homemade. These are the guarantees.''

Well then, Scheckter was asked, who will be leaving Ferrari? ''They are very high on Villeneuve at the moment. But they're very high on Reutemann, too. After all,'' said the South African, ''he's won three Grands Prix this year.'' And Gilles, with only a fourth place to his credit, had heard not a word from Ferrari about the Scheckter deal. Marco Piccinini, who had taken over from Nosetto as Enzo Ferrari's representative at the races, was unable to shed any light on the matter.

After the German race Gilles read of rumours that Walter Wolf and Enzo Ferrari had swapped drivers and he would be going to Wolf, but he was unable to get any firm answers from Ferrari. The uncertainties were bothering but Gilles relegated them to the back of his mind to concentrate on the Austrian Grand Prix. At the Osterreichring in the Styrian Mountains, as he had at Gimli in faraway Manitoba, he took advantage of the elements to overcome mechanical deficiencies.

The race was held in two parts, the first ending after seven laps when a cloudburst sent half the contestants spinning into the fields surrounding the circuit. The race was restarted with everyone on rain tires and Gilles, revelling in the conditions, quickly moved up from his 11th place on the grid. His progress was not without incident, including a spin and an off-course excursion and a pit stop for slicks when the track began to dry. But Gilles's first wet race in a Formula 1 car ended with a visit to the podium, where he sprayed champagne with Depailler and the winner and Reinmeister, Ronnie Peterson. Gilles's third place was Ferrari's only result after Reutemann, who actually led the race for a few laps, was disqualified for receiving a push start after a spin.

After the awards ceremony, where he was greeted by enthusiastic cheers from the large Italian contingent in the crowd, Gilles was invited to give his post-race comments. "The circuit is difficult to learn and very dangerous. The rain didn't worry me. On the contrary, I think that I like it better than when it's dry." And did he think this result might help persuade Ferrari to keep him? "It's not for me to decide. Mr. Ferrari was watching it all on television and he will know what to do."

Encouraged by his Austrian success Gilles attacked the Zandvoort course in Holland with tremendous aggression. He recovered from a huge spin in qualifying to score another point for Ferrari with a solid sixth place, despite poor handling. Andretti won the Dutch Grand Prix, with Peterson close on his heels, and his Lotus teammate was now the only one capable of beating Andretti for the 1978 world championship. Gilles, still uncertain of his future with Ferrari, regarded the situation at Lotus with a certain amount of envy. The Lotus 79s were the class of the field and Gilles was a long-time admirer of Colin Chapman's team.

"Lotus was the team I always heard and read about. When I first started racing, Fittipaldi had just won the championship in a Lotus. I had read about Jimmy Clark in several books and they left a great impression on me. And also, Ronnie was in a Lotus, and I always thought Ronnie was a fantastic driver – on opposite lock and everything. So from very early on, I liked Lotus and always thought it would be fantastic to drive for Colin Chapman."

But after the race in Holland, where Reutemann had finished behind Gilles in seventh, Chapman's great Formula 1 rival made the decison that assured Gilles's future. On September 6, Gilles was summoned into the Commendatore's office where he signed a new contract for 1979. Gilles learned that Ferrari had asked everyone on the team for an opinion and even the mechanics were on his side. Gilles was tremendously relieved: "I cannot help but be pleased after a year of alternating opinions. I think I'm in a position to make the decision to keep me a positive one. I hope to be able to repay Mr. Ferrari's great trust in me starting at Monza."

6

"I don't think of dying, but I accept the fact that it's part of the job."
                                                    – Gilles Villeneuve

Il Gran Premio d'Italia at the Autodromo di Nazionale di Monza, near Milano, should have been one of the best of days for Gilles, but the date of September 10, 1978, brought nothing but grief for everyone in F1 racing.

Gilles qualified a brilliant second to Andretti, delighting the enormous congregation of *tifosi* with a made-in-Italy performance of flat-out motoring in his T3 all around the historic 5.580 kilometers of Monza's challenges. "Viva Ferrari! Viva Villeneuve! Forza Gilles!" went the chorus of approval, and the fans cheered themselves hoarse. Scarcely a murmur was heard for Reutemann, who was 11th on the grid, and the tide of public opinion, at least, had definitely turned in Villeneuve's favour.

The *tifosi*, 120,000 of them on race day, went mad with delight when Gilles rocketed away in a lead that was only to last for a few seconds before the red flag was shown. Behind him the circuit erupted in a terrifying display of flames and black smoke. In a chaos of ten crashing cars Peterson's Lotus was enveloped in a fireball, the driver trapped inside. James Hunt ran back from his wrecked McLaren and, with help from Clay Regazzoni, dove into the flames and dragged Peterson out to safety while a marshal sprayed them with an extinguisher. Peterson was conscious but in great pain from two badly shattered legs. He was rushed to hospital by ambulance, along with Vittorio Brambilla, who was unconscious from a blow to the head from a flying wheel.

There was a lengthy delay while the wreckage was removed from the circuit and spare cars readied for those who needed them. Gilles shut himself in the motorhome for a while, then came back to sit in his Ferrari for nearly an hour, long before any of his rivals showed up. The news that Ronnie Peterson had only suffered broken legs was encouraging; it seemed Brambilla was worse off with head injuries (though he would recover fully); and Gilles was chafing at the bit to take up where he had left off in the race.

Unfortunately, he was too eager, and as the lights turned green for the second time he was already gone. Andretti went with him and the two had a hammer-and-tongs duel all around the first lap to cross the start/finish line side by side. Next time around Gilles was in the lead and the ecstatic *tifosi* nearly drowned out the sound of the cars. The roaring crowd was then silenced when it was announced on the PA system that Villeneuve and Andretti were penalized one minute for jumping the start. But the two pressed on and Andretti finally overtook Gilles, whose tires were unable to keep up the struggle, with a few laps remaining. At the finish the subtraction of the one-minute penalty meant Lauda was the winner, with Andretti classified sixth and Gilles seventh. But Andretti's point clinched the world championship and Reutemann salvaged some of the Ferrari glory with third place.

But there was no joy for anyone the next morning when the shocking news came that, at 6:30 a.m., Ronnie Peterson had died. During the long operation to set the broken bones in his legs, bone marrow embolisms entered his bloodstream and caused an aneurism in his brain. Mario Andretti and Colin Chapman, at first unable to believe the disaster, were distraught. Andretti had won his World Driving Championship and Chapman's team the Constructors' Championship (over Ferrari), but there was absolutely no satisfaction in their supremacy. (For Chapman, it was all too terribly reminiscent of the 1970 Italian Grand Prix at Monza when his Austrian driver, Jochen Rindt, was killed, then became World Champion posthumously.) Ronnie Peterson's wife Barbro, recovering from a recent miscarriage, had not come to Monza but stayed in their flat in Monaco. A helicopter, delayed by fog, brought her to Milan too late to be with her husband and the grief-stricken woman flew directly home to Sweden.

Ronnie Peterson was buried in his home town of Obrebro, north of Stockholm, where his funeral was attended by many Formula 1 personalities and hundreds of fans. The quiet, gentle man was extremely popular and his passing was universally mourned in the racing world. In his eight years in F1 he had ten victories and was generally regarded as one of the fastest drivers of his time, not a methodical, calculating type like Lauda, but a flat-out racer whose pace was dictated by his right foot. His colourfully aggressive style of driving was thrilling to watch and had inspired many, including Gilles Villeneuve.

■ ■ ■

Gilles had never been in a race where a driver had been killed and was deeply affected. "Ronnie's death really surprised me and hit me hard. I always admired him as the quickest driver around. From '73 to '75 he was incredible in the Lotus. And he was bloody quick in '78, too. He had so many accidents in '74 and '75. Wheels falling off and him falling off the track. Never any injuries. Then he had a stupid accident in the middle of the pack at Monza and killed himself. And also, because it was only leg injuries, 'How come he's dead like that?' I thought. 'Was it a doctor's mistake? What happened? What's the reason?' All that really hurt me."

But Gilles kept his own fears at bay in the way that all racing drivers do. "I know there's danger – but it's not in the front of my mind. It's in the back. I didn't want to walk too close to Ronnie's accident. I didn't know at the time if he was dead or alive, but there was a bunch of people around and everything was taken care of. I always try to avoid looking too closely at this kind of thing in case it will hurt me psychologically and I'll start thinking about it after that. It's my job not to think of that so I try to avoid everything. Even if I had known he was dead I don't think it would have changed a thing in my driving. It may sound cruel and heartless to people when they hear me say that. But it's part of the job and I accept the fact that one of these days I will hurt myself very, very much. I don't think of dying, but I accept the fact that it's part of the job.''

There was acrimony in the aftermath of the Peterson fatality and much time was devoted to finding the cause of the Monza crash. The cars of James Hunt, Riccardo Patrese, and Carlos Reutemann had been closely involved and the Formula 1 Safety Committee, comprised of Hunt, Andretti, Scheckter, Lauda, and Fittipaldi, decided that Patrese was responsible for triggering the accident. (Subsequent investigation of photographs showed that Patrese was innocent of the charges.) The twenty-four-year-old Italian had developed a reputation for reckless driving and even before Monza the Committee decided he needed to be disciplined. Now they demanded that the organizers of the next race, the U.S. Grand Prix East, refuse his entry, and he was forced to sit out the event at Watkins Glen.

Reutemann won convincingly at The Glen to gain a measure of revenge against the Ferrari decision not to retain his services. His fortunes had also rebounded nicely with a deal to drive for Lotus in 1979. The Ferraris ran well throughout the weekend, Reutemann qualifying second to Andretti and Gilles fourth. Gilles held second to Lole until the 22nd lap, when his engine broke, leaving him with one more race in 1978, the Labatt Grand Prix du Canada in Montreal.

7

"This is the happiest day of my life!"

– Gilles Villeneuve

"It's a little paradise in the middle of a great river," said three-time World Champion Jackie Stewart when he first saw the new Circuit Ile Notre-Dame. The Wee Scot, at that time the winningest driver of all with twenty-seven F1 victories, was there as a race commentator and, like all the Grand Prix circus, he was highly impressed. "It's one of the most beautiful settings in the world for a motor race, with the metropolis of Montreal right in the background."

When Mosport was declared unsuitable as a Formula 1 venue the people of Quebec, earlier denied their Mont Tremblant race for similar reasons of safety, leapt at the chance to build a new track. In just three months, at a cost of $2 million, the site was developed and readied for the eleventh running of the Canadian Grand Prix. With the mighty St. Lawrence River on one side and the Seaway on the other, the circuit was constructed by following the contours of the road that wound around the island opposite the Montreal waterfront.

The park-like setting included trees, grassy knolls and gardens, a lake and ornamental ponds, and canals running between the futuristic pavilions built for Expo '67, the world's fair held in Canada's centennial year. There were spacious press facilities located in the buildings at the end of the rowing course where the 1976 Olympic Games were held. Just a short Metro ride away from the cosmopolitan delights of North America's most culturally unique city, and much appreciated by the visiting international Formula 1 fraternity, the location was an ideal compromise between the urban and rural venues in other parts of the world.

Twenty-eight drivers from fifteen nations arrived to put the new 4.41-km circuit to the test. But from the moment the cars began circulating the spectators only had eyes for the local hero in the number 12 red Ferrari. They packed the perimeter of the seventeen-corner course, 36,181 of them on Friday and Saturday, to watch their boy from Berthierville in action. His reputation had preceded him and now his countrymen saw it firsthand.

Gilles came howling down the pit straight, foot-to-the-floor in fifth with the 500 prancing horses in the flat-12 behind his back singing a siren song of 11,300 revolutions per minute. He gave a quick glance at the pit board held out by the Ferrari crew but had to file it away for future reflection at an easier place on the circuit, because the first turn was looming up between the guard rails like a speeded-up movie.

The flattened S-section began with a gradual right-hander, then quickly tightened into a kink in the opposite direction just beyond the overhead pedestrian bridge. For the spectators, this was one of the most thrilling places to watch their heroes at work, because the middle of the S featured a bump in the pavement that picked the car up and hurled it sideways. More timid types lifted off briefly, but the bravest (and quickest) did not. Gilles did not disappoint.

Moving at something like 265 kph, Gilles came flying around the right-hander on full opposite lock. Instead of detecting the telltale engine note of a cautionary right foot being exercised, the fans noted that Gilles never wavered. Rather, the engine revs soared as his T3 achieved momentary liftoff on the bump, lurching sideways at least two meters, with the fat rear Michelins pawing aimlessly in the air before regaining traction with puffs of blue smoke erupting from the tires.

From their vantage points on the surrounding hillocks the fans gasped in amazement at the terrifying spectacle. As they looked down into the beehive of activity in the Villeneuve cockpit they saw the steering wheel being yanked vigorously right and left as Gilles grabbed handfuls of lock, in opposition to the directions his car threatened to go. The sound and fury of it all shook the ground and was over in little more than the blink of an eye. Until the next lap.

Gilles blasted down the causeway, a blur of red between the rowing basin on his left and the ornamental lake on his right. He flashed through a speed trap here at nearly 270 kph, then slammed down through the gears into third and braked sharply for the sweeping right-hand turn, followed by a quick left. This brief detour in the otherwise straight causeway made the T3 skitter wildly from curb to curb and Gilles felt the heavy pressure of tremendous g-forces in his neck. Safely through the kink he floored it again up through fourth and fifth, only to have to hit the brakes and double-clutch back down through the gearbox a few seconds later. Through the left-hander in third, then up into fourth for the gradual loop in the opposite direction.

More hectic steering wheel, pedal, and gearlever activity saw
the Ferrari swing sideways around an abrupt left to encounter a
second-gear hairpin to the right, the slowest part of the circuit.
But Gilles was busier than ever, his feet beating a constant tattoo
on the brake, clutch, and accelerator pedals, his right hand flick-
ing up and down from the tiny gearlever as he twirled the steering
wheel right, left, and centre. All the while he was being pitched
violently from side to side, his body straining at the six-point
safety harness as he carved out the apex at each corner in search
of the fastest line.

The hairpin corkscrewed the Ferrari uphill and to the right,
powering it along a parallel course with the turbulent St. Lawrence and slingshotting it along beneath the leafy canopy of ov-
erhanging trees. Gilles snatched third, then fourth, and shot forward
at what seemed suicidal speed in view of what lay ahead. The
short straight terminated dramatically in a sharp curve where the
driver must stamp violently on the brakes, simultaneously snicking down through the gears into second, and effect a hard right
turn. The alternative was to encounter the unforgiving steel of
the guard rail or, should it be forgiving, to wind up flying over
a cliff and into the river.

Gilles managed to hold the middle ground, though hovering
marshals feared he would be unsuccessful and clutched their fire
extinguishers and crowbars expectantly – every lap he went by.
They watched in amazement as the Ferrari disappeared over the
brow of the hill in a tremendous full-blooded powerslide that
surely was not conducive to keeping it on the island.

Thus inclined, Gilles dropped down the hill, went up into third,
and hurled his lurching machine around the ensuing left-hander.
The marshals on the outside of the circuit here made no bones
about their misgivings and moved well back from the barriers.
They were chased by dirt spewn up in their faces by the right
rear Michelin, which also, on several occasions, left a black
streak on the guard rail.

Gilles was long gone, throwing caution to the wind, up into
fourth gear in a thunderclap of sound, down a valley and around
a kink to the right beneath a pedestrian bridge only to be confronted with another S configuration. It coiled sinuously uphill,

beginning with a second-gear left turn, followed smartly by a circuitous right-hander. Here Gilles kicked down the accelerator and was rewarded with an instant rear-end breakaway of alarming proportions. He applied the necessary corrective movements on his Momo steering wheel and brought everything approximately back into line for the momentary straight section.

Third, fourth, and fifth were selected in instants, then the process was reversed just as quickly for another right-left situation taken in second gear. Gilles sailed sideways out of the left-hander and rowed up through the gearbox into top to barrel down the long gentle curve to the left, which afforded a breathing spell of a few seconds before all his faculties would be required to ne-gotiate the final turn on the circuit – the 90-degree bend before the pit straight.

Fifth-fourth-third-second-first, with blasts of flame and bursts of noise from the bundle-of-snakes exhaust. Accompanied also by the screeching of tortured Michelins and squealing of red-hot brake discs, the Ferrari came from top speed to almost a halt in less time than it takes to read about it. Gilles cranked the wheel hard right and tromped hard on the loud pedal to whip the car sideways. He held it in this attitude for a full hundred meters, with the left rear of his car intent on overtaking the front. He played another concert with the gearlever, gradually fed in the required lock to straighten the car out, and was up to 260 kph again by the time he streaked across the finish line to complete one flying lap.

It took him less than a hundred seconds to complete, he made about two dozen gear changes en route, and his average speed was about 165 kph. That was one lap for Gilles Villeneuve on the circuit that was one day to be named after him.

While he won hands down in the entertainment category during practice and qualifying for his home race, Gilles wasn't the quick-est driver. Bouts of rain sweeping in from the Laurentians had doused the circuit on Friday so it all came down to the final session on Saturday afternoon. At one stage Gilles was fastest with a time of 1 minute, 38.230 seconds and the crowd had scarcely finished their cheering when his teammate-to-be Scheck-ter shaved .204 seconds off that.

The Canadian fans had mixed feelings over Scheckter's show-ing since his Wolf car with the Maple Leaf flags was the "home team" and Walter himself, having made much money in con-struction at Expo '67, had many neighbourhood connections. But the fans' dilemma became irrelevant when Jean-Pierre Jarier snatched pole position right near the end of qualifying with a brilliant 1m 38.015s.

It was a splendid effort from the veteran French driver who had been called in to replace Ronnie Peterson at Lotus, beginning at Watkins Glen. There, Jarier had pulled muscles in his back due to an uncomfortable seating position and needed pain-killing pills in Canada. Thirty-two years old, "Jumper," as he was called (because of his predilection for anticipating the start), had never won a Grand Prix in sixty-eight attempts. Now, driving the most successful car in the field, he had an excellent opportunity to join the ranks of Formula 1 winners.

■ ■ ■

"Wait for me, I won't be long," Gilles whispered to Joann, then pulled on his fireproof balaclava, strapped on his helmet, and stepped into his Ferrari 312T-3/78, chassis number 034. Joann, bundled up in a white Eskimo-style parka (loaned to her by Daniele Parent, Gaston's wife), scarf, and mittens, picked up her lap chart and stopwatches and took up her position in the Ferrari signalling station along the pit wall.

The packed grandstands opposite her were bright with the colourful clothing of the fans dressed in full winter apparel. The day was cold and blustery and the overcast skies carried a threat of the first of the three or more meters of snow that falls in Montreal each winter. The weather hadn't deterred 72,632 people from attending, among them Georgette, Seville, and Jacques Villeneuve, many other relatives, a host of Gilles's friends, in-cluding John Lane, the Parents, even Pierre Elliott Trudeau, the Prime Minister of Canada.

The start of the race was imminent, but for Gilles it was the culmination of an exhausting weekend that saw him the focus of attention that rivalled Monza. The media had made tremendous demands on his time, much of it made necessary by his having to explain the nature of his sport to unknowing local journalists. A television crew making a Gilles Villeneuve special had showed up in Berthierville at midnight. He had lunched with Montreal mayor Jean Drapeau, given press conferences till he was hoarse, and there was danger of impaired vision from camera lights and flashbulbs bursting in his face. The sensationalist press was adamant that he was going to be the first Canadian to win the Grand Prix du Canada. Gilles patiently pointed out that no driver had ever won his first Grand Prix in his country's home race.

Overhead a small aircraft trailed a banner reading "Bon Chance Gilles/Good Luck Gilles" and the crowd buzzed in anticipation. But all the ballyhoo and hoopla faded far into his subconscious as Gilles sat on the grid, concentrating deeply to prepare himself for the next two hours of his life. He seemed in a trance, oblivious to all, so much so that when the Prime Minister leaned over to wish him "Bon chance," Gilles gave not a flicker of recognition. Mr. Trudeau, a noted racing fan and sports car buff who owned a vintage gull-winged Mercedes-Benz, moved away as the five-minute signal was given.

The crowds of dignitaries, officials, team personnel, photographers, and journalists filtered from the starting area. With three minutes to go the grid was cleared of everything but twenty-two F1 cars. At the one-minute signal the cars were fired up and Ile Notre-Dame vibrated with the sound of engines being nervously blipped. Thirty seconds later the field moved off on the parade lap, snapping, snarling, and weaving from side to side to warm up the tires. Two minutes later the pack returned to the grid on the pit straight and lined up in front of the starting lights. The red light came on, followed a few seconds later by the green, and the cars surged ahead in an ear-splitting blast of noise.

■ ■ ■

Jumper Jarier did not live up to his nickname on this occasion, but shot off directly on cue, his senses obviously not dulled by a pre-race pain-killing injection. Nor did Gilles repeat his Monza mistake of beating the starting light. But Scheckter tried to do too much too soon and got his Wolf sideways, forcing Gilles to back off for a moment and allowing an opportunistic Alan Jones to sneak his Williams through from the third row into second place. Behind them the frantic jockeying for position saw several cars come together and there were assorted spins and avoidance manoeuvres. But the frontrunners held station and round they came to complete the first of seventy laps, in the order of Jarier, Jones, Scheckter, Villeneuve.

Jarier seemed uncatchable but Jones was experiencing handling problems from a slowly leaking tire. On lap 18 Scheckter found a way by him, followed by Villeneuve one tour later. The crowd cheered lustily for the third-place Ferrari and louder still when it passed the Wolf (which was misfiring slightly) in a decisive manner at the hairpin on lap 25 to assume the runnerup position. Gilles was thirty seconds behind Jarier and was at first unable to make a dent in the Lotus lead. But he pressed on, trying harder and harder, and he saw that he was gradually reeling in the number 55 black-and-gold car.

Shortly after half distance Jarier felt his rear brakes fading. The problem became more pronounced and was soon followed by a dipping oil pressure gauge. An oil-cooling radiator had sprung a leak and the liquid was spilling onto the brakes. He might have continued with reduced stopping power but the life-blood seeping from the Cosworth-Ford engine was what did him in. On lap 49 Jarier coasted into the pits, climbed out of his stricken car, and was embraced emotionally by a crestfallen Colin Chapman. Their cruel stroke of bad luck was greeted by an enormous cheer of joy from the crowd, who realized their man had victory within his grasp.

Thoughts of winning did not rest easily on his shoulders as Gilles inherited the lead. "Those last laps were torture. I could hear all kinds of noises in the car. And I didn't like it because I was having to drive like an old woman, shifting at 10,000 and being careful not to break anything. I would have liked to keep running the way I was earlier behind Jarier. Then, I was trying to put more and more pressure on him. Everything was easy then: you shift quickly, brake hard, and you've got full power on through the corners. I love charging and I try to put on a show for the people who have paid to watch."

The paying customers paid no attention to his reduced pace. They yelled and gesticulated wildly, urging him on, every lap. They didn't realize how hard it was for Gilles to drive slowly.

"It affected my rhythm. I'd just done nearly fifty laps, shifting: bang-bang, and clutching: bang-bang. Then I had to do the whole thing in slow motion, p-u-s-h the clutch, c-h-a-n-g-e the gear, r-e-l-e-a-s-e the clutch."

There were further agonies as he reeled off the last few laps and was easing up so much that several cars he had lapped passed him, among them his Formula Atlantic adversary Keke Rosberg, who was 13 laps in arrears after many pit stops to service his ailing ATS. Gilles was infuriated. "I hated that! You are leading and, even if he's many laps behind, he's passing you and that doesn't look good. The crowd says, 'What's happening here? Somebody passed him.' Many of them don't know what's going on."

Enough of them did to turn the finish line into a madhouse of tulmultuous delirium as Gilles began his last lap. They shrieked and whooped and jumped up and down in a sea of euphoria. But Gilles didn't notice. "I never saw them. I just kept saying to myself, 'Ferrari is the best! Ferrari is the best! It doesn't break. It *never* breaks!' " It didn't, and he rounded the hairpin for the last time saying to himself, " 'Now anything can happen. Anything can blow. I can run out of gas. I can still coast over the line.' "

He crossed the finish line and greeted the chequered flag with both fists punching the air, the sound of his faithful Ferrari completely obliterated by 72,632 howling fans.

■ ■ ■

"To win a Grand Prix is something," said Gilles on his return to the pits. "But to win your first Grand Prix at home is completely unthinkable. I have to thank Mr. Ferrari and all the team. It's an enormous satisfaction. This is the happiest day of my life!" And he was engulfed in a vast crowd of well-wishers. Forghieri and the Ferrari team shook his hand, hugged him, and clapped him on the back. Joann embraced him with tears in her eyes. Everybody else joined in, weeping unashamedly, his mother and father and brother and Gaston Parent and his wife Daniele and John Lane.

Gilles began to feel uncomfortable at their unrestrained emotion. He had no trouble in acknowledging the chants of

"Villeneuve – Villeneuve – Villeneuve" from the thousands of fans who were now jumping the fences to get closer to their new hero. But Gilles didn't want to be a hero to those close to him and he looked embarrassed.

Seville Villeneuve said it was the biggest day of his life – bigger even than the day he married Georgette, bigger than the days Gilles and Jacques were born. John Lane was repeating over and over: "I don't believe it. I don't believe it." "Knock it off!" said Gilles, taking a good-natured swipe at him. He was cold and shivering in his sweat-soaked driving suit. Gaston Parent gave him his brown hunting parka and Gilles struggled through the crowds toward the victory podium where pandemonium reigned.

Gilles was grinning from ear to ear but by the time he got to the presentation area some of his external euphoria had worn off. "I was very happy, but it was like when you sit for a portrait. You smile, but after half an hour your smile starts to fade. When I got to the podium I almost had to force myself to smile." If he was tired of smiling, no one else was. As Gilles took his place on the top step he was joined by the second- and third-place men: Scheckter and Reutemann, both of whom were laughing and joking as if they had won the race.

They congratulated Gilles, genuinely happy for him. Said a gracious Lole, who finished third in this, his last race for Ferrari, "I'm quite happy not to have won this race if Gilles could win. He is a very good driver. Some day he'll be World Champion. He'll give Jody a hard time next year for sure." Scheckter gave no signs of being intimidated but said how wonderful it was for Gilles to win. He had won his home race in South Africa three years previously and was asked how that compared with the wild scenes of celebration around him now. "Half the specators were drunk," said Jody, "and they threw beer bottles at me. It wasn't anything like this."

Walter Wolf bounded up onto the podium and gave Gilles a big bear hug. A wreath was placed around Gilles's neck. The Prime Minister handed him a large trophy topped by a gold maple leaf and said: "I feel warm in my heart for myself and also for Canada." And Gilles, fully cognizant of him now, shook his hand and raised the trophy aloft for the adoring crowd to admire. The huge throng, packed densely in front of him, gave the loudest cheer of the day and was silenced only with the playing of the national anthem.

Tears of joy flowed freely as the strains of ''O Canada'' echoed around Ile Notre-Dame. A look of uncertainty crept over Gilles's face, as if he was struggling to comprehend that this huge out-pouring of emotion was all for him, the kid from Berthier who only liked to drive fast. It passed in a moment and Gilles raised his arms in triumph as the anthem ended.

Mr. Trudeau waved a Ferrari flag at the fans. The proceedings took on a distinctly Canadian flavour when, instead of the traditional magnum of champagne, Gilles was handed an oversize bottle of the race sponsor's product. He shook it vigorously and sprayed the beer over his countrymen.

6

THE TIME OF HIS LIFE: 1979

/

"In my opinion, with Gilles and Jody, it was the best team I had in my life."

— *Mauro Forghieri*

"Villeneuve represents a daring hope which has come true," was Enzo Ferrari's statement following Gilles's victory in Canada. And if Formula 1 had a rookie-of-the-year category Gilles would have won it hands down in 1978. In his first full season, despite a very shaky start, Gilles finished ninth overall in the driver's standings (tied with Emerson Fittipaldi) with 17 points, garnered from his win (9 points), a third (4), a fourth (3), and a sixth place (1). Based on doubling those results, his publicly announced goals for 1979 seemed realistic. He felt two Grand Prix wins and 35 points would help get him into the top five in the drivers' standings. Privately, Gilles was confident of doing even better than that.

After all, he had come from "nowhere" to the winner's podium in just eighteen F1 races, overcoming a great deal of adversity along the way. "I've made a lot of mistakes," he admitted, "and paid the price of being a poor judge of both Formula One cars and drivers. But if I weigh up the pros and cons I must confess that I'm rather pleased with myself. Without wishing to sound presumptuous, I realize I've become really competitive, to the extent of finding myself at the same level as the best drivers." His position at Ferrari now secure for another year, Gilles spoke highly of the team. "I'm convinced that it's the best team in Formula One. I was told that I could expect a lot of problems of understanding, and tension, but I've only seen people who take their work seriously, and have a great will to win."

For the winning to take place in 1979 a lot would depend on Ferrari's new 312T4, which would be essential to keep pace with the Lotus-instigated aerodynamic revolution in F1. The more progressive and affluent teams were developing Lotus-like versions of Chapman's wing-car design. Perfected in wind tunnels, the chassis shape was based on the principles of an inverted aircraft wing, which served to create downforce to keep the car stuck to the track in corners. Since Forghieri's version of the new generation of car wouldn't be ready until later in the season, the team would begin with an updated version of the venerable T3 model, so Maranello was a beehive of activity over the winter.

While the other teams, except Renault, relied on outside suppliers to produce engines, gearboxes, wheels, and so on, Ferraris were built entirely in-house. At this time there were 170 employees involved in fielding two F1 cars: as many as fifty men in the design department, thirty building and maintaining the engines, five on gearboxes, and so on. Personnel at the races included eight mechanics (four per car), two crew chiefs, two engineers, two transport drivers, and Mauro Forghieri. Marco Piccinini, who reported directly back to Enzo Ferrari by telephone, was always on hand, as were assorted public relations people and liaison personnel from Fiat.

On race weekends in Europe two huge, red, Fiat IVECO transporters carried at least three cars (sometimes four at Monza), an extra five flat-12 engines, and enough spares to construct another two cars. Mobile headquarters was a vast, sleek, Fiat-based motorhome where a skilled chef prepared and served meals from a fully equipped stainless steel galley.

Backing up the men from Maranello was a full team of tire technicians from Michelin with stacks of rubber in varying compounds, another crew from Agip, the supplier of fuel, oil, and lubricants, and a contingent of specialists from Heuer watches who manned sophisticated timekeeping equipment. And, unlike any other team, Ferrari had the technically advanced Fiorano circuit at its doorstep for unlimited testing. Between 1977 and 1979 Gilles calculated that he drove at least 60,000 kilometers at Fiorano. "When you look at it," said Gilles, "Ferrari should win every race with facilities like that. Of course it's not that simple . . ."

■ ■ ■

Ferrari's advantages were what brought Gilles's new teammate into the fold. He had come close to signing as a replacement for Lauda in 1978, but Jody Scheckter's contacts with the Italian team went back further than that. "In 1973 I was offered a Ferrari drive. At the time I was with Tyrrell and turned it down. In those days Ferrari meant good engines, good facilities, chaotic management, and pit stops that made Chinese fire drills look tame. I passed then, but when Ferrari offered me a contract this time, I weighed all the prospects and signed it. It was the team best suited to the needs of the moment."

Scheckter's needs included a serious shot at the world championship and he felt the resources of the Italian team would, in the long run, overpower even those of Walter Wolf. And as an enterprising man who always carried a briefcase along with his helmet, he was also attracted by the $600,000 offered to him by Ferrari. That amount included financial input from Agip, Michelin, and other sponsors, and becoming a Ferrari driver helped pave the way for Scheckter's private enterprise to come to the fore. The name Brooklyn was emblazoned across his driving suit for an amount said to be $350,000 from the Italian chewing gum company.

Enzo Ferrari sought Scheckter because he "is a fighter who does not burn himself up by coming on too strongly at the beginning, but like Nuvolari and Stirling Moss measures himself fully and evenly throughout a race." That was the mature, 1979 version of Jody Scheckter, but his Formula 1 career had a troubled start, in much the same way as that of his new teammate at Ferrari.

Born in East London, South Africa, on January 29, 1950 (eleven days after Gilles), Scheckter was reared in an automotive atmosphere around his father's garage, which included a Renault dealership. He worked there as an engineering apprentice and soon took to driving cars quickly (his first was a Renault 8) as well as repairing them. He raced motorcycles for a while, then cars, and in his first national race he was black-flagged off the circuit for dangerous driving. He settled down enough to become South Africa's leading driver in 1970 and was the recipient of £300 prize money and air tickets to England for him and his wife Pam.

He paid his dues in Formula Ford, F3, and F2, doing well enough to be noticed by several Formula 1 teams, and was given a contract by McLaren similar to the one Gilles Villeneuve received. He was entered in a third car and run alongside the regular McLaren drivers, Denny Hulme and Peter Revson, at selected races. At the 1973 French Grand Prix he impressed by taking the lead from the start, then collided with Fittipaldi's Lotus. The McLaren flipped and so did Emerson when his car hit the guard rail heavily. The reigning World Champion, also undoubtedly upset at being challenged by a newcomer, blasted Scheckter as a menace.

In the next event, at Silverstone, Scheckter spun in the middle of the pack and triggered an almighty eight-car accident that stopped the race. Fortunately, Andrea de Adamich's broken leg was the only injury, but Scheckter was threatened with banishment from F1. McLaren then gave him a cooling-off period for several races until the Canadian Grand Prix at Mosport, where he crashed with François Cevert's Tyrrell, putting both of them out of the race.

Between the Canadian and U.S. races that season Ken Tyrrell announced that he had signed Scheckter to replace the retiring Jackie Stewart as teammate for Cevert in 1974. Sadly, this partnership would never be, as Cevert was killed in a horrible practice crash at Watkins Glen. Jody Scheckter was the first driver to appear on the scene of the accident where the very talented, charming, and popular Frenchman was badly mutilated when his inverted Tyrrell rode along the top of a guard rail. The accident had a profound effect on the rest of Jody Scheckter's racing life. He became very conscious of safety, though no less competitive, and arrived at Ferrari with seven Grand Prix victories, four with Tyrrell and three with Wolf.

Scheckter also brought with him a reputation for being tough, blunt, strong-willed, profoundly serious, and testy of temperament. His nickname, ''The Bear'' (or ''Baby Bear'' to those who recalled that Denny Hulme was the original ''Bear''), owed as much to his reputed disposition as to his rugged features and woolly hair. With Ferrari, he went about his racing with a great sense of purpose and intense dedication but was able to relax and become more sociable and exercise a keen sense of humour. He lived well with Pam and their child, Tobia, in a splendid seafront penthouse in Monaco where he had an office and secretary to run The Scheckter Company. In his spare time he consorted with the likes of his neighbour Bjorn Borg and regularly played tennis with him. And he got along splendidly with everyone at Ferrari, especially with Gilles.

■ ■ ■

''In my opinion, with Gilles and Jody, it was the best team I had in my life,'' says Mauro Forghieri. ''When we had car troubles neither of the drivers was crying. They worked and worked to help. And we came out of the problems with points and the ideas of how to improve the car. I think that without saying one word they took the decision to be fair and follow their luck. Whoever was ahead, the other would help. They raced together, but always cleanly. It was a very professional team. Gilles was happy to help Jody. In my opinion he was considering Jody to be a little bit like himself. Jody was like Gilles early in his career. He was a fighter, but a fighter who was understanding what it took to win the championship.''

Marco Piccinini joined Ferrari the same year as Gilles and he, too, remembers 1979 fondly. ''That season with Jody and Gilles was definitely one of the happiest of my career. It was the best combination of drivers and personalities in my eleven years with Ferrari.'' (He left the team at the end of 1988 to begin a business career, but remained on the board of directors.) ''In the beginning, when Jody first arrived, he underrated Gilles. When he came to Fiorano he couldn't really approach the times Gilles was doing. Of course, when he learned more about the car, he became very competitive. So he realized Gilles was a very good driver, but also a very good man. They became very close personal friends and this, I think, contributed to the fact that in '79 Ferrari had a beautiful season.''

Piccinini's previous background was in architecture, but his duties as sports director and team manager at Ferrari required diplomatic skills to maintain harmony. He was to have difficulties in this department later on with Villeneuve and Pironi and in later combinations of drivers, but the Scheckter/Villeneuve alliance made his job easy. His regular reports back to Enzo Ferrari contained mainly good news. ''The championship was only a family business between either Gilles or Jody. This could have generated a lot of problems. We see now what happens when this situation arises in other teams. It never happened to us because, I would say, of the human qualities of those people involved.''

The problems between teammates invariably stem from real or perceived preferential treatment of one driver over another. Some teams avoid this by designating number-one and number-two drivers, but Ferrari usually prefers to let them fight it out and let the results in the races decide supremacy. This, too, can lead to acrimony when an ego is deflated, but the strategy is guaranteed to extract top performances from both drivers.

''Ferrari never had a number one or a number two,'' says Piccinini. ''Mr. Ferrari used to say the number one is chosen the Sunday evening after the race, but the next race is a new story. Of course, if there is a championship situation and we are competing with another team, we may ask one driver to maybe sacrifice some effort to help his teammate. It's not really a matter of one driver over another, but more in the interest of the team.''

Despite the stated Ferrari policy of driver equality, Scheckter was by far the more experienced of the two, he was more highly paid, he did the bulk of the winter testing at Fiorano, and his contract called for him to have first call on the use of the spare car at the races. There is no doubt in his mind as to where he stood when he joined the team. ''I really didn't know much about Gilles when I signed with Ferrari. As long as I was number one I didn't really care who was number two. But Ferrari had enough resources so they had at least two of everything and there really wasn't much difference. We had the same orders: after things settled down in the races, whoever was in front, stayed in front.

If we had no other competition that was the rule. Very definitely, if we were one and two ahead of everybody else, we had to stay in our positions.''

Scheckter, now a prosperous businessman in Atlanta, Georgia, describes how his partnership with Gilles was forged. "The reason that Gilles and I were so successful was because we were very honest with each other. That's the way it had to be. It was like we were living together and although I wanted to win more than I wanted Ferrari to win, I didn't want to get into a fight with somebody in my own house. Gilles and I were the same age (though he always bullshitted his age and said he was two years younger – we used to joke about that) and we respected each other. I respected him for what he was and what he was good at and the good qualities in him. And I believe he respected me for the same reasons. Our relationship grew and there were times when it was very tough. But it developed over time on a trust basis. We had to trust each other. You can trust somebody when you're just having a drink with them, but you get to know people and the trust runs much deeper under wartime conditions. And when you're racing you're at war.''

2

"My preoccupation was keeping myself alive, but Gilles had to be quickest on every lap – even in testing."
– Jody Scheckter

The 1979 Grand Prix wars began in Argentina three days after Gilles's twenty-ninth birthday. He qualified tenth, 1.3 seconds behind Jody, but the 312T3 Ferraris weren't able to match the front-row Ligiers of Jacques Laffite (the eventual winner) and Patrick Depailler. The Argentinians booed Jody lustily for taking Reutemann's seat at Ferrari and weren't displeased when he crashed on the first lap, along with several others. The Ferrari made contact with John Watson's McLaren, lost a wheel, and hit Mario Andretti's Lotus. Several backmarkers piled into them, and the track was blocked and the race stopped while the carnage was cleaned up.

Five cars were unable to take the restart. Nelson Piquet's Brabham had caved in around his feet, spraining his toes, and an angry Scheckter was forced to sit out by the track doctor, who ruled that his sprained wrist, caught in the flailing steering wheel, was not up to the task of driving. Gilles was unable to help the Ferrari cause in the race when he spun out of sixth place, then pitted for fresh Michelins, only to retire near the end in a cloud of smoke from a blown engine.

Though the journalists had little to write about his race in Buenos Aires, Gilles was winning friends among their fraternity off the track. At the events held outside continental Europe the Formula 1 circus tends to be thrown together in closer association, flying on the same planes, staying at the same hotels, eating at the same restaurants, and so on. Many of the dignitaries and superstars remain aloof and seldom deign to socialize outside their coterie of protective hangers-on. But Gilles was never like that. His entourage abroad usually consisted of only Joann and his approachability was much appreciated in an arena of uncooperative prima donnas and/or inarticulate drivers from whom it was a struggle to get anything but perfunctory reports of gear ratios and such. Gilles was always good for a quote and became quite friendly with several scribes. While it was his spectacular style in a racing car that created the Villeneuve legend, his agreeable personality and honourable character traits did much to enhance it. And these latter qualities were what attracted those several journalists who became close to him.

One of them was Peter Windsor, then sports editor of the British magazine *Autocar* (and later an executive with the Williams team), who became a Villeneuve fan. "I got to know Gilles over a two- or three-year period," says Windsor, "and found him to be unbelievably charming and friendly. He loved the physical act of driving but beyond that he was a very sensitive and warm person who cared about people and was never rude to anybody. And he used to joke a lot. At Watkins Glen in '78 he had a piston failure. About a week later I asked him to sign a picture for me and he wrote: 'To Bloody Peter who screwed my piston at Watkins Glen! best wishes Gilles.'

"I mentioned to him early on that we were about the same age," Windsor recalls, "and we used to joke about who was getting older quicker. He always remembered my birthday after that and totally unexpectedly, about three years in a row, he would ring me up at the hotel about five o'clock and say, 'Why don't you come and have dinner with Joann and me tonight.' Our meal was always what he had: steak or hamburger, followed by ice cream with chocolate sauce.''

Windsor and his peers were also taken by the Villeneuve approach to everyday motoring. ''Driving me back to the hotel in Brazil, Gilles would use handbrake turns as a matter of course. He wouldn't stop for anything, be it traffic light or traffic jam. He would use any bit of open space in order to continue his forward momentum. With Gilles it was always full speed ahead.''

Another sometime passenger was Len Coates, a Canadian journalist and automotive writer who began covering Gilles's career in Formula Atlantic and followed him in his first F1 seasons for the *Toronto Star*. Gilles was particularly pleased to have at least one knowledgeable Canadian reporting firsthand to the home media and the two hit it off splendidly, to the point that he and Coates planned to write Gilles's memoirs. The project was never completed but Coates was left with a rich fund of anecdotes.

Coates's first ride with Gilles was through the streets of São Paulo in a Fiat 128, which carried the message ''VILLENEUVE Grande Premio do Brasil F1 1979,'' and Gilles drove it as if it were an entry in that race. As they left the São Paulo Hilton, bound for the Interlagos circuit, Gilles floored the Fiat and, according to Coates, their progress in heavy traffic went something like ''Vroom, vroom, vroom. Screech! Vroom, vroom, vroom. Screech!'' Admiring Brazilians yelled ''Vamos Gilles! Vamos!'' and Coates thought at first Gilles was just playing to the audience. ''It took about three blocks for me to realize that he drives like that all the time. Every stoplight signalled a drag race. Every corner was taken at full throttle. Every tiny gap in traffic became a target for the Fiat.''

At first Coates was a worried man: ''I had to keep reminding myself this was no ordinary mortal at the wheel. I kept repeating: 'He's a Grand Prix driver, one of the best in the world. He's a Grand Prix driver . . .' '' Gradually, as they cut through some of the world's worst traffic without mishap, Coates relaxed his white knuckles and his journalistic bent caused him to observe the driver more closely. "First, he concentrates. He's constantly aware of what's happening around him with the other traffic. Second, there's no hesitation in any move he makes. He has checked the situation, then he moves with deliberation. Finally, Villeneuve understands fully what forces react on an automobile and when we overshot a corner he snapped on the handbrake and we were facing the right direction in an instant."

Following his street-race performance Gilles was able to use his Ferrari to reasonably good effect in the Brazilian Grand Prix. The first three rows of the starting grid were entirely symmetrical, with the Ligiers, Lotuses, and Ferraris in that order. In the race, Laffite and Depailler were first and second for the gloire de France, while Gilles and Jody did their best to uphold Italian honour, finishing fifth and sixth after pit stops to replace worn Michelins. But they were a whole 7.960-km lap behind the Ligiers and obviously not on equal footing with them. Part of the pleasure in the Ferrari pit at the end of the race was due to the fact that this was the last appearance of the Ferrari T3 and the new generation of ground-effects cars would be introduced at the next event, in Jody's native land.

■ ■ ■

When Mauro Forghieri's new Ferrari 312-T4 appeared at the South African Grand Prix some people thought it the ugliest car ever to carry the prancing-horse insignia. With a nose like a hammerhead shark and the tail of some similar species, it did bear a resemblance to a bizarre denizen of the deep, a pregnant one perhaps. It was rather wide, to accommodate the boxy flat-12 (now in its ninth year of service), and featured bulbous side-pods with sliding skirts to aid the ground effect. Though it was not a true ground-effects car because of its width, it proved to be no fish out of water at Kyalami, where it was quick right out of the box.

"The car is much more precise to drive and a lot better under braking," observed Gilles, who was a tenth of a second slower than Jody, who was in turn a shade slower than the polesitter, Jean-Pierre Jabouille in the turbocharged Renault. The Ferrari drivers established a race strategy before the start, according to Gilles. "I told Jody if he was first and I was second it wouldn't matter much. If I was too far behind I would push but if I was close I wouldn't attack. He agreed, but I really wanted to get close to him at the start.'' Their diplomatic agreement meant the start would be the only opportunity for one or the other to establish supremacy. As it developed they had two starts to contend with and they were hectic affairs.

A crowd of 100,000 was on hand, most of them equipped with rain gear as the race began under threatening skies. From the green light the Ferraris shot forward slightly ahead of the Renault. Jody led for a moment, then Gilles edged ahead, but as they came around to end the first lap Jabouille summoned all the extra Renault horsepower on tap and passed the Ferraris. The next time the trio appeared it was in the order of Villeneuve by a nose over Scheckter and Jabouille, but their fierce battle was halted on the third lap when a heavy cloudburst brought forth a sea of umbrellas in the crowd and a red flag from the race officials.

Everyone filtered into the pits to wait until the weather made up its mind one way or another. But the elements seemed to be of two minds: while the sky brightened, storm clouds lingered and drivers were faced with agonizing decisions as to whether or not to use rain tires. As it was, Jody chose to stay on slicks while Gilles opted for the grooved wet-weather variety. ''Forghieri would have liked it better if we both started with slicks,'' said Gilles. ''But five minutes before the restart I decided to use rain tires. The circuit was still quite wet and I thought it would be easy to lose control on slicks. I figured I would be able to make a better start with the wets and build up a lead which would give me time to change back to slicks if the course dried out later on.''

When the lights flashed green again Gilles's strategy gave him a fractional lead over Jody, who was just ahead of Jabouille. Whatever was going on behind them was obscured in a huge cloud of spray sent skyward at the start. Gilles's plan worked to perfection during the opening laps, then became flawed as the South African sun began to poke through the clouds before he had built a proper cushion over Jody. A dry line soon appeared on the circuit, the wet-tire advantage became a liability, and everyone thus outfitted peeled into the pits for tire changes. Gilles was the last to stop, on the 15th lap, and his 15-second lead over

Jody evaporated in the 18 seconds it took the Ferrari crew to effect the change to slick Michelins.

However, Jody's advantage began to diminish as his tires lost grip from having been severely stressed in the early going. By lap 50 the two Ferraris were running nose to tail and Jody, somewhat flustered at the turn of events, administered the coup de grâce to his worn Michelins when he flat-spotted one of the fronts under braking. The ensuing vibration was more than he could contend with and three laps later he came flying into the pits for a tire change. He was back in action after a delay of less than 20 seconds and immediately began to chew away at Gilles's lead, which by the time Jody got back up to speed was 36 seconds. Their situation now reversed, Gilles was having to back off to save his tires and Jody sent his home crowd of 100,000 into spasms of hopeful hollering as the interval between the Ferraris shrunk with every lap. But Jody ran out of laps and on the 78th and final one he crossed the finish line .42 seconds behind his teammate.

"Racing is dangerous!" Gilles joked as he limped up to the winner's dais, having slightly twisted his ankle on jumping out of the victorious car. Then he said, "I am very happy to have scored the last win for the Ferrari T3 and the first with the Ferrari T4!" He had also set the fastest race lap, a new track record, and those who felt the French Canadian's racing progress was dictated only by his heavy right foot were forced to take note of his use of some clever thinking in what was a well-judged performance.

"I waited until the fuel load lightened before pushing the tires too hard," said Gilles, "then when I felt either the front or back tires starting to go off I adjusted my driving style to bring them back again. Jody came close and if I had made a mistake he could have taken me easily. I decided to keep my cool and hold on."

While accepting second-place laurels, Jody admitted to having a less fruitful game plan and was philosophical about it: "I had it coming to me. I went too hard at first. I stayed out too long. I should have come in and changed them earlier."

■ ■ ■

So Gilles arrived at Long Beach in California (where he had crashed out while leading twelve months earlier) with the Ferrari momentum in his favour and was asked how he felt about the possibility of becoming World Champion. ''I might have a chance at it but I don't think of it like that. Just race by race. I hope to win every race I enter. But I don't have the championship in my head. The strategy is to go as fast as I can all the time, so that's what I'll do here. Except on the 30th lap, I will watch not to end up in the guard rail!''

Nonetheless he did just that on only his second lap on opening-day practice at Long Beach, sliding off and bending the front end of his T4. ''It was a stupid mistake, trying to go fast too soon,'' he admitted, then went faster still. In fact, he was fastest of all in qualifying and scored his first F1 pole position. It was an heroic effort from Gilles to wrest the quickest time away from his former teammate, Carlos Reutemann in his well-tried and proven Lotus. With Jody third on the grid, Lole's Lotus was the meat in a Ferrari sandwich. Then, after making something of a hash of the start, Gilles made a meal of the race.

He was unaccustomed to the responsibilities of the polesitter, who is supposed to lead the field around in an orderly fashion on the parade lap and take up his position on the start line to wait for the lights. When Reutemann dove into the pits to have an electrical fault attended to Gilles found himself alone on the front row with no one else in sight. He continued to roll forward and the field was forced to tour around on another parade lap. Gilles was later fined 10,000 Swiss francs for causing the confusion but it mattered not a whit. He got everything right on the second try and led the U.S. Grand Prix West from start to finish.

Jody, who was using a harder compound of rubber than Gilles, had to fight for his second place with the likes of Depailler and Laffite, but Gilles was unopposed in establishing new race and lap records and driving an absolutely faultless race. The magnitude of his achievement was exemplified by the fact that such drivers as Lauda and Tambay crashed into the unforgiving walls around Long Beach and only nine cars finished.

In truth, Villeneuve's supremacy was such that he left a boring race behind him, but the win had him leading the world championship with 20 points (to 18 for Laffite and 13 for Jody) and in a jubilant frame of mind. "People said I was lucky in Montreal because Jarier dropped out. In South Africa they said I only won because of the rain and the problem of tires. But whatever they say, this race was all mine."

3

"Motor racing was a romantic thing for him. We were close friends, doing the same job for the same team, but we had completely different attitudes to it."

– Jody Scheckter

In the middle of the three-week interval until the European season began in Spain at the end of April, some of the Formula 1 teams entered the non-championship event at Brands Hatch in England. Gilles was appointed the Ferrari representative, driving an updated version of the T3, and his opposition included six other Grand Prix regulars and twelve entries from the British Aurora AFX series for used F1 cars. Gilles qualified third behind Lauda and Andretti and ahead of Nelson Piquet, the Brazilian newcomer whose talents were being compared to those of Gilles when he first arrived. Andretti made a poor start and was led by Lauda and Villeneuve. Lauda had to stop for tires and Villeneuve ran wide on a corner to let Andretti through. On lap 27 the Canadian elbowed his way by the veteran American, who was then slowed by gearbox and tire problems. So Gilles won the Race of Champions in a walk, ahead of Piquet and Andretti. While no points were awarded, it was his third race victory in a row and there seemed to be no stopping him.

"He's superb, and I believe he will get better and better," predicted Jackie Stewart. "Gilles has improved out of all recognition," said a previous critic, John Watson, who so far in 1979 had only four points in his Marlboro McLaren. "He is very, very quick and has tremendous potential." (Watson's teammate, Patrick Tambay, had yet to finish in the points.) And, for journalists, Jody Scheckter put on a humorous face. "The team was supposed to consist of me and this Canadian kid. I was supposed to do all the winning. He was supposed to watch me and learn.

"In fact," Jody admits now, "I was mad as a snake! When Gilles won the first two races it was tough. I certainly identified immediately that he was fast. And the Italian press was very much in the mode that they wanted us to fight together. But regardless of that, there's a great deal of pressure, sometimes more pressure from your teammate, because he's got the same type of car. So if he beats you you've got no excuses."

Ferrari issued a statement to the press prior the Grand Premio de Espana, the fifth race of 1979. The press release was partly in response to an intensive media campaign in Italy that was pushing Scheckter to the sidelines in print and advocating Villeneuve for World Champion. The gist of the press release was that the current points leader had the team's blessing in his quest for the world championship and that a possible review of the status of the Ferrari drivers might be necessary as the season progressed. The strong inference was that no preferential treatment was going to be given to the team's senior driver, as had been the case at Lotus the previous season when Peterson had been required to play second fiddle to his team leader, Andretti. So Gilles and Jody were left to fight it out on their own, and they did so in earnest at the Jarama circuit.

In qualifying, the two Ferraris flew around in a private competition that made their every lap look like a showdown for the title. At the end of the first day Gilles held the overnight pole from Jody. On Saturday Gilles improved his time slightly but not enough to catch the Ligiers of Laffite and Depailler. Jody had a huge spin, then a chassis problem, then was held up by slower traffic on his quickest laps. He was in a rage at the conclusion of qualifying, required consoling by Mauro Forghieri, and would start an unhappy fifth on the grid.

The Ferrari drivers' fortunes were reversed in the race. Gilles became tired of running fourth behind Reutemann, tried to outbrake him, locked his rear brakes, and spun in front of the oncoming traffic. Everybody managed to avoid him and Gilles resumed racing only to repeat his spinning performance on the next lap while trying to outbrake Piquet. This time he exited the circuit in a huge cloud of dust, then regained it by means of an entertaining power spin, flooring the accelerator and whipping the contrary rear end of his T4 around to face the right way.

Now in 13th place, he decided to cool his heels for a bit and ponder the situation. Meanwhile, Jody was motoring briskly along in third behind Reutemann. Toward the end his tires went off and he fell back to finish fourth behind the winner, Depailler.

Gilles stopped for new Michelins with 17 laps to go, then tore up the track at record speeds and was credited with by far the fastest lap of the race, 1.56 seconds quicker than the next man, Alan Jones. Gilles lost second gear in his comeback effort and, though he finished out of the points in seventh and Depailler had tied him for the lead in the championship, Gilles was far from displeased. "It was a good day for us," he said. "Although we had tire problems, they were a lot less than in the past." He had proven himself to be the quickest man at Jarama and that mattered a great deal to Gilles – too much, according to Jody Scheckter.

■ ■ ■

"Gilles wanted to win laps. He didn't really want to win the races, he didn't want to win the world championship," says Scheckter. "He was a very intelligent guy but in my opinion he wanted the wrong things out of racing. One of the things that made me feel that I had a chance of winning the championship against Gilles was the stupid things he did.

"In the beginning of my career I think I was as crazy as he was but when I got to Tyrrell I changed around and realized that you aren't going to win world championships doing that. It may have been Ken Tyrrell hitting me on the head all the time and telling me you don't win races by winning laps. But Gilles was so big on fastest laps that in a race when he felt his tires going off he would dive into the pits, put on new tires, and get fastest lap.

"I would argue with him about it, saying you should stay out there with an old set of tires because that's probably the way you're going to get the best result in the end. I used to throw cars around, too, it was my natural style, but as the ground effects developed the tires became overheated and wore out when you slid them.

"Gilles liked this image he had of being a crazy guy and he worked at it. I used to drive up to Fiorano with him and he was usually quite sane all the way. Then, when we got 10 kilometers from Maranello he became a madman, wheels spinning, skidding around, and so on. But Gilles wanted to impress and I used to say that he would get a fever when he got near Maranello and we joked about it. When he came flying into the carpark at the factory he would do a 360-degree wheelspin and the mechanics would all cheer. And I just sat back, it gave me a relaxing feeling to see him do that because I felt if a guy does this kind of thing on the road he's going to make too many mistakes in the races and that's how I can beat him.

"But I wouldn't let Gilles clown around like that on the motorways because at the speeds we travelled it could be as dangerous as racing." And after a few trips to Fiorano, Jody insisted on doing the driving in his own Ferrari 400. However, unless he was creating his own speed, Gilles was always bored on the road. He amused himself with such stunts as holding the newspaper he was reading up in front of Jody's face and saying, "Look Jody, see what they're writing about you. You're famous!"

Often what they read, particularly in the Italian papers, was a source of amusement to the two friends. "We had an open-heart relationship," says Scheckter, "and it annoyed some journalists because they used to invent stories. They'd come to me and say Gilles said this about you and he's much faster than you even though he has a broken gearbox, and so on. But he knew that I was honest, I knew that he was honest, and we never had any personal aggravation. So Gilles and I used to bullshit the press because we both knew what was going on."

■ ■ ■

The press had plenty to write about at the next race, the Grote Prijs van Belgie. Zolder took on an especially gloomy aspect on the first morning of unofficial practice when steady rain fell. The only bright spot in the proceedings, from the enthusiasts' point of view, was the number 12 Ferrari that pounded around on the wet track, sending up great showers of spray down the straights, locking wheels and sliding sideways around corners, and generally darting about like a waterbug. Gilles's perseverance paid off when the rain abated for a while in the afternoon's timed session and he secured the overnight pole. But the elements contrived to hide the fact that the Michelin qualifying tires weren't up to the Goodyear variety.

The extra sticky qualifiers provided phenomenal traction for only two or three laps, making it imperative for the driver to take risks in traffic. Many people within Formula 1 were trying to have them banned (and Gilles later became a prime crusader for the cause), but the rubber companies got a great deal of publicity mileage from pole-setting performances. Qualifying tires were a factor in Gilles's death at Zolder in 1982, but in 1979 they served only to put him further down the grid. In the dry Saturday qualifying session the Ferraris fell back, leaving Gilles sixth and Jody seventh in the field of twenty-four cars.

Race day was warm and sunny. Though the local constabulary displayed their clubs and dogs prominently, they failed to subdue the high spirits of the large contingent of Ferrari supporters on hand in the main grandstand. At the start they waved their prancing-horse banners and flags with great vigour, urging on their favourites, who came around the first time as they had qualified, but in close attendance with the leading group of Depailler, Jones, Piquet, Laffite, and Andretti. Also in the hunt was Regazonni, who was threatening the Ferraris. On the second lap the Ferrari supporters were more subdued as the number 12 car failed to appear on schedule, having been involved in an altercation at the chicane on the far side of the circuit.

"In the chicane, Regazzoni bumped with Jody. Jody had the advantage in the corner but Clay wanted to fight it anyway," was the way Gilles saw it. "I thought something broke on Clay's car but there was nothing I could do. I was a foot behind him and he stopped there. I ran into him with my wing and ran over him with my wheel."

Gilles's eyewitness account failed to mention that he flew high over Regazzoni's Williams, emulating their Long Beach contretemps. Regazzoni was out on the spot but this time Gilles's car was not immobilized, only suffering a broken nose section, and he tore into the pits to have it replaced. Tomaini and the crew gave the car a quick once-over and Gilles tore out again – in 23rd, and last, place.

Depailler, Jones, and Laffite were engaged in an epic struggle for the lead, which each of them held for a time. Jody, having survived the Regazzoni incident unscathed, was flying around most aggressively and bunted Piquet out of the way to take fourth place on the fourth lap. On the fifth, despite nearly full tanks, he set the fastest race time, a new lap record, and very nearly as quick as he had gone in qualifying. Shortly after that his teammate established an even quicker time in what was becoming the drive of the race.

Gilles flew around Zolder at an astonishing pace, carving his way through traffic as if he were on a Sunday drive in the streets of Rio. His aggressive mood was almost palpable, certainly obvious to the *tifosi* in the crowd who were ecstatic at his come-from-behind determination. Never mind that several of those who stood between Gilles and the front had their races accidentally terminated (Mass, de Angelis, Giacomelli, Hunt, and Depailler all crashed) and that half a dozen others fell out for mechanical reasons. The point was that Gilles forced his way past many of them before they departed the race.

By lap 38, Villeneuve had barged his way up to fifth place when his upward mobility was arrested by Riccardo Patrese's notoriously wide Arrows. Patrese, though absolved of blame in the Peterson accident in 1978, had a well-deserved reputation for being distinctly ungenerous when it came to being passed. For 10 frustrating laps the Ferrari sat on the tail of the weaving Arrows. Finally Gilles made his move at the chicane, feinting first one way, then the other, and elbowed his way alongside. The cars banged wheels but the Ferrari came away in front and Gilles set off after Pironi's third place. The 14-second deficit to the Tyrrell was gobbled up in 10 laps and Gilles passed Pironi and then gave chase to Laffite in second.

Jody was now in the lead, having benefited from Depailler's crashing exit (he understeered off the road) and the other Ligier of Laffite being bothered by gripless Goodyears. In seven laps Gilles whittled 11 seconds away from Laffite's 21-second advantage over him, but in the process he was using up precious reserves of the Ferrari's lifeblood – Agip. As the cars flashed by the pits on their last lap Laffite was again edging away from the following Ferrari, which was emitting a curiously strangled exhaust note. In the pits Forghieri muttered, ''He went too fast, he's run out of fuel.''

Across the finish line they came: Scheckter, Laffite . . . Pironi, Reutemann, Patrese. Watson. No Villeneuve. Gilles came walking into the pits, his Ferrari parked 300 meters from the finish line to fulfil Forghieri's prediction: out of fuel.

So Jody got his first win as a Ferrari driver and was now tied for the points lead with Laffite. Such was his good humour in Belgium that Jody appeared in person to receive his award as the least co-operative driver in the previous season. The International Racing Press Association Prix Orange (most co-operative to journalists) commendations went to Andretti, Renault, and Le Circuit Paul Ricard, while Jody, Ferrari, and Monza were selected for the Prix Citron. But now all at Ferrari were wreathed in smiles, even Gilles, who seemed content to have proven he was faster than anyone on the day.

"The least you can do is clap your hands for Villeneuve," said Forghieri, and Gilles did get a big ovation from the *tifosi*, who had witnessed a tremendous drive, tailor-made for Ferrari fans. But, for want of a few tablespoons of fuel, that's all Gilles got at Zolder (he was classified seventh overall) and he confessed privately to Joann: "I hope those four points are not going to be important when this is all over, but I'm afraid they will be. Maybe I've just lost the championship."

4

"Gilles has a rage to win, more than any other driver."
—Mauro Forghieri

At the end of May, Jody and Gilles came to race through the streets of Monaco. And from the opening day of practice and qualifying they were the class of the field. Again Gilles produced the fireworks, hurling his Ferrari through Casino Square with tremendous brio and sending the crowd into throes of delight with his brilliant car control all around the circuit. He was concentrating intensely on the task at hand and extremely busy, but he was able to take note of the crowd reaction and describe the sensations in the cockpit.

"Around the swimming pool I was going very quickly and I could clearly see the crowd was appreciating what I was doing. It's a good feeling to know people like what you are doing. You barely see it, but it does register. I hate it when people are close to the track wearing a yellow jacket or red sweater so that sometimes you mistake them momentarily for a yellow or red flag. Those things you really see because every instinct is tuned for the danger signals.

"The chicane at Monaco is just a blur. *It's so bloody quick!* Every time you go in there you say: 'Wow! – I'm going to crash here!' Then: SHOOOM! ZAP! It's gone. You brake – it's lousy asphalt there so you are bouncing so hard you can barely see – and in almost the same instant, you're through it. But you don't really know what's happening. It's very, very quick. A blur.

"You can hear – actually feel – that you are going quickly because the engine doesn't drop its revs. It's a total sensation: hearing and feeling – like dancing, like a waltz, where every step and every note leads to the next one. When you are going slowly, say when you are learning a circuit, it's jerky, the levels of energy rise and drop. Then it's nothing like a waltz.

"In a way it's like comparing soccer and hockey. In soccer a player runs, then stops dead. The motion ends. But in hockey a player never actually stops on the ice. He goes from braking to accelerating to turning, all very quickly with one action leading to another. When you are really quick in a Formula One car, you are using the deceleration to build acceleration, as if you were creating energy under braking and storing it, putting it in reserve for the acceleration that comes after. When you are going really quickly the energy of accelerating, decelerating, and cornering all becomes constant."

Though Gilles was going very quickly indeed at Monaco, Jody was hard on his heels throughout the Thursday session and with just a few minutes remaining posted the fastest time, well under the track record. Gilles strapped on his last set of qualifiers and went out for a final assault. Jody, having done all he could for the day, sat and watched from the Ferrari pit as Gilles circulated ever quicker until he eclipsed his time by nearly half a second. Said Jody: "There's no point in having a discussion about it. Gilles is simply quicker than me and that's all there is to it."

Jody was wrong. On Saturday he chipped away at the stop-watches and improved his time by almost a second. Gilles was unable to retaliate at first, his car having sprung a fuel leak. He went out for a while in the spare car, then had his regular machine for the last few minutes. He gave it all he had but heavy traffic and the chequered flag left him seven-hundredths of a second slower than Jody. "I think for sure I could have gone quicker with a little more time," said Gilles. "But then again Jody could probably have done the same. I suppose it's all a matter of the drag race into the first corner . . ."

■ ■ ■

Jody won the drag race into Ste. Dévote and he won the Monaco Grand Prix. He smoked his tires at the lights and was gone, followed by Niki Lauda, who shot through from the second row. For one of the very few times in his life Gilles flubbed the start and spent the first two laps looking for a way by Lauda's Brabham. As the cars powered past the pits to begin the third tour of the Rainiers' domain, Gilles darted out from Lauda's slipstream and gained the advantage into Ste. Dévote. He quickly reeled in Jody and sat right on his tail for the next 50 laps. The T4s ran in tandem until lap 54, when Gilles idled into the pits, his car transmissionless.

So Jody was received in the royal box by the Prince and Princess, who plied their honorary subject with the spoils of victory. He sprayed champagne for the second time in two weeks, celebrating not only the win but the lead in the championship: 30 points, versus 24 for Laffite, who failed to score. Meanwhile, Villeneuve was still stuck at 20 and unhappy about it. "I've had bad luck," he said. "I should be ahead by ten points but things have worked the opposite way. Everything's working against me."

But Jody feels he was the author of his own fate. "Gilles was always putting his foot down and running through the gears. He would change gears without taking his foot off the accelerator, which you can do with an old saloon car but you can't do with a Formula One car. When you do that you use more fuel – like he did at Zolder – and the car tends to break down. He probably felt it was faster but the fraction that it helps isn't worth it. And

Monaco has a bump coming out of the corner onto the pit straight. Gilles would go over that flat out so the engine was screaming and when he hit the other side the car had wheelspin and jerked the transmission hard. I used to change gears in between to save the transmission.''

■ ■ ■

In the one-month interval until the French Grand Prix at Dijon there were two major driver changes in Formula 1. Patrick Depailler, a dedicated thrill-seeker, was seriously injured in a hang-gliding accident near his native Clermont Ferrand in France. In his stead, Guy Ligier called in the great Belgian driver Jacky Ickx, whose eight Grand Prix wins included five in Ferraris. Ickx was still winning sports car races regularly (including a record six times at Le Mans) but came back to Ligier from semi-retirement in single-seaters. The other driver change at Dijon, Keke Rosberg in the Wolf, was made necessary by the abrupt and permanent retirement of James Hunt.

The man who was instrumental in getting Gilles Villeneuve into F1 decided he had had enough of it himself. Unlike Gilles, Hunt had fears about racing and, while he never showed it in competition, he admitted to sometimes being physically ill prior to the start of a race. After he helped haul Ronnie Peterson from his flaming Lotus at Monza in 1978 Hunt was so disturbed he was ready to quit then and there. He was calmed by Teddy Mayer, Walter Wolf, and Jody Scheckter and did restart the race, though he drove slowly for a few laps and finally stopped.

In replacing Scheckter at Walter Wolf Racing for the 1979 season Hunt had announced it was to be his last year. But the Wolf was uncompetitive and following the Monaco race Hunt moved to cash in his chips while he was still ahead of the game. After seven Formula 1 years and ninety-two races he had ten wins and a world championship to his credit. Now, one month before his thirty-second birthday, he moved to the safety of the other side of the fence and became a television commentator for the BBC coverage of F1 racing.

■ ■ ■

The Grand Prix de France was an historic day in the republic when a French driver in a French car won the race. It was Jean-Pierre Jabouille's first F1 win and the Renault EF1 motor in his Renault RS11 chassis marked the first victory for a turbo engine.

But hardly anyone remembers July 1, 1979, at Le Circuit Dijon-Prenois for those reasons. They remember it for the electrifying or terrifying (depending on the point of view) wheel-to-wheel, no-holds-barred duel between Jabouille's teammate, René Arnoux, and Gilles Villeneuve. It was one of the fiercest battles ever seen in the history of motor racing.

The 3.800-km track in the heart of French wine country resembles a Mexican sombrero with a slightly battered brim. Certainly it gave the F1 drivers a severe battering in ground-effects cars that were negotiating its succession of switchback curves and up-and-downhill plunges at terrific speeds. Jacky Ickx, fresh from manhandling high-powered Porsche sports cars, confessed the g-forces generated by his unfamiliar Ligier were difficult to bear. By the end of the first day he needed to have his helmet tied to the roll bar to keep his head erect. Other drivers began to sprout neck braces, several complained the cornering forces nearly caused them to black out, and even the prospect of 80 laps in the race gave them a headache.

Their extra horsepower put the Renaults on the front row, with Jabouille just ahead of Arnoux. Gilles was next up after a typically energetic performance, while Jody was an unhappy fifth fastest, complaining of heavy traffic and an understeering T4. The news of the all-French front row lured well over 100,000 loyal spectators to Dijon on Sunday and, though the overcast and cool weather was less than perfect for the crops in the surrounding vineyards, it was ideal breathing weather for turbo engines.

Prior to the start Gilles announced his race strategy. "For me it is very important to get a good start. Somehow I must at least split the Renaults on the first lap. I am not interested in three or four points. This one I want to win, nothing less. I need those points to close on Jody and Jacques. If Jabouille gets into the lead I think it will be impossible to catch him."

The turbo motors were difficult to get under way abruptly and that played into Villeneuve's hand. Jabouille lagged, Arnoux nearly stalled, and Villeneuve took full advantage of their hesitation to blast away in the lead. He did a rather ragged version of a Mexican hat dance all around the first lap, intent on putting as much distance as possible on the sure-to-catch-up Renaults. His scorching pace, ahead of Jabouille, Scheckter, Piquet, and Jumper Jarier, continued for several laps until after five of them he was nearly as many seconds ahead of his pursuers. That Gilles's charge was being made at the expense of his Michelins became evident when Jabouille began to close the gap. Proof positive of pending tire troubles came when Jody had to pit for replacement rubber and was never to get any higher than seventh place, where he finished.

But Arnoux, whose tardy start had dropped him back to ninth place, was certainly not finished. His comeback surge brought him quickly back into contention and by lap 15 the race was between one red Italian car and two yellow-and-black French ones. The Ferrari was behaving ever more luridly – less from the driver's albeit flamboyant style than from rapidly deteriorating tires. It oversteered madly on right-hand corners and behaved exactly the opposite way on left-handers. Jabouille's constant hounding of Gilles paid off on lap 46 when he dove past him at the end of the pit straight and took the lead he kept to the finish.

And thus began the Villeneuve-Arnoux battle. There was a vociferous contingent of *tifosi* on hand in the heart of France, but they had to do their hollering best to make much of a dent in the cheers for Little René. A great crowd favourite, he had come up the hard way into Formula 1 like Gilles. He served a lengthy apprenticeship in the lower echelons of the sport, even doing time as a humble racing mechanic before making it to the big league on driving merit alone. Rumpled and a bit rough around the edges, Arnoux had much of the street urchin about him. His facial expression varied between a look of pure deviltry and perpetual astonishment (the latter aspect seemingly more predominant post-Dijon). Somewhat shy and retiring outside a racing car, he was the reverse behind the wheel, being brave, tough, and determined in much the same way as the man in the Ferrari in front of him.

On lap 71, with just nine to go, Arnoux set the fastest lap of the day, over one full second quicker than the next man, Jabouille, and the French fans screamed mightily at the prospect of a Renault one-two finish. With five laps remaining the second Renault shoved its nose rudely up the Ferrari's gearbox. Two laps later and three to go till the end, the deed was done and Arnoux led Villeneuve over the line. The joyous fans thought it was all over but the shouting – but it had only begun.

Gilles noticed that René was not able to pull away from him, and, indeed, the Renault was stuttering slightly, suffering from fuel pickup problems. It put the cars on a more level playing field, any remaining performance differentials being overridden by the sheer guts of the drivers. The Ferrari pulled alongside the Renault on the inside line for the approach to the Double Droite de Villeroy, the right-hander at the end of the straight. The Ferrari braked at the last possible instant, locking up all four tattered Michelins in fearsome looking puffs of smoke. The Renault held its position, refusing to budge, and the two cars rounded the corner as if welded together.

Nobody – including the two drivers – was able to count the number of times the cars actually clashed together in those final kilometers, how many times their wheels interlocked, how many times they both slid off the circuit, only to regain it in unison and bang together once again. Through the 'S' de Sablieres they careened, around the Gauche de la Bretelle as one, through the Parabolique in unison. Arnoux inched ahead but slid wide and forced Villeneuve into the dirt. Villeneuve held his ground in the flying dust and banged his way back onto the tarmac.

Through the Double Gauche de la Bretelle and out onto the Courbe des Gorgeolles they caromed off each other and into the Virage de la Combe. In a final fit of demonic late-braking Gilles nosed ahead. Arnoux threw all remaining caution to the wind and attempted a suicidal-looking counterattack around the Courbe de Pouas – but it wasn't enough. The Ferrari crossed the finish line on the Ligne Droite de la Fouine after one hour, 35 minutes, and 35.01 seconds of racing. It took the Renault twenty-four one-hundredths of a second longer.

On their cool-down lap the two protaganists, who had just engaged in what was surely the most heart-stopping battle in the 321 races since the world championship series began, raised their arms in a mutual salute of appreciation. The frenzied crowd, their loyalties forgotten, cheered them madly as one. The Ferrari and

Renault cruised into the pits together to be engulfed in a sea of tumult and pandemonium. Somewhere in the crowd Jabouille was being crowned the winner of his first Grand Prix, but all eyes were on the place and show men. The sweat-soaked drivers dismounted, embraced fondly, and congratulated each other.

"No," said René, grinning from ear to ear, "I am not sad to be third. All you needed was for one or the other of us to become frightened and there might have been a terrible accident. But Gilles drove a fantastic race. I enjoyed it very much!"

Gilles was equally high-spirited, laughing and joking. "I tell you, that was really fun! I thought for sure we were going to get on our heads, you know, because when you start interlocking wheels it's very easy for one car to climb over another. But we didn't crash and it's okay. I enjoyed myself amazingly!"

Gilles went back to take a shower in his motorhome, where he was congratulated by his lawyer, Boris Stein, and Gaston Parent, who were over from Montreal to attend to some business for Gilles in Geneva. John Hogan of Marlboro sent word that there would shortly be a screening of a video replay of the Dijon duel in the Marlboro tent. As Gilles and his entourage trooped through the paddock they met up with the Arnoux contingent and the two drivers walked arm-in-arm through the paddock. In the tent, while the others sat in chairs arranged around the screen, Gilles and Rene sat on the ground in the front row. They laughed and giggled, shouted and cheered their performance, louder than anyone in the audience. And from then on Gilles and René were good friends.

■ ■ ■

For René Arnoux, still fighting the Grand Prix wars in his forties, Dijon in 1979 is one of his best racing memories. "I think only two people could do this kind of thing: Villeneuve and me. For me it is the best memory of Gilles. He was a very good guy on the track and in life, too. I liked him because he was a very natural person. He was a very popular guy because he said everything that was in his head. This is very important for me. If Gilles told you something, that's the way it was. No mistake. He spoke every time what he thought."

After his stint at Renault, Arnoux drove for Ferrari for two seasons, then was fired after an internal dispute, at least partly because he dared to criticize the cars. "I remember whenever Gilles was unhappy with his Ferrari he told the truth. He told everybody it was a shit car."

"I think Ferrari has got a wonderful driver," was Enzo Ferrari's reaction to the Villeneuve display at Dijon. His former employee, Mauro Forghieri, has mixed feelings about it. "I think it is the big story in the sport for Gilles. It was a very good story for automobile racing. A nice picture. Nice television. I was angry that day, but what could I do. In my opinion it was too much risk-taking. But as the team engineer in the pits I can stay cool and use my head. The one inside the racing car has a different view."

Most of the rest of the world, having viewed endless replays of the battle on television, thought it was wonderful, if very frightening to see. Mario Andretti termed it a minor incident: "Just a couple of young lions clawing each other." But the Grand Prix Drivers' Safety Committee, Jody Scheckter president, condemned Villeneuve and Arnoux for unruly behaviour. The two were hauled on the carpet before the Committee at the next race, in England, and roundly censured. Jody had spoken to Gilles privately before that.

"When I saw François Cevert killed it was the first time I ever thought about dying in the sport. You have a lot of drivers talking about the excitement, romance, and glamour of the danger. For me that was the ugly part of the sport, an unfortunate part. And I believed I had to do everything in my power to drive as slowly and carefully as possible to give myself more chance – just to keep alive. At first I was always keen to prove myself. Then the truth slowly trickled down to me. But Gilles was always wanting to prove himself, for every lap. I never knew him to say I will take it easy now. It was always the maximum.

"Because I had such a good relationship with Gilles I could talk to him quietly and tell him he was a silly ass. He was intelligent enough to know that it was a stupid thing to do and that you don't last long doing that kind of stuff. But he liked that image of knocking wheels together and the idea of being crazy. He wouldn't admit it was foolhardy but I think he realized it. At

Silverstone we spoke to the two of them in front of everybody. We asked them for their points of view. Then we were tough on them.''

Arnoux recalls the heated session vividly. ''At Silverstone a lot of drivers – Scheckter, Fittipaldi, Regazzoni, and Lauda – said it was too dangerous. 'You guys are completely crazy! You could have a big crash. Etc. Etc.' After Lauda said it was too dangerous, I said, 'Yes, maybe for you and Gilles. But not for me and Gilles.' I said to Niki, 'There is no possibility for you to do that because you would take your foot off the accelerator!' Gilles said to them all it is not dangerous and you are completely stupid to have a meeting for that!''

Two years later Gilles was still talking about it. ''That is my best memory of Grand Prix racing. Those few laps were just fantastic to me – outbraking each other and trying to race for the line, touching each other but without wanting to put the other car out. It was just two guys battling for second place without trying to be dirty but having to touch because of wanting to be first. It was just fantastic! I loved that moment.''

Post-Dijon there was a journalistic furore in the racing press as to whether Villeneuve and Arnoux were heroes or idiots. Of those people who wrote the latter: ''Well, they're a bunch of old women, aren't they!'' says Denis Jenkinson, the dean of British motor-racing journalists who has been covering the sport for over forty years. ''You see the press have never *raced*! They just sit up there in the press room and watch it and say, 'Oh dear, that's too dangerous.' What a load of rubbish!''

Jenkinson, alias ''DSJ'' in the magazine *Motor Sport*, was himself a very brave racer, performing such feats of courage as being a passenger in motorcyle sidecar competition and acting as navigator for Stirling Moss in the Mille Miglia, which they won at an average speed of nearly 100 miles per hour over 1,000 miles of Italian roads. Jenkinson has a shortlist of the drivers he has most admired in each era: Alberto Ascari, Stirling Moss, Jimmy Clark, Gilles Villeneuve, and Ayrton Senna. ''That's the lot. That's my top echelon and he's in it. Villeneuve just drove with tremendous spirit all the time. I loved him for that. He was a hero.''

5

*"The crowds loved him because he, of all the men out
there, was so clearly working without a net."*

—Nigel Roebuck

After Dijon, Boris Stein and Gaston Parent were going to Geneva
to structure Gilles's various commercial enterprises under the
umbrella company Caracer S.A. The business included setting
up a will for Gilles and during the trip to Switzerland with their
client, Stein and Parent were made to realize the need for having
their own affairs in order. Gilles and Joann were with them in a
small rented Volkswagen as they left Dijon late in the evening.

"I was sitting in the front," Joann recalls, "and the lawyer
was driving. Gaston was in the back beside Gilles. Before we
left Gaston told the lawyer not to let Gilles drive, no matter what
happens don't let him get behind the wheel. Gaston fell asleep
and immediately Gilles tapped the lawyer's shoulder and said,
'I'm driving now.' And the lawyer, who had never been in a car
with Gilles, thought, well, this guy's a racing driver so he should
know what he's doing. Gaston soon woke up, because obviously
nobody could sleep, and started yelling at Gilles. But the lawyer
didn't say a word and I thought he was really calm. Then I saw
that his face was white and realized he couldn't speak."

"I told Boris not to give him the goddamn key," says Parent.
"Then there he is sitting beside me in the back and Gilles took
off. And those are the words: Took Off! Shit! We were in the
mountains and the road was full of those flashing lights that mean
dangerous curves, slow down and all that. He had his foot to the
floor all the way. To hell with the flashers! Gilles would come
up behind the back of a truck. You could almost feel the back
of the truck hitting the car. Gilles would pull out for a look on
either side, then he'd pass, very often right in the gravel on the
wrong side. God! I left half my stomach back there. When we
made it to Geneva that night Boris tells me that now he knows
what I meant. But it was too late. My ulcers were very bad."

■ ■ ■

The next Grand Prix necessitated a journey across the English Channel to Silverstone, but Gilles might just as well have stayed at home. The Ferrari T4s were much less competitive on the ultra-fast circuit where real ground effects were the only way to go. Jody qualified 11th and Gilles 13th. In addition to his reprimand from the GPDA Safety Committee, Gilles came away from Silverstone with no points, the victim of fuel vaporization, tire troubles, and bad handling. But Jody stayed around long enough to collect fifth place behind Regazzoni's winning Williams.

Jody's result strengthened his lead to six points over Gilles and he was putting pressure on Ferrari to give him better support in the championship hunt. "After Dijon I complained like mad to Piccinini and Forghieri to give me more of the best and to hold Gilles back. My point was that I was leading but they were still letting us race each other and we could wind up with neither of us winning. But they wouldn't do anything."

There was more aggravation for Jody in this regard at the German Grand Prix. Hockenheim's configuration, with longer straights and fewer fast curves, masked the ground-effects deficiencies of the T4s and Jody started fifth. Gilles qualified ninth on the grid, powersliding around in entertaining fashion. In the race Gilles's progress was even more wild and uneven when the rear wing began to fall apart and he pitted while running in fifth place to have it and four tires replaced. On his return he recorded the fastest race lap and was soon circulating in close company with his teammate. Jody had no idea whether Gilles was on the same lap or not and looked for his pit to advise him of Gilles's position. No message was forthcoming and Jody became increasingly agitated, gesticulating vigorously each time he passed the Ferrari pit. Finally the signal board advised him that Gilles was no threat to his fourth place and Jody duly finished there. Gilles was classified eighth and out of the points again, while Alan Jones won for Williams.

■ ■ ■

Across the border at the Grosser Preis von Osterreich the three championship contenders, Villeneuve, Laffite, and Scheckter, finished second, third, and fourth behind the runaway winner, Alan Jones. But the second-place man provided the main interest in the race with a spectacular start that seasoned observers called the most brilliant seen for perhaps twenty years in Grand Prix racing.

Both Ferraris were handling badly in early qualifying but the bugs were ironed out on the second day to the point that Gilles was fifth quickest. His time came despite a lengthy off-road excursion that ended with his car thumping an earth bank. Jody was an unhappy ninth on the grid and after practice he took Forghieri down to the Williams pit for a closer look at a proper ground-effects car. The Saudia Williams FW07, making full use of generous funding from Middle East sponsorship, was obviously now the car to beat. Here it had carried Jones to the front row beside the turbocharged Renault of Arnoux.

The narrow start/finish area at the Osterreichring (the scene of many first-lap accidents in later years) was a precarious stage for the drama that unfolded as the Austrian Grand Prix began. Gilles was on the inside of the third row of the grid, alongside Regazzoni and behind the second-row men, Lauda and Jabouille, who in turn sat behind Jones and poleman Arnoux. As the field sat waiting for the green light all twenty-four drivers concentrated intently on getting the timing of their getaways absolutely right and when it came on they rocketed away in unison – all except for Gilles.

His T4 sprang forth as if shot from a cannon, zooming past Jabouille's yellow-and-black Renault on the inside, then squeezing between the similar car of Arnoux and the pit wall in a space hardly wider than the Ferrari. Snicking through the gears, foot to the floor, Gilles powered up the hill into the lead, ahead of a somewhat startled following of Jones, Lauda, Arnoux, Regazzoni, and the rest. "I was half expecting a yellow car to come through at the start," said Jones, "but no way a red one. I was really taken aback and thought, where the hell did he come from!?"

Jones knew Gilles's start was a triumph of quicker reaction time, not Ferrari superiority, and the Williams advantage would soon tell the tale on the sweeping curves of the Austrian venue. The Australian assumed his rightful place on lap five and was never headed again. Gilles then did strenuous battle with the Renaults until their turbopower carried them through. But Jabouille dropped out early with gearbox problems and Arnoux had to pit for extra fuel in the late going, leaving Gilles a solid second place at the finish. Jody had been running third, but complained of fading brakes. Jacques Laffite pounced on this deficiency and snatched third place on the very last lap.

The Austrian results tied Villeneuve and Laffite at 32 points, behind Scheckter's 38, and Gilles was highly pleased with second place on such a circuit. He was all smiles and joked in understatement about how his race began. "I made quite a good start, I think. And I drove absolutely as hard as I could throughout the race. But there was no way I could hold back Alan or René. Of course, no one likes to be second. But today I am happy with it."

■ ■ ■

Villeneuve's fighting spirit was now the talking point in the Italian press, where it was decided that Scheckter had given way to Laffite too easily in Austria. Beyond their driving performances, the pro-Villeneuve faction pointed out that Scheckter was still unable to speak Italian whereas Villanova was becoming quite proficient in the language. Gilles, they said, was a much more friendly man and better liked within the team. They had each won two races and Scheckter had more points, it was claimed, only because he finished more often. Why then, went the printed questions, was Villeneuve not given number-one status? As it developed, both drivers improved their Italian reputations in the next race, among the sand dunes along the coast of the North Sea.

The Grote Prijs van Nederland was the scene of continued success by Jones, who won from Scheckter and Laffite. Gilles saw his championship hopes fade but his in-car antics, albeit in a losing cause, again made headlines. He qualified sixth, immediately behind his teammate. Before the race both of them made practice starts, coming to a halt on the circuit, then roaring away in a glorious blast of Ferrari sound and fury. In the start proper Gilles got it right but Jody faltered, his clutch having overheated, and was immediately swamped by the pack.

Gilles's blazing beginning took him beyond Regazzoni, Jabouille, and Arnoux but his audaciousness caused grief among those he overtook. They were four abreast along the pit straight and "Regga" was crowded into the wall by Arnoux. The Williams lost a wheel and tricycled along at something like 160 kph before coming to a mercifully safe halt. Clay was livid, if unhurt, and gained a measure of satisfaction when the Renault of Arnoux was rendered hors de combat with one wheel askew.

While the number 11 Ferrari of Scheckter began an uphill fight from 18th place, its number 12 counterpart hung onto the gearbox of the leading white Williams for 10 laps. As they hurtled by the pits at top speed toward the notorious right-hand 180-degree Tarzan corner, Villeneuve darted out to the left from Jones's slipstream, intent on taking him under braking. The tough Australian refused to budge as the Canadian pulled alongside on the entry into Tarzan. In a colossal clash of wills the two colonials held their ground all the way around the curve. Gilles, on the outside, looked for a moment as if he had overdone it, his vigorous application of the brakes snapping the tail out of line. But he corrected it at the last moment, stomped on the power again fractionally faster than Jones, and inched ahead as they exited the curve. The crowd, which had been holding its collective breath, gave a tremendous cheer at such a display of bravado on one of motor racing's most difficult corners.

Gilles forged ahead and 10 laps later had four seconds in hand over Jones. By now the charging Scheckter was up to third, his tremendously aggressive comeback having included the disposal of Pironi's Tyrrell around the outside of Tarzan in a manner similar to that of Gilles. But all was not well in the cockpit of the leading Ferrari. Several times it skittered precariously around Tarzan following locked brake slides on the approach to the corner, and Jones was soon in close attendance again. "It was oversteering worse and worse and I thought the tires had just gone off," Gilles said later.

It was indeed a tire problem; the left rear was slowly deflating and on lap 47 it caused him to spin at the chicane on the back section of the circuit. The Ferrari gyrated viciously, sending up clouds of smoking rubber and forcing the closely following Jones to brake violently in avoidance. As was his custom, Gilles sorted out the spin satisfactorily and continued, though now in second place to Jones, who went on to an untroubled victory ahead of a splendid second for Jody. Gilles's race was only a lap and a half from being run but his grand exit was one of the most spectacular ever seen.

Coming past the pits the deflating tire suddenly lost all its remaining air and collapsed like a spent balloon. The T4 twitched back and forth violently, surely destined for a resounding crash into the barriers at Tarzan. Worse than that, it seemed on a collision course for the previously crashed and abandoned Arrows of Patrese. Gilles sawed away at the steering wheel, the useless rear tire unable to provide adequate purchase for full-scale panic braking. At the last moment, he deliberately cranked the wheel hard to induce a spin to scrub off speed. The Ferrari slewed sideways, then backwards in a cloud of smoke from three surviving Michelins, supplemented by a spectacular shower of sparks from the culprit wheel. The car ground to a halt on the grass just short of disaster, its engine stalled. The appreciative crowd hooted and yelled their approval of such masterful car control, but the show was only starting and everyone gaped in astonishment at what followed.

Gilles jabbed away at the starter button and finally got the flat 12 to fire up again. He jammed the gearlever into reverse and shot back onto the circuit, selected first, and clanked away toward his obvious goal – the pits – nearly four kilometers away. The crippled Ferrari clawed its way around Zandvoort, the right front wheel pawing the air and the remains of the left rear banging and crashing around in a shower of sparks and mangled rubber. Gilles was soon nearly up to a speed worthy of an able-bodied machine, but even Enzo Ferrari's stoutest fabrication was unable to withstand such punishment.

Halfway round the circuit the rear wheel wound itself up into a ball and dragged behind like a flailing anchor. The rear of the chassis sat down on the road and an even greater display of sparks and flying bodywork issued forth. Finally the remains of the Ferrari lurched drunkenly into the pits, where Gilles presented the wreckage to Forghieri. He remained in the cockpit, dancing on the end of his safety harness tether as he signalled the crew to get busy and replace the offending wheel.

Gaston Parent was standing by. "Gilles was blowing his stack, yelling, 'Put a fucking wheel on there! Let me go out again!'

Finally they made him see the back of the car was a disaster. Then people criticized him for dangerous driving again. His argument was that he didn't know it was so bad. But, believe me, Villeneuve would have gone out again on three wheels! That was the way he was.''

■ ■ ■

"Blind madness!'' ''Inconceivable habitual exhibitionism!'' ''Stupid, dangerous behaviour!'' were some of the negative comments in the press on Villeneuve at Zandvoort. But those with long memories paralleled his performance with the likes of Bernd Rosemeyer in 1937 and Alberto Ascari in 1953 – both of whom persevered on three wheels. And the man with the longest memory of all, Enzo Ferrari, absolved Gilles of any wrongdoing. ''Villeneuve still makes some ingenious mistakes, but is a man who wants to come out on top at all costs. He has been justifiably criticized, but we mustn't forget that his enthusiasm and passion have had a predecessor: Tazio Nuvolari. In 1935 Nuvolari won the Brno Grand Prix in Czechoslovakia driving on three wheels.''

And Nigel Roebuck, writing of Gilles in *Autosport* (as he was doing more and more frequently), spoke for all enthusiasts: ''Thank God there will always be a few people in this world who simply know not how to give in. It was foolhardy, yes, but it came from the same pure competitiveness and spirit which has characterized all his races. He likes to *win*, rather than not lose.''

Denis Jenkinson was another to speak for the defence then, as he does now. ''Get the car back to the pits, by all means. It might be mendable and you go on racing. I can understand those people who chastised him at Zandvoort – those people who never raced. It's as simple as that. If you're a *racer* and you're out there *racing*, if it will move – drive it!''

These were exactly the sentiments of the racer in question when he gave his account of the 1979 Dutch Grand Prix. Had he come into the pits when he first felt something wrong with the handling, ''I would have lost all chance of winning.'' And after his spin: ''Strapped into the car all I realized was that it could still move. I knew that something was badly wrong, but as long as it moved I thought there was a chance of it being repaired. For me, as long as the car is running, I will drive it.''

6

*"His judgement at high speed, his reflexes, his tenacity
and sheer excitement in his driving made all of us go out
on the circuit just to see him in action."*
— Denis Jenkinson

On the eve of the Italian Grand Prix Villeneuve considered his
chances of overtaking Scheckter for the title. If Jody won at
Monza he would be World Champion, but Gilles could still do
it if he won all three remaining races. "I know there is an outside
chance that I could get it but I have resigned myself to not
succeeding. In this game you just don't get that kind of luck.
But I'll still keep fighting . . ."

The Renaults were on the front row at Monza, with Jody on
the second beside Jones and Gilles on the third beside Regazzoni.
But for the enormous throng of *tifosi* in attendance, the French
and English cars were incidental to what was a two-horse race
— prancing horses, that is.

Jody gave them what they wanted to see by leading the first
lap from Arnoux, while the crowd favourite in the number 12
Ferrari was third ahead of Laffite, Jabouille, Regazzoni, and
Piquet. On lap five the latter two touched and Piquet's Brabham
crashed mightily on the super-fast Curva Grande. There were
flames and fears of a repeat of the previous year's accident to
Peterson, but Piquet, amazingly, was only shaken up. His car
split in two, ending up with the engine ablaze on one side of the
road and the lucky Brazilian sitting some distance away in the
remains of the cockpit.

Arnoux had turbocharged his way past Jody but lap 13 was
his unlucky one — the Renault motor began to misfire and René's
first time as a Grand Prix leader ended. There was no sympathy
for the retiring Renault as the joyous *tifosi* now found their cars
running one-two, with Gilles riding shotgun to Jody's world
championship-clinching first place.

Faithfully, Gilles held off a challenge from Laffite, who thereafter retired with a blown engine. And when Gianclaudio Regazzoni moved his Williams into third behind Maranello's finest,
all was as it should be in the fiftieth annual Gran Premio d'Italia.

Clay's win here in 1975 had been the last Ferrari victory at Monza. It seemed Enzo Ferrari might hear the cheer back in his villa when Jody crossed the line .46 seconds ahead of Gilles.

"I don't know how I feel. Ask me tomorrow!" was all Jody could say about his title-winning race. On the victory stand, overlooking a tumultuous sea of Ferrari flag- and banner-waving *tifosi*, he and Gilles were cheered as equals. Jody was the World Champion in a Ferrari but his teammate was the undisputed winner of the affections of prancing-horse afficionadoes. And Gilles, after being thanked profusely by the team for his contribution, announced that he was looking forward to the last two races in North America, when team orders would no longer be in effect.

"It wasn't a present for Jody, you know," said Gilles. "I was trying hard." And several times in the last five laps he pulled alongside his teammate as if to signify that it was honour, not inferiority, that was keeping him in check. He joked about it: "I suppose the thing I should say is that I never felt as if I could touch Jody, he was that good . . ."

And Jody was keeping a watchful eye on his teammate. "I must say that during the last few laps – as much as I trusted Gilles – I was looking in my mirrors more than usual. On the last lap I slowed right down in one section, then just went as fast as I could for insurance to keep ahead to the finish line. I would have been very surprised if he had tried anything, but I always look for surprises.

"At Monza I lived the best moments of my life when I switched off the engine and got out of the car. I saw the crowd going wild, climbing the fences, waving Ferrari flags. It was great. I felt a keen sense of pleasure and it grew in me so that I glowed inside. When I won, when I began to realize the fact and allowed a year's tension to drain out, I had a lump in my throat as I walked through the paddock with all the police around me. When I get a lump in my throat it's quite something . . .

"That night we all went out to dinner with the mechanics and Gilles said I had taught him some things. He said I had done a great job and now he realized the championship was really what it was all about. He was the star all the time in the press, which made it a lot tougher on me. But Gilles said now that it was all settled he realized having your name in the paper wasn't worth toilet paper if you didn't win."

While Gilles was gracious in defeat he was convinced it was fate, not Jody, that beat him. "This has been a dreadfully unlucky year for me," he said after Monza. "I don't think I could have gone any harder than I have, but I just did not get the breaks, while Jody did. That is the only difference between us. The turning point for me came in the race in Holland. If only I could have finished in the points there, I'm sure it would have been a different story for the rest of the season. Jody has been a very lucky man, but that's the way it goes in motor racing. Jody might have become World Champion but I know who has been driving the hardest this year, and in the States and Canada I'll be doing my best to prove it."

■ ■ ■

Gilles had another chance to prove himself before the North American races, at a non-championship event on the Autodromo Dino Ferrari. Named after Enzo's late son and previously used mainly for motorcycle racing, the circuit just east of Maranello would host the Italian Grand Prix in 1980 and this race was intended as a dress rehearsal. Not everyone took it seriously – only fifteen cars showed up – but the 40,000 spectators were only interested in the home team anyway. Gilles did not disappoint, taking pole position over Jody, while Reutemann (Lotus-Ford) and Lauda (Brabham-Alfa Romeo) sat on the second row and were the main opposition.

Gilles led Jody at the start but after a few laps both Ferraris began to slip and slide with tire problems. Lauda passed Jody with no problem but Gilles was less accommodating. It took Niki several laps of trying before he gained the advantage. His lead lasted less than a lap before Gilles had repassed him. They traded places once more, then the Brabham braked unexpectedly, breaking the Ferrari's nose in the process.

Gilles pitted post-haste for a new nose section and tires, returned to the circuit, and promptly set fastest lap in a time nearly as quick as his pole position. He continued to circulate at the highest possible speed and in his customarily entertaining fashion and the 40,000 members of the Gilles Villeneuve fan club on hand were exceedingly pleased. Though Niki (who dedicated his win to Enzo Ferrari, with whom he was effecting a reconciliation of sorts), Carlos, and Jody stood on the podium for first, second, and third, and Gilles was only seventh, he received by far the loudest cheers of the day.

■ ■ ■

"La Fièvre Villeneuve" was the publicity rallying cry for the Grand Prix of Canada. And from the intense pressure on him at his home race it was a wonder that Gilles did not succumb to his own fever. He was towed around to an exhausting series of promotional appearances organized with split-second precision. A typical day included: a dawn breakfast meeting with the race sponsor, Labatt; a 9:00 a.m. interview on Radio-Canada; a helicopter dash to an 11:30 reception in the town hall at Berthierville; a 12 o'clock rendezvous with the Premier of Quebec; head-table guest at publicity lunch an hour later; an afternoon press conference; an hour at a radio phone-in show; back to a Montreal department store for a featured appearance; an evening organized by an association of Italian businessmen.

On another day's excursion into Ontario, Gilles was caught speeding from a press conference in Hamilton to another in Toronto. His car was stopped by an off-duty policeman who happened to be wearing a T-shirt with the number 12 on it. His misdemeanour cost Gilles only an autograph but all the dashing about, speech-making, and photograph-posing were fatiguing. "The way things have been going it will be like a holiday for me once the racing begins. I can't wait to get into the car. It's quiet there!"

Of the event he had won in 1978 Gilles gave a prophetic forecast. "The pressure will definitely be worse on me this year. But I won't take the race any differently than any others. I certainly don't think I can take any more chances than I already do. We are not as competitive now as we were a month ago. It seems we are lacking some adhesion; part of it is tires but not all of it. The problem is hard to find. But Montreal is my favourite race on the circuit. It's the type of track that, even if a car is not working properly, you can still squeeze out a good finish."

■ ■ ■

Gilles had one less competitor when Niki Lauda walked away from another Grand Prix of Canada, this time permanently. (Or so he thought, because he unretired himself again in 1982.) For some time Niki had been questioning the wisdom of continuing in his profession. In Montreal he was mindful of how his life had so very nearly ended in his 1976 accident. "The priest came in and gave me the last rites. He crossed my shoulder and said 'Goodbye, my friend.' I nearly had a heart attack! I wanted someone to help me live in this world, not pass me on to the next. So I clung onto the voices and to my wife's strength. I would not let myself become unconscious because I was afraid I would die."

His motivation waning, he had demanded a $2-million contract with Bernie Ecclestone to continue with Brabham in 1980 and had finally gotten it. "And that was the moment I realized the bubble had burst," Niki wrote in *To Hell And Back*. "Scarcely had I won the day against Bernie, when I found the whole business no longer interested me. And the prospect of two million dollars didn't really change matters. Previously, I had hoped that a fortune like that would motivate me again and bring a new sense of excitement to my career."

Lauda had also hoped for inspiration from Brabham's new Ford-engined cars, which were debuted in Montreal. He tried one for fifteen minutes or so but found the thrill was gone. He had spent eight years driving 12-cylinder machines from BRM, Ferrari, and Alfa and "they always gave me a sense of pleasure, with their high revs, shrill note, and sheer aggression." The Cosworth-modified Ford's noise was "flatter, muted. Everything seems slower; boring somehow. . . . All at once the curtain comes down. I have only one thought: you don't belong here. Go and do something else." And he did. On Friday afternoon Niki was on a plane out of Montreal, bound for Los Angeles to buy a new Lear jet for Lauda Air.

As Lauda left the Bonaventure Hotel in Montreal he met Arturo Merzario, one of the drivers who had pulled him from his burning Ferrari at the Nürburgring. "At the Ring my life was saved for the first time," he said to Little Art. "I've just saved it for the second time, today."

Ecclestone hired a spectating driver, Ricardo Zunino, to fill the vacancy and the Argentinian, wearing Lauda's helmet, qualified carefully near the back, then finished a creditable seventh in the race. The behind-the-scenes machinations at Brabham were largely unnoticed by the crowd at Le Circuit Ile Notre-Dame, who concentrated on the boy from Berthier. He kept them busy, flying around at a terrific rate on the slightly revised track. Two S bends had been straightened out and two other curves were smoother and quicker. The circuit was faster for everyone, particularly Alan Jones, whose better ground-effective Williams bested Gilles's T4 for pole by over half a second.

The World Champion-elect languished back in ninth place on the grid but Jody was noticeably more relaxed and smiling now that his ambition had been achieved. He had nothing to lose and resolved to enjoy himself. Meanwhile, Jody's former employer, Walter Wolf, was reduced to the role of ordinary spectator, Keke Rosberg having crashed the only remaining example of the Wolf in qualifying. With Walter in the process of winding up the operations of his Formula 1 team, Gilles was left to fly the Canadian flag alone – which he did, fabulously.

■ ■ ■

At the green light Gilles nearly did a drag-racing wheelie as he catapulted ahead of Jones. Behind them Jody went wider than the tarmac in an effort to catch them but only managed to kick up a dust storm. He fell back to 12th place, which by the end of the afternoon became fourth, behind Regazzoni. However, everyone else tended to get lost in the shuffle that was the epic struggle at the front. Villeneuve and Jones fought fiercely for all 72 laps of a memorable Canadian Grand Prix.

Gilles's strategy, as ever, was simply to go flat out all the way, while Alan Jones had a more circumspect plan of action, worked out previously with his boss, Frank Williams. "Before the race I talked with Frank and we decided that if Villeneuve beat me from the start I would sit behind him and save the car as much as I could, at least until lap 30."

When the required distance into the race had been reached Jones found the second part of his plan, to pass Gilles, was not going to be easy. Time after time the white car nosed alongside the red one only to be shouldered back into submission. The Williams was undoubtedly the quicker machine, but the man behind the wheel of the Ferrari made up the difference.

Finally, on lap 50, Jones made a slightly faster exit from the chicane to gain precious centimeters for the run down the straight leading to the hairpin. Jones took the inside line under braking, but Gilles stuck to him like glue and the two cars rounded the right-angle corner in unison. Jones proved to be as keen an adversary as Arnoux at Dijon and the cars banged wheels. On the inside, the Williams was better placed for the exit and accelerated away in the lead. There was an audible moan from the 100,000 enthralled spectators, but Villeneuve continued to entertain, scrabbling around on worn tires to finish less than a second behind Jones.

On the podium Jones raised Gilles's arm in tribute, having thoroughly enjoyed their spirited race-long dispute. Both drivers found the duel immensely satisfying and Alan Jones, himself exhibiting a touch of "Villeneuve Fever," spoke for everyone when he said, "Jeez, this little guy just won't give up."

Later Jones elaborated. "I just couldn't believe it. That guy just would not accept that he was beaten. I sweated like hell pulling out a couple of seconds on him, relaxed a fraction through a couple of corners, and there he was in my mirrors again. That bloody red shit-bucket was all over me! I just had to keep running flat out all the way to the finish because I knew if I let him past me there would be no second chance to get ahead again!"

The winner's team leader, with one proviso, was also complimentary to Gilles. Said Frank Williams: "Although I don't particularly agree with his daredevil style, he has done more for Grand Prix racing this season than all the other drivers combined."

■ ■ ■

Gilles contributed even more to the sport and to his own growing legend the next weekend at Watkins Glen. The patented Villeneuve display began on Friday when the track was soaked and few cars even ventured out of the pits. In fact, most drivers thought the flooded tarmac was simply undriveable. Gilles did not share their opinion and Denis Jenkinson was there. "When we saw him going out in the rain, we said, 'This we've got to see!' Some members of the press, who think they know it all, don't bother to go out when it rains. But I was out on a corner in the rain watching him and all the hardball members of the press were with me. We had to see this. It was something special. Oh, he was fantastic! He was unbelievable!''

Another hardballer on hand was Nigel Roebuck. ''Gilles was the one bloke who made you go and look for a good corner in a practice session because you knew that where everybody else would go through as if on rails Gilles would be worth watching. That day in the rain at Watkins Glen was almost beyond belief! It truly was. You would think he had 300 horsepower more than anybody else. It just didn't seem possible. The speed he was travelling didn't bear any relation to anybody else. *He was 11 seconds faster!* Jody was next fastest and couldn't believe it, saying that he scared himself rigid! I remember Laffite in the pits just giggling when Gilles went past and saying, 'Why do we bother? He's different from the rest of us. On a separate level.' ''

Jeff Hutchinson, another British journalist, was also a greatly impressed witness. ''The spectacle of him pushing that Ferrari to the limit, with great roostertails of water cascading off its rear wheels, just for the sheer fun and thrill of it, made the wet feet and miserable wait worthwhile. He lapped at an average speed of just over 100 mph!''

''That was fun!'' said Gilles, grinning widely as was his custom after such feats. But he was of the opinion that he might have been quicker. ''I was flat in fifth on the straight, about 160 mph. It should have been faster but the engine had a misfire and was down about 600 revs. But for that I could have gone quite a bit faster, but then maybe I would have crashed.'' However, his car was less manageable on dry Michelins and on Saturday Gilles's best efforts produced only third on the grid behind Jones and Piquet. With a grin he said, ''I will just have to make one of my usual good starts.'' And he did that, with the help of more rain that fell half an hour before the start, forcing most people to start on wet tires.

Gilles was past Piquet in a flash and alongside Jones under braking for the first corner. ''I was trying really hard to get up beside Jones and then I thought I was going to spin as we went into the corner.'' He put two wheels off the circuit but managed to straighten it all out and lead Jones for the next 31 laps. Villeneuve was in the best possible position because everyone else had heavy spray to contend with, their only navigational aids being the tiny red tail lights on preceding cars.

Before the race was half over the number of Grand Prix cars put out of action by the wet conditions exceeded the total destroyed overnight in The Bog. And the flames from those hijacked and torched vehicles – nine of them – were snuffed out in the dampness of race day but the distasteful odour from The Glen's ghetto of madness lingered in the air. While the visiting press were again dismayed by this strange aspect of life in the New World, one native from north of the U.S. border was doing his best to distract them.

Gilles continued to sail around in the wet at a high rate of knots with Jones rather far astern. While Gilles held his own at the front, Jody did better than that following an early spin that relegated him to the back of the field. He passed everyone in sight bar the two leaders and was up with them, in third behind Jones, on the 13th lap. The track was drying now and Jody stopped for slick tires as did many others. By lap 30 Gilles and Jones had lapped the entire field but the changing conditions favoured the Goodyear-tired Williams and two laps later it went by the Ferrari.

Gilles pitted for dry tires, losing half a lap to Jones in the process. But that was erased once and for all when Jones made his stop. He was delayed when a wheel nut gave trouble to the Williams crew. Then, in their anxiety to get Jones out of the pits ahead of Gilles, the team sent him away before the nut was properly tightened. He only made it 500 meters before the offending wheel dropped off. There were no three-wheel heroics from Jones as the Williams slid off the circuit to a permanent halt. Nor were there from Jody Scheckter, whose Ferrari shed a tire exactly as Gilles's had done at Zandvoort. Jody parked it and walked back to the pits – the first time he had done so all season.

Thus Gilles won his third race of 1979, the fourth of his Formula 1 career, and he finished just four points short of Jody's world championship total of 51 points.

7

TRYING TIMES: 1980

I

"Villeneuve's approach to motor racing is possibly too passionate – too instinctive and immediate – to ever bring him a world championship, but it does explain why he is worshipped across the world like no other driver."

– Nigel Roebuck

The final points score showed Gilles to be the second-best driver in the world in 1979, but he was without doubt the racer of the year. In the season total of 975 racing laps he led almost a third of them – 308. Jones was in the lead for 216 laps and the World Champion, Scheckter, just 170. Gilles had six quickest race laps, versus two each for Regazzoni, Laffite, and Arnoux, while Jones, Depailler, and Piquet had one each. Gilles was leading in seven of the fifteen races but he only won three. Jody led in only four races but also won three. (For that matter, Alan Jones won four races, yet finished third in the championship.)

The difference between the World Champion and the runnerup came down to that most fundemental racing truth: to finish first you have to first finish. Enzo Ferrari said, "A Formula 1 car today is made up of 8,200 parts and in order to achieve a positive result it's necessary for everything to work perfectly." While his "Prince of Destruction" was too hard on those parts too often, Enzo affirmed that "We are fond of both Villeneuve and Scheckter. They both have the same urgent needs."

Reflecting on his 1979 season, Gilles admitted how his sense of urgency might have been his downfall. "I was fairly unlucky in comparison to Jody. But I admit it is up to each driver to make his own luck and Jody did well to conserve his. Perhaps I still have something to learn in this area. But I am a better driver than I was a year ago and I hope I'll be better a year from now. You should always be gaining a bit. Experience. Speed. Everything. I'm sure I'm smarter now than I was. I didn't spin as often."

But Gilles was unlikely to change his philosophy: "I will never ease off, except when I am first. I have never got out of a car and said, 'I could have tried harder.' " And winning still wasn't the only thing. The pleasure for him lay in the act of racing, not just the results. "Take Long Beach. That was a pretty easy run, I can tell you. The car worked perfectly and all I had to do was keep going, making certain I didn't make a stupid error. But, take Montreal, when I finished second to Jones. I put *everything* I had into that race and I got tremendous satisfaction from finishing second. And that final lap with Arnoux at Dijon was fantastic!

"Last year, I believe that I proved to myself and to the people in racing that I was quick in a Formula One car. Now I've proved I belong here and that's very important to me. I want to be considered worthy of being one of the few people in the world who can be Grand Prix drivers. I can't say how long I'll be with Ferrari. Most drivers don't stay with any one team for more than about three years. Then they usually figure they can get a better car, or a better deal somewhere else. And quite often the engineers will become disenchanted with a driver and will want to start looking around."

But Forghieri was not looking around, and after his happiest season ever at Ferrari he paid tribute to both his drivers. "Scheckter: a serious professional, an expert driver. Villeneuve: a knowledgeable driver with a tremendous will to succeed." And Marco Piccinini was equally pleased with his French-Canadian driver. "I got along fine with Gilles. I was sometimes in a difficult situation because I was involved in negotiations with the drivers and represented management. With Gilles I never had any specific problems because he always had clear ideas and knew what he wanted. He was very determined about what he wanted but it was always possible to discuss it on a realistic basis with him and to reach a very quick and lasting understanding."

Gilles was becoming a main cog in the wheel of the team and beginning to appreciate how the mind of the founder worked. "Mr. Ferrari likes his drivers to compete with each other and he expects full effort from everybody on the team. But he doesn't want the drivers to do anything dangerous. He just wants to make sure we get the most out of ourselves. I can't imagine him being a racing driver, although I know he used to be very good at it. When I see him in his office, behind his big desk, he looks more like an organizer, maybe even a godfather. But he's a kind man and sometimes I think he sees himself as a father to his drivers. He keeps a picture of his son Dino in his office and I know it was very difficult for Mr. Ferrari when his son died."

In discussing his future, Gilles maintained that he would race for "another six, seven, eight, or maybe ten years. Really it's hard to say right now, but I guess I'll drive until I'm forty." It would depend on how long he was able to remain competitive. "I think it's absolutely pathetic when people struggle on, being paid by a professional team, when they are over the hill. I think that I would hate myself tremendously if the best I was capable of doing was running sixth. I feel I would have to give up right then."

Thus, when the time came to stop he would recognize it and act upon it as Hunt and Lauda had done, even if it was in mid-season. "I know people say, 'Well, shit, for the sake of all their sponsors and the people who want to see them, they should have stayed.' Sure, but the people at home and in the grandstands don't risk anything. Maybe this will make people understand how demanding racing is. James was very good for Formula One in his way, and so was Niki. They were two very important people. There are never enough superstars, so Formula One loses by losing both of them.

"When you decide you don't want to do it anymore – then why keep on racing? If you stay to finish the season when you don't want to do it, that's when things really get dangerous. It's not like golf or tennis where, if you make a mistake, maybe your arm hurts for a week. Here, you can get killed.''

For now, and the foreseeable future, the positives far outweighed the negatives for Gilles. "First, I love motor racing. If I didn't like racing cars, there is nothing that would make me do it because it's far too dangerous. I love driving the car right to the limit, feeling it drifting and knowing the car is right at its maximum. Hitting that limit, the absolute flat-out fastest that a car will go through a corner, is a tremendous feeling – an absolutely fantastic sensation. It doesn't matter if there's anyone watching or even if there's a stopwatch on me. By itself, it is enough.

"Then there's the super feeling of achievement in beating someone else. It's egocentric, but boiled right down, it's what racing is all about – beating the other guy. There is the money, too, and I don't deny I like that. But if there were no money in Formula One, just enough to live on, I would still do it. As it happens, there is money, so I'm like everyone else. I want to get as much as possible. Everyone does. I think I'm basically a lazy person, so I hope to make enough money so I can retire and spend it doing nothing. But I'm not doing it mainly for the money.''

He was always matter of fact about what he did in a racing car, no matter which language he spoke: "J'ai fait ma jobbe." (I did my job.) "When I say racing is my job, it is a job when you look at what you owe your team and your sponsors. They pay you to do that job. They pay you to be quicker than the next guy. In that sense it is just a job and when a race is over and I've won, I've done my job. Period. Then I'd like to go home to Joann and the children.''

2

"If he could come back and live his life again, I think he would do exactly the same – and with love."

– Jody Scheckter

Home for the Villeneuves was no longer the villa at Plascassier. It belonged to a Belgian who had built it for his retirement and Gilles wanted a more permanent residence, closer to his main place of work. At the time the autoroute through the south of France was unfinished in the Cannes area and Gilles's many trips to Fiorano from Plascassier were made more laborious. Having to take one of the heavily travelled corniche routes to make his autoroute connection cost Gilles at least an extra hour of his valuable time. Joann suggested they move to Italy but Gilles was adamant the children should be brought up in French. So a compromise was reached with a decision to locate in Monaco. Racing drivers have always lived there, for tax reasons as much as for the glamorous lifestyle, and this is what brought the Villeneuves to the principality.

Gilles's Montreal lawyer, Boris Stein, advised Gaston Parent that the residence in Plascassier would cause Gilles to be taxed heavily under the French system. Parent helped with the house-hunting and eventually they came up with an apartment next door to the building where Jody Scheckter lived. The vacant apartment belonged to the late Ronnie Peterson and they rented it from his widow Barbro. "But Gilles didn't like the idea of his kids living in an apartment block," says Parent. "He wanted his two feet on the ground and the kids', too."

Gilles's idea was to establish the Peterson flat as his official residence but have the family continue to live in Plascassier. Through Walter Wolf, Parent had met a senior official in the French police, who suggested this was unworkable because with his high profile Gilles's scheme was bound to be discovered by zealous French tax authorities interested in having his contributions to the republic's treasury. So the hunt for a permanent Monaco home began.

Available dwellings were in short supply in this confined area of a mere 150 hectares of some of the world's most expensive real estate. The search continued for some time until a vacant villa was found in Monte Carlo, the easternmost section of the principality. The property, off a twisting street high up on a terrace, lay in ruins behind high walls. It was called La Mascotte and belonged to a jeweller whose heirs had been fighting over its ownership since his death seven years earlier. The roof leaked, the interior was a wreck, and the gardens were overgrown in unkempt foliage. But the Villeneuves saw possibilities – it had grounds for the kids to play in, even space for a small swimming pool. Prince Rainier, who has the final say in all real estate transactions, gave the project his blessing, no doubt pleased to have another illustrious subject in his domain.

Gaston Parent handled the transaction. "They wanted a million-two or three for it. I said that's beyond our reach. So they said make an offer. I said $750,000 and it was accepted. It cost half a million bucks to repair, so we got back to a million-two, but at least it paid off. It's worth several times that now."

The interior was gutted, the plumbing, heating, and electricity were redone, a large garage, workshop, office, and separate apartment were blasted out of the rock in the basement, and a pool was installed in the garden, one of the very few private pools in Monte Carlo. Gilles insisted on having North American appliances and ordered refrigerators, stoves, and dishwashers through John Lane in New York. While their new villa was taking shape the family spent six months in the Peterson apartment and Gilles began to accumulate more essentials for the good life as he saw it.

He had Gaston Parent ship over his 4×4 Ford Bronco from Canada and the outlandish device, perched high atop huge knobbly tires, became a curiosity along the Cote d'Azur. It was painted in Gilles's personal colours of yellow, orange, and red, the rather garish graphic identity conceived by one of Parent's artists.

Gilles still had winter sport in his blood and rented a chalet (he later bought it for $450,000) high up in the Alpes Maritimes at Pra-Loup, a ski resort area, and first took up skiing in the winter of 1978-79. Ray Wardell and John Lane and their families spent Christmas with the Villeneuves, and Wardell remembers how quickly Gilles took to the slopes. "He had never skied before so he fooled around on the nursery slope for half an hour. Then he said, 'Let's go,' and within one day he was off and running straight from the top."

At Pra-Loup Gilles had a chance encounter with the Canadian men's alpine ski team, which was training for the World Cup season. The Crazy Canucks, as they were called because of their daring approach to ski racing, became very upset when some lunatic on a snowmobile began tearing their well-groomed hill to shreds. Of course it was Gilles, whom they had all heard about, and he was quickly forgiven and everyone compared professional notes. The car racer and the ski racers had much in common and Gilles developed friendships with Ken Read and Steve Podborski in particular and brought them to several Grands Prix as his guests.

"Gilles had a tremendous amount of respect and admiration for Steve and Ken," Joann remembers. "Gilles would come up to me and say, 'Do you realize what these guys are doing on a pair of skis? – going down a hill at ninety miles an hour – they really must be crazy!' For him it was something really unbelievable. He admired their dedication, all the work involved, the hours of training and exercise, and their success."

The Canadian Press voted Gilles the Athlete of the Year for 1979. He polled 270 points to the runnerup, Ken Read, who had 151. "I guess that puts me in pretty good company, eh?" said Gilles. Like the Crazy Canucks, who were accorded major celebrity status throughout Alpine Europe long before it happened in the land of the Maple Leaf, Gilles's huge popularity abroad was largely lost on the unknowing populace back home. Only after his death did his countrymen begin to understand that Gilles was quite likely the best-known Canadian in the world.

Both Read and Podborski were badly injured in high-speed falls in their careers and could easily relate to the dangers Gilles faced. In spite of that, all three felt the rewards of their sports were worth the risk. After Gilles was killed Steve Podborski, who became the World Cup Downhill Champion in the 1981-82 season (the only non-European to do so), was one of those able to help Joann and the children through difficult times and he gave ski lessons to young Jacques, who showed considerable aptitude for the sport. Podborski recalls that Gilles always maintained he wouldn't really feel alive if he wasn't racing.

Yet Gilles felt he had to curb those extracurricular activities that might interfere with his racing career. "Of course, I have to be careful, which is sad because I'd like to go flat-out on the hills. I think if I had started at ten or twelve years old I would have been good at skiing. In some ways it's like car racing. If there was no risk of an injury that could ruin a racing season I would like to be crazy in it. Going balls-out would be genuine fun but I have to be sensible.''

Nevertheless, tearing up an Alp in a Bronco à la Villeneuve was fraught with hardly less danger than falling down it on skis. And many of Gilles's mountaineering expeditions involved looking for adversarial situations to tackle on four wheels. "Of course four-wheeling is different in Europe," Gilles pointed out. "There are no swamps in Europe. It's more like mountain-climbing. I don't go as if I'm out on a Sunday picnic. The fun of it for me is to get through some place where nothing should be able to get through.''

Gilles had a few more sedentary pursuits. He still dabbled in music and bought a piano. His trumpet was always near at hand, but, said Gilles, "I bought a flute, blew into it a few times, then gave it up." He had more than a passing interest in photography, however, and began printing and developing his own photos. "I started because I take a lot of pictures of the children and four-wheeling, and so on, and I could never get enlargements I liked. I hate going into a photo lab and going into long explanations of what I want enlarged on a particular negative. Plus I can also take nude pictures and develop them myself!''

He was also developing a passion for helicopters. Walter Wolf, his neighbour at Plascassier, called Gilles over one day and invited him to go for a ride in his Bell Jet Ranger helicopter, which was painted in the blue-and-gold Wolf corporate colours. Gilles took over the controls and was immediately hooked. Wolf said Gilles was the only man he'd ever seen who could hover a helicopter after only two hours of observation. Gilles took lessons at a helicopter school in St. Hubert, Quebec, and after a saturation session of long days he got his licence in a record three weeks, as opposed to the usual three months. Gaston Parent worked out a leasing arrangement with one of Walter's companies, which owned the craft. The deal provided an option to buy, for $235,000, at the end of the two-year lease.

■ ■ ■

Fortunately for Villeneuve's increasingly costly lifestyle, Gaston Parent was fulfilling his promise to sell Gilles ''like a can of beans,'' and his helmet and driving suit bore the logos of sponsors who were contributing to that lifestyle. Though he neither drank nor smoked, Gilles was a high-speed billboard for beer (Labatt), wine (Giacobazzi), and cigarettes (Marlboro). Besides badges and decals for sparkplugs (Champion), petroleum products (Agip), and tires (Michelin), signage for kitchen appliances (Smeg) and clothing (Matras) competed for consumer attention on Gilles's person so that the small prancing-horse insignia of Ferrari was buried in a patchwork quilt of commercial messages. But his Ferrari fortunes were improving, too.

"We never renegotiated the contract with Ferrari," notes Gaston Parent. "Gilles would just go in and talk to the Old Man and say he wanted more money. He would agree. Once a month Gilles would bill Ferrari for his out-of-pocket travel expenses and they would pay them, too, no argument. Besides the basic Ferrari salary we had a point money deal. For instance, at the race he won in Montreal in 1978 his nine points for finishing first paid him $9,000 a point – $81,000."

But Villeneuve's market value had soared beyond the $250,000 to $300,000 he was now getting from Ferrari. Traditionally it was one of the lower-paying teams because the prestige of driving for the famous prancing-horse outfit meant drivers would accept less. Prior to the 1980 season Teddy Mayer asked John Lane to sound Gilles out about his driving for McLaren. The offer was in the neighbourhood of $750,000 for the season, most of which would be paid by McLaren's major sponsor, Marlboro, which was then paying Gilles approximately $100,000 to carry its logo. When Lane presented Mayer's proposition, Gilles was very surprised at the amount but declined the offer. He asked Lane to tell Mayer he was flattered and would remember the McLaren interest in him, but he was already committed to Ferrari.

As one of the highest-profile Formula 1 drivers, Gilles was now worth his weight in gold to the sponsors who poured the financial fuel into the world's most expensive sport. Each race was covered by hundreds of journalists (sometimes over 1,000) who generated upwards of 20,000 newspaper and magazine articles around the globe. Television networks brought the races into the living rooms of over half a billion viewers in more than 100 countries. When statisticians factored in these figures with the number of Grand Prix events each season they arrived at an enormous international armchair audience equal to about one-third of the planet's population.

Marketing people took these numbers, factored in a glamorous and exciting sport in which heroic drivers from many nations laid their lives on the line in races in a dozen countries, and came up with an advertising El Dorado. It helped Marlboro, a division of Philip Morris Inc. of New York, become the top-selling brand of cigarette in the world. The company's anuual investment of many millions of dollars in Formula 1 drivers, teams, and races was explained by Aleardo Buzzi, president of Marlboro Europe. "We looked for an image to match our Marlboro man, the lonely cowboy on a horse. We transformed the horse into a mechanical one. What we wanted was to project an image of adventure, of virility, of courage . . ."

And in the public eye the number-one symbol of what Grand Prix racing should be was the daring French Canadian driving the most famous racing cars of all.

3

"To Gilles Villeneuve, fear – the limiting factor in most human reactions – was something which he rarely considered. Had he done so, he would not have been the kind of racing driver who left us the memories we treasure now."

– Jeff Hutchinson

Fan mail for Gilles poured into Maranello. The letters came from children, teenagers, and adults, people in all walks of life from all over the globe. One boy wrote: "I called my cat Gilles and it disappointed me because it fell asleep." A student told Gilles how his professors had given him permission to be absent from college due to "Villeneuve Fever." He was excused to go and watch Gilles practice. A kart racer wrote that he had started winning when he set himself a new goal: to reach the "Gilles Limit." One wife confessed that "in bed we see Gilles's poster."

It was one of Brenda Vernor's tasks at Ferrari to answer the fan mail, usually with postcards showing the driver and his car.

She got Gilles to sign them and the postal avalanche for him kept her hopping. Besides the thousands of letters there were regular communications from the over 400 Ferrari fan clubs around the world. Of these, Brenda estimates there were 150 Ferrari Gilles Villeneuve clubs and many of them remain. Now secretary to Piero Lardi Ferrari, she remembers fondly ''my happy days with Gilles. The times we used to have together. I'm so sorry he's not here any more.''

Born in England, Brenda Vernor first met Enzo Ferrari in 1962 when she visited Maranello with Mike Parkes, who was employed by the team for a time as a driver and engineer. After Parkes was killed in a road accident in 1978 Enzo hired her as his personal secretary. ''The Old Man had a very special soft spot for Gilles. We all did. He was such a perfectionist. He ate, slept, and drank cars. Gilles was very introverted, you know, though he used to talk to me quite a bit. And he was one who would say what he really thought. And in a car he would just put his foot down and as long as the car went, he went.

''I remember once when he was here for testing and there were no hotels open so I invited him to stay at my place. I gave him my bed and cooked for him. The only thing he would eat was beef-steak with chips or tortellini alla penne. Then the Old Man gave him a 308 Ferrari for his personal use and I went up in the mountains on a trip with Gilles. I was bawling my head off – 'Stop this bloody car!' – because of the way he was going around the corners. I thought, 'My God! if another car is coming we're not going to be here tomorrow!' And he was laughing all the time, saying, 'What's the matter, Brenda?'

''Jody would sometimes lend him his car and when Gilles went flying out the gate burning about 40,000 lira worth of tires, Jody would yell, 'My bloody tires!' They were always playing tricks on me. They would lock things up in my office and hide the keys. I'd have to phone Monte Carlo and ask Gilles what he'd done with my keys or my typewriter ribbon. The things they did, those two.''

■ ■ ■

Jody and Gilles bickered incessantly, though in a good-natured way, and their language was much saltier than the way they spoke for public consumption. Gaston Parent was often a witness. ''Jody is a very funny, arguing character. If Gilles said something was black, Jody would say it was white. They argued about anything and everything: a beautiful girl, about the tires, about how to take a corner. If one wanted left, the other wanted right. At a race Jody would say, 'You stupid son of a bitch, why didn't you take it easy?' Gilles said, 'Fuck you. You race your way and I'll race mine.'

''I flew with them in the Wolf helicopter to Fiorano for training. Every time we took off Jody left his heart on the ground and picked it up again on the way back. We were coming back to Monaco when a red light started flashing. Jody said, 'What the hell does that mean?' Gilles says, 'No problem. Not important.' The light kept flashing and Gilles drops us down at the airport to go through customs out of Italy. Gilles goes into the airport to sign the papers and Jody pulls out the flying manual and looks up flashing red lights. It said that it means the battery is over-heating and might explode. It's a warning and you've got thirty seconds to land!

''Gilles comes back and Jody tears into him. 'Villeneuve, the fuckin' battery is kaput! You aren't gonna take off and kill us all!' Gilles says, 'Take it easy, there's no problem,' and we take off to 3-4,000 feet. We were over the sea coming into Monaco and the light starts flashing again. Then Jody almost flies out of his chair, right out of his shoes. 'Villeneuve, what the fuck are you doing? Stop!'

''Because Gilles is cutting the motor off – and we're going sh, sh, sh, sh, sh – then he starts it up again. He's cooling the battery. The rotor is still turning but we drop – zzzzzz – until he starts the motor again. He cooled the battery all the way into Monaco like this and Jody is having a heart attack. He got out of that helicopter as white as a sheet and said, 'Fuck you, Villeneuve, I'll never get back in that goddamn thing again!' And he didn't.''

Gilles piloted the helicopter the way he drove his cars, and for a while it served to tone down his penchant for highway madness, though in some ways he regarded the Bell as a substitute for the Bronco. He delighted in going on exploration flights up fog-shrouded valleys into the mountains. On more than one occasion he had to navigate by following telephone wires and once, in a blizzard near Pra-Loup, he discovered his absence of altitude when the helicopter gently grazed a snow-covered hill. But he lost none of his zest for speed on the road.

■ ■ ■

The French journalist Jean-Louis Moncet lived in Nice while working for Télé Monte Carlo and met Gilles through their mutual friend, Patrick Tambay. Gilles was excited to learn that Moncet covered the Monte Carlo Rally and quizzed him at length about it. At the time Gilles had a Fiat 131 and he was particularly interested in the times that car had recorded in the Rally. As Moncet recalls: "He asked me for a route book of the Rally – the special stages – and he wanted to do it himself, on those very twisty mountain roads. And he did it, all alone. He did the special stages, the most famous ones, and kept his times. He was very fast."

In October of 1979 Gilles tried the real thing, competing in the Tour of Italy with the official Lancia rally team. Gilles, paired with German rally star Walter Rohl, won the event in a turbo-charged Lancia Montecarlo and their teammates Patrese and Geistdorf were second. The Lancias were both later disqualified for using unofficial motorway routes between the seven special stage-timed sections.

"You know we in the French press were very close with Gilles," says Jean-Louis Moncet. "He was so pure and honest. Sometimes he would say, 'I made a mistake.' Not many do that. Thinking of him now I am sad because I never saw a man like that. And a car was pure gold in his hands. I've never seen a driver like that. For a while Johnny (Rives) and I had the idea to write a book only on the Grands Prix of Gilles because in each race you have a fantastic anecdote about Gilles."

Johnny Rives, who has been covering racing for the French sports newspaper *L'Equipe* since 1957, states flatly: "He was the greatest Formula One driver I ever saw. I loved his mind. It was pure. What stood out in Gilles was his complete openness – his freshness, his bluntness even. He didn't hide his opinions. The only thing on his mind was racing. He loved engines, wheels, steering wheels. Once at a private test at Dijon, Gilles was dozing, his eyes closed, in the cockpit while they worked on his car.

Then Tomaini tapped him on the helmet and Gilles shot away down the pit lane sideways in blue smoke! Another time he couldn't find the keys for his Ferrari 308 so he broke the door open and took off in a cloud of smoke! That was Gilles. I loved him."

The majority of Formula 1 journalists jumped on the Villeneuve bandwagon, though there were some with reservations and others who simply did not approve of his relentless charging. He was accused of a lack of intelligence, mindless hooliganism, and frequent lapses into imprudent behaviour. Gérard "Jabby" Crombac, founder and editor of the French magazine *Sport Auto*, disapproved of Gilles's "lack of mechanical sympathy. When he got the Ferrari 308GTB he would pop the clutch to spin around in circles. Jimmy would never have done that," says Crombac of his close friend, the late Jimmy Clark.

Nigel Roebuck of *Autosport* had a special rapport with Gilles and was closest to him of all the journalists. "Literally, he was one of three or four racing drivers I've known who I would have wanted as a friend even if they hadn't been racing. Normally when you talk to racing drivers you find there isn't much else there. It's the only connection. But Gilles and I hit it off. We used to spend hours on the phone chatting about anything and everything."

Because of his approachability and candour, Gilles's personal relationships with journalists were generally very good. But Italian freelancer Giorgio Piola found him less than forthcoming in interviews. "He wasn't very co-operative. If something went wrong he would only give short answers – the car is shit, etc. This made it hard for the Italian journalists who have to write a lot about Ferrari. He was not very articulate. Maybe it was his culture."

Most of the Italian press corps eventually became Villeneuve fans, as Pino Allievi, of the newspaper *Gazzeto Dello Sport*, points out. "There were plenty of people who wrote against Villeneuve at first. They wrote exactly the opposite of what Villeneuve was. Only a couple of people like Franco Lini and myself liked him. It was very nice after a couple of years to see how they had changed. He was a very kind guy and had a very good image in Italy. It was a very positive thing for his image to see a driver with his lifestyle, going to the races with a motorhome with the family and children. Also, we have a long tradition of motor racing in Italy, of fighting drivers. Villeneuve went directly into the heart of the people for that. He took a lot of risks.''

Franco Lini, who has been covering racing for forty years, recalls that some of his fellow Italians began by saying, ''Villeneuve is a crazy man, a crashing man who destroys cars. Then they all changed their minds.'' Lini, now writing for *Il Giorno*, became friendly with the whole Villeneuve family and proudly notes that Melanie still calls him ''Uncle Franco.'' The Italian fans loved her father, says Lini, ''because he was always fighting, throwing the car into the race. They realized he was full of combativity.''

■ ■ ■

''One time,'' Jean-Louis Moncet relates, ''we went with our wives, Patrick, Gilles and I, to see the film of Sam Peckinpah which is called *Convoy*. Gilles was mesmerized by the film, fascinated by the big trucks being driven fast. At the end of the film he said, 'We stay for one more seance.' And one more. We saw that picture three times! Everyone stayed, our wives, too. And when we got out of the cinema Gilles got in his Ferrari 308GTB and was making tête-à-ques (spins) in the streets of Cannes!''

Gilles's spins weren't always deliberate. On a business trip to Europe in late 1979 John Lane dropped in for a visit at the Villeneuve apartment in Monaco. They talked late into the evening and Lane suddenly found himself running late for a flight out of Nice. Gilles was going to take him in the helicopter but wasn't allowed to leave the Monaco heliport because it was close to sunset and he didn't yet have his instrument-rated licence for night flying. So Gilles drove his guest to the Nice airport in time to catch his plane. The trip is etched indelibly in John Lane's memory.

''He took me in the 308 up the Grand Corniche road behind Monaco, where Grace Kelly was later killed, and it was one of the most exciting rides I ever had in my life. We got up to the toll booth on the autoroute and Gilles went through there at about 50 mph and just threw the money at the machine. The guards all

seemed to know him and just yelled Bonjour to him and away
we went. We came to this big sweeping curve, flat out in fifth,
probably about 145 mph, and we hit a patch of ice. Well, I
thought I was going to die, but at least I would go while sitting
next to one of the best drivers in the world.

"And I watched him as we were spinning, he went from fifth
to fourth to third to second – whip, whip, whip – down through
the gate as we did at least three complete revolutions in the middle
of the road. Then Gilles popped the clutch and away we went
again, without stopping. It was the only firsthand example I had
of just how superhuman he was at controlling a vehicle in a spin.
He had this favourite gesture, whenever he was referring to a
big moment, of tapping his heart. So he did that and then he
laughed.''

Gilles thought his ability to extricate himself safely from spinning situations could be attributed, at least partly, to a well-
developed survival instinct. "I think the will to survive is probably crucial. When I'm spinning down the road it's this will to
survive that makes me try and work out where the car is going.
I'm always looking for the way out in situations like this. Some
drivers freeze with their foot on the brakes when they start to
spin. I'm not like that. I want to go on driving – and that means
extricating myself from this sort of problem!''

His Ferrari road car, a development model of the 308GTB
Enzo had given Gilles for his personal transport, was well used
when he got it and even more so when he was finished with it.
Enzo also gave Joann a little Autobianchi car for her own use.
"Actually, I'm the only wife of any driver Mr. Ferrari did that
kind of thing for," says Joann. "He also gave me a beautiful
broach, one of only five he had made up specially by a jeweller,
with the Ferrari horse in diamonds. I hardly ever saw Mr. Ferrari
but I think he was kind to me because Gilles was so special to
him. And I think he respected us for our close-knit family image.''

Ferrari also kept Gilles supplied with a current Fiat model, so
they were a three-car family. But Gilles lusted after the top-of-
the-line, 12-cylinder Ferrari Berlinetta Boxer and planned to
negotiate one in a future contract. His appetite had been whetted
by the Boxer owned by Walter Wolf: "I asked Gilles to take my
BB to the Ferrari factory for repairs. But it needed more work

when he brought it back! Gilles always waited until the last minute on his trips to Fiorano. For normal people the trip from Monte Carlo is roughly five hours and if you were really quick you might make it in three and one-half hours. Gilles always did it in two and three-quarter hours. It's no wonder I needed a new car after Gilles took it in a few times for maintenance.''

In the opinion of Gaston Parent, Walter is fortunate he did not accompany Gilles on those trips. On one occasion Parent was with Gilles on a visit to Roberto Nosetto, formerly the Ferrari team manager and now head of the Autodromo Dino Ferrari at Imola. ''We were talking to Nosetto, a big admirer of Gilles, when all of a sudden Gilles says we've got to go because Jody is coming for supper at eight o'clock in Monaco. He'd forgotten about it and now it's 4:30 in the afternoon at Imola. So we get in this 308 and I hated to do that because you always felt your ass was dragging on the ground.

''Whanggg! Jesus! – he floored that thing and his foot never left the floor. I was sitting there with my eyes closed. I didn't want to look because even on the curves on the autostrada there'd be the guardrail and a truck and he'd squeeze between them. I swear to you there was no more than an inch on each side. Whew! No time to lose. It's usually a five-hour drive, even at his speed. Now he wants to do it in three and a half!

''Anyway, we make it to this fork in the road where you branch off to Genoa and Monaco. And I guess they got a report because there were a whole bunch of policemen just before the toll gate. They all had little white sticks with red reflectors on them and were waving them to stop us. And all of a sudden there are about fifteen of these guys in uniforms and I said to Gilles, 'Oh, oh.' He slams on the brakes and goes sideways and we stop about three feet from the head cop. The guy got mad as hell and took his stick and I thought he was going to hit the car. I look at Gilles and he's very serene. Doesn't say a word.

''He reaches into his briefcase behind the seat and he pulls out four postcards with his picture on it. And he pulls out his passport and driver's licence and opens the door. He hands this stuff to the policeman and looks him straight in the eye. The policeman looks at the cards and says, 'Oh ho! Villanova! Villanova!' And all the policemen are crowding around him. Gilles just sat there and signed the cards with his name. Then he closed the window and we took off at the same speed we came in – Whanggg!

"Whenever we came to a toll gate he'd just grab a handful of Italian change, open the window, and throw the stuff at the box. Whether he hit it or not I don't know. Then whanggg! – again. And all the time he's sitting there very relaxed, driving with one hand on the wheel and looking for a candy with the other. He loved to suck sweet stuff, candies or chewing gum all the time. So he'd be looking for a candy. I was so nervous and I started feeding him the candies so he'd keep both hands on the wheel. Anyway, we made Monaco at 8:15 and ate with Jody. And I figured from that day on I would never ride with Gilles. I never did."

But Parent was a passenger with Gilles in Jody's Ferrari 400 on another trip in Italy. "Jody pulls into this gas station to get benzina. He rolls down the window and looks at the gas guy. Jody's the World Champion. The guy didn't move. Just looked at Jody and pumped gas. Then Villeneuve lowers his window and the guy sees him and says, 'Hey! Villanova!' and a crowd gathers around on Gilles's side of the car. Jody opened the door and started to shout: 'Look, you sons of bitches! You bastards! I'm the World Champion – not him.' And he gets back in the car and says to me, 'Can you believe this?' He was laughing, but only half joking I think."

In spite of his professed concern for safety, Jody was himself no slouch on the roads of Europe, and on one occasion the tables were turned and Gilles thought Jody was the crazy one. The journalist Peter Windsor was with them en route from Monaco to Fiorano with Jody at the wheel of his Ferrari 400. "We came into a tunnel doing probably 220 kph," Jody recalls. "Suddenly there were lights flashing in front and it was a potential disaster. There was a police car stopped in one lane and another vehicle stopped in the other. Everybody – including me – thought it was all over!" There was no time for braking and at the last second Jody managed to jerk the wheel of the 400 to one side and they scraped through the tunnel with centimeters to spare. Peter Windsor was speechless but, says Jody, "Gilles complimented me on being so cool under adverse conditions."

4

"I know that some day I am going to have a really big crash."

—*Gilles Villeneuve*

Both Ferrari drivers had trouble keeping their cool in the decidedly adverse conditions afforded by the new 1980 T5 Grand Prix car. "It was a very bad year for Ferrari," in Jody's estimation, "one of the very worst. The cars ate rubber, had bad ground effects, and so on, while everybody else had gained all kinds of speed. What Ferrari did was take the T4, which was a very good car, and they modified the front in one of those workshop modifications where everything was theoretical. So when the car comes out you've got this new car which is much worse than the old one.

"All that year Gilles was faster than me most of the time. I was trying very hard, I thought, but subconsciously I don't know if I was because I seemed to be running around in 25th place all the time. After going through all I did in my career I couldn't be putting my life on the line just to become 25th. I announced my retirement in the middle of the 1980 season but I think I probably made my mind up even before I won the championship. But Gilles did well in a couple of those races."

Big things were expected of Gilles. In England the bookmakers made him the 3-to-1 favourite to win the 1980 championship. Jones was second at odds of 7 to 2, followed by Jody at 4 to 1 and Reutemann at 5 to 1. As it developed the Jones/Williams combination won handily over Piquet in his Brabham and Reutemann in the other Williams. Gilles managed only two fifth and two sixth places to score six points (to Jones's 67). In the twelve-month period between the 1979 and 1980 Grands Prix in Canada Gilles failed to run a single race non-stop. But he never gave up and in nearly every race he had his uncompetitive Ferrari T5 in places where it had no right to be.

In Argentina in January Gilles qualified eighth on the grid, which now was staggered, the first car a few meters ahead of the second on each row. This new measure was intended to cut down the incidence of first-corner accidents by separating the cars more, and Gilles immediately put it to the test. On the first lap he went wide on a corner and slid wildly across the grass, but quickly gathered it together again and resumed racing without interruption. His off-course excursion was due in part to the deterioration of the newly resurfaced track. Then he had another grass-cutting agricultural misadventure, sliding off the circuit and coming perilously close to a marshal's post. He continued, fighting on tirelessly until he was up in second place behind Jones. But on the 36th lap he crashed out of the race permanently in a heavy accident.

The Ferrari went straight on instead of turning right at the first corner past the pits, ripping through the catch-fencing and thumping the barrier very hard. The T5, though outclassed, was obviously strong – Gilles hopped out of the stricken machine unhurt and explained what happened. He had tried to turn right but the car failed to respond. "I noticed the steering wheel position had changed on the straight and when I got to the corner, the car just understeered straight off.

"It was frightening. I was going about 200 kph and took my foot off, but that didn't slow me down. I saw the guard rail coming at my face fast and I'm heading straight at it. I know if I bang it I can hurt myself. So I reacted – squashed the brakes and at the same time jerked the wheel – so I made the car spin to the side and hit that way. A driver can make a mistake in a corner but not to go off that way on the straight. Something broke for sure." Indeed it did, front suspension/steering failure being the diagnosis.

While mechanical failure over which they have no control is very worrying to all drivers, Gilles had a hard-nosed philosophy about accidents and was not afraid to talk about it when asked. "I know that some day I am going to have a really big crash. I've had a few, but not as many as people think. And it's important to me that people don't think I have a reputation for crashing. In fact, I'm worried more about my reputation, the car, and the team than I am about my own personal safety.

"I was more afraid before my first accident. When I was driving Formula Atlantic in Canada I used to be afraid of those steel guard rails around tracks like Mosport. When I hit the rail there in my big crash and broke my leg it was a good lesson, because I'm not afraid of guard rails anymore. I guess everybody is afraid of the unknown.

"Then I had my big crash in Japan and walked away from it. Maybe the next time I'll get carried away on a stretcher. But I'm not afraid of it. I'm not afraid of getting broken bones. You just spend a couple of months in the hospital and they get better so you can get out and get back into a racing car. But I don't try to analyse the risk factor too much. I believe if you think about it too hard you can end up convincing yourself it's much too dangerous!

"It's funny, but you are very conscious of accidents happening at very high speed, yet shortly afterwards, when you are out of the car, you can recall them in graphic detail. After that front suspension broke in Argentina, it was an incredibly quick accident. But when I think of it now, it all unfolds in front of me in remarkable slow motion."

■ ■ ■

On the tighter Interlagos circuit in Brazil, where the more ground-effective cars had less advantage, Gilles used his Villeneuve effects in qualifying and sat third on the grid behind Jabouille's Renault and Pironi's Ligier. But Gilles knew his race chances were poor and his best hope for temporary glory would be a banzai start.

At the green light both Jabouille and Pironi got away promptly on cue but Gilles did even better, blasting through the narrow gap between the Renault and Ligier to lead the first lap. Thereafter he dropped back, pitting for new Michelins on lap seven, then carving his way up through the field again only to spin to a halt late in the race. The spin was once again deliberate, this time to stop the car after a bolt worked loose in the throttle assembly and caused it to jam open.

Some people thought this was poetic justice, as there were inferences that Gilles must surely be jumping the starting lights. "I don't steal," said Gilles. "My Ferrari simply has a much better accelerator. Why on earth shouldn't I take advantage of that? If I weren't prepared to do that I might just as well sit comfortably at home and watch the Grand Prix on television."

He was being facetious, because his starting prowess was a major arrow in Gilles's racecraft quiver. Alain Prost, beginning his brilliant Grand Prix career with McLaren in the ride that had been offered to Gilles, said: "He always made the fastest starts. No one else could compare. I thought he must have some kind of trick."

Prost later became the most successful Formula 1 driver ever, and he was known as The Professor for his analytical approach to racing. But Gilles, too, was a keen student of every facet of the game and studied continually how to play it better. While his flamboyant style of driving usually looked distinctly impromptu and off the cuff, he was methodical and detail-conscious in the extreme. On race day every move was calculated to provide maximum benefit.

"There's a tremendous feeling of anticipation before the start. I like to pay very close attention to the details of all the procedures of getting ready. The second-by-second ritual helps to get your mind working in an orderly way. The paddock gates are opened at a certain time, you have to get the car out and the gates close, you sit on the grid, and so on. I usually like to stay quiet as long as possible so I don't come out of the motorhome until the last minute. I want to spend as little time as possible sitting there doing nothing.

"Then I usually sit in the car because I want to get my mind cleared out for racing. The only people I want to talk to are members of my team. If you get out, people want to come around and slap you on the back and talk to you. They're mostly the inconsiderate fans who insist on talking or having their picture taken standing beside you. I stay in the car to avoid that – unless I have to go to the bathroom!

"When we start our engines the excitement really starts to build up. Even though I'm tucked down inside the car, all wrapped up in driving suit, helmet, gloves, and fireproof underwear, I'm fully aware of everything that's going on around me. The noise and colour are fantastic. I can almost feel my nerve ends tingling all over and the adrenalin is pumping through my body so fast, I'm almost shaking.

"I know some drivers say it's like being with a woman. I don't agree with that. The physical senses are greatly heightened for sure, but it's because of expectation of the race about to start. It's all mental condition. In a few seconds before the starting lights, everything in my mind seems to come together and all the senses start working – feeding in information just like a lot of different terminals will supply information to a central computer.

"The starting grid for a Formula One race is a very dangerous place to be. Sitting there, I'm always studying, trying to anticipate what might happen. I try to keep all sorts of alternatives in mind. I keep reviewing all the possibilities of what the people around me might do. I feel that if every eventuality has run through my mind, I'll be prepared to act instinctively if anything should go wrong.

"It helps if you're up near the front of the grid, because you can get away from potential trouble just by accelerating out of it. But when you're in the middle of the field, trouble can come at you from almost any direction. And if you've run everything through your mind, reflexes and instinct will help keep you out of trouble."

■ ■ ■

To help him quickly leave behind potential trouble, Gilles had a head start on most of his rivals. In his road cars, from the earliest days in Berthierville, Gilles was a "street racer." Every stop sign or traffic light was a challenge to get away from as quickly as was humanly and mechanically possible. He honed the necessary qualities of concentration, anticipation, reaction, and co-ordination of the clutch, accelerator, and gearlever functions to the highest degree. He was probably the only Grand Prix driver to have actually drag-raced and Gilles felt experience in conditioning himself to react to the lights gave him a big advantage. And he sought further ways to enlarge on that talent.

Others made practice starts in F1 cars, coming to a halt on the circuit, then powering away, leaving strips of black rubber behind them. But Gilles took it one step further. On one occasion Daniele Parent, Gaston's wife, asked Gilles how he was able to get away so quickly at the start. Gaston remembers his answer. "He said to her with a grin on his face, 'You didn't notice, eh? Nobody notices. They all say I'm reckless because before the race I go like hell, come to the place where I'm going to start, then slam on the brakes so I leave two big black marks on the track. But when I go to my place on the grid I put my tires on the black marks and when the race starts I have rubber on rubber for better traction.'

"Look at the tapes or films of his races," Parent continues. "You're going to see that Gilles nearly always had those two big black marks under him. I remember once he did it in Montreal, came around at full speed and braked hard on the grid. Everybody said what the hell's he being so stupid for. He's crazy. He's nuts. But there was a purpose to it."

Gilles was forever looking for the advantage, and while his great natural talent was always commented upon, few drivers concentrated more on developing their God-given attributes. Peripheral vision, the ability to see to either side as well as in front, was another focus of Gilles's attention. He needed glasses for reading and sometimes wore them, though few knew it and he preferred they didn't. He took pains to hide any signs of weakness. But he knew that exercising the muscles of the eyes could improve vision. And, typically, he was less interested in being able to read print more clearly than being able to gain sharper insights while sitting in a racing car.

In his snowmobiling days he found that conquering the visibility problems gave him a head start on winning. He developed the ability to ascertain shapes even in maelstroms of blowing snow, sometimes by squinting or using only one eye. Maintaining this visual contact with his surroundings was essential sensory input necessary to maintain control of a sliding snowbmobile at 150 kph. And Gilles looked for ways to clarify and enlarge upon the view from his Ferrari.

He had an ophthalmologist in Montreal design him a set of exercises for his eyeballs and he practised in private at home. The apparatus consisted of a green ball suspended on an elastic band and two green circles, the same size as the ball, which represented the mirrors on his Ferrari. The ball was hung from the ceiling or suspended from a light fixture, with the green circles placed equidistant on either side of it on a wall. When the ball was set in motion Gilles would lie on the floor in front of it doing pushups, to simulate the motion of a T5 at speed, and count out loud as the ball swung from side to side between the circles. He moved his eyes to follow the ball, then focused on a circle, then back to the ball, then the other circle and so on, stretching the muscles in his eyes.

In this way Gilles estimated his field of peripheral vision was extended about 10 degrees to better supplement the function of the mirrors of his car. He was having to use his mirrors much more often in the "brouette" (wheelbarrow), as he was now calling the tardy T5, though often it seemed the mirrors were the only part of the car that worked. It could be extremely frustrating but Gilles started every race full of optimism and concentrated on remaining cool under fire.

"To some drivers the start of the race means they stop being sick and get themselves mentally organized. I don't have any physical or mental problems. As soon as the race starts I become cool. The concentration is very strong and the reflexes are ready, but now that the race is on I feel like I'm doing my job. The thoughts are flowing fast and smooth. At least as long as everything is running well.

"I'm always trying to brake deeper, yet get the power on out of a corner earlier. Apart from winning, of course, I'm aiming for consistency of lap times. Ideally I'd like to run a race with every lap as close to my fastest lap as it can possibly be. There's a tremendous sensation when everything is going well during a race. When things are clicking into place it's like a computerized ballet at high speed. Movements become precise and logical and you get the feeling that things are happening in their proper sequence.

"Mechanical problems can change all that. You develop a sense of feeling when the brakes start to go. Or there's a tire wearing a bit thin. Or the suspension is going out of tune. Since your feelings extend right through the car, you become quickly aware of mechanical problems.

"You can imagine how frustrating it can be when everything is going along so beautifully, then a problem crops up to completely change the rhythm of your race. I go from a mood of real satisfaction to one of frustration and despair. You can imagine why sometimes when we go into the pits with a lot of problems and everything is going very badly, we're not very friendly toward people who want to chat."

5

*"As you watched you were staggered by his natural pace,
yet also a little scared for him."*

−*Nigel Roebuck*

He was finding it more and more difficult to put on a happy face as the 1980 season wore on. There were frequent engine failures in practice and qualifying, and in the South African Grand Prix, after the now obligatory pit stop for new tires, the transmission ground Gilles to a final halt as he was leaving the pits.

His spirited sideways attack of the streets in Long Beach ended in the expiration of the driveshaft, which was unable to keep pace with the Villeneuve punishment. Jody finished fifth in that U.S. Grand Prix West to score his only points in 1980 and the last of his career, but the race at Long Beach ended the career of Clay Regazzoni.

The accident, which literally shook the ground for some considerable distance around the scene, was called one of the most violent in the history of Grand Prix racing. Regazzoni's Ensign suffered total brake failure at the end of the 180 mph Shoreline Drive and crashed head on into a tire barrier, then a concrete retaining wall. The front of the car was bent almost at right angles, trapping Regazzoni for nearly half an hour before he was taken to hospital with broken legs and severe spinal injuries. The very popular Swiss recovered wonderfully well and, though confined to a wheelchair, continues to lead a busy and productive life. He pioneered teaching driving to paraplegics and continues to travel with the Formula 1 circus as a television commentator.

In the Belgian Grand Prix at Zolder, Villeneuve wrestled his wheelbarrow to a sixth-place, while Didier Pironi won his first Grand Prix. At Monaco Pironi's upward spiral continued when he put his Ligier on pole and the French driver, who led much of the race before crashing, liked the place because he felt "a driver could express himself here." That being the case, Gilles was certainly the most expressive driver at the Grand Prix de Monaco. Said Gilles: "Practice here is always very satisfying. The race itself is a joke because you can't pass, but practice, simply as a driving exercise, is really enjoyable."

In giving himself pleasure, Gilles provided splendid entertainment value for the crowds lining the streets of the principality. He particularly enjoyed Monaco because his limit, which he so dearly loved reaching, could be measured in concrete terms – or rather, rubber-against-metal terms. When his rear tires kissed the barriers Gilles knew he couldn't have come any closer to perfection. In the Thursday qualifying he estimated that he touched the guard rail somewhere between twenty and thirty times, this highwire act being achieved on slick tires on a damp track.

Near the end of the session, in his haste to catch the superior Ligier of Pironi, Gilles made a "stupid" error and had to make an excursion down the escape road at Ste. Dévote. The T5 stalled and Gilles hit the fire extinguisher button by mistake. While the apparatus busied itself snuffing out an imaginary conflagration Gilles ran back to the pits for the spare car and resumed his rapid touring. The rain continued but so did Villeneuve's assault on the timepieces, and at the end of the day he was second fastest.

On Saturday Gilles actually hit the leading Ligier, damaging the Ferrari's right front tire. Pironi was travelling slowly after setting his quick time and Gilles complained that he hadn't given him enough room to get by. Still, he was sixth on the grid, while Jody was a lowly 17th. In honour of his world championship, Jody's car bore number 1 this season and Gilles's was number 2. But now, at the race where they had been on the front row the previous year, the two adopted Monégasques were much lower in the pecking order.

The traditional first-lap accident at Ste. Dévote was of larger than usual proportions with a great deal of flying wheels and wings. Included in the airborne debris was Derek Daly's Tyrrell, which flew over a couple of cars. No one was hurt but several vehicles were put out of action and Villeneuve's avoidance manoeuvre took him on another sidetrip down the escape road. He rejoined the fray in a fierce powersliding turn, effected by smashing the accelerator and cranking the wheel, the angry-looking gesture reflecting his state of mind at being back in ninth place.

From then on the lap charts showed Gilles making steady progress, which accelerated astonishingly as rain began to fall and most of his peers slowed down. While other drivers waved and shook their fists at the organizers to stop the race, Gilles beavered away at the job in the wet and, despite two tire stops and a spin at Mirabeau, persevered his way up to fifth at the finish.

■ ■ ■

The next race, the Spanish Grand Prix at Jarama, was a non-event, though Alan Jones won it. The results were declared null and void and no points were awarded in a bizarre permutation of the long-simmering struggle for power in Formula 1 between two rival factions. The authority of the Federation Internationale de Sport Automobile (FISA), the official governing body of world motor sport, was being challenged by the Formula One Constructors' Association (FOCA). The FOCA group went ahead and staged the Spanish race, minus Ferrari, Renault, and Alfa Romeo, who supported FISA (and referred to the FOCA teams disparagingly as "assemblatori" or "garagistes" because they didn't build their cars in-house).

The quarrel abated to the extent that the French Grand Prix went ahead on schedule, but the five-week interval between races for Ferrari made little difference. Gilles qualified 17th and Jody 19th, positions that were very hard earned as the T5s slid griplessly around the Circuit Paul Ricard. Gilles finally gave in to the hopelessness of it all and just threw the car around spectacularly to amuse himself and thrill the crowd. He got serious at the green lights and his storming start saw him rocket past no fewer than eight cars in the first few hundred meters and he was up to seventh on lap 2. He finished one position lower than that after his pit stop.

Despite his car's non-competitiveness, and the fact he could have sold himself to the highest bidder among nearly all the rival teams, Gilles had decided to stay with Ferrari for another year. "I like it here," he said. "Things are bad right now for sure but I have confidence in Ferrari. I like continuity in my life and there is no point in changing for the sake of it. Anyway, I feel we will be very competitive next year." Part of that competitiveness would come from a new turbocharged engine that was being tested regularly and might even be ready for a 1980 race.

■ ■ ■

Gilles was spending more and more time at Fiorano and enjoying the challenge of developing new technology. A regular *collaudo* (test) session lasted from 10:30 in the morning until five at night and Gilles was hardly out of the car during that time. He talked about the requirements of testing. "Mechanical knowledge is quite important, even though some drivers get away without knowing how a car works. I don't think many of the new young drivers do. But the ones who came up the hard way have it. I have my snowmobiling background, designing, building, and welding together my own machine. I can bend pipes and sheet metal and I did my own engine in Formula Atlantic. So I can put nuts and bolts together even if I'm not a true mechanic.

"But when something is wrong with the car I can relate to it. If it isn't handling well, I understand enough about basic geometry to be able to discuss roll centres and camber adjustments with the engineer. You can't be too knowledgeable in this area, but there's a point after which you don't need to know. It doesn't matter if I know the clearance between the pistons and cylinder walls or how they assemble the transmission. That wouldn't help me to drive any faster."

However, his speed and a new, narrower Fiorano-developed chassis did nothing to improve things in the British Grand Prix at Brands Hatch. Gilles considered the dips and dives through the rolling countryside of Kent to be "the nicest circuit in Europe." But he wound up 19th on the grid; Jody was 23rd and second last, though he kept running till the end and finished 10th. Gilles stopped twice for tires, then retired with a blown engine.

This result, or lack of it, occasioned a reflection from Gilles on his situation. "This year I am driving harder to try to make even sixth place than I did last year when I was winning. And the quicker you go the more difficult it becomes. You brake harder, corner faster, and you have less time to correct a mistake. I think I can overcome some of the Ferrari defects by trying that much more. The problem is that it is not always easy to see who is trying hard. When I won a race easily last year people would say, 'What a fantastic driver.' Now they don't even notice that I'm battling twice as hard."

While he could understand a lack of appreciation of his efforts from the public, he was unable to tolerate anything of the sort from his team. When he felt his boss was being misinformed as

TRYING TIMES

to the reasons for the lack of results, Gilles became rather perturbed – or, as Gaston Parent phrases it, "He was madder than a sonofabitch because the car was a pile of shit! Gilles thought that Forghieri and Piccinini were afraid to blame the car. After the races they would phone the Old Man and tell him it was the driver or the tires. It was never the Ferrari. So the Old Man would make the wrong decisions based on the wrong story. And Gilles finally blew his stack."

Gilles had installed a telex machine in his Monaco villa to better communicate with Parent in Montreal. He taught himself how to type, albeit very slowly with two fingers. "So he sits there for hours at the telex in Monaco on the Monday after the race and taps out a long message to the Old Man. It was in French and it was full of mistakes and it was at least three feet long when he was finished. He told the Old Man what was happening and he sent it to Brenda. Brenda thought Gilles was the greatest thing going and she made sure Ferrari got it. And after that the Old Man told him every Monday morning after the race he should send him a telex."

After a short period of acrimony over this arrangement, especially when Jody also began sounding off through the telex medium, the atmosphere within the Ferrari family became even-keeled once more and everybody soldiered on in search of mechanical improvements.

For Gilles, his telex became a favourite toy, and both Parent and Brenda Vernor treasure his messages, filled with errors in fractured French and often humorous, and keep them as mementos. "When I used to send him a telex I would say 'Bonjour mon amour Gilles,' " Brenda recalls. "And his daughter Melanie used to get angry. She didn't know who it was and Joann would tell her that it was okay. It was Brenda. Gilles would reply, 'Hello My Love,' and we did a lot of joking."

6

"Unfortunately, he was one of those guys you were always wondering when he was going to have an accident he wasn't going to walk away from."

– Jeff Hutchinson

In early August, Gilles attended the funeral of Patrick Depailler, who was killed in a pre-race testing accident at Hockenheim. His Alfa Romeo inexplicably veered off the circuit, much the same way as Jimmy Clark's Lotus had done there twelve years earlier, and this time, too, there was a great sense of loss in the racing fraternity. Depailler was a likeable, happy-go-lucky character, as well as a brave and capable driver. In some ways he and Gilles were kindred spirits, and Patrick was given to pursuing challenges such as motorcycling, skiing, sailing, and the hang-gliding that injured him badly the previous year. Gilles was disturbed by the death of a man he'd known since Atlantic racing. But his comment after the funeral was "Let's get on with it."

At the very subdued Hockenheim race for the German Grand Prix Gilles qualified 16th, made another demon start and was up to seventh by the fourth lap, then fought back from his pit stop to fifth at the flag. Jody qualified 20th, finished an unlucky 13th, but was surprisingly nonchalant and happy, for he had officially announced his retirement from racing.

In the Austrian Grand Prix Jochen Mass had a very big practice accident that left him trapped upside down in his Arrows in a corn field. The car somersaulted off one of the Osterreichring's fastest curves and Gilles was one of those to stop and rush to help extricate him. The rollbar on the Arrows did its job and Mass escaped with a severe bruising. The race marked the Formula 1 debut of Nigel Mansell (who became a Ferrari driver in 1989), who persevered, despite painful burns to his backside from fuel leaked into the cockpit, until the engine of his Lotus expired. Gilles, too, had his usual eventful race, passing six cars in the first four laps, dropping down the order, then fighting back after a tire change to seventh.

New Michelin qualifying tires helped Gilles to seventh on the grid at the Dutch Grand Prix. He was up as high as third in the race before two pit stops for tires left him seventh at the end. The Zandvoort weekend was marred by two big crashes at the infamous Tarzan corner. In practice John Watson's McLaren went brakeless into the barriers at high speed and the Irishman was lucky to walk away with only a pain in his back. Much worse was the crash of another Irish-born driver, Derek Daly, whose Tyrrell suffered a broken brake caliper when he tried to slow for Tarzan. The Tyrrell hit the tire barriers at something like 150 mph, flew up into the air, and settled in a heap on top of the piles of tires. Miraculously, Daly was completely unhurt after this worst of several accidents he endured in 1980.

■ ■ ■

After thirty successive years at Monza the Gran Premio D'Italia moved to the Imola circuit near Maranello where the Autodromo Dino Ferrari boasted elaborate new pit, garage, hospitality, and paddock facilities. Ferrari's "home" circuit was beautifully situated in a park where the hills of Tuscany meet the plane of Lombardy. And the 5-km route for the Formula 1 cars sampled a bit of both, twisting up into the vineyards on the hillsides and plunging back down into the urban outskirts of Imola.

The track manager, Nosetto, had consulted with Gilles and Jean-Pierre Jabouille on circuit modifications for the Grand Prix and the driver/designers appeared to have done an excellent job, except for a rather unpopular chicane, Acque Minerali, that slowed the cars down almost to a halt. Much of the circuit was in an amphitheatrical setting affording excellent viewing opportunities for the vast crowd of *tifosi*. An estimated 150,000 of them showed up to watch their heroic gladiators in the red cars engage sundry foreign forces in combat.

Gilles gave the Ferrari fans something new to cheer about on Saturday when he droned around for a few laps in the brand new 126C turbocar. He was actually faster than in his normal T5 but decided to use the tried and proven car in the race, for which he had qualified fifth. However, that turbo engines were the way of the future was demonstrated by Arnoux and Jabouille, who had their Renaults on the front row. Jody qualified 15th and was very fortunate to be able to start the race.

At the Austrian race a visiting Niki Lauda had wondered why Scheckter didn't stop racing then and there after announcing his retirement. But Jody felt he had to honour his contract (he had signed for two years with Ferrari) and that the immediate withdrawal of a World Champion – à la Lauda and Hunt – was conduct unbecoming to the sport. Jody had second thoughts about this at Imola after experiencing one of the worst crashes of his career.

"It was my fault," he admits. "I went out on cold tires and hit a bump on the fastest curve, then just went straight into the wall backwards. It was a really big accident, smashing the car right up to the engine. I went through the most g-forces ever when it hit the wall – BUMP! – and I remember my neck was very bad from whiplash." Jody's accident was at the superfast Tosa curve where his teammate came to grief in the race.

The hugely partisan collection of fandom virtually ignored the fact that the Renaults and Piquet's Brabham led at the start. They even paid surprisingly little tribute to Bruno Giacomelli's Alfa Romeo in fourth. All that mattered was that their beloved Gilles was fifth at the end of the first lap and they voiced their approval in decibel levels that rivalled the collective engine notes of twenty-four F1 cars at speed. When the number 2 Ferrari came by ahead of Giacomelli two laps later the public outcry from the assembled throng in the stands opposite the pits *was* louder than the mechanical noises. And all around the circuit the hue and cry of "Forza Gilles" and "Villeneuve – Villeneuve – Villeneuve" followed his progress.

It all ended on the fifth lap when Gilles, travelling at an estimated 180 mph, flew off at Tosa and pitched into the cement wall at unabated speed. The enormous impact destroyed the left side of the Ferrari, scattering wreckage high in the air. The front wheel struck Gilles a heavy blow on the helmet – but the accident was not yet over. The momentum shot the remains of the car back across the grass and onto the circuit in front of oncoming traffic, where it then spun to a smoking halt. Cars took frantic evasive action and all came through unscathed except Giacomelli's Alfa, which ran over a piece of Ferrari suspension and stopped with a punctured tire.

Gilles sat motionless in the cockpit for several agonizing moments before he raised his arms and began waving them. Finally, after about thirty seconds, the very worried Tosa crowd gave a mighty cheer of approval as Gilles unstrapped his harness, climbed out, and trotted away, though somewhat unsteadily. He was taken to the track clinic and examined, then released to go and lie down in his camper. He complained of being sore all over and had a severe headache and the next day went to the hospital in Bologna for a brain scan. No damage was discovered, though he wasn't allowed to fly his helicopter for twenty-four hours, and within a few days he was completely recovered.

An exploding right rear tire had caused the accident and Gilles was his usual phlegmatic self in recalling what followed. "I knew what had happened even before the car began to spin, because I heard the thumping of the flat tire. I knew where I was, how close the wall was and everything, and I thought, 'This one is going to hurt.' Everything went black when I hit the wall and I could not see for maybe thirty seconds. I could hear the cars going by and I thought I was thrown in the middle of them. I was afraid someone would hit me and that's why I raised my arms, so they could see me."

Then he gave his standard speech about his fear, or lack of it, and how he was more frightened about the unknown or falling out a window than crashing in a racing car. However, it was comforting to know how well his car stood up to the impact. "People say a Ferrari is not a good car to have an accident in. Well, I went in there bloody hard and I've just seen the wreckage of the car. The whole cockpit section and footwell area is hardly damaged. I'm reassured by that."

But privately Gilles was terrified by one aspect of the accident. The impact, the biggest he'd ever suffered through, and the wheel on the helmet had momentarily stunned him. Worse, it left him completely blinded for at least half a minute. He told confidant Nigel Roebuck that he had never considered being blinded and the experience shook him badly. Gilles was ready to accept pain when he hit something, but the thought of losing his sight was very disturbing. He consulted with his eye doctors following the accident and thereafter needed to wear his glasses more often for reading.

Jody, wearing a neck brace and in considerable pain, laid it on the line again at Imola and finished a plucky eighth. Enzo Ferrari paid tribute to him as "one of the most honest men ever to drive for Ferrari." The Ligier driver Didier Pironi, who finished sixth at Imola, refused to verify the rumours that he was replacing Scheckter in 1981, saying only that "I am going to a team where they don't have a number-one and number-two driver and I am very happy about that."

When asked for his comments about Pironi as a possible team-mate, Gilles said, "Who will be number one? The stopwatch will decide that . . . I don't know Pironi, other than to say hello. But he's very quick. I've got to beat him, haven't I?"

The next day Ferrari officially announced that Didier Pironi was indeed his new driver for next year and the Frenchman had signed a contract in May. When he heard this Guy Ligier, well known for spectacular outbursts of temper, gave vent to one of considerable proportions. Ligier maintained that Pironi had committed himself to stay with his team for another season – now he had gone back on his word.

■ ■ ■

At his home Grand Prix, Villeneuve was a disastrous 22nd on the grid, though everyone agreed it was more than the car deserved. Gilles had a practice shunt that knocked his rear wing askew but was less put out by that than the fact that Jody was unable to qualify for the first time in his career. After 111 Formula 1 races Jody's humiliation in Montreal was testimony to just how far Ferrari had fallen, and Gilles worked off some of his frustrations by thrashing about to a remarkable sixth fastest during a wet spell of practice. Sending up a wake like a speedboat in the nearby St. Lawrence, he sailed around Ile Notre-Dame at speeds out of all proportion to the conditions. "All I can say is that it better rain on Sunday," he said.

It was dry on race day, however, and also quite cold, but Gilles forecast improving conditions for himself. "I don't think the people of Montreal will expect me to win as they have in the past. They expect a good race and that's what I hope to give them." He did that by motoring flat out for all 70 laps. He earned himself a splendid fifth place before an appreciative audience who knew his result was the triumph of a resolute driver over an inadequate machine.

The 1980 Grand Prix of Canada was also notable for race-winner Alan Jones clinching the world championship after his rival, Nelson Piquet, dropped out. Earlier the two unyielding combatants had started a first-lap chain-reaction accident that caused the race to be stopped. The restarted event was then disastrous for Jean-Pierre Jabouille, who crashed heavily when the front suspension of his Renault collapsed, sending him straight into a barrier. He had to be cut from the wreckage and the multiple fractures to his right leg prevented him from ever racing properly again. Though he began the next season with Ligier as a teammate to his brother-in-law, Jacques Laffite, Jabouille stopped driving after three races and thereafter worked in F1 with several teams in various capacities.

Gilles qualified 18th and Jody 23rd in the season finale at Watkins Glen. Gilles retired from the race when he slid wide and damaged the suspension on the 49th of 59 laps. Before retiring permanently from the sport, Jody stayed around long enough to collect 11th place. After acknowledging his last chequered flag Jody made a grand exit from the number 1 Ferrari, stepping up and out of the cockpit and walking down the nose, which promptly bent under the strain. The Ferrari mechanics sprayed him with champagne, and Jody, with ten wins, fourteen seconds, and nine thirds in his career, walked away from the sport a happy man.

Gilles summed up his year. "It's been a long, frustrating season, but not totally unexpected. Everybody seemed to think I would win the title this year – everyone but myself. Ferrari was much more confident than I was. But I think I was more realistic. This was going to be a transition year for Ferrari. We would be developing the turbo car and I knew many of the others would be a little ahead of us. I didn't expect to win the championship but I did figure I would win a few races. I'm not discouraged, though. It's a temporary problem.

"You are tempted, when you have a lot of bad luck and things aren't going well, to drive easier and slower just to see the chequered flag. But I don't want to do that. In a car, you've got to be yourself. If you act differently than you would naturally act, that's when you ask for trouble. So no matter what the press or anyone says, I won't change my attitude. I will always drive the same. Which means I will try to go balls-out all the time and, if it brings me the championship, well, I would be very happy for it. I have won four Grands Prix in my career and I've set myself a goal of winning three world championships and twenty-seven Grands Prix like Jackie Stewart. I guess I'd better get going!"

8

TIME FLIES: 1981

I

*"In Formula One you're part of a racing stable and the
number-one driver is the stud."*

– Didier Pironi

Enzo Ferrari's statement that he made engines with wheels on
them was entirely appropriate for his 1981 126C car, though
sometimes it seemed as if the wheels were square. While the V6
turbocharged engine was the most powerful in Grand Prix racing,
the chassis was usually the worst handling, making the prancing
horses decidedly unruly to handle. While their power made them
hard to pass in the races, the Brabham, Williams, Ligier, and
McLaren cars did that often enough to relegate Gilles to seventh
in the final standings with 25 points, half those scored by the
World Champion, Nelson Piquet. In the title chase Piquet in his
Brabham edged out Jones and Reutemann in their Williams cars
and Laffite in his Ligier. But the number 27 Ferrari, as driven
by Villeneuve, swept the opposition aside in the sheer spectacle
sweepstakes.

The number 28 Ferrari was also driven with aggression and
vigour, and Didier Pironi quickly showed he was well equipped
for the task of being the teammate of Gilles Villeneuve. He scored
nine points in the season, was sometimes equal to Gilles in pace
and occasionally ahead, and from the beginning was surprised

at how he was treated by Gilles. "By the time I joined Ferrari the whole team was devoted to Villeneuve. He wasn't just their top driver, he was much more than that. He had a little family there. But he made me welcome and made me feel at home overnight. Gilles made no distinctions. You were expecting to be put in your place but Gilles was great and treated me as an equal in every way. Maybe I was number two in the season, but with Gilles's backing I was never discouraged."

He was two years younger than Gilles and came from an entirely different background. A Parisian, he studied engineering and took a degree in science with the intention of taking over the family business. His father owned a prosperous construction firm with some 300 employees, but Didier caught the racing bug from his cousin, José Dolhelm, went to driving school, and thereafter devoted himself to the sport.

Money was never a problem for him and he was always able to obtain the best equipment. He used it well, becoming French Formula Renault champion in 1973 and two years later won the European title in that category with twelve wins in seventeen races. He won the prestigious Monaco F3 event, showed well in F2 and in his Formula Atlantic appearances in Canada, and co-drove a Renault to victory at Le Mans in 1978. In the same year he began his F1 career with Tyrrell, then switched to Ligier in 1980 and won the Belgian Grand Prix that season.

Stocky and muscular of build, he was an accomplished practitioner of such sports as squash, tennis, and water skiing and he enjoyed piloting aircraft. He lived well in Paris and enjoyed a sophisticated lifestyle. He loved cars and speed but his great passion outside motor racing was off-shore speedboats, and it was in this sport that he was to die, in a race along the English coast in 1987.

A thoughtful, somewhat aloof, and introspective man, Pironi took his racing very seriously and prided himself in hard-working professionalism. He was politically minded and active and was elected president of the Grand Prix Drivers Association when Jody Scheckter retired. Unlike Jody and more like Gilles, Pironi had a romantic approach to racing and was honoured to drive for Ferrari and admitted to being very emotional on his first meeting with the Old Man. Pironi had great confidence in his ability and relished the opportunity to compete alongside the man with the reputation of being the quickest driver of all.

In the beginning his rivalry with Gilles was a friendly one, though keenly felt and always there. Pironi's philosophy held a realistic view of the potential power struggle between teammates, and in describing it he spoke prophetically of how his relationship with Gilles was to end. "In Formula One you're part of a racing stable and the number-one driver is the stud. He's the one you're compared with in every race because you have the same machinery, which means that your so-called partner is your biggest competitor. So when one is praised and the other forgotten he feels wounded and resentful."

■ ■ ■

In 1981 the FISA-versus-FOCA war reached an uneasy truce with the Concorde Agreement (named after the street in Paris where the governing body is located), which gave the Bernie Ecclestone-led FOCA faction control over the sport's commercial side. In return, Jean-Marie Balestre's FISA technical committee tried to keep the F1 designers on a leash. New rules called for six centimeters of ground clearance and the elimination of sliding skirts. In 1980 the skirts had been developed to create more of a vacuum beneath the car, hence even greater downforce and the cornering-on-rails syndrome. For 1981 the idea was to reduce cornering speeds for safety reasons and put more control of the cars back in the hands of the drivers, but the rules worked only for a short time.

The designers outmanoeuvred the rulemakers by having fixed skirts on the chassis that passed the ground clearance requirements in the pits. But they devised a system, controlled by the driver with a lever in the cockpit, that lowered the car on the track to create even more downforce. It was started by the innovative Brabham designer Gordon Murray and when Piquet showed how well it worked early in the season, everyone else fell into line. Though certain vehicles were banned and/or disqualified, the situation prevailed throughout the year. The resulting cars virtually sat on the ground, handled like go-karts with rock-hard suspension, cornered more quickly than ever, created enormous g-forces, and were hated by the drivers who were unhappy passengers in potentially lethal machines over which they had even less control.

When Goodyear dropped out of Formula 1 racing everyone began the season on Michelins, but the equalizing effect at the first race, in Long Beach, wasn't enough to bring the ill-handling Ferraris into mainstream competitiveness. Gilles manhandled his version up to the third row in qualifying, lit up his tires at the start and passed everyone in front to lead into the first corner, then was waylaid by a snapped driveshaft after 17 racing laps.

Gilles was using the rally driver's technique of left-foot braking to keep to a minimum the throttle delay inherent in a turbo engine. With his right foot on the accelerator to keep the revs up, he dabbed the brake pedal with his left foot to flick the tail of the 126C out even further in turns, a spectacle much appreciated by the 80,000 fans on hand. Pironi qualified six places behind Gilles but his V6 turbo engine fell victim to a fuel pickup problem and he, too, was sidelined.

Also on hand in Long Beach was Gilles's brother Jacques, the reigning Formula Atlantic Champion. The Atlantic cars raced through the streets as a preliminary to the main F1 event and Gilles was a keen spectator, watching his investment run, for he was helping Jacques financially. Gilles paid for his course at the Jim Russell race-driving school at Mont Tremblant and made other contributions through Gaston Parent, who was acting as manager for the younger Villeneuve. Jacques had turned down an offer to race F3 in Europe to stay in Atlantic another season and hoped for continued success. But it wouldn't be easy. As Jacques explained, "A lot of people expect me to win all the races, just like Gilles did." In his race Jacques was second to the Australian Geoffrey Brabham, son of the man who founded the Formula 1 team.

In Brazil, Gilles qualified seventh, made his usual speedy start, but bumped into the back of Prost in the process and caused a pileup among several following cars. Gilles continued with the front wing of his car askew, which made the handling trickier than ever, but his turbo blew up before half distance. His demise came just after Pironi had spun in front of Prost, who was lapping him, and both cars crashed out spectacularly.

In a preview of what ultimately happened in the Ferrari team, the Brazilian GP was won by Reutemann over Jones. Lole was the designated number two on the Williams team and ignored pit signals to let his teammate past. Jones was very displeased and said, ''Now I know the situation, I shall treat him just like any other driver and bang wheels to get past him instead of sitting back and praying he's a gentleman.''

In neighbouring Argentina, Villeneuve's race ended in a big spin when a driveshaft broke again, while it was Pironi's turn to suffer an engine failure. Prior to his final exit, Gilles had been vastly entertaining with lengthy opposite-lock powerslides that had him engaged in comprehensive grass-cutting with the rear wheels, the performance accompanied by showers of sparks from suspension extremities grinding against curbs and blasts of fire-spitting from the turbo exhaust. Several photographers, most of whom tended to feature him more than anyone else, admitted they missed many great shots because they were so busy watching him they forgot to snap the shutter.

2

''But the person behind the public figure had insecurities.''

– Joann Villeneuve

In the two-week interval between the South American races several of the French-speaking drivers went to a Club Med on an island off the coast of Brazil. Jean-Louis Moncet was there. ''It was the first time there for everybody. Gilles was with Joann, Alain Prost was alone, Didier was with his girlfriend Catherine, Jabouille with Genevieve, Jacques Laffite with Bernadette, and we were all happy to swim and play with dune buggies. One day after our arrival Joann did not like this place and she became sad and Gilles was obliged to leave with her. They went back to Europe. Gilles was upset by the fact that Joann did not like the place.''

In fact, after eleven years, the Villeneuve marriage was showing signs of stress. The life of a racing driver's wife is never easy; now that Gilles was a celebrity it became even harder for Joann. "I first knew him when he was just a kid really. I didn't marry a racing driver. I didn't marry a star. I married a guy from Berthierville who didn't even have a job. To the public Gilles was a superman, a hero, a legend, all of those things. But the person behind the public figure had insecurities."

Besides worrying about his age and hiding the extra two years and not wanting to wear his glasses in public, Gilles had other vanities. He was very sensitive about his height and would not allow Joann to wear high heels for fear she would appear taller than him. He was also bothered by what he perceived as thinning hair. He combed it from back to front to cover his supposed receding hairline and always brushed it that way with his hand immediately on taking off his helmet. He asked Gaston Parent to investigate hair transplant techniques.

"So we went to a doctor, an aesthetician," says Parent. "And the doctor said, 'You're crazy. There's nothing wrong with your hair.' Gilles was vain about his appearance. Though he dressed very casual, in jeans all the time, he took care and he was always clean and presentable and took two or three showers a day.

"With Joann and the shoes, he didn't want her to dominate him in height or in any other way. In the French-Canadian world the tradition is that the man is the boss. Your woman is your woman and if you marry her it's because you can pay for her and her job is to look after the home.

"Gilles was very jealous of everything he owned. In Monaco he had a dog called Bella, a German shepherd that Walter Wolf gave him. Bella would always sit by Gilles and if Bella got up and came and sat by you, he wouldn't like that. Gilles was a very possessive man."

On one occasion John Lane greeted Joann by kissing her on both cheeks in the European manner and Lane, despite being a close friend of the family, was reprimanded by Gilles for being too familiar with his wife. In public Joann had to discourage any such displays of affection and even when she went out with the girls: "He was possessive and jealous. One day I was having lunch with Pam (Scheckter) and some others, a ladies' luncheon. After I was there for two hours he called and said, 'What are you doing? Lunch should be over now. It doesn't take you two hours to eat lunch.' "

Gilles hired a live-in English nanny to help look after the children at the villa and teach them English. But he wouldn't allow the girl to eat with the family, cook, or help with any of the housework. That was Joann's job, and she grew to resent all the demands being made on her. "Gilles was an extremely demanding person. It wasn't so bad in the beginning, but later it got worse because of the life he had outside the family where, whenever he demanded anything, it was handed to him on a silver plate."

Joann began to fight for her rights and those of the children. "About the things I felt were really important, I would nag him. It was one of my bad points, I guess, but one of the subjects we would fight about was the kids. I was determined he should be a good father to them. He wasn't an early riser and the kids were in school from eight in the morning till four in the afternoon and he would only see them for a little while in the evening before they went to bed. I said, 'The kids hardly ever see you. Don't wait until you're fifty when it's too late. It's unfair to them and the minimum you can do is get up and drive them to school.' And after my nagging about it so many times he finally understood and agreed to do it."

The rest of the day, when he was at home, Gilles spent downstairs in the garage or in his office, often until the early hours of the morning. A regular patron of the newsstand in Casino Square, he bought armfuls of magazines and sent away for manuals on cars, boats, and aircraft and pored over them. He spent hours on the phone talking to people like John Lane and Gaston Parent and/or ordering parts for his various toys, like a winch for his Bronco, the better to haul it out of difficulties in the mountains. Visitors from North America often carried bits and pieces of vehicles in their luggage when they visited the Villeneuves.

Gilles's dangerous playthings, or at least the way he played with them, were another bone of contention with Joann. "At first the kids and I used to go with him in the Bronco and it was no fun at all sitting there for seven or eight hours with the kids screaming in my ears. The pleasure for him was bouncing around to see if he could get into trouble, then get out of it again, and then he would enjoy repairing the damage. He seemed to spend a lot more time repairing than anything else. One day he almost killed the kids and that was that. He went out on his own after that.''

Another divisive factor was the way Gilles was spending money. In his words, ''If you've never had it before I guess the money changes everybody a bit. I'm not the same as I was a few years ago, that's for sure. Now I can afford to buy all the little toys I couldn't afford before. Whatever I want, I just go out and buy it. That's fun.''

But Joann, who had suffered more than him during their years of impoverishment, was much more financially prudent than her husband. Perversely, Gilles was very careful about the amounts of money he would dole out to her. At one point Gaston Parent suggested that Gilles invest in a diamond stone for Joann, who was very pleased at the idea. Gilles told them it was out of the question, then went out and spent more than twice the money involved on a speedboat.

''Suddenly he was a millionaire and some of the things he did were crazy,'' avows Jody Scheckter, who continued to be very close to Gilles. ''It was like money had no meaning to him. At his villa he just went, 'I want a swimming pool here, a garage there,' and so on, and they had to be blasted out of solid rock. When he decided to become a photographer he went into Nice one day and bought maybe $8,000 worth of stuff. Then he developed a picture or two and said, 'Geez, this takes too long.' Finished. He wanted to work on his cars so he bought probably $20,000 worth of tools. Then he took a gearbox apart once. Then there was his boat, that was complete madness. At least to me it was, but he got his enjoyment out of it. I'm the other extreme, I don't buy anything. I had a rowing boat. But Gilles ordered two full-house V8 motors from the States for the bloody thing. I only went out with him once. I told him to stop and let me out. I was scared stiff!''

Gaston Parent was involved in the boat purchase, a 36-foot Abbate, and he remembers, ''That boat was a goddamn fight like you wouldn't believe. She wasn't too happy about that. He paid

$185,000 for it from Abbate himself in Italy. He became a good friend of Gilles's and custom-made it for him. Then it wasn't fast enough for Gilles so he imported two 700-horsepower motors from Detroit. He bought a chrome exhaust system in California that cost $18,000. Gilles had the boat painted in his own colours and then the police wouldn't let him start it up in the port of Monaco. The two motors were so loud he had to go right out to sea, in the Mediterranean, to start them up.''

"The boat was a pain, literally," says Joann. "The kids and I would be black and blue when we got out of that boat. You couldn't sit in it, you stood hanging on. So I had both kids in my arms holding them so they wouldn't fly out. He was having a great time while I was trying desperately to stay in the boat with the kids. He would just bounce it through the waves to see how long it would take before the engines blew up or the boat broke. In the end he was going out by himself because even the kids didn't want to go out in the boat anymore."

"Everything in his life was done at 200 miles an hour," claims Patrick Tambay, one of those closest to Gilles. "Skiing, driving the speedboat, playing backgammon . . . And his spending was the same, whether it was buying Christmas presents for the kids or playing blackjack at the casino. 'Gilles, you're crazy!' I used to say to him, but that's the way he was."

Whenever they played Monopoly, Gilles "handled himself as if he was driving his Formula One car," and was, according to Tambay, "very decisive, never hesitating, taking risks, going forward, forward all the time. Once his mind was made up he would go for it – as he did in his driving." Gilles's headlong approach to Monopoly made him either a big winner or a big loser – and he was not happy in the latter role.

3

"I like life as a Ferrari driver."

– *Gilles Villeneuve*

The Ferraris finally came good at a new event on the calendar, the Grand Premio di San Marino. The race at Imola, named after the tiny republic nearby and ostensibly held to raise funds for a recent Italian earthquake disaster, was really just an excuse for another Formula 1 race in Italy. The *tifosi* were not disappointed as their Gilles put one of their Ferraris on pole and led the event for the first 14 laps. Pironi, too, showed the flag to good advantage by qualifying sixth and taking over the lead for many laps before slowing with worn tires to finish fifth.

The race was intermittently wet and dry and Gilles lost his lead when he pitted twice to change to appropriate tires to suit the changing conditions. One factor, his amazing aggression, remained constant in the drive. He slid around in superb style, setting the fastest lap of the race, only to fall back to seventh with a slipping clutch near the end.

Villeneuve scored his first points of the year with a fourth in the Belgian Grand Prix, but the race at Zolder was remarkable for acrimony and tragedy. On Friday the crowded pit lane was the scene of an ultimately fatal accident to an Osella mechanic, Giovanni Amadeo, who slipped from the ledge along the pit wall and fell between the wheels of Carlos Reutemann's Williams. Reutemann was moving slowly at the time but Amadeo was thrown against the wall and succumbed to severe injuries later. Reutemann was thoroughly distraught by the incident but managed to win the race.

Crowded conditions at Zolder were also at the root of an unsavoury and dangerous drivers' protest at the start of the race. The Concorde Agreement called for a maximum of thirty cars on the track at each Grand Prix and a pre-qualifying session for any extra cars. When thirty-two machines showed up in Belgium the organizers refused the GPDA request for a pre-qualifying session. Many mechanics, upset at the accident to one of their number, supported the drivers and it was decided to make a show of solidarity by delaying the start in front of the television cameras. After the warmup lap the grid was chaotic with drivers and mechanics milling about, but the organizers continued the countdown to the three o'clock start.

While the ringleaders of the protest stood around, among them GPDA president Pironi and Villeneuve, the other cars were flagged off on another warmup lap and the rest eventually fell into line. Gilles, who professed himself to be apolitical, had reluctantly joined in the protest. ''It's not the kind of thing I would normally get involved in. I don't believe in strikes, far from it, unless it's the only way to get ahead.''

The delay on the grid meant the cars were overheating and as Gilles moved into position, the last car to do so, Patrese's Arrows, stalled. His team's chief mechanic, Dave Luckett, ran out to his aid and – as the race began – was struck by Siegfried Stohr in another Arrows. Mercifully, Luckett received just a broken leg and finger and facial cuts, but it was only the weaving action of Didier Pironi's Ferrari that brought the field safely to a halt before anyone ploughed into the rescue effort on the starting grid.

The race was safely restarted but Jones bunted Piquet off the track and the fuming Brazilian was quoted as saying, ''He's absolutely crazy! The next time he does that I'll kill him.'' The whole atmosphere at Zolder was one of tragically dramatic foreboding that foretold of what was to happen there the next year.

■ ■ ■

Prior to the Monaco Grand Prix, Gilles announced he would be staying with Ferrari for the foreseeable future. ''I signed my contract on May 11, and it's firm for 1982, with a strong option for 1983. I am pretty sure that I will stay for that year also. More than ever, I am sure that Ferrari is the best team and that my prospects are better here than anywhere else. I did not re-sign because of the money – I could have got the same, or more, from several other teams. I like life as a Ferrari driver.'' And, after Monaco, he liked it even better.

In qualifying, Villeneuve astonished everyone by clocking second to Piquet's Brabham. With their throttle delay, an interval before the power kicked in, the turbos weren't supposed to be suited for Monaco's short straights and its point-and-squirt configuration. The cumbersome chassis also worked against him, but Gilles pounded these negatives into submission, extracting every ounce of prancing horsepower, feeding it to the road in mighty powersliding bursts and chucking his 126C about with tremendous brio. Pironi (who had also re-signed with Ferrari) tried to emulate his teammate but hit the barriers three times, forcing Forghieri to send an emergency call to Maranello for a fourth chassis.

At the start, Piquet led Gilles through Ste. Dévote and the two sped safely away from the traditional accident, which involved several following cars. Other incidents and his own relentless aggression saw Jones up to third behind Gilles after 15 laps, and three tours later Gilles moved over to let the Williams through, the Ferrari beginning to be hampered by fading brakes. On lap 54 the leader, Piquet, perhaps distracted by Jones looming large in his mirrors, came out second best in an argument with Cheever, whom he was lapping, and crashed into the barriers. Jones seized the advantage and opened a gap of half a minute over Gilles, then began to experience a misfire.

On lap 67 Jones pulled into the pits, where fuel vaporization was diagnosed and he was sent out again with the problem unremedied. Gilles was now just six seconds behind him and began to lessen the interval, pushing ever harder and sending the attendant horde of Villeneuve fans into hysterics of screaming lungs, hooting airhorns, wailing yacht sirens, and waving flags and banners. There was an explosion of joy as the Ferrari passed the Williams in front of the pits on lap 72 and an even greater one when Gilles acknowledged the chequered flag on the 76th lap.

A portion of the outpouring of Ferrari euphoria was reserved for Pironi's fourth-place finish, but Le Petit Grand Homme in the number 27 car was again the hero of the day. Sweating profusely in the pressroom, he described the unexpected victory – the first for a Ferrari turbo motor, Gilles's first in two seasons, and his first ever in Europe. He paid tribute to the strength of his car. "When I first came to Ferrari I kept breaking driveshafts all the time and Enzo Ferrari used to get really mad with me. He didn't want to hear about that anymore so he had some very special, big driveshafts made for me. I always have them now. Actually I'm quite proud of my driveshafts.

"I tell you, my car, it was very hard to drive with the suspension so stiff it was like a go-kart. I bumped my head all the time on the rollbar and now I ache all over. It was one of the most tiring races of my life – but I am very, very happy with this win. When my brakes started to go I had to be very brutal with the car, but it lasted okay. I am very lucky today.''

4

"By the time I stop racing my son will be seventeen and he will know so many girls in Monaco there's no way we'll be allowed to leave here!"
— Gilles Villeneuve

Jacques Villeneuve had to leave the Monaco Grand Prix when he developed a bad headache. His English nanny took him up the hill to the villa before the race was half over. John and Elizabeth Lane were guests of Gilles and Joann that weekend, and Lane notes that "When Gilles was racing Jacques became almost a basket case. He would sit there and you could see him gritting his teeth with his jaw muscles working and eventually he would have to leave. Melanie was always screaming and cheering for her dad and she would stay to the end of the race. But not Jacques."

For several years Jacques had been experiencing nervous head-aches and was having difficulty in school. Joann thinks it was because of the pressure his father put on him. "Gilles was very demanding with Jacques and not at all with Melanie. He spent more time with her and in his eyes she was perfect. He wanted his son to be more than perfect and accepted from his daughter all the little faults children have and thought they were nice and cute in her. But not in Jacques. I was the only one who really saw the difference in the way he treated the kids. I didn't have any problems with Jacques. He would sit calmly at the table and not drop his glass of milk. But when Gilles was there he would drop the glass of milk. He would get very nervous just trying so hard to please his father.

"Towards the end he was becoming a better father. He began to realize that he was too demanding and he had to treat them both more equally and fairly. But the kids sensed there was a lot of tension and friction between us. It made them unhappy and unsettled them."

Joann, too, became very unsettled when what had begun as petty bickering and quarrelling had now escalated into full-scale marital strife, at first in private, then in public. "He would pick a fight with me before we'd go outside: 'Why are you wearing that terrible dress?' And obviously it would put me in an awful mood and I couldn't cope with it. Or he would say, 'Oh what a terrible meal you've cooked' – this is after telling me fifteen minutes before that we have seven people coming to dinner. But he could always put himself on show and be charming. I could never figure out how he could do that and it was infuriating to me. He would criticize me in front of others and was forever creating situations that he was very good at coping with and I wasn't."

Still, the two mostly managed to put on a smiling front while in the public eye and seemed a happy couple at the Monaco Grand Prix. On their way to the race from their villa, they zipped down through the streets on the family moped, with Gilles beeping the horn and Joann waving to the crowd. Following the race they were the guests of honour at the traditional post-race gala awards banquet, usually hosted by Prince Rainier and Princess Grace. This time the royal couple were away in America attending their son Albert's graduation from college. So the Villeneuves had an even larger share of the spotlight that evening, Joann charming and beautiful in a full-length white evening gown and Gilles, much to the surprise of many, in a tuxedo. In fact, his formal evening wear was purchased earlier for an audience with the Prime Minister of Canada, Pierre Elliott Trudeau.

"Trudeau was a great fan of Gilles," says Gaston Parent, who one day received a call from the Prime Minister's office requesting Gilles's attendance at a diplomatic supper. The guests of honour were to be President Reagan of the U.S. and President Barre of France. "So I called Monaco," says Parent, "and told Gilles he's got to get a tuxedo and go to dinner with the Prime Minister of Canada. 'No goddamn way! Tuxedo? You've gotta be kidding!' Gilles hated to wear a tie. Anyway, I told him he had to be there because it was like a command performance. So I told Joann to go to Paris and buy the best dress and Gilles went into Nice and bought a tuxedo from a tailor.

"They fly into Montreal and he's saying he doesn't think he's going to go to Ottawa. He wants to go and play with his 4×4

in Berthier. We argued and finally I put them in my car and drove them to a hotel in Ottawa where they got dressed. They made a fantastic couple, they looked beautiful. Joann had flowers for her dress, a black one from Christian Dior. So I drove them right to the Prime Minister's residence on Sussex Drive in Ottawa and they stayed at the dinner till after midnight. The next day they said they had a terrific time and enjoyed themselves the whole night. When Gilles died I made a film about him and in it Trudeau paid homage to him.''

5

"I know that no human being can perform miracles. But Gilles made you wonder sometimes."

– Jacques Laffite

There had been tears of joy in the Ferrari pit in Monaco; in the following days at Maranello, Brenda was inundated with mail and telegrams from adoring fans. They had been counting the days since Gilles's last win – 601 of them – and were now overjoyed. One letter was typical: "When Gilles came across the finish line I started to cry from the simple joy of it.'' But the next race brought forth an unprecedented outpouring of tear-stained tributes as Gilles scored his final, and most outstanding, Formula 1 triumph.

After two days of qualifying for the Spanish Grand Prix at Jarama, Gilles was seventh on the grid, beside Andretti's Alfa Romeo and behind Giacomelli's Alfa, Prost's Renault, Watson's McLaren, the Williams duo of Reutemann and Jones, and the polesitting Ligier of Laffite. Gilles's fourth-row grid slot was only achieved after some right-on-the-limit lappery in an ill-handling Ferrari 126CK, which he compared to "a hopeless fast red Cadillac. It wallows all over the place with no grip at all. I thought half a dozen times for sure I am going off the road. And yet, the chassis is incredibly forgiving. I can get so sideways I am almost looking over the rollover bar! And still it comes back.''

His careening "Caddy" was using up tires at an extraordinary rate. Said Gilles: "Look out for me in the first few laps. After that, the tires will be screwed and that will be that.'' Well, the tires were indeed screwed, but that wasn't that. And the Ville-neuvism that took place under the blazing Spanish sun, in temperatures of over 100 degrees Fahrenheit, ranks with the most sensational drives ever seen in Formula 1.

To prepare himself, Gilles followed the advice of two French doctors who were studying the drivers and recommended a large intake of fluids to avoid dehydration. As Gilles put it, ''You're in the car for two hours dressed like you're going to the North Pole when it's 30 degrees (Celsius) outside and even more inside the car.'' Particular attention to physical fitness was not part of his usual regimen – ''It's enough if you jog two or three times a week to develop good breathing and good stamina.'' Now he readied himself for a duel in the sun by drinking plenty of water and a special mineral salt supplement prescribed by the doctors.

At the green lights the two white cars of the feuding Williams teammates surged to the front, Jones having a slight advantage over Reutemann as the field floored it en masse toward the first corner. Right up with Jones and Reutemann was the irrepressible red slingshot that was Villeneuve's Ferrari. It zig-zagged arrogantly past the rather startled likes of Laffite, Watson, Giacomelli, and Prost, the latter further disturbed to have the Ferrari rudely chop the front wing of his Renault as it whizzed past.

As Jones exerted his authority over Reutemann on the opening lap, Gilles began to pressure his former teammate from behind. Coming across the line for the first time on his 264.96-km Jarama journey he had his front wing tucked beneath Lole's rear one. Under braking for the Virages de Fangio at the end of the straight, the Ferrari brazenly zipped out from behind the Williams and into second place. Behind the leading trio the order was Andretti (who had also made a brilliant beginning from the fourth row), Prost, Watson, Giacomelli, Piquet, Pironi (who had bent his front wing against Patrese's Arrows at the start), Patrese, and Laffite (whose overheating clutch saw him swamped at the start).

Jones was a comfortable eight seconds ahead on lap 14 when he suffered self-confessed ''brain fade,'' locking up his front brakes and undergoing an off-course excursion. Jones resumed running in 15th place, worked himself up as far as eighth, then fell out of the main chase with gearbox troubles.

Thus Gilles led the Gran Premio de Espana with Reutemann in very close proximity, several times alongside but with never quite enough poke to pass. Gilles's frontrunning cause was aided by Piquet, who collided with Andretti, effectively eliminating Mario from further serious play, and Prost took himself out of the action on lap 28 when he slid his broken-nosed Renault off the road. Pironi pitted for attention to his disfigured nose and new front tires and soldiered on to finish 15th.

Reutemann continued to investigate ways past Gilles while the pack behind them underwent further shuffling. Piquet, physically exhausted from hanging onto a Brabham with increasingly less adhesion, finally lost it on lap 44 and crashed. Five laps later Jolly Jacques Laffite, driving an inspired race, used lapped traffic to sneak ahead of Watson into third and set off in quest of the lead that, based on his pole position, he felt was rightfully his. But then, so did Reutemann, and he hovered behind Gilles like a hawk, waiting to pounce at the slightest opportunity. However, Lole's claws had lost some of their sharpness as he was sometimes having to hold his Williams in third gear. This weakness and a brave bit of late braking brought Laffite second place on the 61st of 80 laps. One lap later Reutemann was outmanoeuvred by Watson while lapping slower traffic and that was the final change of order among the frontrunners.

For the last 18 laps the first five roared round and round like a high-speed freight train, a Ferrari engine leading cars of Ligier (Laffite), McLaren (Watson), and Williams (Reutemann), with a Lotus caboose manned by Elio de Angelis, who had a small lead over teammate Nigel Mansell, who was sixth.

While his followers cornered as if on rails, Villeneuve's tired tires afforded him ever more precarious purchase on an increasingly dirty track surface. He doddered drunkenly on tiptoe through each of Jarama's sixteen bends, then as the power of 550 prancing horses beneath his right foot was given full rein, the Ferrari surged ahead on the straights. His virtuoso performance created a concertina-like effect as the impatient queue behind him closed up in the corners, then fell back in momentary exasperation, before squeezing in behind him yet again.

The pace was frenetic, the heat intense, and the tension electric as the final laps were reeled off. Gilles had only to lose concentration, fumble a gear change, or slide a millimeter off line and he would instantly switch from victor to vanquished. Time and again the blue-and-white Ligier would emerge from a tighter hairpin abreast of the scarlet Ferrari. Threatening to climb over them both were the red-and-white McLaren, the green-and-white Williams, and the black-and-gold Lotus as the epic technicoloured struggle continued round the Spanish circuit at undiminished pace.

On the last lap Gilles held off a final desperate challenge from Laffite as they rounded Tunel corner and was given the chequered flag 1 hour, 46 minutes, and 35.01 seconds after he began. The others shot by in the blink of an eye: Laffite .22 seconds later, Watson .36 seconds behind Laffite, Reutemann .43 seconds behind Watson, and de Angelis crossed the finish line .23 seconds later. The first five were covered by a blanket of 1.24 seconds, making the Spanish Grand Prix of June 21, 1981, the second closest race in history after the Italian Grand Prix of September 5, 1971, where six-tenths of a second at Monza covered the winner Peter Gethin over the pursuing Peterson, Cevert, Hailwood, and Ganley.

"One time Gilles went right across the white line on the edge of the track – all four wheels – but he came back! I don't know how – but he came back," said Carlos Reutemann. "I honestly think it was the greatest drive I've ever seen by anybody," said Brabham designer Gordon Murray. "That chassis is awful, worse by far than that of any other driver. His driving was just unreal. To get that car around 80 laps without making a mistake is an achievement. To do it when you are leading and under constant pressure is unbelievable!"

On the victory podium the exhausted winner was congratulated and crowned by King Juan Carlos of Spain. Afterwards, Reutemann was heard to say: "It was ridiculous. It was like a train." And Gilles laughingly agreed: "I was embarrassed about it. In fact, I couldn't understand why they didn't pass me – after all, three of them were ahead of me on the grid! All the time I was thinking they could run rings around me if they wanted to . . . Laffite's car was worth two seconds more, at least, each lap. It was very, very hard for me. I had to take many big chances. I never let go. It was the best race of my life."

In the Ferrari pits the crew and Joann had watched Gilles's progress on television monitors and they were exhausted from jumping up and down and screaming. Toward the end Mauro Forghieri had climbed onto the roof of the Ferrari transporter to get a better view of the finish. When he returned to earth he was exultant. "Gilles was fantastic, a veritable marvel! I'd like to see who has the courage to criticize him now. In the past years he has taken an enormous amount of unmerited criticism and he has been accused of going off the road when the fault was really not a driver's error. Gilles, like Clay Regazzoni and all the people who have real courage, is thoroughly genuine."

And the next day, in Maranello, Enzo Ferrari said: "Gilles Villeneuve on Sunday made me live again the legend of Nuvolari."

6

"Oh, it's just typical of old Gilles. You've got to give him credit because the guy just never stops trying."

— Alan Jones

Gilles retired from the French Grand Prix at Dijon with electrical troubles, but in practice and qualifying he supplied the electricity. In fact, he was also literally wired up by two French doctors who were engaged in scientific investigations of what made racing drivers tick. Using the Ferrari drivers as guinea pigs, the doctors had previously found Gilles and Didier had to contend with forces of between 2.4g and 2.9g in cornering and 2.9g under braking at the Fiorano circuit. Doctors Richalet and Bertrand from a hospital in Creteil, France, also categorized the various stresses in Formula 1 driving as physical (through acceleration, deceleration, and vibration), thermal (from heat build-up), energetic (work using the arms and legs and bracing the body), and emotional (social pressures, as well as consternation in the cockpit).

In the Monaco race they had monitored Didier Pironi's heart rate and found that race-induced stress made his pulse soar from a normal of 60 beats per minute to between 180 and 207 through the race, the high point registering his exasperation about being blocked by Cheever. In Gilles's case, at Dijon, the medical people were shocked to find his heart rate barely blipped above an average of 127 despite his ever-vigorous on-track activities.

On Saturday morning he had a nasty shunt, running off the road at 140 mph and piling into catch-fencing, a pole of which clubbed his helmet, cracked it, and cut him slightly on the face. In that incident his heart monitor registered a flash reading of 168. Later, when he was trying for a quick time in his spare car, his highest reading was 182 and the doctors concluded that Gilles was indeed some kind of unflappable phenomenon. (A previous study on Niki Lauda had shown the brave Austrian's racing pulse to average 190.) Gilles's was an amazingly low-keyed response to what was surely one of the world's most stressful situations. The reading on the heart-rate Richter scale also seemed to support the prevailing theory that Gilles was always more worried about setting a quick time than crashing.

But his antics in that final qualifying session at Dijon considerably increased the pulses of onlookers, among them Nigel Roebuck, who was stationed at the same corner where Gilles had gone off in the morning. Roebuck noted the time on his watch – 1:45 p.m., and fifteen minutes to go in the session. "At its clipping point at the top of the rise the Ferrari was already sideways, its driver winding on opposite lock. As it came past me, plunging downhill now, the tail remained out of line, further and further, and still Gilles had his foot down hard. By the bottom of the dip I knew the position was hopeless. I have a clear picture of that car, virtually broadside, full lock on, Villeneuve's helmet pointing up the road – at 90 degrees to his car!" Of course, contrary to all expectations save his own, Gilles continued on nonplussed, lap after lap. Standing with Roebuck was a marvelling Charles Cevert, brother of the late François, who remarked: "Not often do you see a car sideways at close to 130 mph – for over 100 yards!"

There were more Villeneuve-inspired theatrics at Silverstone in the British Grand Prix. Gilles qualified eighth and by the end of the first race lap he was third behind Pironi and Prost and obviously keenly intent on relieving his teammate (who had outqualified him in fourth) of second place. On the next three corners Gilles pulled alongside Didier, who was reluctant to play second fiddle and refused to give way. Thus blocked, Gilles had to back off suddenly and Arnoux sneaked into third place.

At the end of the fourth lap Gilles climbed the curb at the Woodcote chicane and spun across the circuit, wreathed in a great cloud of tire smoke. The Ferrari emerged from the momentary obscurity intertwined with the Williams of Alan Jones and the two buried themselves in the catch-fencing. All the others managed to avoid the accident, except Andrea de Cesaris, who locked up his brakes and lost his McLaren against the unforgiving sleepers to join Jones – safe, though sidelined.

But the instigator of the incident was not finished racing. Gilles floored the engine, unwrapping his car from the fencing, and slid smartly across the grass and back onto the circuit, accelerating away at surely suicidal speed. For his Ferrari was a shambles of bent wings, punctured tires, and flapping bodywork. Again, practising his if-it-moves-drive-it philosophy, seen before at Zandvoort, Gilles's intended destination was the pits for repairs, but he made it only as far as Copse corner before the red wreck ceased to function.

Prior to the race the reigning World Champion, Alan Jones, was asked which driver he most respected: "Villeneuve. The thing about him is that he's aggressive and tough, but he's also sensible and responsible, which actually adds to his competitive spirit. He *thinks*. Very few drivers would have won in that Ferrari in Spain, horsepower advantage or not." Jones went on to say that a lot of other drivers made him nervous because "the car's taking them for a drive half the time."

Jones, well known for his short fuse, might have been expected to modify his assessment of Gilles after Silverstone. At the time the British journalist Mike Doodson was working closely with Jones (including ghostwriting a column for him) and got a first-hand report of the Australian's reaction. "When Gilles came around Woodcote at his usual ludicrous rate of speed," says Doodson, "about 120 per cent of the actual possible speed around there, Jonesy was a completely innocent victim. I asked him later, 'What do you think of that complete idiot Villeneuve?' Now Jonesy was one who very quickly lost his temper with anyone who got in his way. And if you look back at that incident, it could have cost Alan Jones the championship that year. Yet he showed no animosity toward Gilles at all. Jonesy said, 'Oh, it's just typical of old Gilles. You've got to give him credit because the guy never stops trying.' ''

■ ■ ■

In Germany all of Villeneuve's trying produced only 10th place after a stop for tires, and in Austria his aggression caused another accident. In qualifying he forced his porpoising Ferrari around the daunting swoops of the Osterreichring to claim an astonishing third on the grid. But with Goodyear now back on the scene as supplier to several teams Gilles predicted his Michelins would be second best in the race, good for no more than 20 laps before new rubber would be required. As it turned out he didn't get that far.

At the start everyone, including Arnoux and Prost ahead of him in their Renaults, knew that Gilles would get the jump – and he did, leading over the line at the end of the first lap. His rate of progress proved to be more than the Ferrari could handle into the Hella Licht chicane and he understeered off down the escape road, regaining the track in sixth place.

On the 12th lap Gilles approached the quick Bosch Kurve at a heady rate, which would require a significant contribution from his brakes if he were to negotiate the corner safely. Alas, the retarding effect was inadequate and the Ferrari thumped the guard rail heavily, ricocheted off it, and parked itself in a ditch, much the worse for wear. Gilles climbed out, walked back to the paddock, and a short while later was airborne in his helicopter. He hovered for a moment over the remains of his car, then headed off in the direction of Monaco.

Of the Austrian incident, Gilles said: ''There are races if you don't run a risk you'll never win. I agree that I am rash and impetuous sometimes. That's the way I am. Obviously if I had taken the Bosch Kurve more slowly I would not have gone off the circuit. But if I had gone slowly I would not have been a Formula One driver. I would not have been Gilles Villeneuve.

''Of course, if you're leading and you have it all under your right foot, you can back off and go at your own pace. But if you are not leading, you must charge balls-out to try to be first. There's no point of just hanging in there. The point is to charge all the time, unless you are first. That's the whole point of racing.'' Gilles had choice words for those drivers who did not share his theory of racing, referring to them as parade drivers, wankers, or chauffeurs de ballet. But his personal philosophy accounted for a severely truncated Dutch Grand Prix.

In Holland, the Ferraris were hopelessly off the pace in qualifying with severe handling problems, the extent of which Pironi demonstrated in a frightening accident that threw his car off the Zandvoort circuit at high speed and pitched it into the catch fencing. He was 12th on the grid and in the race tangled with Patrick Tambay, now driving for Ligier in place of the retired Jabouille. Pironi stopped with damaged suspension on lap 4 but Gilles, who had qualified 16th, didn't get that far.

Prior to the race he was in a sizable snit over the state of his equipment. ''I don't really want to spend the rest of my life fighting a non-competitive car. You have no idea how irritating and frustrating it is to have a car which is capable of no better than 16th on the grid.''

Mauro Forghieri laughs about it now, though he saw rather less humour in it on that day in Zandvoort. ''In his car we had a new experimental engine, with modifications to the pistons and so on. Only this one engine, and it was very important to stay in the race to test it. So I said to Gilles, 'Forget the race today. Just do 300 kilometers of testing.' Gilles said, 'Okay, no problem. I will do what you say.' Off they go and we saw Gilles overtake four cars in the first few meters at the start. The fifth was Giacomelli's (Alfa Romeo) and Gilles hit it and flew up into the air and into the tires at Tarzan.

''Gilles walked back toward us and he was not wanting to come to me and tell me what happened. He was walking around the pits twenty-five meters away from me to his motorhome. He was embarrassed. But I didn't say one word to him because I knew him. That was the character of Gilles.''

7

''. . . people look at me as if I'm a monkey in a cage.''
— *Gilles Villeneuve*

The weekend before the Italian Grand Prix, Villeneuve was able to put his powerboat experience to some practical use when he took part in a race on Lake Como north of Monza. The event, sponsored by his friend Abbate the boatmaker, was for craft of that make with 180-horsepower engines, as compared to the 1,400 horsepower generated by the twin Ford V8s in Gilles's version at Monaco. Didier Pironi, who was the importer of Abbate boats for France, had a powerful private boat similar to that of Gilles and was an accomplished aquatic racer, making him the favourite to win.

The event consisted of two heats on a course marked out near the sumptuous Villa d'Este hotel. The Formula 1 competitors included Riccardo Patrese, Marc Surer, Bruno Giacomelli, Jumper Jarier, Beppe Gabbiani, Pironi, and Villeneuve. Giacomelli won the first heat, while Gilles clouted a buoy when trying to pass Patrese and finished fourth. Gilles won the second heat after punting Patrese and nearly swamping him and was declared the overall winner. Said Gilles: "It was really good. I enjoyed it. I could get that boat at some incredible angles. It was nice to win something again."

Gilles was less happy about the onshore developments, which saw his helicopter, parked near the Villa d'Este, looted of his briefcase that contained all his credit cards, air tickets, helicopter and driving licences, passport, and other valuables. He spent the following week organizing replacements. Then there was more plundering in the paddock camping area at Monza where, despite a police guard, the radio equipment was removed from the Villeneuve helicopter. Gilles was particularly livid because he was not allowed to fly without the radio. Eventually he was able to leave with the helicopter of Parmalat (the sponsor of the Brabham team) acting as a guide.

Villeneuve was convinced the culprits were overzealous souvenir hunters, rather than just ordinary thieves. (After Gilles had posed on the podium wearing a Michelin cap at Monaco, Nigel Roebuck was offered, and declined, 2,000 French francs to retrieve the Villeneuve-worn chapeau for a fan.) By now he was by far the most revered, and pursued, of all F1 drivers, and the untoward incidents in Italy served to remind him of the pitfalls of being a very public personality. While he had no qualms about being recognized for his qualities behind the wheel, he was in many ways a reluctant celebrity off the track. He never lost his essential shyness and close public scrutiny bothered him.

"You have absolutely no freedom or privacy and it seems to get worse every year. They let more people into the paddock and pits and you simply don't have a minute alone. I hate that. If I'm in the motorhome people look at me as if I'm a monkey in a cage. You can't put your nose outside to talk to somebody or go and buy French fries, you can't go to watch the Formula 3 race or – whoosh – hundreds of people are all over you. I'm happy to sign autographs and I do it a lot. But there are so many people now and they're so anxious they don't even give you time to do it properly. They grab the pen right out of my hand and yank my arm when I'm trying to sign.

"So at the tracks I'm a prisoner, really, either staying in the motorhome or in the cockpit. Even if I go to the garage, there are fifty people calling for an autograph. If I start signing, then there's 300, so it's difficult to know what to do. At home in Monaco, privacy is no problem. People recognize me, but there are so many kings and princes and movie stars around that nobody takes much notice. That's good.

"Back in Quebec, it's a bit of a problem. I would like to keep a low profile and be able to go out and see old friends. But people recognize me and want to talk, or they point and stare. It's not all that annoying, I guess, but there's no privacy. With my family and genuine friends, nothing changes. I try to keep it that way when I'm in Berthier, so I'm like everybody else. That's the way I want it.

"All most people know about my life is what they read about or see on TV – the glamour side of it. But they don't see all the work behind the scenes, all the testing and so on. Then there's the travelling and the constant pressure of having people all over you all the time. It's never peaceful and I can't really have a normal life. I like the driving, sure, but sometimes I get very tired of it all."

■ ■ ■

His life was now further complicated by an intensifying relationship with a lady friend. Previously, Gilles had joked about the pit-popsies, race groupies, birds, or crumpet, as they were variously called, the eager women who lingered on the fringe of Formula 1 racing, waiting to meet the drivers. Connections were made much less frequently than popular opinion had it. "I suppose," said Gilles, "the problem is that they can't get the right passes, because I've talked to other drivers and they say the same thing – *we* never see all these beautiful women who are supposed to be hanging around. The theory is that all the women are going to the Formula 3 races because it's easier to get in and meet the driver!"

In fact, Gilles did have a flirtation or two with women in Italy, in company with Didier Pironi. Through an Italian fashion photographer they met models and went out on the town with them in Milan. "Gilles could be naughty," says Jody Scheckter. "He didn't necessarily need to be led astray and could be motivated by things other than speed sometimes. That was one of the boy things Gilles and I talked about. There were a couple of people he took out but it wasn't a girl-in-every-port thing with him. I do know there was one he fancied in particular."

The woman Gilles met on a flight to Canada was no race groupie. In fact, she didn't know anything about the sport or Gilles's position in it. She was from Toronto and worked with her three sisters and her father in the family insurance business. She exchanged business cards with Gilles on the plane and on his subsequent trips to Canada they went out together. Gilles met her family and found a kind of serenity in that environment so far removed from the racing world. Her father flew aircraft and was mechanically oriented, so he and Gilles developed a rapport.

Joann had no inkling of another woman until after her husband's death, and Gilles went to great lengths to keep his romance a secret. Gaston Parent, against his will, was drawn into the deception and was asked by Gilles to help arrange covert rendezvous. There were flights and hotel rooms for her to certain races where she stayed for a day or two until Joann arrived. Gilles asked Parent to get his new lady a fur coat and Parent went with her to a furrier in Montreal where a fine coat of wolf fur was purchased.

The duplicity bothered Gilles and he was increasingly torn between his marital obligations and the other woman in his life.

His guilt and stress contributed to even greater conflict with Joann, and Gilles became even harder to get along with at home. At the time Joann was bewildered by his behaviour, but she understands it better now. "I think he was petrified of having me find out about it because he knew exactly what it meant. He knew how strongly I felt about the marriage commitment, that I wouldn't tolerate anybody else.

"He never admitted anything to me. Eventually I said to him, 'Look, this is not a normal situation. Do you have someone else in your life? If that's the case then don't go crazy about not knowing what to do, just get a divorce.' And he said, 'No, no, you're the only person I love. You're the only person I want.' And maybe at the time that's what I wanted to believe."

■ ■ ■

Gilles's life was not made any easier by the events at the Italian Grand Prix, where the helicopter pilfering was merely the finale of an unhappy weekend. Pironi, who was to finish fifth in the race, got off to a bad start when he was the victim of a huge accident in Friday qualifying. His Ferrari unexpectedly lost grip on the 150-mph Lesmo curve and he was thankful to escape with only bruised ribs. On Saturday Gilles coasted into the pits with an about-to-expire turbo, intent on resuming qualifying in his spare Ferrari. The team had four cars on hand but Gilles was extremely vexed to find that Pironi had complained of a vibration in his own spare and was now using Gilles's to qualify in eighth place.

Gilles assumed a distinctly glum expression for the rest of the day. "I was bloody mad! Didier is out in my car improving his time. I sit in the pits with one of my sets of qualifying tires completely unused! I'm sure I would have been fifth on the grid, no higher than that, but certainly not down in ninth." He was particularly disappointed about not being able to perform for the *tifosi*. And in the race their chants of "Gilles – Gilles – Gilles" fizzled to a whisper when Gilles trundled into the pits after only six laps with fire and smoke issuing from a blown turbo.

8

"He's somewhat crazy, but surely a phenomenon."
– Nelson Piquet

In Montreal, prior to what was to be his final appearance before his home fans, Gilles was disgruntled enough to sound off publicly about Ferrari. "The car was badly designed right from the beginning. There's no excuse. The engineers did a bad job. I was lucky to win in Monaco and Spain. We had the power, but even with power you have to have the handling in the corners. You have to be realistic in this profession and I know I don't have a chance of winning in Montreal. People might say I'm pessimistic and don't have the will to win. But it's not just the will of winning that makes you win a race. I just don't have the equipment. If you gave John McEnroe a ping-pong racket and told him to play Bjorn Borg, all the will in the world isn't going to make McEnroe win.

"I renewed my Ferrari contract, but the contract is only a piece of paper. Nobody can make me drive for Ferrari if I don't want to. They could sue me, or there would be some kind of gentlemen's agreement, or I would pay them to let me go. But unless I change my mind here, or in the last race at Las Vegas, I'll be driving for Ferrari next year. Things can change though. Somebody could offer me $50 million to drive for them and I would do anything for $50 million!"

As it transpired, someone was prepared to offer him a lot of money to leave Ferrari and did so, in the pits at Ile Notre-Dame. In the traditional end-of-season game of musical chairs, Gilles had previously had overtures from several teams. Meanwhile, McLaren had been talking to Niki Lauda about his coming out of retirement for 1982. In Montreal the name of Villeneuve came into the McLaren equation. In his capacity as a friend of Gilles and of McLaren, John Lane was approached by Teddy Mayer and Ron Dennis (who later took over from Mayer and made Marlboro McLaren the powerhouse of Formula 1) and asked to act as an intermediary with Gilles. Lane had breakfast with Gilles and Joann on Friday morning before the track opened at Ile Notre-Dame.

Gilles told Lane he was open to offers and Lane suggested they start at the top and ask for $5 million. Lane presented that number to Ron Dennis, who countered with half that amount. They hit upon the scheme of using the pit signalling boards to conduct further negotiations.

"So we were out in the pits," Lane recalls, "between the morning and afternoon sessions, and we had to be careful because Marco [Piccinini] was standing there. The two pits were adjacent and Ron went over to the wall and put 2.5 on the McLaren board. I casually pointed it out to Gilles and he says, 'They can't be serious! What do I do now? Can we get more?' I told him I thought so, we'd only had two opening shots. So Gilles sauntered over and leaned against the armco barrier beside the McLaren board. He reached down into the box of numbers, pulled out a 3, took the 2 off the board and replaced it with the 3. So the board is now showing 3.5.

"Then Marco saw Gilles and wondered what he was doing fooling around with the McLaren board. Gilles told him he was just playing a joke and Marco went away. So I went over to Ron and said, 'Look at your pit board.' Dennis says, 'Does he keep his suit, too?' Gilles hadn't mentioned it but I said, 'Yes, he keeps his suit.' Dennis says, 'Tell him he's got a deal. I want him to be in Lausanne (the Philip Morris/Marlboro headquarters in Europe) right after this race.' But from that point on Gilles started having second thoughts about it. And that night he said, 'I don't feel right about this.' Gilles always had a very strong ethical approach. He had great integrity. His word was his bond and he had given his word to Enzo.''

After Montreal, Gilles went back to Monaco and Gaston Parent met with the Marlboro McLaren people in Switzerland. Parent started the bidding for Gilles's services at $3.5 million and numbers as as high as $5 million were mentioned. The negotiations went on over two days. Finally, Parent gave them a deadline to meet, it was missed, and the deal was off. Gilles, who confessed he was terrified about the prospect of having to tell Enzo Ferrari he was leaving, was greatly relieved that he wouldn't have to consider breaking his Maranello ties.

Previously, Gilles had severed his Marlboro connections after a disagreement over the amount of his retainer with them. The cigarette company sponsored several individual drivers in what was called the Marlboro World Championship Team. Marlboro was instrumental in moving Didier Pironi to Ferrari and was paying him $250,000 per season, part of which was to augment his Ferrari salary. But Gilles, whose Marlboro retainer was for $125,000, demanded that John Hogan pay him as much as Pironi or he would quit. When the extra sum wasn't forthcoming Gilles removed the Marlboro identity from his person. But his public statement was: "Why should I be a member. Half the grid are on it – so that's a reason for being different. Besides, they wouldn't be able to afford me!"

"Gilles was an awkward son of a bitch as far as retainers were concerned," according to Marlboro's John Hogan. "He was just awkwardly expensive and probably had a slightly inflated view of his own worth. He was a very nice man, very honest and straightforward. But I think he was basically a little naive with regards to the whole politics of the thing in Formula One."

Despite their problems, Gilles was still relying heavily on Joann for help in career planning. "Even when we were really fighting he still asked for my advice and trusted my opinions. Maybe I'm the one to blame for telling him that honesty is the best policy. But he listened to me and continued with Ferrari instead of breaking the contract, which in my mind I still feel was the right thing to do. Even though I know perfectly well that if Ferrari had been displeased with him, contract or no contract, he would have been right out the door."

■ ■ ■

Gilles's competition in Montreal included his brother, as Gaston Parent had arranged a deal for Jacques to replace Siegfried Stohr in the Arrows team. Gilles gave Jacques plenty of advice, beginning with his opinion that it was a mistake for him to try to make his Grand Prix debut in an Arrows, the cars being midfield runners at best that season.

Jacques, now twenty-five, was showing great potential in Atlantic and was being compared by some on equal terms with Gilles at that stage of his career. But of their relative merits, Gilles said, "I don't think he's going to be as good as I am. But that's quite natural. If you asked him the same quesion, he would probably say that he's better than I am!''

And on the track, said the elder Villeneuve, "He's no different than anyone else. If I have to push him, I'll push him.'' In truth, Gilles actually tucked his Ferrari in front of his brother's Arrows and tried to tow him along to a faster time. But the two also nearly had a disastrous coming together.

"I could tell his engine was very slow throughout qualifying,'' said Gilles, "and because of that we almost crashed. Coming out of the hairpin I was about fifty feet behind him and gaining. Jacques went to the left and I thought he was slowing down to let me pass. But it was his engine that was slowing him down and just as I was about to pass on the right Jacques moved over. He didn't see me. That would have made a good show for all the people had we crashed!''

Jacques failed to make the qualifying cut, being delayed by an overheating engine on Friday, then crashing on Saturday. Then Gilles had his own private crash. On Friday he was thrilling the crowd at the flat-in-fifth complex of right-left-right S-bends beyond the pits where the bump would send the Ferrari airborne and put it back on the track, very sideways and considerably off line. Each time Gilles managed to rescue himself from near disaster and continue at unabated speed. But on Saturday the car finally got away from him, launched itself over the curb, and bounced off the guard rail, ripping off the nose and damaging the suspension.

Gilles took the experience in stride, of course, but spoke out about the risks inherent in the current F1 machinery, particularly Ferrari. "The trouble is these cars have no suspension movement and my car moves six or seven feet out of line over the bumps. The cars just keep bouncing and it's very dangerous.'' And Gilles was only able to bounce his way to 11th on the grid.

■ ■ ■

The start was delayed ninety minutes while Bernie Ecclestone rewrote the insurance waiver (which released the organizers from responsibility from damage or injury resulting from an accident), slanting it more toward the benefits of the teams. The need for correct documents in this regard seemed particularly advisable in light of the dreadfully wet conditions that now prevailed over Ile Notre-Dame.

At the green light it appeared that everyone was intent on getting the proceedings over with as quickly as possible, but most of the getaway action was obscured in the vast wall of spray sent skyward by ninety-six furiously spinning rain tires. Cars fishtailed around madly in the aquatic conditions and somewhere in the murk Gilles hooked Arnoux's Renault with the nose of his Ferrari, sending his Dijon sparring partner into the rails and causing a closely following Pironi considerable delay. As the school of machines swam by the pits to complete the first of the scheduled 70 laps, Jones and Piquet were in front and Gilles surged by in ninth. The nose of his Ferrari looked rather out of joint, a souvenir of the Arnoux incident, but seemed to have no apparent speed-retarding effect. Nor did the bent appendage seem to alter the handling as the number 27 car was, as usual, sideways.

The 46,000 sodden Canadians on hand peered through the downpour with increasing delight. It might be raining on their parade but it seemed the local boy was going to make good. Gilles was leapfrogging up the order in spectacular style, a bright flash of red splashing through the roostertails of those who stood between him and the front. By lap seven he was third overall.

Gilles was on a major fishing expedition for a high finish and his methods weren't always subtle. He came powerboating up behind the Lotus of de Angelis, which braked abruptly and was harpooned up the gearbox by the Ferrari. Both cars spun but continued, Gilles regaining the road by means of a neat 180-degree power turn and maintaining course despite the front aero-foil being further askew. It was modified even more when the Ferrari bashed the rear of Andretti's Alfa and now the front wing began to fold up over the cockpit as a result of the considerable wind pressure being generated by the continued application of an unrelenting right foot on the floor.

There were other incidents galore and, in all, ten cars fell foul of the treacherous conditions, spinning and/or crashing out of the action. Meanwhile, Gilles kept it on the island and continued to brighten up the day with his antics. But there were fears he would be black-flagged to have the decidedly dangerous-looking nose section removed. The problem was resolved when the offending piece of bodywork finally detached itself and flew over Gilles's helmet to land in a shower of sparks. One of the Ferrari's rear wheels ran over the debris but the driver pressed on with undiluted vigour. The handling now completely haywire, with daylight frequently appearing under the front wheels on sharper corners, the number 27 slid across the finish line in third place.

The sopping wet chequered flag was shown on the 63rd lap, after the maximum two hours of racing had elapsed, and all were relieved to see it. The winner, Jacques Laffite, was pleased at his result but admitted it was no fun. "I didn't like racing today. The rain, it was impossible to see." The runnerup, John Watson, called the fourteenth Grand Prix of Canada "the worst conditions I've ever driven in. At times you could see virtually nothing."

And the third-place man – the undoubted hero of the day who collected the Walter Wolf Trophy for exhibiting the best fighting spirit in the race? "Well," said Gilles, "as for the rain I didn't mind it a bit. Even if it had snowed I would have been able to get by. There's always some speed you can do – even if it's only ten miles an hour!"

But what of his visibility problems, compounded by the wayward wing? "When it broke and came up in front of me I couldn't see a thing, which in this case was good for me because if the black flag came up I wouldn't have been able to see it!"

But Gilles had not been running around with his nose up in the air oblivious to the problem. When his forward view was completely impaired he used his peripheral vision to navigate, using the yellow markings along either side of the track as reference points. Realizing the black flag was imminent should the wing problem persist, he waited until no car was following too closely, then deliberately drove onto the ribbed concrete curbing to dislodge the offending bodywork.

"Nothing in the world would have made me stop," he said later. "I wanted to finish in the first three so I could go up on the podium and if I had stopped in the pits it would have undermined all my effort. It was a risk I took and I knew the consequences. That's my way of racing and I can't see any justification for doing it any other way."

While there were again accusations of irresponsible behaviour after Montreal, most were tempered with admiration. "He's somewhat crazy, but surely a phenomenon. He's able to do things which nobody else could achieve,'' said Nelson Piquet. ''Villeneuve showed that the man is more important than the car,'' said Eddie Cheever. And James Hunt observed, ''I can say I was the first person to discover him.''

Gilles finally did run afoul of rules and regulations at the 1981 season finale, the Caesars Palace Grand Prix in Las Vegas, where Piquet clinched the driving title over Jones, Reutemann, and Laffite. A brilliant qualifying effort saw Gilles placed third on the grid but he failed to position his car exactly in the designated slot at the start and was set for disqualification. He ran second, then third for a few laps, but soon stopped out on the circuit with terminal fuel vaporization before the authorities could act on his starting misdemeanour.

9

''What makes you think I'm going to be around next year?''

— Gilles Villeneuve

At his end-of-season press conference Enzo Ferrari talked about his two drivers. ''Didier Pironi is undoubtedly one of the best drivers in Formula One, but during the year he had 90 per cent of our bad luck. It looks as though we gave him all the bad equipment, but this is not so. He was just unlucky. I expect a great season from him in 1982.

''There has been a lot of talk in the press about mistakes by Villeneuve. But anyone who works anywhere makes some mistakes, that is understandable and acceptable. I have no complaints about Gilles's season. Yes, he made a few mistakes, but after Monaco and Jarama everyone said that Ferrari were possible World Champions. We were not. We won there because of Villeneuve's ability, nothing else. Anyway, I like Gilles as he is, with his incredible aggression and willingness to take risks.''

And Gilles spoke to the press about his fourth season with Ferrari, responding first of all to his public criticism of the cars. ''It wasn't anger really, more impatience, I've shown from time

to time. But contrary to what some people think, there hasn't
been a lot of shouting within the team this year. Yes, the car
could have been better. When you consider all the facilities we
have at Ferrari, to have the worst chassis in the field is pushing
things a bit far.

"I get along with Didier as well as I did with Jody and I think
Didier's joining the team has been as good for the team as it has
been for me. And there's never been any bad feeling between
Mr. Ferrari and me. We talk regularly, and not only by telex.
When I go to Fiorano we talk a lot more together, much more
this year than previously. It's built up gradually. When I first
drove for him I scarcely knew him at all, but now we get on
very well.

"I can talk with him very openly and honestly. I've even had
to tell him that on certain circuits the car is the worst in the field.
Anyway, I don't need to tell him: he knows it already, he can
see it on television. The only way I would ever leave Ferrari
would be if I was certain of driving a better car. But how can
you be sure? At the risk of having nothing better I'd like to
continue with Ferrari for as long as possible. Contrary to what
some people have said of him, he's the most humane of all
Formula One team patrons."

Gilles made no reference to the McLaren pit board negotiations
in Montreal, but did mention that opportunities had been turned
down. "Yes, I could have left Ferrari. Let's say I could have
gone to just about any of the established top teams, but they were
talking to me rather more than I was talking to them! Maybe if
I hadn't re-signed so early in the season I'd be on the market at
the moment and I might have been able to get more money from
Ferrari, but that's not important. Certainly, during the season,
when the car was no longer competitive, I had second thoughts.
But these were only temporary regrets. What's done is done and
it's not the end of the world."

■ ■ ■

In Las Vegas the pits were rife with rumour about the big money
being offered to lure the likes of Niki Lauda, Jackie Stewart, and
James Hunt back to the sport. It had been reported in the British
press that Stewart had been offered a £3 million stipend to race

with Brabham in 1982. Hunt's amount was £2.6 million and he was seriously reconsidering his future, though he said, "I don't need the money, and when I retired it was for reasons of self-preservation and that doesn't change."

While both Stewart and Hunt decided against racing again, Lauda was due for a comeback with McLaren – accepting the drive that might have been Gilles's. And all the big numbers being bandied about to bring former stars back into the F1 fold made Gilles Villeneuve – the number-one drawing card in the sport – seem underpaid. In 1981 his total income, including his Ferrari salary and sponsorships, amounted to about $1.2 million, though the Canadian press was full of more optimistic amounts ranging up to $2.7 million. The newspapers were also fascinated by the $2.5-million insurance policy on Gilles's life and the annual premium of $30,000.

The press was about a year ahead of the truth because Gilles was set to realize their prediction in 1982. The arrangement with Ferrari was for $65,000 for each of the sixteen races on the calendar, plus bonuses for finishing in the points. His driving suit deals, with Giacobazzi, Smeg, a new sponsor, Piemme ceramics, Labatt, and so on, would be worth about $1.5 million.

Caracer, Villeneuve's Geneva-based umbrella company, administered various financial offshoots, including a company in Liechtenstein that owned all the commercial rights to the Villeneuve name with the exception of licensing and royalties, which were handled by a firm in Holland. Any surplus funds were invested in selected industrial stocks by investment counsellors in Geneva, but the gnomes in Switzerland were left with little to work with by their client in Monaco.

■ ■ ■

Not all of Gilles's spending was frivolous, and he went to great lengths to settle an old debt, as Gaston Parent recalls. "One day he came to me and said, 'Make out a cheque to Canadian Tire for $4,000.' I told him, 'You can't just send money to a corporation like that. Why should I do it?' And he says, 'Look, when I didn't have a cent and I needed tools I would go into a Canadian Tire store and steal something. I owe them, $4,000 should cover it, and now I want to pay them back.' Nobody else knew it, but years and years later it still was on Gilles's conscience.''

Without revealing the real intention, Parent approached Canadian Tire with several disguised payback schemes. Eventually the company accepted a ghostwritten ''Gilles Villeneuve'' column that appeared under the Canadian Tire banner in the Canadian motorsport monthly, *Wheelspin News*. Parent charged only a token $25 per column and the corporation collected on the publicity value of the Villeneuve name.

''Gilles was happy about that, he didn't want to owe anything to anybody,'' says Parent, ''and he was generous to his family, too. He arranged to have a pension paid to his parents, $2,000 per month. He felt that he owed his family, especially his mother who had worked hard all her life, and he got her to sell all the sewing machines in the house from the clothing business. The money is still going to her, because the father's gone (Seville died of heart failure in 1987), and Joann's mother gets $1,000 a month.''

■ ■ ■

In late November of 1981 Gilles took part in a race between F1 cars and an Italian air force F104 fighter aircraft at the Istrana airport. The competition was for a flying kilometer distance along a runway and a huge crowd turned out to watch the new World Champion Nelson Piquet and Riccardo Patrese in Brabhams, Bruno Giacomelli in an Alfa Romeo, and Gilles in his 126C. They were to test themselves against the time set by the supersonic Starfighter in three runs apiece.

At the end of his first run Gilles threw his car into a spectacular high-speed pirouette, spinning through 360 degrees with turbo flames shooting from the exhaust and smoke spiralling up from his tires. The crowd loved it. Before his third and final run Gilles had the front and rear wings removed from his car for more straightline speed and wound up fastest of the day, beating all comers, including the jet.

Gilles became friendly with the air force general who organized the jet race and was looking forward to taking him up on an offer to accompany him on a flight in which they would break the sound barrier. Meanwhile, Gilles sought further aerial adventures, as Gaston Parent recalls. "He came to me and said he didn't want to buy the Bell helicopter from Wolf. He said he wanted to fly at night and you can't fly a single engine then. You need two engines to fly on instruments and he wanted to buy a bigger helicopter. He came up with an Agusta, which is worth a million and a quarter.

"And I remember sitting with him in his little office downstairs in Monaco and saying, 'Jesus Christ, that's a million more than you can afford!' I said, 'Why don't you just buy the Bell from Walter and just fly during the day? You don't have to fly at night.' But he's like a kid about this new toy. He's already got all these folders on Agusta and on colour radar and all the right stuff. I told him it was impossible, just looking at the insurance for that helicopter was too much. I was saying, 'Why not wait until next year?'

"And I will always remember his answer to me. His sentence was very simple: 'What makes you think I'm going to be around next year?' "

9

TIME RUNS OUT: 1982

I

"Gilles Villeneuve was someone I took a great liking to. I liked everything about him, although I questioned the risks he used to take. He was the craziest devil I ever came across in Formula 1."

— *Niki Lauda*

His new Agusta 109 seven-passenger helicopter cost Gilles $900,000, discounted from $1,150,000 in exchange for him wearing an Agusta patch on his driving suit. Still, he had to mortgage the villa to arrange the financing and Joann was very unhappy about that. She made the sacrifice, of her home, in hopes of having him realize how far she was prepared to go to make him happy. And while he was very pleased with his new toy, it took him even further away from home – faster.

"It's the fastest in its class, cruises at 175. I love it!" he said, and the brilliantly hued machine, painted in his colours, became a fixture in the skies over Monaco and at the races. He performed a variety of hair-raising stunts, such as stalling the craft, and the worse the weather, the better for Gilles. "What I prefer is flying with practically nil visibility, say 150 meters. Now that really is sport!"

Niki Lauda wrote about Gilles's aerial exploits in his memoirs. "Gilles Villeneuve was someone I took a great liking to. I liked everything about him, although I questioned the risks he used to take. He was the craziest devil I ever came across in Formula 1. . . . A typical Villeneuve episode: I am in my hotel room at

Zolder. It is pitch dark outside. Suddenly I hear the chatter of a helicopter. I throw open the window and see a chopper hovering outside, using its headlights to find a suitable landing pad. Absolutely crazy! Illegal, impossible, mad. Of course, who could it be but Gilles.''

On the road, Gilles and Didier Pironi were livening up their trips to Fiorano with high-speed hijinks. The teammates devised a contest intended to determine which of them was the greater daredevil. The idea was for the driver to get the Ferrari 308 into top gear and keep it there, foot to the floor, without touching the brake for as long as possible, while the co-pilot timed him with a stopwatch.

''The guy who kept it up the longest was the winner,'' explained Pironi. ''When Gilles was my passenger and I started to wilt a bit I would look over at him and he looked very calm and composed. Later he said he was afraid but managed not to show it. That's how he got his reputation as the man who never knew fear. He told me once, 'Every time I get in the car I think about all the things that can go wrong – how many things my life depends upon.' ''

Nevertheless, they ate up the motorway miles at speeds of around 155 mph for lengthy periods of time. On one occasion they averaged 136 mph over a ninety-five-mile stretch of Italian autostrada filled with heavy traffic. At the end of their forty-two-minute trip the speedsters were met by armed police at the toll gate. As it developed, the police were seeking a stolen Ferrari and were delighted to meet Pironi, who was driving, and Villeneuve. Autographs were given and Enzo Ferrari's two drivers reported for duty at Fiorano well ahead of schedule.

The two were getting along famously, as Pironi reported: ''We have a lot of things in common. Our characters are similar and we have a very nice relationship – much better than I had before in other teams.'' And Pironi believed they were treated as equals by the team. ''Absolutely. We exchange all information. Usually we have a meeting between ourselves before we go to the engineers to discuss changes and so on.''

■ ■ ■

Their 1982 Ferrari 126C2 cars were a technological leap forward that brought the team closer to its main competition in chassis design. While Forghieri looked after the ever-powerful turbo engines and the transmissions, Dr. Harvey Postlethwaite was responsible for bringing the new carbon-fibre construction methods to Maranello. The Englishman whose Wolf design had been so successful (and whom Jody Scheckter had helped persuade Enzo to hire) was given carte blanche by Enzo Ferrari to bring his cars out of the aerodynamic and handling dark ages. One of the first things Postlethwaite noted when he came to the team was just how remarkable it was that Gilles was able to win in Monaco and Spain with the decidedly inferior 126C. He called the wins "Brilliant, just brilliant! Quite out of this world. I *know* how bad that car was."

Since coming to Ferrari during the previous season, Postlethwaite had observed Gilles closely and became an unabashed fan. "I think he was the most disarmingly honest person I've ever met. He had no hangups about anything whatsoever. In front of the Old Man, in front of anyone, he'd come into the pits and say that the car was shit, that it had no ground effect, no down force, and he was wasting his time. He wouldn't get out and kick the wheels. 'I'll drive it,' he'd say, 'all day long. I'll spin it. I'll put it in the fence. I'll do whatever you like. I'll *drive* it because it's my job and I love doing it. I'm just telling you that we're not going to be competitive.' "

Like everyone who ever rode with Gilles, Postlethwaite had tales to tell of near misses on the roads, though the experience left him less terrified than most. "It wasn't frightening to drive with him, because you knew you were sitting alongside the best driver in the world. Gilles would drive down the outside of a line of traffic with no gap in it and a truck coming the other way, just to get himself warmed up! And I'm not joking either. He just *knew* that he would find a gap. He had complete blind faith in his own ability."

■ ■ ■

In January the Formula 1 circus convened in South Africa to start the 1982 season – whereupon its star attractions promptly went on strike. The ringleaders of the walkout were Didier Pironi, Gilles Villeneuve, Jacques Laffite, and the newly unretired Niki Lauda. The drivers were upset becaue their 1982 FIA Super-licences were issued in conjunction with their current team only and they felt that their freedom to shop around for better rides was being encroached. Another clause in the licence indicated that any adverse comment or action by a driver might result in the loss of his licence. They wanted immediate changes made and GPDA president Didier Pironi presented their demands to Balestre and Ecclestone, thus throwing FISA and FOCA together against a common adversary – the drivers.

On the Thursday before the race the drivers barricaded themselves in a hotel and stayed there for twenty-four hours, sleeping on mattresses brought to a conference room. United in a common cause, rival racing drivers developed a camaraderie never seen on the track. Elio de Angelis and Gilles (whom most were surprised to find was musically inclined) entertained with impromptu piano concerts and the others gathered round them for singsongs. Whenever Lauda received a telephone report from Pironi, who was negotiating out at the track, Villeneuve would herald the news with a dramatic fanfare on the piano. Meanwhile, Bruno Giacomelli drew cartoons and everybody told jokes about sleeping together, Patrick Tambay's being that if Villeneuve and Alain Prost ever produced offspring it would be the world's fastest baby.

While the drivers kidded around the organizers, team managers, and other people in power were not amused and threats were issued: new drivers would be flown in to replace the strikers, the teams would be sued by the organizers, the drivers would be fired, they would never be allowed to race again, and so on. When Balestre finally agreed to negotiate with the drivers in the near future the strike was called off and practice began. But not for Patrick Tambay, who was replacing the injured Marc Surer in an Arrows and who decided he'd had enough and announced his retirement.

"I don't have faith in Formula One any more," said Tambay before he left South Africa. "Apart from the amazing time we've just had, I hate the atmosphere these days . . . the way the drivers are treated by the governing body, the way the cars handle to the extent that they're virtually undriveable, and the fact that I'm only a replacement driver for a couple of races.''

About the only positive thing Tambay could find was that ''the fantastic communal life here has meant that we've got to know one another better.'' And finally, said the man who would replace his friend Gilles Villeneuve in a Ferrari in just a few months, ''A lot of things are going to have to change before I come back again.''

Gilles was a prime mover in the strike, had read the new Superlicence application forms thoroughly, and noted that the wording effectively made the team bosses owners of the drivers. He pointed out that he had seen a similar problem in the National Hockey League in North America, where the players' individual freedoms were put in jeopardy by their teams. His point of view put him in direct confrontation with Bernie Ecclestone, who following the strike prevented his driver, World Champion Nelson Piquet, from taking part in the opening practice session at Kyalami. Ecclestone's Brabham cars appeared on pit row all bearing the number 2 for Riccardo Patrese to use. Ecclestone claimed that Piquet was ''unfit to drive'' after a night of sleeping on the floor during the strike.

Ecclestone's position of power as head of FOCA intimidated most people, but not Gilles. He was never involved in a physical altercation in his life but seriously considered tangling with Ecclestone at Kyalami. Their mutual antipathy had festered for years. Now they got into a heated argument, Gilles maintaining that the fans came to see the drivers rather than the cars and Ecclestone vehemently claiming the reverse.

Bernie Ecclestone was in a rage that can only be called towering, despite his small stature. (The hardly five-foot-tall Denis Jenkinson once referred to the FOCA leader as being, ''like myself, half actual size.'') Ecclestone's dudgeon seemed as high as the South African sky and he was particularly incensed at the tall opinion the drivers had of themselves. ''It is people like Borg and McEnroe who bring in the crowds,'' said Ecclestone. ''If these drivers think they can do the same, I suggest that what they do is dress up in all their gear, rent the New York Shea Stadium, which holds 56,000 people, and see how many of them turn up. Then we would really find out what the public wants.

"We have been watching Ferraris for fifty years," he continued. "Ferrari has had God knows how many drivers. They come and go but still all that people want to see is a Ferrari. They cannot see the bleeding driver anyway!. . . Really, I ask you, what asset are they?"

In Gilles's opinion, "The sport is more important than anything. More important than any of the people in it. Of course I say what I think. I always have, even if it upsets people like Ecclestone and Balestre. Why should I be afraid of them? The fans aren't here to see politicians and manipulators. They're here to see Alain and Mario and Carlos and me. I am very secure in my feelings about racing. I make a lot of money from it, but one thing I can tell you for sure: if the money disappeared overnight, I would still be in racing, because I love it. The entrepreneurs would be gone."

As it developed Gilles and his peers were the ones who lost money over the strike, Villeneuve being fined $10,000 by FISA, along with Pironi, Patrese, Prost, Giacomelli, and Laffite. Twenty-three others were fined $5,000, the big six being charged double the going rate because they had led the previous insurrection at Zolder.

When the South African Grand Prix was finally run, Prost's Renault won, while Gilles's turbo blew up after six laps. He had qualified well, in third, while Pironi was sixth on the grid and had to stop for tires in the race and finished far back. The new Ferraris worked well enough, it seemed, but still had an appetite for rubber, which this year was being supplied by Goodyear.

2

"You can't lift off if you're on a quick lap. No way. All you can do is hope he's looking in his mirrors."

— Gilles Villeneuve

For the Brazilian Grand Prix, Gilles Villeneuve qualified on the front row alongside Prost, but he was worried about how he had had to do it. With only two sets of qualifying tires per car the driver was required to take desperate chances in slower traffic. "You sit in the pits for half an hour, you come out cold, you go slow and then you go banzai for one lap to set a bloody time. Jesus Christ! It's dangerous! Then you find someone in your way. You can't lift off if you're on quick lap. No way. All you can do is hope he's looking in his mirrors."

Didier Pironi had trouble in practice and qualifying, making mistakes and spinning frequently, and finished an unimpressive eighth in the race. Prior to coming to Brazil he had suffered a big accident in testing at the Paul Ricard circuit. While he maintained he only had a sore knee now, Gilles thought otherwise and spoke of it to Nigel Roebuck. "After practice Gilles took me to one side and said Didier's had a really bad time. 'It was a huge accident and it's frightened him. He'll get over it but don't give him a hard time for being slow here.'

"I thought that was extraordinary," says Roebuck, "because most teammates never miss an opportunity to score off each other. But here Gilles was saying give the guy a break. It was very generous of him and I was very impressed with that. I have no doubt whatever that, until Imola, Gilles believed they were good friends. That's why Gilles was so shattered later."

Gilles also spoke to Roebuck about his hatred for the current breed of F1 car with its ground effects and lack of suspension. He was wearing a neck brace in Rio to protect against the g-forces, which were of sufficient strength to nearly cause blackout. Moreover, the vibrations in the suspensionless 126C2 made it hard for him to see and there was very little pleasure in driving. He got a headache every time he was in the car. "It's not driving, it's just a matter of aiming for the corner, flooring it, and hoping you're on the right line – because you can't see it and you can't correct it. There's no satisfaction in these bloody things. . . . I like it when a car's cornering speed has something to do with the ability of the driver, not how well the skirts are working."

Gilles fretted that the spectators were being shortchanged by the current slotcar-like machinery in Formula 1 and he proposed a formula of his own. "The ideal for me would be something like a McLaren M23 with a 5-liter engine, 800 horsepower, and fat tires. . . . And that would be a fucking great spectacle, I can tell you! Corners would come down a gear and we could get things sideways again. People still talk about Ronnie Peterson in a Lotus 72 and I understand that. I'm with them. That's the kind of entertainment I want to give the crowds. Smoke the tires! Yeah!''

He was nostalgic, too, for a return to some of his early racing days, starting with Atlantic. ''You know, get a good car, do some testing, and then go and blow everyone off at Trois-Rivières or somewhere. And then after that do a Can-Am race . . . the cars are fantastic, they look great, have lot of power . . . the crowd would love it. So would I.'' Gilles often said he dreamed about the perfect race: ''I would win the pole, drop to last after getting a flat on the fifth lap, then pass every car to win the race with half a minute to spare.''

There was even room for Indycar racing in his mind's eye and he had spoken to Enzo Ferrari about it. His idea was to make a ''raid'' on the Indianapolis 500. Gilles thought Ferrari should build a car for the oval circuit and he would do the race – one time only – and he would win it, easily.

Again in Rio, some journalists were treated to a private Villeneuve performance, as Mike Doodson recalls. ''Jeff Hutchinson and I were given a ride out to the circuit with Gilles and Joann in a little Brazilian-made Fiat Gilles had borrowed. Joann sat in the front beside Gilles and we were in the back. Gilles was talking about helicopters and, of course, Jeff is a great aviator so they were in deep conversation all the way.

''Gilles only knew one way to drive. If they'd welded the accelerator to the floor on all his cars, road or racing, nobody would have noticed the difference. His policy driving the fifteen kilometers to the circuit was under no circumstances to lift off the accelerator. The idea was to keep your foot down hard and if the road was blocked you go around the object, even if that involved going out into the opposite line of traffic and risking going under an enormous truck – which we did a dozen times in fifteen kilometers.

''This car did not have seat belts and Gilles was supposed to be a happy family man. Here he was with his wife in front, putting all our lives at risk and not improving the situation by talking about flying to Jeff, which involved looking over the back seat and staring Jeff in the eye for half the time we were travelling.''

Hutchinson found the trip equally memorable. ''Gilles was explaining to me how he got his instrument-rating licence in the helicopter, how it was snowing and how the rotors were getting iced. Terrible weather somewhere in Canada. We were talking away and I didn't get terribly scared, perhaps because he was talking so lucidly about flying a helicopter.

''I did get rather worried when we went into a dark tunnel at about eighty miles an hour, heading for a bus that was doing maybe twenty miles an hour and with another car doing about forty in the lane beside us. There came a point when most people would have lifted off. But Gilles never hestitated. Just about a foot from the back of the bus, and about a foot from the car next to us and despite the speed differentials, Gilles slotted sideways and went straight into the gap and we passed the bus.

''He had this game where he'd try to get all the way to the circuit without using the clutch once, just shifting at maximum revs. We actually made it all the way to the traffic jam just outside the entrance. When we hit the traffic jam he just dove into the central median and we went into the circuit.

''Then in the race I was standing at the hairpin when he went off after leading until nearly halfway. It was obvious his tires were getting bad and he was going to have to come in and change them at some point. He was losing ground to Piquet, who was much quicker. Suddenly Gilles went off in this incredible cloud of dust. He climbed out with his usual smile on his face and I asked him why on earth he didn't stop. He said, 'Oh, it's much better to go off in the lead than to go into the pits and finish sixth.' That summed up Gilles. The only thing he knew was leading. Of course, that attitude doesn't win championships. But he was the most exciting driver that I've ever watched. He was 100 per cent racer.''

While the journalists were pleased to be able to report on Villeneuve, whose antics often highlighted otherwise dull races, some continued to be critical of his methods. One of them is Rob Walker, the aristocratic Englishman who has spent a lifetime in Formula 1, as an entrant of drivers such as Stirling Moss and more recently as a journalist for America's *Road and Track* magazine. After Rio, Walker said, "The only fault I find in Gilles is when the adrenalin runs high, which is most of the time with him, he is inclined to do things that not only endanger himself, but his fellow drivers."

World Champion turned TV commentator James Hunt went further and felt the man he had discovered in Formula Atlantic was too much of a speed freak for his own good. "Villeneuve has a brilliant natural talent. I've always thought very highly of everything about his motor racing – his speed, car control, approach, enthusiasm. He lives for motor racing and that may be his biggest problem. He drives with enormous aggression and flair, but he seems unable to combine that with common sense. I worry for him because he does things on the track which are not in keeping with his personality off the track. He has a very intelligent and ordered approach to life, but his performance in the car sometimes belies that."

■ ■ ■

When Gilles spun out in Rio he handed the win to Piquet, but the Brazilian was so exhausted at the end of the race he collapsed and needed medical attention to attend to a severe case of dehydration. Lack of water, too, was at the root of his and second-place Keke Rosberg's subsequent disqualification from the Brazilian Grand Prix, of which Prost was then declared the winner.

Some FOCA teams, in an attempt to catch the flying turbo machines, had fitted their cars with water reservoirs, ostensibly to cool the brakes. It was established practice to top up oil and water levels after a race, before the cars were scrutineered, thus bringing them back up to the regulation minimum weight of 580 kilograms. And, hoping to offset the turbo horsepower advantage, certain cars ran underweight by up to fifty kilos, racing without water in the "brake coolers," then filling them up before scrutineering. Obviously, the trick worked in Rio for the Brabham and Williams cars, but FISA declared it illegal and the FOCA/FISA feud was in full flower again.

At Long Beach it was Gilles's turn for disqualification after an exciting third-place finish behind a triumphantly on-form-again Niki Lauda and a typically hard-charging Keke Rosberg.

Gilles (sporting a rather wide-looking rear wing) and the Flying Finn engaged in a battle royal reminiscent of their Atlantic days. After swapping positions energetically several times they powered down Shoreline Drive in tandem, the Williams in front of the Ferrari, and Gilles left his braking too late. The Ferrari slewed sideways and backed into the escape road. Gilles selected first gear, tromped the accelerator, and made a tire-smoking re-entry, much to the approval of a large audience that cheered the display lustily.

But all his effort went for naught when Ken Tyrrell protested that Mauro Forghieri's unconventional rear wing was too wide. When the scrutineers agreed and Gilles's third-place result was thrown out, Marco Piccinini responded with another protest over the first- and second-place McLaren and Williams water-cooling trickery. This was disallowed and thus Niki Lauda resumed his winning ways in only his third race after his comeback, while Keke Rosberg was now en route to winning the 1982 World Championship.

■ ■ ■

It was at Long Beach that the Villeneuve marriage reached its crisis point. Joann had seriously offered to give Gilles a divorce. "I thought it was the best solution. He was not happy and I was miserable so I asked him to consider it. I don't know what went through his mind at the time. But he definitely did change after that. He did ask the lawyers to work on it but he wasn't prepared to go all the way. He said, 'No. No divorce.' "

Gilles asked Boris Stein and Gaston Parent to make a written report on how a divorce settlement would work, giving half the estate to Joann. In Long Beach, they met behind the pits with Gilles and he read the statement. He re-read it, then asked for the copies each of them had, tore them up into tiny pieces, and threw them in the garbage.

Gilles had dinner with John Lane, who had been through a divorce before he met Gilles, and they discussed Joann. "His comment," Lane recalls, "was that he loved her but couldn't live with her. All they ever did was fight. We went back over their marriage, which hadn't begun in the best conditions. They were just kids then and had been through tremendous changes in their lives.

"He compared Joann to the girl from Toronto and I said that living with another person is not going to change things in the long run. Eventually everybody changes and it's your ability to adapt to those changes that makes a relationship work. We talked about all the ramifications, about how your friends react when you divorce, about how the Catholic Church would not approve. Gilles wasn't very religious but we talked about it. He and Joann had just come back from a trip to the Caribbean together and Gilles said they actually had had a good time. They enjoyed themselves, so maybe it could work after all. In the end he said, 'Well, I'm going to go back and try. I'm not throwing in the towel yet.' "

■ ■ ■

At Long Beach, Didier Pironi had raced only six laps before crashing, but a week later he walked down the aisle with his girlfriend, Catherine Beynie. The best man at their wedding was Ferrari team manager Marco Piccinini. When he was not invited to the Pironi betrothal Gilles thought it was just an oversight on Didier's part.

Part of Pironi's honeymoon was spent in testing at Imola in preparation for the upcoming San Marino Grand Prix. Several teams were in attendance but the Ferraris were quickest, Pironi fastest with 1m 30.81s on Goodyear qualifying tires, while Gilles was second best with 1 minute, 31.58 seconds set on race rubber. Gilles sent the 20,000 *tifosi* home happy with one of his patented 360-degree spinning performances in front of the pits to end the session.

The San Marino Grand Prix of April 25, 1982, was to be Gilles's last race. It was memorable also for the fact that ten FOCA teams boycotted the event as a protest against the disqualifications in Brazil. Thus, only fourteen cars were in the competition at Imola, really only two as far as the vast crowd of *tifosi* was concerned, and the number 27 Ferrari in particular was greeted with mighty cheers each time it took to the circuit.

And whenever he was out of the car Gilles was surrounded by hordes of admirers. Besides the usual plethora of "Forza Gilles" and "Viva Villeneuve" banners around the track, there was a very large sign that read "Dio Perdonna . . . Gilles No" – God Forgives . . . Gilles Does Not, a slogan that was meant as a deification of the *tifosi* hero but which actually foretold of what was to unfold at Imola.

3

"He was totally dedicated to what he believed: to motor racing, to his family, to his friends. That's why he was so upset with Pironi. It was treason."

– Franco Lini

Despite having the full weight of the crowd behind them, the Ferraris couldn't match the qualifying pace of the Renaults. Arnoux was on pole with a time of 1 minute, 29.765 seconds and Prost was beside him half a second slower. Gilles's time of 1 minute, 30.717 seconds got him third on the grid – and that final grid position of his life is now commemorated by a Canadian flag, re-painted on the pavement on the third starting spot at Imola each year.

Pironi's time of 1 minute, 32.020 seconds was fourth fastest, and in trying to achieve it he had a big accident. The number 28 Ferrari went off the road and backwards into a barrier at very high speed, and he didn't know why. "The car suddenly snapped out of control. Maybe it was suspension failure, maybe a tire. I'm not sure."

Arnoux powered away in the lead at the start with Prost in tow, but the Ferraris overtook the second Renault before the first lap was finished. Prost retired with piston failure on lap seven and the San Marino Grand Prix became a three-car race. The Renault-Ferrari-Ferrari trio roared round in that order until lap 27, when Gilles overtook René and stayed there for four laps. The Renault regained the lead again and on lap 35 Didier overtook Gilles and stayed in front of him for half a dozen laps, then Gilles regained second place. The three frontrunners were separated by less than a second until lap 44, when the French machine spewed out smoke and then flame going past the pits, and the Italian cars took over the race.

The hordes on the hillsides around the Autodromo Dino Ferrari erupted in a roar of approval as Maranello's finest circulated nose-to-tail – with their idol in the number 27 car surely on his way to another Grand Prix win. Then the number 28 usurped the lead on lap 46 and three laps later it was 27 in front again, despite having been rudely chopped by 28 on the entry to the corner at Tosa. The fans loved it – the home team was obviously putting on a show just for their entertainment.

The crew in the Ferrari pit was without Mauro Forghieri, who was unable to be there because of a family problem. The Ferrari pit board "SLOW" sign was shown to Villeneuve and he promptly eased off, slowing down by two seconds per lap to save the cars from unnecessary punishment and particularly to save fuel, which testing had shown would be marginal over the length of the race.

But on lap 53 Pironi was in the lead again, having speeded up surprisingly. Four laps later Villeneuve scrabbled sideways through the Acque Minerali chicane and seemed to be pressing after Pironi rather hard. On lap 58 he moved alongside Pironi under braking at Tosa and was again cut off in no uncertain terms and the crowd began to sense that the Ferrari manoeuvres were not being made lightheartedly.

Lap 59, one to go, and Villeneuve dove into Tosa ahead of Pironi and that appeared to be that. Number 27 immediately slowed down again as they went past the pits on their final lap. Then, as the matching set of red cars sped toward Tosa at 180 mph – through the right-hander that today carries the name Curva Villeneuve – number 28 pulled out of the slipstream of number 27 and chopped in front in a brutally aggressive move that left the crowd gasping. There was neither room nor time left for a response and the cars crossed the finish line with Pironi in the lead.

On the victory podium Pironi waved to the crowd in triumph. Michele Alboreto was all smiles at having finished third in his Tyrrell. But the second-place man on the rostrum was there under protest. He wouldn't speak to Marco Piccinini and the team manager had to get Joann to persuade Gilles to join his teammate in front of the Imola crowd. Gilles wore an expression of mingled fury and despair that was frightening in its intensity. It was very obvious to even those who didn't know him that something was desperately wrong.

Joann certainly knew exactly what was wrong because during the race her timing analysis showed the Ferraris were running up to three seconds slower when Gilles was leading. It became obvious to her that Didier was intent on pursuing his own interests, not those of the team. Immediately after the awards ceremony, without having exchanged a word with Pironi, Gilles stalked off the podium, walked straight to his helicopter, and flew away to Monaco.

Didier Pironi joked about his victory being the perfect wedding present but his jubilation was conspicuously muted. Realizing all was not well with his teammate, he made a defence of his result. "Even Gilles knows that the 'Slow' sign means only to use your head. It has to be interpreted as keeping your eye on your brakes, your tires, your fuel, and so on. It certainly doesn't mean you, if you think you can win, don't do it. I do hope Gilles won't bear me any rancour. Time heals all wounds."

■ ■ ■

But time, the thirteen days of it remaining in Gilles Villeneuve's life, did not heal his wounds. Two days after Imola, Nigel Roebuck phoned him in Monaco and had a lengthy talk with Gilles. "I was very upset by that phone conversation," Roebuck remembers. "It frightened me. I didn't blame him for being angry. It was quite justifiable. But what frightened me was that he was saying that at the next race in Zolder he would take the same chances against Pironi as he would with any other car. He was so adamant that he would never exchange another word with Pironi again."

Roebuck's "Fifth Column" feature in the next issue of *Autosport* carried much of what Gilles told him on the phone. Roebuck called the piece "Bad Blood at Maranello" and it began with Gilles explaining why he had left Imola in such a hurry. "I left because otherwise I would have said some bad things. He was there, looking like the hero who won the race and I looked like the spoiled bastard who sulked . . . I haven't said a word to him and I'm not going to again – *ever*! I have declared war. I'll do my own thing in the future. It's war. Absolutely war.''

Gilles then recounted all the times he had obeyed ''slow'' orders at Ferrari. He pointed out that he had dutifully sat on Jody's tail the whole way at Monza in 1979, ''knowing that this was my last chance to win the world championship. I hoped like hell he would break! But I never thought of breaking my word. I know all about team orders at Ferrari.

''After the race I thought everyone would realize what had happened, but no. Pironi says that we both had engine problems and there were no team orders. And what really pissed me off was that Piccinini confirmed that to the press, saying there were no team orders. My engine was perfect and there *were* team orders.

''When René blew up at Imola I took the lead and we got a 'slow' sign from the pits. You get a 'slow' sign and that means 'hold position.' It's just not true there are no team orders at Ferrari . . . Imola was going to be my race because I was in front of Pironi when Arnoux dropped out. If it had been the other way around, tough luck for me . . . I would not have tried to take the lead away from him. Jesus, we've been living together at Ferrari for a year and a half. I thought I knew the guy. Our relationship had always been good and I trusted the guy.

''People seemed to think we had the battle of our lives! Jesus Christ! I'd been ahead of him most of the race, qualified a second and a half ahead of him. Where was my problem? I was coasting those last 15 laps. *He* was racing. I think I've proved that, in equal cars, if I want someone to stay behind me . . . well, I think he stays behind.

''I guess it looked like I was mad at finishing second. Okay, I'd have been mad at myself for not going quick enough if I'd been plain beaten. Second is one thing, but second because he steals it, that's something else.''

About the same time as that conversation took place Enzo Ferrari took the unprecedented step of making a statement on the controversy, which now raged throughout the racing world. Ferrari said that Pironi did not interpret the pit signals correctly and he well understood Villeneuve's disappointment and agreed with him.

It was Marco Piccinini's task to try to smoothe the troubled waters after Imola, and he remains reluctant to apportion blame. "I have never said who was right or who was wrong and it would certainly not be productive at this stage. And also, the two people involved are not alive any more and it would not be loyal and not correct.

"I have a clear view of what I think happened and was sorry about what happened afterwards. Maybe it was because of the reduced pressure they had, with only fourteen cars racing and both Renaults stopping. Maybe that led them to forget they were in the same family. That's what I think happened.

"Pironi was very sorry for the situation which was generated and the two drivers met with Mr. Ferrari, his son, and myself after the race in Mr. Ferrari's office at Fiorano. We discussed the situation and I think at the end of the day something was also linked to the environment – the press, their friends, etc. – of each driver which maybe generated a certain degree of mis-understanding."

Though Gilles vowed never to speak to Pironi again, he momentarily forgot himself that day at Fiorano. After Gilles landed in his Agusta, Pironi walked by and said, "Salut, Gilles." Gilles nodded his head and replied, "Salut," then immediately cursed himself privately. While he couldn't comprehend what he viewed as Pironi's act of treachery, because he would never have considered it himself, hatred did not come easily to Gilles. His mind was in a turmoil of conflicting emotions.

Also at Fiorano, Mauro Forghieri spoke to Jody Scheckter, who had flown in with Gilles and Gaston Parent. "Jody asked me what I thought, if the people in the pits should not have shown the sign that the winner should be Gilles. I agreed and told this to Gilles and tried to make him quiet, but Gilles was taking everything inside himself. He was happier to know that I was on his side but it was not enough for him because the Grand Prix was lost."

■ ■ ■

One positive effect created by the Imola situation was that it brought Gilles and Joann closer together again. Gilles always trusted his wife's judgement and intuition and often brought her along to meet his new acquaintances. From the beginning, Joann had reservations about Didier Pironi, thinking that he seemed very politically motivated and was, she suspected, something of a schemer. When she first gave this verdict to Gilles he disagreed. Then, just recently, when the Villeneuves weren't invited to Pironi's wedding, Joann became even more suspicious of her husband's teammate. Again she told Gilles she did not think Pironi was what Gilles thought he was. Gilles remembered all that now. And he also recalled that Joann had misgivings about the people who were supposed to be the backers of Team Villeneuve.

Gilles had been greatly excited when some businessmen from Milan approached him the previous year about him forming Team Villeneuve. They proposed backing him with major sponsorship from a large tobacco company (not Marlboro). Gilles took the idea and flew with it, spending a great deal of time making plans. At first, he would be the driver, then perhaps it would become a two-car team. He even talked about the day when he might retire and his son Jacques would drive for Team Villeneuve.

The Team Villeneuve backers were going to provide Gilles with enough money to do whatever he wanted, to build his own factory with a test track just like Fiorano and construct his own cars. Gilles planned to bring in his old friends: Ray Wardell was to be involved on the engineering side and Jody would be the team manager. Both were keen on the idea, as was Gaston Parent, who along with Boris Stein drew up the necessary papers. Behind the scenes Gilles had approached several Formula 1 technical people about joining his organization. Jody had already located an interim facility near the Paul Ricard circuit in the south of France, near Marseille. Gilles had even designed the interior facilities and was looking forward to putting the plan into effect, possibly as early as the 1983 season.

But the week after the Imola race the whole concept was undermined at a meeting in Milan where the truth came out. Jody had done some background research into the person responsible for securing the sponsorship and found he had misrepresented himself. He didn't really have the international tobacco money behind him at all, and the group was using the Villeneuve name to perhaps secure it, or at least further their own interests. Gilles recalled that when he had taken Joann out to dinner with the businessmen in question she came away feeling suspicious and that something was not correct.

The collapse of his Team Villeneuve dream was another blow to Gilles, another betrayal. The only person he was sure he could trust was his loyal wife, and he turned back to her. In the short remaining time they had together Joann felt they were on the way to reconciliation, heading back to where they were in the beginning. He badly needed her moral support again and Gilles's attitude toward her changed for the better.

The Imola incident also served to rekindle Gilles's friendship with Jody after a period of estrangement. The Scheckters had given a party in Monaco and Joann went alone because Gilles was out of town. When he returned Joann told Gilles about the gathering and confessed that she had had a bit too much to drink. Gilles went down the hill to lecture Jody and was very angry that he had allowed Joann to overindulge. "It was really a school-boy argument," says Jody. "But there was a time when I saw less and less of him and I felt awkward about it, though I didn't really have anything to feel awkward about."

Jody was fully aware of the problems between Gilles and Joann and could sympathize with both of them. "You have a choice as a racing driver to be either a nice relaxed family man where your wife bosses you around or you try to be a winner doing everything you know to maximize your chances. You have to be selfish. I think Gilles was selfish in certain areas outside racing. He may have spent a lot of time with his toys and less with his family.

"Being a racing driver's wife is a horrible job. You have to get your kicks out of being pretty in the pits and doing your husband's washing, because that's what it consists of. You're the star racing driver's wife, but you're really the star of nothing. There are women who want to do it because of the stardom of it. But it's a horrible, lousy job."

Besides the deep sense of betrayal he felt after Imola, Gilles was undoubtedly bothered by the fact that his reputation as the fastest driver was tarnished. One of the reasons he got along so well with Scheckter as a teammate was that Jody was content to let Gilles be quicker while he, Scheckter, concentrated on winning the championship. After he had done that, Jody coasted through his second year at Ferrari and never threatened Gilles's stardom. But Pironi had hurt his pride.

"The way he did it," says Jody, "when he jumped him at Imola, made it worse. Gilles was naive. Yes, you must trust people, but you must also always keep your hand on your gun.

"Gilles always wanted to be the fastest person in the world. He didn't do everything he did for the good of his health. He just hated to get beaten and that was the big thorn in his side. He always put himself under a lot of pressure and Pironi had been pushing him, getting faster and coming closer to him. Then when Pironi beat him the way he did, he was outraged."

Gilles and Jody discussed the Imola incident at great length and Jody tried to calm his former teammate before the Zolder race. Jody remembered his own anger at races and knew the dangers of a blind rage. The sport is dangerous enough without having one's judgement impaired by anger.

"I've been crazy and felt so mad I could have jumped out of the car at 100 miles an hour. I've changed gears without taking my foot of the accelerator, wanting to destroy the car. I used to get really upset in practice and qualifying, that was the worst time. The races were more controlled aggression. But in practice and qualifying I tried so hard to be good and took a lot more chances. You're really desperate and there's only a few laps and it gets real dangerous. When you roll the dice a little more often they're going to come up negative sometimes. But you just don't care, you hold your foot down."

4

*"Everyone agrees that Gilles always was risking more
than any other driver. That was how he made his career."*
                                                    – Eddie Cheever

The Grote Prijs van Belgie, which would have been Gilles Villeneuve's 68th Grand Prix, began with practice and qualifying on Friday, May 7, 1982, at the Omloop Terlamen Zolder. Much of the attention was concentrated on the Ferraris, for the Ville-

neuve/Pironi controversy was now the talking point of Formula
1. The tension in the team's pit was obvious, with Gilles briskly
going about his business looking more preoccupied than usual
and studiously avoiding any contact with Didier. He was also
reluctant to discuss the matter with journalists. "Nothing has
changed since Imola," said Gilles. "I still don't talk to him and
I'd rather not say anything more."

There was one exception, when Gilles took Nigel Roebuck
aside. "I was standing near the Ferrari pit and he beckoned me
over. We started talking about the car and I gave him a copy of
the story I'd written. Then Pironi came into the pits and got out
of his car. Gilles saw him coming and said, 'Let's get out of
here.' He wasn't going to stay in the pit as long as Pironi was
there. He wouldn't look at him, let alone talk to him. It was as
serious as that.

"The next day he came over to me and told me about the
article. 'That's exactly what I wanted to say. I'm glad that it's
in print. That's my side of it and I think the facts bear it out.
And thank you for doing it so fairly.' That was the last time I
ever spoke to him."

On Friday Gilles set a best time of 1 minute, 17.507 seconds,
which was fifth fastest of the day (behind the 1.15.903 set by
Arnoux's Renault), while Didier was slower than his teammate
at 1.18.796. Gilles complained that his car was quite undriveable
on the harder-compound Goodyear tires. "In fact," he said, "I
scared myself several times. We just don't have enough grip, but
it was better on softer tires."

Gilles also mentioned that the steering seemed to lock momentarily in the straight-ahead position as he was going through
the left-right curves over the hill toward Terlamenbocht, and
because of that it was not easy to go flat through that section –
where the accident was to take place. He was also irritated by
the traffic problems, with up to thirty cars on the 4.262-km circuit
at one time. There were tremendous speed differentials between
faster and slower cars as drivers were cruising to warm up their
qualifiers, slowing down after their quick laps, waiting for gaps
in traffic to go for a quick time, and so on.

"It's no worse than usual, I guess," said Gilles, "which means
it's very bad. Every time I was on a quick lap I came across

someone going slowly. Like I've said a million times before, it's crazy having only two sets of tires to get your time with. You're forced to take fantastic risks.''

The incident report for Friday quoted Gilles talking about the difficulties. ''The French Canadian expressed himself absolutely amazed at the early braking habits of some of the slower drivers, and confessed to having a couple of nasty moments when he nearly collected a Renault and a March.'' The March was the number 17 car driven by Jochen Mass; Gilles had had to brake hard to avoid running into the back of it.

On Friday, too, the Grand Prix Drivers Association held a meeting to work on the safety problems in F1. President Didier Pironi and vice-president Niki Lauda formed a committee of drivers to investigate ways of lessening the hazards in the sport, particularly those encountered in qualifying. One of those nominated to the working committee was Jochen Mass.

Also on that first day in Belgium, Gilles was interviewed in the newspaper *Le Soir*. He was asked about the danger of racing. ''It's normal to have one or two accidents in a season. I know I risk finding myself in hospital. This does not frighten me, because I am aware of the risks. But there are times when one cannot do anything. If at Zolder my car skids, all I can do is call mama and cross myself.''

Gilles was alone at Zolder and the motorhome was not at the circuit. Joann only missed half a dozen of her husband's F1 races and this time she had remained with the children in Monaco to make preparations for Melanie's first Communion, on Sunday. Gilles was staying at a hotel near Zolder and on Friday evening he had dinner with a Belgian acquaintance who lived in Canada and had helped him secure some sponsorship back in Formula Atlantic. His dinner companion noted that Gilles still sensed there was a conspiracy against him and he was distracted and preoccupied to a very noticeable degree.

■ ■ ■

On Saturday the final hour of qualifying began at one o'clock. The Renaults of Prost and Arnoux were fighting over the front row while the Ferraris seemed set to be close behind them on the grid. With a little over a quarter of an hour remaining Pironi's was the faster Ferrari with a time of 1.16.501, while his teammate was slightly slower at 1.16.616. Gilles's time worked out to an average speed of just over 200 kph. As the minutes ticked away more and more cars took to the circuit in attempts to improve their positions, among them Jochen Mass, whose best time of 1.19.777 had him on the last row of the grid.

With less than fifteen minutes to go Gilles was still out on the circuit using his last set of qualifying tires. He had already established his fastest time but continued to circulate on the used tires, trying to improve. As Gilles came by the start/finish line Mauro Forghieri showed him the "IN" signal on the pit board.

"I called him into the pits because his tires were finished. He had already done three fast laps on them before and was close to the best time of Pironi and there was nothing more he could do. He knew he couldn't do any better and was coming in. Gilles was coming in to the pits on the lap on which he had his crash. But even when the car was coming into the pits it was travelling at over 200 kilometers per hour. That was Gilles."

Gilles came over the brow of the hill and into the left-hand kink before the Terlamenbocht corner at a speed estimated later to be 225 kph, just about 140 mph, and saw the March in front of him. Competing in his 100th Grand Prix, Jochen Mass was a careful and considerate driver and was watching for following cars. He was in fifth gear but cooling his tires and moving much slower than the oncoming Ferrari. "I saw Gilles in my mirrors and expected him to pass on the left. I moved right and couldn't believe it when I saw him virtually on top of me. He clipped my right tire, bounced off the front tire and was launched into the air."

The accident was of aircraft proportions and, unlike when a car skids and then hits a solid object, there was no loss of speed, no deceleration before impact. The Ferrari just kept flying and was airborne for over 100 meters before it slammed down nose first into the earth, buckling the front of the car in on the driver. But the energy was scarcely dissipated and the accident went on and on.

The car catapulted high into the air again and began a series of horrific cartwheels, at one point touching down on an earth bank some distance behind the guard rails on the right side of the entry to Terlamenbocht. On its return to the circuit the un-controlled red projectile very nearly landed on the following March. Mass was just able to swerve onto the grass to avoid being crushed.

The Ferrari chassis began to disintegrate with pieces flying in all directions. The driver, the seat, and the steering wheel became detached and were hurled nearly fifty meters through the air to the left side of Terlamenbocht and ploughed through two layers of catch-fencing. Gilles's helmet flew off and rolled to rest some distance away from his body.

A doctor was on the scene in seconds and began to try to revive Gilles with mouth-to-mouth resuscitation. He banged his chest and gave him heart massage. More doctors arrived and were surrounded by marshals as the frantic lifesaving attempts contin-ued. Jochen Mass stopped and rushed over to the gathering crowd. As the black flag was shown around the circuit Didier Pironi halted at the accident scene and ran toward Mass, who turned him around and led him away. René Arnoux and Derek Warwick joined them and the shaken drivers walked back toward the pits.

Among the medical personnel attending to Gilles was the presi-dent of the FISA Medical Commission, Professor E.S. Watkins, who is on hand for emergencies at each Grand Prix. Also head of neurosurgery at the London Hospital, Sid Watkins "was very upset . . . not because it was in any way avoidable once the circumstances which produced the accident had fallen into place – but because I knew him very well. He was always rational and reasonable, a thoroughly nice person to deal with. When I first met Gilles he was extremely polite, a gentleman. I remember he said, 'I hope I never need you.' When I identified his car as we arrived on the scene of the accident . . . well, I just thought of those words."

Gradually everyone filtered back into the pits and many drivers hid their feelings behind their helmets as they walked into the paddock behind pit lane. But some didn't and wept openly, among them Alain Prost, who said: "I've lost my motivation for the race. He was my friend."

The last portion of the accident was seen on television monitors and its enormity was immediately apparent. The disaster was shown in endless replays and many people burst into tears on viewing it. Gloom and grief spread along pit row and throughout the paddock. The deeply shocked Ferrari team packed away the equipment and left for Maranello. Marco Piccinini stayed on, saying "a miracle is still possible."

The crash occurred at 1:52 p.m. and just eleven minutes later a helicopter took Gilles to the University of St. Raphael Hospital in nearby Louvain. At 5:40 p.m. the doctors at the hospital announced that he was unconscious and suffering from severe injuries to his neck and brainstem, officially a fracture of the cervical vertebrae and the severing of the spinal cord. His vital functions were being maintained by a life-support system.

Then came a final official bulletin from the hospital: "Gilles Villeneuve died at 21:12 (9:12 p.m.)."

■ ■ ■

That day of May 8, 1982, is forever imprinted in the minds of millions of people the world over. And for the racing journalists, who are really fans who get to report on their favourite sport, the Zolder experience was a catastrophe. Many of them sent news of the accident out to the world through their tears. "I distinctly remember crying," says Nigel Roebuck, "and we're not supposed to cry when racing drivers get killed. But Gilles was very important to me as a friend and, quite seriously, I've never felt anything like the same about racing ever since. I very nearly packed it up.

"I was terribly upset to lose a friend, but at the same time I was also losing the one focal point in racing, the one bloke in racing who made it worthwhile. Because it was such an awful time in Formula One, with all the wrangling between FISA and FOCA, so many rows in the pits and the paddock, a lot of acrimony wherever you went. Gilles was the one reason for still going to Formula One races."

Alan Henry, a British journalist who was close to Ronnie Peterson and co-authored a book about him, later wrote a full-length profile of Gilles. "It wasn't just the loss of the bloke that I felt personally, because I'd gone through the pain barrier before and felt inured to a certain extent. The thing about Gilles was that his death signified the passing of a certain approach. He was the last person who had the totally uninhibited joy of driving a racing car."

Peter Windsor was a teenager when Jimmy Clark was killed in 1968 and his death left Windsor "physically ill" for some time. "I was devastated. By the time of Gilles's accident I'd lived through a lot of tragedy and sadness: Mark Donohue, Tom Pryce, and others I was close to. But when Gilles died it was terribly upsetting. What made it worse were the circumstances at Imola. Gilles trusted Didier totally as a friend. What happened at Imola was like a stab in the heart to Gilles."

"I'm convinced that the situation with Pironi was what killed Gilles," says Rob Walker. "I've no doubt in my mind. It certainly was on Gilles's mind at the time."

Another to share Walker's opinion is John Blunsden, who has covered F1 for *The Times* for many years. "One of the most important skills for drivers to develop and use regularly is the ability to suppress their emotions at critical moments, and one of the most crucial moments is in final qualifying. I have a very deep-rooted feeling that Villeneuve was driving with a great deal of emotion that day. I think he threw caution to the wind.

"Perhaps 99 times out of 100 you can get away with it. But in this case all the circumstances which can cause a near miss to become a calamity suddenly slotted into place. He had no power over the circumstances then, he was just one of the players on the scene. He took a gamble that it would not happen. It did happen. And that was it. Curtains."

Derick Allsop was also at Zolder, in only his second year as Grand Prix correspondent for the *Daily Mail*. In 1988 Allsop was co-writer of Nigel Mansell's autobiography as Mansell prepared to become a Ferrari driver. Allsop learned that Mansell was honoured to be driving the number 27 Ferrari because Gilles was the driver Mansell most admired and he prided himself in being friendly with him. Allsop himself had trouble with Gilles's death.

"It was the first fatality I'd had to deal with and it affected me in a very profound way. I felt a very guilty man that weekend. Because I was living off this sport. When I went to the circuit the next day, the Ferrari garage was all shut up and yet the race just continued. It all went on. I couldn't quite cope with that. It seemed somehow sacrilegious. I know how the drivers all know what they face. They're very fatalistic about it. And time, I'm afraid, does harden you. But I struggled within myself that weekend in Belgium. I struggled with my conscience. Could I go on with this sport? I must admit I really didn't want to go on. I remember that clearly. Yet, somehow I did.''

The Belgian Grand Prix went on as scheduled, the first race since 1976 that was run without a Ferrari. A proposal that there be a minute's silence for Gilles before the start was rejected on the grounds that it might affect the concentration of the drivers. Before the start Eddie Cheever spoke of the accident: "In a situation like that I know I would have been scared stiff. But I am sure that when Gilles felt his Ferrari take off, his last thought was anger, plain and simple, because he knew that he had spoiled that one quick lap.''

"I think Gilles was the perfect racing driver,'' said Niki Lauda. "He had the best talent of all of us.'' But Lauda also thought Gilles's propensity for risk-taking was a contributing factor in his accident. After criticizing Jochen Mass for not giving Gilles more room to pass, Lauda went on: "Having said this, I must say that Villeneuve was perhaps the only driver around who would have chosen the risky option of overtaking a slower car going flat out off the ideal line. The chances of a misunderstanding were simply too great.'' (A FISA inquiry later attributed the cause of the accident to an error by Gilles and absolved Mass of any blame.)

John Watson won the Belgian race from Keke Rosberg and it was Rosberg who said, "Metaphorically, we were all wearing black armbands at Zolder on Sunday.''

The next day Rosberg was driving past the Zolder circuit alone. "It's the emptiest place in the world. After all that activity and intensity, there's not a soul about. It's dead. Nothing but litter. And parked out there was Gilles's helicopter. Then it hit me. Very hard.''

5

*"We can only console ourselves with those fleeting
memories of the man who left us in the way he would have
wanted to be remembered: giving us everything he'd got."*
— Alan Henry

On that Saturday, Jody Scheckter was recovering from a hernia
operation at his home in Monaco. "A friend of mine called me
from Zolder and said, 'Gilles has had an accident, a big one,
and it doesn't look good at all.' So I phoned Joann and shot up
to her place very quickly. From then on it was chaos and disaster.
You don't even want to think back on it."

Joann was baking cookies in her kitchen when Jody called.
"He told me it was very serious. I went into shock and Jody
gave me some tranquilizers he had for his operation. He couldn't
travel so his wife Pam went with me to Belgium. The doctors
took me into an office and told me there was nothing more they
could do. They'd been on the phone with several specialists, in
Montreal and elsewhere. I wanted them to try and operate, to do
something, anything. They told me I had to make the decision
to cut the life-support machines off. I told them they were crazy.
Eventually Gilles died. From then on everything is blurred for
me. A lot of people helped. Jody was very, very good. Very
strong."

Despite being in constant pain from his operation, Jody devoted
himself completely to the very difficult tasks that followed. "I
thought it was my duty to Gilles. I wanted to look after Joann
and make sure she was protected. And the children. I didn't care
about anything else. I needed to do it. Probably I was under
shock as well."

John Lane flew over to Monaco as soon as he heard the bad
news and remembers how Jacques and Melanie reacted. "They
were just ten and eight years old at the time and seemed to be
doing much better than I expected. That first night they both went
upstairs to bed and later I went up to check on them. They were
asleep. When I saw Melanie I started crying. She had a picture
of her dad with her. She was holding it in her arms."

Ray Wardell also came to Europe immediately and joined Scheckter and Lane, attending to the logistics of bringing the body back to Canada. The three organized themselves so that Joann was never alone. In Canada, Gaston Parent's wife Daniele began making the funeral arrangements. Gaston was unable to function: "When he died, when he passed away, I went into a shell. I didn't want to see anybody. I didn't want to go anywhere. I didn't want to do anything. I just closed myself off."

The government diverted a Canadian Armed Forces 707 jet from Frankfurt to the Brussels airport where the coffin, draped in a Maple Leaf flag, was marched slowly onto the aircraft by six Canadian soldiers. Among those who made the seven-hour flight to Montreal with Joann and the children were Bruno Giacomelli's girlfriend, Linda Marso, who helped Scheckter, Wardell, and Lane look after Joann, who was suffering terribly with grief. Also on board were Marco Piccinini and the Canadian French-language radio journalist, Christian Tortora, whose task it had been to pick out the coffin. Tortora remembers that the children spent the flight drawing and writing poems about their father, and Jacques drew pictures of racing cars.

In Montreal a large crowd waited at Dorval airport. Joann refused the offer of a helicopter ride, preferring to accompany the body by car to Berthierville, where her husband lay in state in the town cultural centre for two days. An estimated 5,500 people filed silently by the open bronze casket where Gilles lay dressed in a white cardigan with a single red rose on his chest. At his feet were his pock-marked red-and-blue helmet and his orange driving gloves. Nearby lay a model of a Ferrari made of red flowers with a card reading: "Papa et Mama."

All the church bells in Berthier peeled. Nearby, in their neat white home, Georgette and Seville Villeneuve received condolences from around the world. "When he was out there, I was with him," said Seville. "I'd take the corners with him, put the pedal down. At the end of the race, I'd be more tired than him. It's terrible after working so hard to be cut off like this. He's too young. It's too soon. He had another ten years he wanted to race. It's tough to take but I know that he loved racing and if he died from that, at least he died doing what made him happy."

Also with the Villeneuves was their other son, and on that ill-fated Saturday Jacques Villeneuve had had a premonition. "For some reason, when the phone rang I had the feeling it was something about my brother. I can't explain why. I just knew. It was about ten in the morning here and I knew he was racing that weekend. My mother-in-law heard the bad news on the radio and called me. I went fast to my parents' place but my mom had heard it on the radio, too. She took it really hard. My dad and I were so busy taking care of her and so on that it didn't really hit us then. It didn't really get to me until later and finally I realized it. It hit me hard and I just cried all night long. It just hit me that I had lost my best friend."

■ ■ ■

The funeral was held at 3 p.m. on Wednesday, May 12, 1982, in L'Eglise Ste-Genevieve-de-Berthier, the church Gilles attended as a boy. Loudspeakers broadcast the service to several hundred people outside, while in the white-and-gold interior of the church 900 invited people attended the ceremony. Among them were Prime Minister Trudeau, Quebec Premier René Lévesque, and other government officials. Previously, the Prime Minister had said: "In the name of all Canadians I offer my deepest sympathy to his wife and children and to his relatives and friends. Fate has determined that we will never again have the opportunity to applaud the achievements of this man who has made us so proud."

The racing world was represented by Jean Sage, manager of the Renault team, Walter Wolf, Jacques Laffite, and Peter Windsor, as well as Marco Piccinini and two other representatives from Ferrari. "At Zolder it was very, very sorrowful and painful," said Marco Piccinini, "because Gilles was a very dear person and not only a colleague but also a friend. All my experience in Formula One with Ferrari had been with him so he was part of the environment and to lose his personality, his comments and presence and his enthusiasm, was really like losing a major part of the way of life then."

Jean Sage mentioned how Renault would have liked to have Gilles, as would every Formula 1 team. "Gilles was extraordinary. He has a permanent place in our pantheon. Most consider him the best competitor in formula cars of our time."

Jackie Stewart was also at the funeral and had talked with Gilles at Imola. "He was stunned by that race. I think he was a very clean, almost innocent man, with no maliciousness in him. It was very sad that the last two weeks of his life were so tormented and disillusioned."

In the church Joann was wearing a simple black dress. On it was pinned the diamond prancing-horse broach given to her by Enzo Ferrari. Back in Maranello the Old Man had spoken sadly. "He left us because of something incomprehensible. His fatality has deprived us of a great champion – one that I loved very much. My past is scarred with grief: father, mother, brother, son. My life is full of sad memories. I look back and see my loved ones. And among my loved ones I see the face of this great man, Gilles Villeneuve."

The Requiem Mass was presided over by the Reverend Eugene Dumontière, who praised Gilles Villeneuve's courage, tenacity, and simplicity. Prime Minister Trudeau escorted Joann out of the church in the procession that moved behind the coffin. Thousands of people stood in respectful silence on the bridges overhead along the autoroute as the funeral procession drove back to Montreal, where the body was cremated.

The lasting memory for most people was the eulogy delivered by Jody Scheckter: "I will miss Gilles for two reasons. First, he was the fastest driver in the history of motor racing. Second, he was the most genuine man I have ever known. But he has not gone. The memory of what he has done, what he has achieved, will always be there."

EPILOGUE

A week after Gilles's death the city council of Montreal officially named the Ile Notre-Dame track Le Circuit Gilles Villeneuve to "perpetuate his memory, honour the great qualities of bravery and professional conscientiousness he exemplified and recognize the reknown his exploits and talents mean to the City of Montreal."

In Berthierville the town created the Parc Gilles Villeneuve and in it erected a life-size bronze statue of Gilles, dressed in his driving suit complete with sponsors' patches and holding his helmet in his hand. Above the statue are the flags of Berthierville, Quebec, and Canada. The inscription reads "Gilles Villeneuve, 1950-1982. Merci, Gilles."

Nearby is the Musée Gilles Villeneuve, a two-storey building crammed full of artifacts, including one of his snowmobiles, one of his Formula Atlantic cars, the bodywork of one of his Ferraris, even a well-used brake disc from a 126C2. Also on view are his driving suit, helmet, gloves, and shoes and some of his tools. Besides the hundreds of trophies, photographs, plaques, and framed tributes, there is a licence plate from one of his road cars, his trumpet, and the sheet music for "Dark Eyes," a piece he once played.

There is a Gilles Villeneuve monument, featuring the Canadian maple leaf, at the Zolder circuit in Belgium. In Fiorano the main street leading to the test circuit was officially named Via Gilles Villeneuve and near the entrance to the track a monument was built, featuring a bronze bust of Gilles atop a circular metal representation of a racing tire. Today it has become a shrine, always decorated with fresh flowers and visited regularly by solemn fans who take photographs and stand before it in respectful silence.

Written tributes such as "Gilles Forever" still appear on the streets and walls of buildings around Fiorano and Maranello, painted there by the *tifosi*, for whom the legend seems to grow. And thousands of visitors from abroad make the pilgrimage to the Ferrari memorabilia shop and bookstore across the street from the gates of the factory. There, the best sellers are the Gilles Villeneuve pins, buttons, banners, models of his number 27 car and helmet, and several picture books devoted to his career.

At the Monza and Imola circuits the souvenir stalls are hard-pressed to keep up with the demand for framed photos, plaques, miniature bronze busts, and replicas of Gilles's driving suit. Each year at the San Marino Grand Prix the "Gilles Vivo" (Gilles Lives) slogans appear all around the Autodromo Dino Ferrari and the Canadian flag on the third spot of the starting grid, where Gilles started his last race, is sacred ground.

At Ferrari, where they still get letters addressed to Gilles Villeneuve, thousands of messages of condolence and outpourings of grief were received by Brenda Vernor. The international press published many of the tributes sent by mourning fans. Six months after his death a twenty-one-year-old woman wrote: "Hello Gilles: I still cannot believe that you are no more. . . . I did not know Nuvolari but I will talk to my daughter with pride about you. I will be able to tell her that I delighted in you and cried for you. I have within me the sense of an infinite emptiness that I feel nothing will be able to fill except my tears. I hope that up there you have found a circuit and when the starting light is green, go Gilles. You will always be first. When I look up towards a starry sky, I see you in the most beautiful star. The brightest one. And I am sure that for you up there, you think of us, you think of me, who died in my heart with you. One day I shall bring you a rose because you were my first shattered dream."

■ ■ ■

After the tragedy in Belgium, Enzo Ferrari tried to have the number 27 permanently retired as a lasting tribute to Gilles. He asked for it to be replaced by 37 but it was not allowed by FISA. The team entered only one car, for Pironi, at the next race, in Gilles's adopted home town. Pironi finished second in that fortieth Grand Prix de Monaco and in the program for the event Clay Regazzoni had written a final tribute to the man being mourned by all Monégasques.

Following the accident in Long Beach in 1980 where Regazzoni was left paralysed for life, Gilles was full of admiration for the driver now confined to a wheelchair. Gilles confessed, "I couldn't bear to have a crash like that. That's dreadful. I couldn't race again."

Now Clay Regazzoni wrote: "So long, Gilles. You were young, loyal, daring, simple and you loved to express yourself in our sport like no one has done in recent years. You had just attained the heights of glory and like a lightning bolt destiny cruelly stole your life. You leave an immense void. Your talents were fantastic exhibitions which the many fans you loved and for whom you always gave your best, will miss. They never will forget what you did and you will leave unperishable memories for automotive sport aficionados. Joann, Melanie and Jacques, like us, will always be proud of you. Adieu, Gilles."

There was more sadness in Formula 1 as the 1982 season continued. At Le Circuit Gilles Villeneuve in June, scarcely a month after the circuit was renamed, a starting line accident claimed the life of the young Italian driver Riccardo Paletti when his Osella rammed a stalled car on the grid: the Ferrari of Didier Pironi.

Pironi was unhurt in Canada and won the next race, the Dutch Grand Prix, which he dedicated to the memory of Gilles Villeneuve. Also in Holland, Patrick Tambay took over the number 27 Ferrari as the replacement for his late friend. Tambay accepted the offer only after deliberating whether replacing Gilles "might be an inhibiting factor, in both sentimental and psychological terms. It was very hard for me to accept replacing Gilles. For a while it seemed the negative aspects might outweigh the positives. I felt I was driving under Gilles's shadow and that everyone was thinking of him.''

"Taking Gilles's place,'' said Tambay at the time, "has been almost more of a duty as well as being an honour. Nobody will ever forget because we are talking about a wound which can never heal, but with time it will become less painful. It will have to be handled with a great deal of understanding, hard work, and friendship. But no one will ever be able to fill a gap such as Gilles left, not in any way at all.''

Three months to the day after Gilles's death, Didier Pironi's F1 career was ended in a horrific accident during practice for the German Grand Prix at Hockenheim. He was now leading in the world championship (he finished second overall to the winner, Keke Rosberg) and driving harder than ever. Having already set the fastest qualifying time, Pironi was circulating at very high speed, though it was raining and visibility was extremely poor. Alain Prost's Renault was hidden in a ball of spray, Pironi failed to see it in time, and hit it from behind. Pironi's car was launched high into the air in a manner disastrously similar to Gilles's fatal crash at Zolder. The Ferrari was travelling at an estimated 150 mph, the Renault at less than 120 mph, and the number 28 car landed 300 yards further on. When Prost, Eddie Cheever, and Nelson Piquet stopped to help him they were appalled at the extent of his leg injuries and Piquet was sick at the sight.

Patrick Tambay went on to win that 1982 German Grand Prix, his first Formula 1 victory, and it was an extremely emotional day for him. "I thought of Gilles and Didier. I was thinking about them non-stop. They were with me throughout. It was very difficult.''

Pironi's legs were badly mangled in the Hockenheim crash and during the following year he underwent thirty-one different operations. Enzo Ferrari promised him a drive when he was fit enough to return and Pironi continued to have hopes of resuming his F1 career. But it was not to be. His life ended in a powerboat crash in the summer of 1987.

Didier Pironi was genuinely sorry about the controversy following Imola. His home was filled with photos of him and Gilles,
and after his death in 1987 his companion (his marriage had
earlier ended in divorce), Catherine Goux, gave birth to twin
boys. She named them Didier and Gilles.

■ ■ ■

At his annual press conference in 1982 Enzo Ferrari paid homage
once more to the driver for whom he had such great affection.
"It seems fitting to remember the driver whom we shall see no
more and who had achieved such fame with Ferrari through his
magnanimity and his daring. . . . I was fond of Villeneuve; in
my eyes he was one of my family. I now draw comfort from the
letter I have received from his widow, in which she says: 'Dear
Ferrari, I was deeply touched by your generosity which has lifted
a great burden from my shoulders. Thanks to you, I can more
easily devote my full attention to my children, who are my source
of strength in this very difficult period. I want to thank you for
everything and hope to come and visit you in Maranello with my
children in the near future.' "

After the funeral Joann brought her husband's ashes with her
back to the villa in Monaco. Friends continued to provide moral
support for her and the children and the matter of settling the
estate was attended to. There were complications in the form of
the international legalities involved with a Canadian citizen re-
siding in Monaco and with business interests subject to the laws
of several different countries. Jody Scheckter spent a great deal
of time over the next year working to collect money from Gilles's
various sponsorship deals. John Lane stayed in Monaco to assist
in sorting out Gilles's personal effects. Gaston Parent, as the sole
protector of the will, worked with Boris Stein to administer the
Villeneuve trust account to assure that Joann, Jacques, and Melanie were well provided for.

Mentally and physically exhausted, Joann went through a very
difficult period of adjustment and drew strength from the many
people who rallied to help her. She concentrated on comforting
the children and putting on a brave front for them, and with her
help Jacques and Melanie proved to be resilient and adaptable.

They were enrolled in a private school in Switzerland and Joann studied fashion design in Nice for two years. Then she interrupted the course, intending to resume it in the future, and devoted herself completely to the children and to perpetuating the memory of their father. Melanie is interested in a career in international law, while Jacques, against his mother's best wishes (though his father would no doubt approve), has decided to embark on a racing career.

The family is still very much in the public eye in Europe and when Gilles Villeneuve's wife and children visit the Grand Prix races they are treated as full-fledged celebrities by the fans and greeted with warm affection by the members of the racing fraternity. For the children, it is a return to the world where they grew up. For Joann, it is a bittersweet time as she remembers those days when her husband would whisper to her, "Wait for me, I won't be long."

GILLES VILLENEUVE'S RACE RESULTS

1973
Formula Ford: Provincial Series (Quebec)
Won seven of ten events; Quebec Champion; Rookie of the Year

1974
Formula Atlantic (March 74B-Ford BDA): Player's Challenge Series (Canada)

May 26: Westwood, B.C.		Result: 3
June 2: Edmonton, Alberta.	Grid: 6;	Result: 22
June 16: Gimli, Manitoba.	Grid: 15;	Result: DNF
July 1: Mosport, Ontario.	Grid: 14;	Result: Accident
August 11: Halifax, Nova Scotia.		Result: DNF
September 1: Trois-Rivières, Quebec.	Grid: 13;	Result: Accident (Non-championship race)

Final Standings: Player's Challenge Series
1. Bill Brack 128
2. Tom Klausler 117
3. Wink Bancroft 74
16. Gilles Villeneuve

1975

Formula Atlantic (March 75B-Ford BDA): Player's Challenge Series (Canada)

May 25: Edmonton, Alberta.		Result: 15
June 1: Westwood, B.C.	Grid: 8;	Result: 5
June 22: Gimli, Manitoba.	Grid: 19;	Result: 1
July 6: St. Jovite, Quebec.	Grid: 4;	Result: 2
August 17: Halifax, Nova Scotia.	Grid: 7;	Result: 14
August 31: Trois-Rivières, Quebec.	Grid: 3;	Result: DNF (Non-championship race)

Final Standings: Player's Challenge Series
1. Bill Brack 112
2. Bertil Roos 94
3. Tom Klausler 92
5. Gilles Villeneuve 69

1976

IMSA Camel GT Challenge (Chevrolet Camaro) with Maurice Carter

January 31/February 1: Daytona Beach, Florida.   Result: DNF

Formula Atlantic (March 76B-Ford BDA): Player's Challenge Series, (Canada); IMSA Series (U.S.A)

April 11: Road Atlanta, Georgia.	Grid: 1;	Result: 1
May 2: Laguna Seca, California.		Result: 1
May 9: Ontario, California.	Grid: 1;	Result: 1; Fastest Lap
May 16: Edmonton, Alberta.	Grid: 1;	Result: 1; Fastest Lap
May 30: Westwood, B.C.	Grid: 1;	Result: DNF
June 13: Gimli, Manitoba.	Grid: 1;	Result: 1
July 11: St. Jovite, Quebec.	Grid: 1;	Result: 1; Fastest Lap
August 8: Halifax, Nova Scotia.	Grid: 1;	Result: 1; Fastest Lap
September 5: Trois-Rivières, Quebec.	Grid: 1;	Result: 1; Fastest Lap (Non-championship race)
September 19: Road Atlanta, Georgia.	Grid: 1;	Result: 1; Fastest Lap

Final Standings: Player's Challenge Series
1. Gilles Villeneuve 120
2. Bertil Roos 72
3. Bill Brack 67

Final Standings: IMSA Series
1. Gilles Villeneuve 80
2. Price Cobb 45
3. Elliott Forbes-Robinson 45

Formula Two (March 762-Hart): European Series

June 7: Pau, France.   Grid: 10;   Result: DNF

1977

Formula Atlantic (Chevron B39-Ford BDA): Phillips International Formula Atlantic Championship (South Africa)

January 15: Roy Hesketh, Natal.	Grid: 10;	Result: 3
January 29: Kyalami, Transvaal.	Grid: 2;	Result: 5
February 5: Goldfields, OFS.	Grid: 5;	Result: DNF
February 19: Killarney, Cape Town.	Grid: 5;	Result: Accident

Final Standings: Phillips International Championship
1. Ian Scheckter 27
6. Gilles Villeneuve 6

Formula Atlantic (March 77B-Ford BDA/BDN): Labatt Challenge Series (Canada)

May 22: Mosport, Ontario.	Grid: 1;	Result: 2; Fastest Lap
June 26: Gimli, Manitoba.	Grid: 2;	Result: DNF
July 3: Edmonton, Alberta.	Grid: 1;	Result: 1
August 7: Halifax, Nova Scotia.	Grid: 1;	Result: Accident
August 14: St. Félicien.	Grid: 1;	Result: 1
September 4: Trois-Rivières.	Grid: 1;	Result: 4 (Non-championship race)
September 25: Quebec City, Quebec.	Grid: 3;	Result: 1

Final Standings: Labatt Challenge Series
1. Gilles Villeneuve 114
2. Bobby Rahal 92
3. Bill Brack 87

Can-Am (Wolf Dallara WD1-Chevrolet): SCCA Citicorp Challenge Series (U.S.A. and Canada)

July 10: Watkins Glen, New York.	Grid: 4;	Result: DNF
July 24: Road America, Wisconsin.	Grid: 1;	Result: 3
August 21: Mosport, Ontario.	Grid: 6;	Result: DNF
September 4: Trois-Rivières, Quebec.	Grid: 3;	Result: DNF

Final Standings: SCCA Citicorp Challenge
1. Patrick Tambay 159
2. Peter Gethin 108
3. Elliott Forbes-Robinson 71
12. Gilles Villeneuve 16

World Endurance Championship (BMW 320i): with Eddie Cheever
August 20: Mosport, Ontario.　　Grid: 11;　Result: 3

Formula One (McLaren M23-Ford Cosworth DFV): World Championship
July 16: Silverstone, England.　　Grid: 9;　Result: 11

Formula One (Ferrari 312 T2): World Championship

October 9: Mosport, Canada.	Grid: 17;	Result: 12
October 23: Fuji, Japan.	Grid: 20;	Result: Accident

1978

Formula One (Ferrari 312 T2/T3): World Championship

January 15: Buenos Aires, Argentina.	Grid: 7;	Result: 8
January 29: Jacarepaguá, Brazil.	Grid: 6;	Result: Accident
March 4: Kyalami, South Africa.	Grid: 8;	Result: DNF
April 2: Long Beach, U.S.A.	Grid: 2;	Result: Accident
May 7: Monaco.	Grid: 8;	Result: Accident
May 21: Zolder, Belgium.	Grid: 4;	Result: 4
June 4: Jarama, Spain.	Grid: 5;	Result: 10
June 17: Anderstorp, Sweden.	Grid: 7;	Result: 9
July 2: Paul Ricard, France.	Grid: 9;	Result: 12
July 16: Brands Hatch, England.	Grid: 13;	Result: DNF
July 30: Hockenheim, Germany.	Grid: 15;	Result: 8
August 13: Osterreichring, Austria.	Grid: 11;	Result: 3
August 27: Zandvoort, Holland.	Grid: 5;	Result: 6
September 10: Monza, Italy.	Grid: 2;	Result: 7 (Finished second in race. One minute penalty assessed for jumping start.)
October 1: Watkins Glen, U.S.A.	Grid: 4;	Result: DNF
October 8: Ile Notre-Dame, Canada.	Grid: 3;	Result: 1

Final Standings: World Championship
1. Mario Andretti 64
2. Ronnie Peterson .... 51 (posthumously)
3. Carlos Reutemann 48
9. Gilles Villeneuve 17

1979

Formula One (Ferrari 312 T3/T4): World Championship

June 21: Buenos Aires, Argentina.	Grid: 10;	Result: DNF
February 4: Interlagos, Brazil.	Grid: 5;	Result: 5
March 3: Kyalami, South Africa.	Grid: 3;	Result: 1; Fastest Lap
April 8: Long Beach, California.	Grid: 1;	Result: 1; Fastest Lap
April 15: Brands Hatch, England.	Grid: 3;	Result: 1 (Non-championship race)
April 29: Jarama, Spain.	Grid: 3;	Result: 7; Fastest Lap
May 13: Zolder, Belgium.	Grid: 6;	Result: 7; Fastest Lap
May 27: Monaco.	Grid: 2;	Result: DNF
July 1: Dijon-Prenois, France.	Grid: 3;	Result: 2
July 14: Silverstone, England.	Grid: 13;	Result: 14
July 29: Hockenheim, Germany.	Grid: 9;	Result: 8; Fastest Lap
August 12: Osterreichring, Austria.	Grid: 5;	Result: 2
August 26: Zandvoort, Holland.	Grid: 6;	Result: DNF; Fastest Lap
September 9: Monza, Italy.	Grid: 5;	Result: 2

September 16: Imola, Italy.	Grid: 1;	Result: 7; Fastest Lap (Non-championship race)
September 30: Ile Notre-Dame, Canada.	Grid: 2;	Result: 2
October 7: Watkins Glen, U.S.A.	Grid: 3;	Result: 1

Final Standings: World Championship
1. Jody Scheckter 51
2. Gilles Villeneuve 47
3. Alan Jones 40

1980
Formula One (Ferrari 312 T5): World Championship

January 13: Buenos Aires, Argentina.	Grid: 8;	Result: Accident
January 27: Interlagos, Brazil.	Grid: 3;	Result: 16
March 1: Kyalami, South Africa.	Grid: 10;	Result: DNF
March 30: Long Beach, U.S.A.	Grid: 10;	Result: DNF
May 4: Zolder, Belgium.	Grid: 12;	Result: 6
May 18: Monaco.	Grid: 6;	Result: 5
June 29: Paul Ricard, France.	Grid: 17;	Result: 8
July 13: Brands Hatch, England.	Grid: 19;	Result: DNF
August 10: Hockenheim, Germany.	Grid: 16;	Result: 6
August 17: Osterreichring, Austria.	Grid: 15;	Result: 8
August 31: Zandvoort, Holland.	Grid: 7;	Result: 7
September 14: Imola, Italy.	Grid: 8;	Result: Accident
September 28: Ile Notre-Dame, Canada.	Grid: 22;	Result: 5
October 5: Watkins Glen, U.S.A.	Grid: 18;	Result: Accident

Final Standings: World Championship
1. Alan Jones 67
2. Nelson Piquet 54
3. Carlos Reutemann 42
10. Gilles Villeneuve 6

1981
Formula One (Ferrari 126C): World Championship

March 15: Long Beach, California.	Grid: 5;	Result: DNF
March 29: Jacarepaguá, Brazil.	Grid: 7;	Result: DNF
April 12: Buenos Aires, Argentina.	Grid: 7;	Result: DNF
May 3: Imola, Italy.	Grid: 7;	Result: 4; Fastest Lap
May 17: Zolder, Belgium.	Grid: 7;	Result: 4
May 31: Monaco.	Grid: 2;	Result: 1
June 21: Jarama, Spain.	Grid: 7;	Result: 1
July 5: Dijon-Prenois, France.	Grid: 11;	Result: DNF
July 18: Silverstone, England.	Grid: 8;	Result: Accident
August 2: Hockenheim, Germany.	Grid: 8;	Result: 10
August 16: Osterreichring, Austria.	Grid: 3;	Result: Accident

August 30: Zandvoort, Holland.	Grid: 16;	Result: Accident
September 13: Monza, Italy.	Grid: 9;	Result: DNF
September 27: Ile Notre-Dame, Canada.	Grid: 11;	Result: 3
October 17: Las Vegas, U.S.A.	Grid: 3;	Result: DNF

Final Standings: World Championship
1. Nelson Piquet 50
2. Carlos Reutemann 49
3. Alan Jones 46
7. Gilles Villeneuve 25

1982

Formula One (Ferrari 126 C2): World Championship

January 23: Kyalami, South Africa.	Grid: 3;	Result: DNF
March 21: Jacarepaguá, Brazil.	Grid: 2;	Result: Accident
April 4: Long Beach, U.S.A.	Grid: 7;	Result: Disqualified (Finished third)
April 25: Imola, Italy.	Grid: 3;	Result: 2
May 8: Zolder, Belgium.	Killed in qualifying	

GRAND PRIX CIRCUITS

Circuit maps courtesy of the Fédération Internationale de
l'Automobile

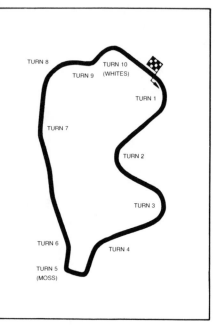

Mosport Park: Ontario, Canada

2.459 miles / 3.957 km

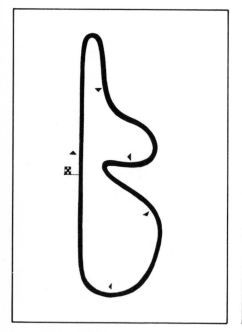

Fuji International Speedway:
near Gotemba, Japan

2.709 miles / 4.359 km

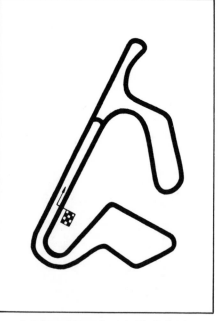

Autodromo Internacional do Rio de Janeiro:
Jacarepaguá, Brazil

3.126 miles / 5.031 km

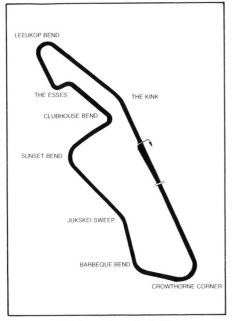

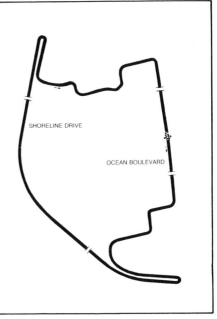

Kyalami: Johannesburg, South Africa

2.55 miles / 4.104 km

Long Beach: Long Beach California, U.S.A.

2.020 miles / 3.251 km

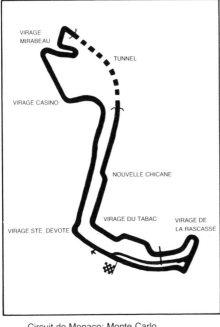

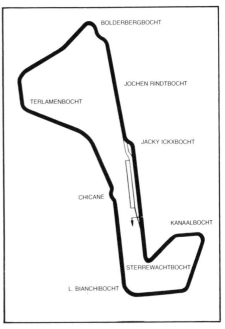

Circuit de Monaco: Monte Carlo

2.058 miles / 3.312 km

Omloop Terlaemen Zolder:
near Hasselt, Belgium

2.648 miles / 4.262 km

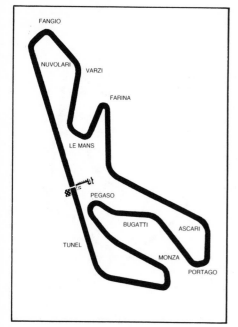

Jarama: near Madrid, Spain

2.115 miles / 3.404 km

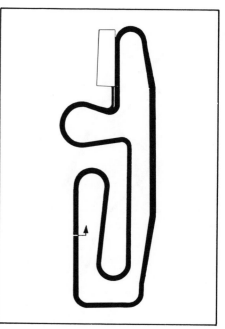

Scandinavian Raceway:
Anderstorp, Sweden

2.505 miles / 4.031 km

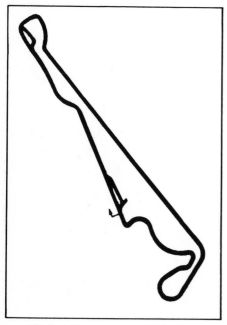

ASA Paul Ricard: near Marseille, France

3.610 miles / 5.810 km

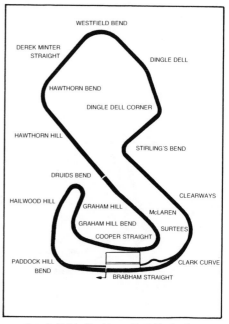

Brands Hatch: Fawkharn, Kent, England

2.614 miles / 4.206 km

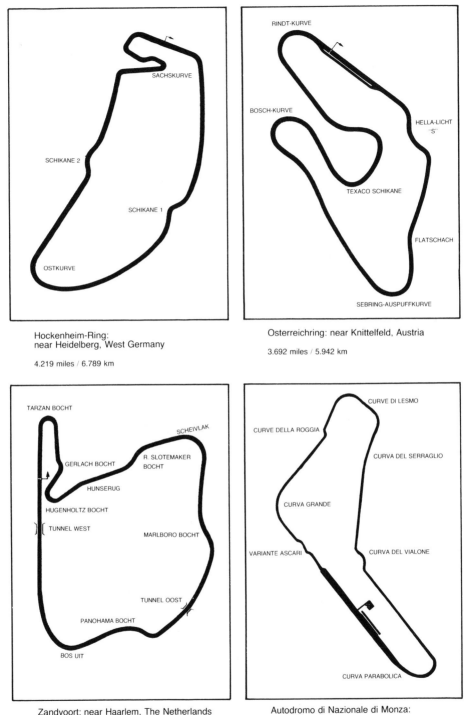

Hockenheim-Ring:
near Heidelberg, West Germany

4.219 miles / 6.789 km

Osterreichring: near Knittelfeld, Austria

3.692 miles / 5.942 km

Zandvoort: near Haarlem, The Netherlands

2.626 miles / 4.226 km

Autodromo di Nazionale di Monza:
near Milan, Italy

3.604 miles / 5.800 km

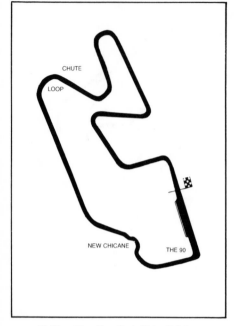

Watkins Glen: New York State, U.S.A.

3.377 miles / 5.435 km

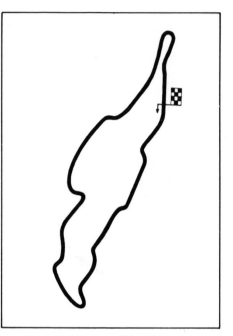

Circuit Ile Notre-Dame (Gilles Villeneuve):
Montreal, Quebec, Canada

2.796 miles / 4.500 km

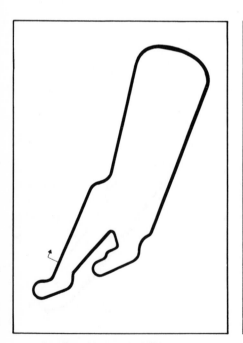

Autodromo Municipal de la Ciudad de
Buenos Aires: Buenos Aires, Argentina

3.708 miles / 5.968 km

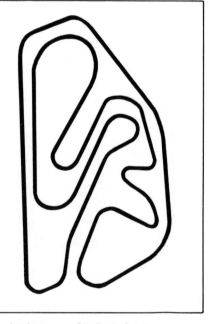

Interlagos: near São Paulo, Brazil

4.946 miles / 7.960 km

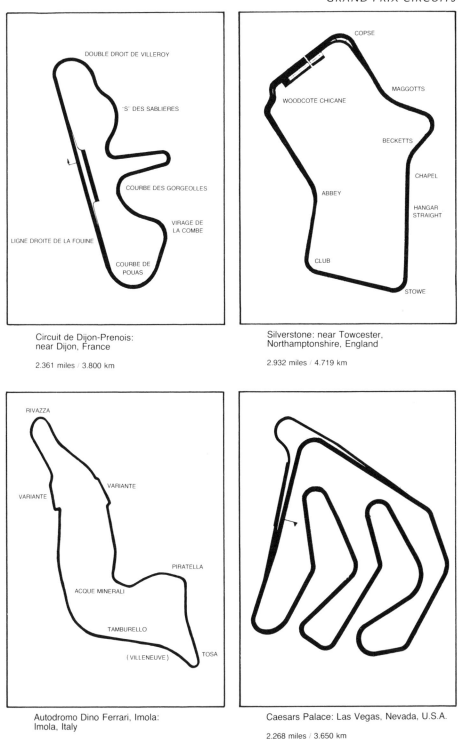

Circuit de Dijon-Prenois:
near Dijon, France

2.361 miles / 3.800 km

Silverstone: near Towcester,
Northamptonshire, England

2.932 miles / 4.719 km

Autodromo Dino Ferrari, Imola:
Imola, Italy

3.132 miles / 5.040 km

Caesars Palace: Las Vegas, Nevada, U.S.A.

2.268 miles / 3.650 km

INDEX

342